Current Topics in Early Childhood Education

Volume VI

Editor
LILIAN G. KATZ

Associate Editor
Karen Steiner

 Clearinghouse on Elementary and Early Childhood Education, University of Illinois at Urbana-Champaign

ABLEX PUBLISHING CORPORATION
Norwood, New Jersey 07648

871322

Printed in the United States of America

This publication was prepared with funding from the National Institute of Education, U.S. Department of Education, under contract no. NIE 400-83-0021. The opinions expressed in this report do not necessarily reflect the positions or policies of NIE or the Department of Education.

ISBN 0-89391-289-1 (C)
ISBN 0-89391-290-5 (P)   ISSN 0363-8332

Ablex Publishing Corporation
355 Chestnut Street
Norwood, New Jersey 07648

Contents

Acknowledgments

The editors are greatly indebted to Rhoda Becher, Nancy Coombs, Betty Jean Dunbar, Merle Karnes, Polly Kemp, Jane Maehr, Chalmer Moore, Sherri Oden, Ross Parke, Mara Sani, Bernard Spodek, Nancy Travis, Jeanette Watson, David Weikart, and Charles West for their careful reviews and thoughtful comments on the papers in this volume.

Preface

The chapters included in this sixth volume of *Current Topics in Early Child-hood Education* address a wide variety of the concerns and interests of those who work with young children, their families, and their teachers.

Many of the topics considered here are of continuing interest in the field and shed new light on areas examined in previous volumes in the series. For example, the chapter by Bhavnagri, on the topic of mother-child interaction in different cultural settings, follows in the line of Kilmer's contribution in Volume III on the subject of infant-toddler group care. Fogel's discussion of the role of adults in infant development likewise updates and expands this concern for the child's earliest environment. Schunk's discussion of the role played by social comparison in children's motivation and achievement echoes papers contributed by Deci and Ryan in Volume IV and, even earlier, by Condry and Koslowski in Volume II.

Each previous volume in the *Current Topics* series has also included at least one chapter on family and school relationships; in the present volume, Becher continues in this vein with an extensive review of research accumulated over the past decade. The chapter by Jones on education for teachers of young children continues a second tradition of keeping abreast of changes in the vital area of teacher education and professional development. Similarly, Shinman's review of research on preschool education in the United Kingdom follows in the line of earlier reports of preschool education research from other countries, such as those contributed by Ashby in Volume III and Good-now and Burns in Volume V. Saracho and Spodek review important work on learning styles; this work continues from an earlier chapter by Sigel and Saunders, also included in Volume III. Finally, the critique by Simons and Simons of the Montessori approach continues a tradition set in the very first volume of *Current Topics* by Franklin and Biber's chapter on alternative perspectives on teaching and curriculum in early childhood programs.

Yet other papers collected in this volume concern topics given special interest in recent days. The chapter by Plummer and her colleagues, for example, synthesizes research relating to grade retention in the early childhood and primary levels, as well as within elementary education as a whole. Oertel's discussion brings us a report of an important trend in West Germany to involve social education in the development of early childhood education curricula. Finally, the chapter by Lukasevich and Summers brings us a self-conscious look at our own field and its data sources by employing the technique of bibliometric analysis. We hope that these new kinds of inclusions begin new traditions in our *Current Topics* series, and we look forward to receiving suggestions for future volumes.

Lilian G. Katz, Ph.D.
*Director, ERIC Clearinghouse on Elementary
and Early Childhood Education*

1

Mother–Infant Interactions in Various Cultural Settings

Navaz Bhavnagri

University of Illinois

INTRODUCTION

Every human infant is dependent on his or her caregiver for survival. This relationship with the caregiver is considered of critical importance in the socialization of the child, a process that in turn affects his or her future adult personality. Since the mother–infant relationship is, of course, a universal one, it is therefore a relevant cross-cultural phenomenon. Issues relating to this particular relationship thus concern not only the child's development, but also relate to international development as well.

In many cultures, the biological mother is the primary caregiver in early infancy. Therefore, the scope of this discussion has been limited to the biological mother–infant interaction. However, some cultures do make use of multiple caregivers; these may include fathers, older siblings, co-wives, members of the kinship group, and so forth. Research on infant care draws most heavily on the Western industrialized nations, where the mother–infant interaction is viewed as being of paramount importance. This paper intends not to condone that bias, but is necessarily limited to the literature on infant care most likely to produce an effective cross-cultural comparison.

As Third World countries move toward modernization, urbanization, and industrialization, there is often an introduction of goods, commodities, and services that may directly or indirectly influence traditional childrearing practices. Among the questions raised by change in Third World countries are the following: What are the effects of introducing powdered milk formula and early supplementary solids on existing mother–infant interactions, particularly in terms of breast-feeding and weaning practices? What are the effects of introducing baby carriages and infant seats on existing close and continuous mother–infant body contact and on vestibular stimulation for the infant? What are the long-term consequences of introducing infant cribs in societies where mother and infant normally sleep together? Does the introduction of outside-the-home employment support or hinder the prevalent traditional child care system? How can progress, such as the provision of desirable health care services, be brought about without disrupting the existing efficient and traditional childrearing practices?

Systematic studies of mother–infant interactions over a period of time in various cultural settings are essential to address these concerns. Such research would also eventually help in identifying infants in the Third World with developmental risks and in designing family support programs to reduce risks and foster growth and development.

In addition to advantages for the Third World to be gained from research, industrialized and Westernized countries may find alternatives or solutions by studying childrearing practices in other cultures. Further investigation might clarify, for example, how women in other cultures have combined caregiving and work, and how that union has affected their interactions with their infants. In addition, the long-term consequences of the use of multiple caregivers in other cultures might be systematically studied so as to identify which specific aspects of this childrearing practice are comparable to the Western practices of family day care, group infant day care, or babysitting. Yet another research question might address the differences among cultures in what is considered "appropriate" infant behavior. Families in industrialized societies could benefit from such research by gaining greater awareness of a wider range of childrearing practices, some of which they may wish to incorporate into their own lifestyles.

Scope of Comparative Child Development

Leiderman, Tulkin, and Rosenfeld (1977) make a distinction between cross-cultural studies and comparative child development by stating (a) that cross-cultural studies examine the interrelationship of various systems on a cultural level and (b) that childrearing practices and child development may be included in this investigation but are not the primary focus. The research reported in the present discussion falls under the category of comparative child development. While comparisons are made across cultural groups, they are focused only on those aspects of a given culture that appear to be directly relevant to child development and mother–infant interaction.

Comparative child development is a relatively new field, emerging as it has in the 1960s (Field, Sostek, Vietze, & Leiderman, 1981; Werner, 1979). Until this time, the view of child development was based on a tiny sample of the human race, namely, the children of the Western world, and of that sample, principally middle-class Caucasians. Lozoff (1977) reported that children and their caretakers studied in the context of modern industrialized societies, such as those in the United States or European countries, are a select group and probably unrepresentative of the human species in most other cultures and during most of human history. The discussion here attempts to balance this earlier bias by focusing mainly on mother-child interactions in non-Western cultures.

Werner (1979) lists six key issues that should be addressed by the field of comparative child development. Two of these six are pertinent to the topic of mother-child interaction. The first of these issues Werner establishes as "the constraints set by ecology and the economic, social, and political maintenance systems of societies on the behavior of children and their caretakers," while the second he defines as "the adaptive significance of child-rearing goals and practices across a wide range of cultures" (p. 4). These issues directly and indirectly address the topic of mother-child interaction, thereby communicating that the relationship is a topic of significant importance in the field of comparative child development.

Another issue demanding some preliminary attention is the definition of infancy. There is no universal consensus as to the exact span of a human being's existence that can be definitively labeled "infancy." Some developmental psychologists (e.g., Stone & Church, 1973) consider only the first 15 months to be infancy, labeling the period between 15 months and 2½ years the toddler years. Others (e.g., Mussen, Conger, & Kagan, 1979) extend infancy through the first 24 months. Some have a still broader definition of infancy, including the first 3 years (White, 1975). This problem is further confounded when one is discussing the issue in cross-cultural terms. Some cultures may not have a term equivalent to "infancy" in their language. Some may be broad categorizers and thus may label infants as "children," while others may have many specific categories based not necessarily on chronological age but rather on developmental age (for example, "sitters," "stand-uppers," "walkers," "solid food eaters"). For the purpose of this discussion, in order to provide the broadest possible coverage, the period of infancy has been arbitrarily defined as the time from birth to 3 years.

Organized into three major sections, the remainder of this examination will address theoretical perspectives relevant to the topic of mother-infant interactions in different cultural settings, empirical research on mother-infant interaction in various cultural settings, and issues and trends in the mother-infant relationship within different cultural contexts.

THEORETICAL PERSPECTIVES

The theoretical models and constructs discussed in this section are drawn from various disciplines: ethology, evolution, population psychology, culture and personality theory, cross-cultural psychology, ecology of human development, and biosocial psychology. These perspectives have been chosen because they address the variables that influence childrearing practices in a cross-cultural context; as such, they are particularly relevant to the Third World. The intent of the following discussion is therefore to provide alternative ways of viewing and comparing mother-infant interactions within a larger ecological context and to provide a framework for generating more relevant future empirical research.

Ethology

Ethology is especially concerned with those animal behaviors that have evolved as an adaption to the environment, thus facilitating the species' survival within the context of a particular environmental niche. This field draws heavily on Darwin's theory of evolution. Patterns of behavior — both infantile and parental — that favor the maintenance of physical proximity, protection, and nurturance are of particular interest to ethologists.

John Bowlby (1958) borrowed these ethological concepts and applied them to mother-infant interaction. For example, Bowlby's conceptualization of attachment is what ethologists would call "bonding." Mother–infant attachment consists of a bonding of infant to mother that endures more or less throughout the extended period of the life span. Mary Ainsworth (1977a) discusses this attachment theory in the context of comparative child development research, asserting the following:

> If different societies have different practices and different patterns of maternal behavior, cross-cultural comparisons will certainly complement within-group comparisons in throwing light upon the development of qualitative differences. Cross-cultural studies, perhaps more clearly than intracultural studies, may clarify how infant-mother relationships of different kinds influence later important interpersonal relations . . . (p. 64)

Ainsworth (1967) applied this ethological approach in her study of infants in Uganda, discussed here at greater length in the empirical research section.

Evolution

Konner (1977a) labels his theory the "evolution of human behavior development" and discusses the contribution of Darwin's theory to social evolution. He compares major differences in the evolution of social behavior as the transition takes place from a hunter-gatherer existence to an industrial way of life. Several differences in social behavior discussed by Konner are related to mother–infant interactions. First, he notes that mothers in hunter-gatherer societies hold their infants vertically in a sling, while Western mothers typically position their children horizontally and do not use a sling. As a result, the Western neonate experiences fewer motor challenges, less tactile and vestibular stimulation, and more challenges to temperature maintenance.

Second, Konner compares the nursing behavior of infants and mothers in terms of frequency of sucking, weaning, and type of sucking. With respect to frequency of sucking, mammals may be classified into two groups — namely, "continual" and "spaced" feeders. Continual feeders are those whose infants cling to them, such as most primates, bats, and marsupials, and those whose infants follow them. Spaced feeders, such as rabbits, are those who leave their infants in nests. Continual feeders have more dilute milk, with lower fat and protein content, and they suck slowly. Spaced feeders have more concentrated milk and suck quickly. Human milk and infant sucking rate are consistent with Konner's classification of humans as continual feeders. Infants of hunter-gatherers suckle several times an hour, but human infants in Western societies now are typically spaced feeders. Weaning in higher primates, including hunter-gatherers, is precipitated by the birth of a subsequent offspring, but in industrial societies there has been a dramatic drop in the age of weaning. Finally, a distinction may be based on the type of sucking: hunter-gatherers do not expose their infants to nonnutritive sucking, a practice common in industrial societies.

Third, as Konner notes, hunter-gatherers exhibit immediate extensive stimulation of the infant at birth and continuous mother–infant contact during the hours and days after birth. Comparatively, infants in industrial societies experience far less proximity to mothers due to nonrooming hospitalization policies at birth, separate sleeping arrangements in the home, and the distance of the mother's work place from the infant care site. Making and breaking of contact with the infant, once controlled almost exclusively by the infant, is in industrial societies largely controlled by the mother.

Fourth, according to this theorist, the mother–infant bond is mitigated for the mother by the presence of other adults and for the infant by the presence of a multi-age juvenile play group. Same-age peer relations are nonexistent among human hunter-gatherers. In Western societies, same-age peer groups are prevalent and have replaced multi-age play groups.

Finally, Konner states that infants learn through observational learning, direct teaching, and play. Over the course of technological development from the hunter-gatherer lifeway to an urban-industrial lifeway, the percentage of information transfer accounted for by teaching has greatly increased and that accounted for by observational learning and play has correspondingly decreased. Furthermore, the information transfer in the urban-industrial context is more from adult to child, or adult to same-age peer group, and less from older to younger child.

The consequences of cultural evolution, if any, are still not well understood, but they are nonetheless relevant to an understanding of the effects of technological change on human development and infant-adult relationships in the Third World as well as in industrial societies. Systematic research is needed to investigate adaptive patterns of and stress on the mother and the infant as they shift from traditional childrearing practices to a more "modern" approach.

Population Psychology

Another model for the comparative study of psychosocial adaptation, offered by LeVine (1977), is also based on Darwin's evolutionary theory. While Konner's (1977a) theoretical discussion primarily identifies the significant changes in infant-rearing practices over time, LeVine attempts to explain the reasons for these changes, adapted by entire populations over time. LeVine postulates that cultural evolution within human populations produces standardized strategies of survival for infants and children, strategies that reflect environmental pressures from the past, encoded in customs and transmitted socially rather than biologically. For example, he explains that the practice of carrying the infant on one's body a great deal of the time (until the child is 18 months of age or older) may severely limit exploratory behavior and may thus affect the emotional and cognitive development of the child. Whatever those intangible effects are, however, they are not visible to the African Gusii or Hausa mothers whom he observed, whereas the very tangible risks of the child's being burned in an open fire, trampled by cattle, or falling from a cliff are. These mothers respond more to tangible risk and have little or no awareness of the possible psychological consequences of continuous physical restraint. Therefore, it seems that prolonged carrying of an infant is a cultural adaptation to protect the infant from a hazardous environment.

Based on his observations, LeVine (1977) cites the two following parental goals:

1. In populations with high infant mortality rates, parents will have the physical survival and health of the child as their overriding concern, particularly in the early years, and childrearing customs will reflect this priority.
2. In populations with relatively scarce or precarious resources for subsistence, parents will have as their overriding conscious concern the child's capacity for future economic self-maintenance (broadly defined), particularly after his survival seems assured, and childrearing customs will reflect this priority. (p. 21)

LeVine's theory thus offers an explanation as to how childrearing practices have evolved, and illuminates the underlying parental concerns and aspirations on which these practices are grounded.

Psychocultural Approach

John Whiting's (1977) model of psychocultural research is a heuristic model built from a variety of other theories. It is eclectic in that it is based on psychoanalytic theory, Henry Murray's (1949) theory of personality, and learning theories advanced by Hull (1943) and Miller and Dollard (1941). More recently, Whiting has incorporated concepts from ethological attachment theory and stress theory as well. Whiting's psychocultural model of 1977 offers greater conceptual detail than does his earlier model (Whiting, 1963).

The child's learning environment, or what Whiting has called "child-rearing practices" (1963, p. 5) is the component of his conceptual scheme most directly related to mother–infant interaction. The arrows in Figure 1 represent the direction of causation. One can infer that the various aspects of the maintenance system are antecedent to mother–child interaction and that the consequence of mother–child interaction is the kind of adult the child will turn out to be.

Despite the broad theoretical underpinnings on which this model is based, it still has some limitations. The linearity of this model (i.e., the assumption that environment affects the maintenance system, which affects the child's learning environment, which affects the individual, which affects the projective expressive system) and the unidirectionality of causality may be oversimplifications. Real, observable phenomena do not always follow a sta-

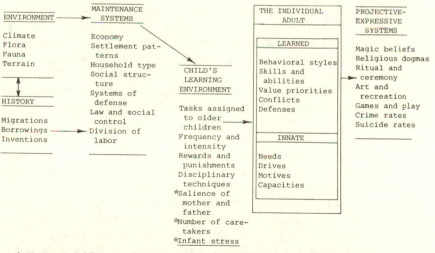

* These variables are directly related to mother-infant interaction.

Figure 1: A model for psychocultural research. *Note.* From "A model of psychocultural research" (p. 30), by J.W.M. Whiting, 1977, in P. Leiderman, S. Tulkin, and A. Rosenfeld (Eds.), *Culture and infancy.* New York: Academic Press. Copyright 1977 by Academic Press. Reprinted by permission.

ble pattern, predictable in a linear fashion, but rather are highly variable and dynamic and exhibit multiple causality. This variability is particularly true in mother-infant interactions (cf. Osofsky & Connors, 1979). Recent literature emphasizes the bidirectionality of such interactions, showing that the infant affects both the caregiver and the total interaction (e.g., Thomas & Chess, 1977; Wolff, 1971). Frijda and Jahoda (1966) cite similar objections to Whiting's model. In his later writings (1977), Whiting has defended his model by making the following statement:

> In some, if not many, instances, the true direction of causation may be the reverse [of that indicated]: there may be feedback loops and steps in the assumed sequence may be skipped. The arrows do, however, represent a commonly occurring sequence. The primary reason for making such oversimplified assumptions about causation is that they give rise to a readily testable set of hypotheses. (p. 29)

Despite this defense, the psychocultural model as proposed by Whiting may not be the most appropriate one for research on mother-infant interaction. What is needed is a model that focuses on the dynamic process of interaction and on the impact of such interaction on both the caregiver and the infant.

Whiting's (1977) work addressing the contribution of stress theory to psychocultural research is also interesting. He reports animal research indicating that stress experienced during infancy has two very important effects on growth and development: "(1) It increases the rate of growth, and (2) It makes the animal bolder in exploring a strange environment when it reaches maturity" (p. 37). Whiting then explores stress as a variable differentially affecting human infants in various cultures. He finds that in some cultures infants are customarily subjected to physically stressful events, such as having their earlobes or their nasal septa pierced, having their heads molded for cosmetic purposes, or being vaccinated or circumcised during infancy. In other cultures, infants are carefully protected from such stresses. Yet others promote the psychological stress of infants being separated from their mothers. Since infant stress exists cross-culturally, Whiting includes it as one of the variables in a child's learning environment.

Also following a psychocultural perspective, Minturn and Lambert (1964) compare the mother's warmth, stability, and responsibility for baby care among six cultures within Kenya, India, Okinawa, Mexico, the Philippines, and the United States. The mothers of the Mexican and Indian samples appeared to express less warmth than did other samples, perhaps because living in a household with other families, as they did, necessitates a training for emotional control that acts as a damper to spontaneous expression of emotions. The African mothers were more emotionally unstable than were the mothers of other societies — that is, they were unpredictable in their expression of hostility and warmth. Regarding responsibility for baby care, the

American mothers assumed more responsibility as compared with women in the other five cultures, who could depend on female kin and older children for daily infant care.

Cross-Cultural Psychology

Triandis (1979) has developed a model for cross-cultural research based on systems theory, with hierarchical levels of analysis that indicate inter-relationships among systems of variables (see Figure 2). For example, mother–infant interaction, a variable in the "interindividual system," is influenced by other ecological, individual, and sociocultural variables. Triandis's model, when compared with Whiting's (1977), appears multidirectional and dynamic in nature, and its theoretical framework is organized such that both the interpersonal and intrapersonal aspects of social interaction are highlighted. While Whiting's model elaborates more the psychocultural aspects of child-rearing practices, Triandis's model employs a social-interactionist perspective in which the individual is seen as actively influencing and being influenced by his or her ecology. Therefore, Triandis's model offers a framework more suitable for the study of mother-infant interaction in a cross-cultural context.

Ecology

Urie Bronfenbrenner, in his book *The Ecology of Human Development* (1979), proposes a theoretical model that views the human being interacting with his or her continuously changing environment throughout the life span. This model is a synthesis of Lewin's (1935) field theory and systems theory. In it, the ecological environment is viewed as a set of nested structures like concentric circles extending outward, with the individual in the center enveloped by the phenomenological environment.

In order to more comprehensively understand the human being's development, Bronfenbrenner has hierarchically organized human ecology into four subsystems: the microsystem, mesosystem, exosystem, and macrosystem. The microsystem includes the interaction between the developing person and the immediate environment. The mother–infant interaction at home exemplifies events occurring in the microsystem. The mesosystem consists of inter-relations among two or more settings in which the developing person actively participates. In the case of the infant, such interrelationships might occur among the home, the infant day care setting, and the homes of other multiple caregivers. The exosystem includes settings that do not themselves contain the developing person but that contain events affecting or affected by the individual. With respect to the infant, the exosystem might include the parents' places of work and worship, older siblings' friends, services of a local health

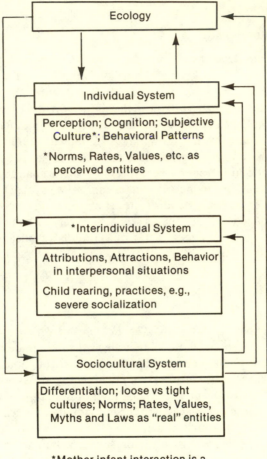

Ecology

Individual System

Perception; Cognition; Subjective
Culture*; Behavioral Patterns

*Norms, Rates, Values, etc. as
perceived entities

*Interindividual System

Attributions, Attractions, Behavior
in interpersonal situations

Child rearing, practices, e.g.,
severe socialization

Sociocultural System

Differentiation; loose vs tight
cultures; Norms; Rates, Values,
Myths and Laws as "real" entities

*Mother-infant interaction is a
variable related to the
interindividual system.

Figure 2: Relationships among systems of variables in cross-cultural studies. *Note.* From "Cross-cultural psychology" (p. 559), by H.C. Triandis, 1979, in M.E. Meyer (Ed.), *Foundations of contemporary psychology.* New York: Oxford Press. Copyright 1979 by Oxford Press. Reprinted by permission.

clinic, local stores where parents shop for the baby's needs, and so on. Finally, the macrosystem includes the overarching institutional patterns of the culture. Such patterns include the economic, social, educational, legal, and political systems of which microsystems, mesosystems, and exosystems are the concrete manifestation. At this level, a national policy on children or health could, for example, have an impact on various institutions that in turn would directly or indirectly influence interactions between mother and infant.

Bronfenbrenner's model is recommended as a basis for studying the mother-infant interaction because it is comprehensive in scope and thus applicable to any culture. Despite its comprehensiveness, the model also takes into account the impact on the developing infant of specific ecological variables within a given culture. In addition, it promotes understanding of the mother–infant interaction within a larger ecological context by compelling the researcher to identify variables in the mesosystem, exosystem, and macrosystem that influence the mother-infant interaction (embedded in the microsystem).

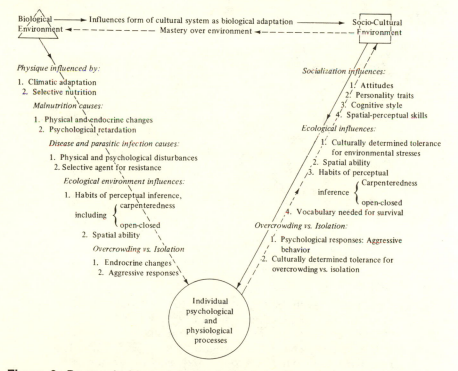

Figure 3: Dawson's biosocial psychological system. *Note.* From *Cross-cultural research methods* (p. 183), by R.W. Brislin, W.J. Lonner, and R.M. Thorndike (Eds.), 1973. New York: Wiley. Copyright 1973 by John Wiley & Sons. Reprinted by permission.

Biosocial Psychology

Dawson (as cited by Brislin, Lonner & Thorndike, 1973) has developed a model focusing on biological and social factors within the environment that influence the individual (see Figure 3). To study these environmental influences, Dawson has developed the Traditional-Modern Scale of Attitude Change (T-M). He has used the T-M scale in studies of childrearing attitudes and processes among Hong Kong Chinese, Australian Arunta, and West Africans of Sierra Leone (Dawson, 1967, 1969a, 1969b; Dawson & Ng, 1972).

Empirical research on mother-infant interaction so far has not been based on Dawson's model. However, research based on other models (e.g., Whiting, 1963; Super et al., 1981) makes reference to the variables listed in Dawson's model as background information.

Lester and Brazelton (1982) have developed a psychobiological model for cross-culturally studying infant behavior, asserting that this model is a holistic, dynamic conceptualization focusing on the processes of development. In this interactive model, the infant is perceived as being influenced

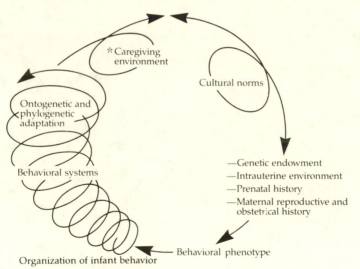

*This variable is directly related to mother-infant interaction.

Figure 4: A psychobiological model for the cross-cultural study of the organization of infant behavior. *Note.* From "Cross-cultural assessment of neonatal behavior" (p. 51), in D.A. Wagner and H.W. Stevenson (Eds.), 1982, *Cultural perspectives on child development.* New York: W.H. Freeman. Copyright 1982 by W.H. Freeman & Sons. Reprinted by permission.

by the environment and in turn influencing the environment (see Figure 4). Specifically, Lester and Brazelton state the following: "The neonate is viewed as a competent organism that is skilled, selective, and socially influential, who actively interacts with and makes demands on the caretaking environment" (p. 52).

Since the major thrust of the model is to study the infant's individual behavior and not a dyadic interaction, the analysis could be said to be at the level of the individual system, according to Triandis's model (1979). Lester and Brazelton (1982) have used their model in studying African infants from Zambia; Gusii from Kenya; Zinacanteco, Maya, and Chiapas from Mexico; Ladinos from Guatemala; and Latin infants from Puerto Rico. In each of the studies they attempted "first, to view infant behavior in its appropriate cultural context, both as a shaper of and as shaped by cultural expectations; and second, to highlight the complex interaction between genetic and environmental influences on neonatal behavior" (p. 28).

Summary

This review of the theoretical literature demonstrates that the same observable phenomenon of mother-infant interaction is cognized, classified, perceived, and interpreted differently by each theoretician based on the paradigm of his or her own discipline. It becomes apparent that each paradigm, by itself, may limit understanding and create blinders (cf. Kuhn, 1970, p. 77). This limitation suggests the value of more collaborative interdisciplinary efforts in comparative child development research.

All the theoretical perspectives reviewed in this section directly or indirectly refer to childrearing practices in a cross-cultural setting. Although none of the models is designed to study mother-infant interaction exclusively, each does facilitate the understanding of a wide spectrum of variables influencing this interaction. The following section on empirical research focuses on a number of the variables mentioned above; some of the research discussed stems from the theoretical frameworks already described.

EMPIRICAL RESEARCH

The empirical research discussed in this section is limited to non-Western cultures and to recent data. Very early ethnographic records, which make tangential and cursory references to mother–infant interactions, are not reported here. The discussion is organized according to the geographical location of the groups studied and with respect to similarities in the traditional cultures of these groups. A matrix (see Table 1) indicating the relationship of

Table 1   A matrix integrating theoretical perspectives with major empirical research

Region or Country	Group	Investigator	Theoretical Perspectives
Kenya	Gusii	Whiting and Whiting (1975)	Psychocultural
	Gusii	Whiting (1963)	Psychocultural
	Gusii	Dixon, Tronick, Keefer, and Brazelton (1981)	Psychobiological
	Kipsigis	Super and Harkness (1982)	*
	Kikuyu	Leiderman and Leiderman (1977)	*
Uganda	Ganda	Ainsworth (1967, 1977a)	Ethological
	Ganda	Geber (1958); Geber and Dean (1957)	*
Zambia	Urban Zambian	Lester and Brazelton (1982)	Psychobiological
	Zambian	Goldberg (1977)	*
Botswana	!Kung San	Konner (1977b)	Evolutionary
Japan	Ainu	Munroe and Munroe (1975)	*
	Urban Japanese	Caudill (1972); Caudill and Frost (1972); Caudill and Plath (1966); Caudill and Schooler (1973); Caudill and Weinstein (1969)	*
South Pacific	Fias	Sostek, Vietze, Zaslow, Kreiss, Waals, and Rubinstein (1981)	*
	Marquesans	Martini and Kirkpatrick (1981)	*
Latin America	Colombians	Super, Clement, Vauri, Christiansen, Mora, and Herrerra (1981)	
	Guatemalans	Klein, Lasky, Yarbrough, Habicht, and Sellers (1977)	*
	Guatemalans	Lester and Brazelton (1982)	Psychobiological
	Mexicans	Brazelton (1977)	Psychobiological

Note. Theoretical perspectives are named only for research explicitly stating such an orientation. Other research, unlabeled, could be viewed as eclectic in approach.

the research to specific theoretical perspectives, where applicable, is also provided.

Kenya

Gusii.   The Gusii are a tribe living in the densely populated highlands of southwestern Kenya. They believe that face-to-face confrontations may call up strong feelings; therefore, such interactions are regulated. A typical adult–adult interaction often occurs with completely averted gaze. Conversations occur with the participants at a 90-degree or greater angle to each other.

Early parent–child relationships among the Gusii are characterized by avoidance of eye contact and restraint in playful interactions. There is continuous physical contact between the mother and her infant, but the infant is rarely held in a face-to-face posture, and therefore, there is little eye contact. Affectionate and social behaviors are rarely directed toward the baby, nor is the infant regarded as capable of communicative intent other than to signal hunger or distress. Whiting and Whiting (1975) found Gusii children to be the least attention-seeking of all children studied.

Whiting (1963) has also reported that the infant's most intense relationship is with the mother, who nurses the child. The mother usually breastfeeds without looking at or fondling the child, and she often continues conversing with others. All day, when the mother is working, the infant is carried and cared for by a child nurse. The primary parental goal is to safeguard the health of the child; enhancing social and cognitive development is not one of the mother's parental goals. These goals are in agreement with LeVine's (1977) observations as to how parents go about prioritizing goals for their children. According to the psychocultural perspective upon which Whiting's (1963) study is based, the findings mentioned above would be categorized as the "child's learning environment" (see Figure 1).

Dixon, Tronick, Keefer, and Brazelton (1981) videotaped 2- to 12-week-old Gusii infants' face-to-face interactions with their mothers. This research reports that the mother–infant interaction would begin with the prescribed stylized greeting, a smile followed by a short pause. The infant would attend brightly and would often smile. Mothers would often initiate a repetitious verbal pattern using single words or phrases. "Baby talk" in its most exaggerated form and dramatic changes in mothers' inflections were not heard. The mother smiled pleasantly and was alert, but had little variation in facial expression. Gaze generally was directed toward the infant, but it had a grossly distracted quality. Mothers' movements were generally small head movements rather than large shifts in body position.

The infants responded to their mothers' attention with smiles and cooing-vocalization, accompanied by big kicks and generally positive affect. Dramatic aversions of gaze or posture were very rare. When mothers left at the end of the taping sessions, few infants showed the dramatic change in affect common in similar American sequences; instead, they competently redirected their attention to objects in their surroundings.

The investigators concluded that, while American and Gusii mothers play with and talk to their infants a similar proportion of time, their styles differ. For example, Gusii mothers' frequency of looking away from their infants is greater than that for American mothers. LeVine (1977) would explain this specific behavior as a cultural adaptation in childrearing practices to reduce mothers' emotional attachment to infants who have a low probability of surviving. However, several of the investigative procedures employed make it appropriate to classify this study as characteristic of Lester and Brazelton's psychobiological model. Specifically, in addition to videotaping, the investigators gathered medical, social, and psychological information on the mothers during pregnancy. Pediatric assessments and Brazelton's Neonatal Behavioral Assessment were also administered to newborns, followed by naturalistic observation and cognitive assessments over the next 15 months.

Kipsigis.   The other highland tribe reported on in the research are the Kipsigis of western Kenya. During their first 3 to 4 months, Kipsigis infants are amost always in physical contact with their mothers; then a child caretaker takes over a large share of the daytime care. Super and Harkness (1982) report that, unlike American families, Kipsigis do not make major modifications in their living quarters or family routines to accommodate their infants' routines, particularly sleep. Also, unlike her American counterpart, the Kipsigis mother does not need to rely on the baby's sleeping for a chance to disengage from continuous infant care; sibling caregivers, co-wives, and other relatives are always at hand to look after the child. Consequently, the Kipsigis 4-month-old infant sleeps just over 12 hours on an average each day, as compared with 15 hours of sleep for an American infant. Kipsigis infants do not develop long periods of sustained sleep: The longest episode of sleep is about 4.5 hours, as compared with 8 hours in American infants. This sleeping pattern affects the infant's other behavior patterns as well. Thus the Kipsigis infant has briefer and less regular cycles of activity and rest, while the American infant has fewer but longer periods of sleeping, feeding, and playful interaction.

Kipsigis infants are upset when their mothers leave them for short periods, but this response does not last long. However, their stranger anxiety is more sustained and intense than that of American infants. This may be the case because the cast of characters for daily life remains stable and relatively small for the Kipsigis infant, despite the fact that two or three individuals are routinely involved in care. Super and Harkness (1982) conclude that the Kipsigis and American babies are learning the emotional structure of their cultural niches through the above-mentioned practices.

Kikuyu. A third Kenyan tribe whose mother-infant interactions have been observed, the Kikuyu, are located in the temperate highlands near Nairobi. Leiderman and Leiderman (1977) report that Kikuyu infants are cared for by the mother up to 5 months of age and are then looked after by a child caregiver or other adult females. The average age of caretakers other than the mother was found to be 13.9 years for the low socioeconomic level, 10.6 years for the middle socioeconomic level, and 20.2 years for the high socioeconomic level. The reason for these differences in age was that the families of the lowest level could not afford to send their older daughters to school; therefore, they were available at home to take care of infants. The highest group could afford to hire nonfamilial help to assist the mother in infant care. The families in the middle level tended to send their girls to school, but since they had insufficient extra cash resources to hire non-familial older caretakers, they were forced to rely on their younger children as caretakers.

Leiderman and Leiderman (1977) were interested in exploring the effects of these caregiving arrangements on the child's cognitive and social-emotional development. They found a significant positive correlation between the caretaker's age and the infant's mental test performance for the second 6 months of life. Presumably, greater social maturity gained by the caretaker with increasing age does have an influence on the child's cognitive performance.

The infants in this polymatric system also tended to react more negatively to a stranger's approach and more negatively to the mother's departure than did infants in monomatric caretaking arrangements. Thus the investigators concluded that social, demographic, and economic factors relating to the caretaking arrangement affect both cognitive and social-emotional development in the child.

The investigations also found that, when compared with the mother, the child caretaker in all three economic groups was providing more playful language and social interaction. The mother's daytime role—demanding because of household responsibilities, agricultural work, and the utilitarian aspects of life resulted in relatively little time for social interaction with the infant. Thus, the Kikuyu mother leaves much of this interaction to her older children. The above findings indicate that a village school intended to help children may actually disrupt infant and child care systems during critical periods of the child's life. This possibility needs to be kept in mind by social policy makers in developing countries.

Uganda

Mary Ainsworth studied childrearing practices among African Ganda tribes, reporting these findings in the volume *Infancy in Uganda: Infant Care and the Growth of Love* (1967). In a more recent article (1977a) she compares mother-infant interaction in Ganda families and in American families from Baltimore, Maryland. With respect to feeding and weaning practices, Ainsworth found that, in 1954 and 1955, 27 out of 28 Ganda babies were breast-fed, while in her American sample only four infants were breast-fed and the remaining 22 were bottle-fed.

Weaning, she found, was a gradual process among Ganda infants, with the daytime feedings dropping out first and the infant still being given the breast on demand during the night. Ganda babies were weaned between 32 and 57 weeks, while the four breast-fed American babies were weaned between 18 and 35 weeks, with the bottle substituting for the breast. Interestingly, the American bottle-fed babies did not show the active initiative in instituting feeding that was so characteristic of breast-fed Ganda infants. Among the American breast-fed babies, only one of the four, who was breast-fed consistently on demand and for comfort, showed this active initiative. The remaining three breast-fed American babies probably did not show this initiative because of their early weaning to the bottle (it is difficult for a bottle-fed baby to take much initiative in securing his or her own bottle).

Ainsworth also found that there were multiple caregivers available for Ganda infants; however, the mother was the main caregiver. Among the American sample, the mother was the only primary caregiver. Despite the availability of multiple caregivers among the Ganda, infants were left alone for much of the time, even when they were awake. Nearly all Ganda infants were free to move about the floor when not being held. This was not the case for most of the American sample, who were frequently confined to cribs, infant seats, jump chairs, or playpens when they were neither asleep nor being held. Three of the Ganda mothers reported that they were impressed with the convenience of cribs and baby carriages, in which they could leave their babies most of the time without supervision. This interest exemplifies the impact of Western commodities on traditional childrearing practices. (One wonders what effect the introduction of these, as well as other Western commodities, actually has on traditional childrearing practices.)

According to Ainsworth, these differences influence the infant's organization and integration of attachment behavior. Specifically, her hypothesis is as follows:

> Under circumstances in which an infant through his own active attachment behavior, including sucking and rooting and also reaching, grasping and approaching, can gain contact with an actual or potential attachment figure who is also his food source, his feeding behaviors become an integral part of the organization of his attachment relationship. The circumstances under which this integration is possible are: (1) When the baby is fed contingent on his own behavior, including both his signalling behavior, as in thoroughgoing demand feeding; (2) When the baby is breast fed so that the food providing source and

the attachment figure are one and the same; and (3) When weaning is deferred until after an attachment has already been established. (p. 128)

Geber (1958) and Geber and Dean (1957) have done several longitudinal and cross-sectional studies on Ganda children from birth to 3 years, using the Andreé-Thomas neonatal examination and Gesell Developmental Schedules and comparing these children with other ethnic groups. The African newborn is precocious in his or her development, which corresponds to the development of European infants 4 to 6 weeks old. Throughout the first 6 months, Ganda babies are developmentally ahead of Western babies by 2 to 3 months. This precocity is lost gradually, and by age 3 Ganda children's developmental quotient drops considerably as compared with Western samples.

Zambia

Lester and Brazelton (1982) report that Zambian neonates have an undernourished uterine environment and require delicate handling. Nonetheless, mothers' expectations are for vigorous neonates who will respond well to vigorous handling. Hence, mothers actually ignore the limp initial behavior of their infants and handle them as if they were more responsive. After hydration and initial feedings, the babies do become rapidly responsive, as the mothers anticipate.

Goldberg (1977) studied mother–infant interaction in urban Zambia and produced findings reflecting childrearing practices similar to those of Kenyan and Ugandan peoples. These included multiple caretakers (including siblings but with the mother as the primary caretaker), a great deal of physical contact, and little vocalization to the infant. Although Goldberg used presumably culture-free tests (since they tapped prelinguistic behavior), she later expressed the self-criticism that the instruments were in fact inadequate to deal with the problem of mothers' and infants' lack of familiarity with the testing materials and testing situation.

Goldberg also found that Zambian infants were reluctant to perform on object permanence tests, in which an object is hidden from the child in order to test the infant's ability to understand that the object still exists when it is out of sight (cf. Piaget, 1975). Goldberg speculates that this reluctance stems from the infant's perception that hiding the object represents an adult's restriction on exploratory behavior. Thus, the performance of Zambian infants on Western cognitive tests may reflect the manner in which the infants have been socialized. Furthermore, on items requiring an upright position intended to test for head and neck control, Zambian babies may perform better than their European counterparts. The fact that Zambian babies are normally held in an upright posture, while European babies are usually held supine, imposes a bias on test results. Goldberg's delineation of sources of cultural bias in infant testing represents a careful assessment of the value of these research tools in non-Western contexts.

Botswana

Konner (1977b), utilizing his evolutionary perspective, studied infancy among !Kung San hunter-gatherers (previously referred to as Bushmen) in northwestern Botswana. He reports that !Kung San infants have far more physical contact with their mothers and other caretakers than do American or English infants. However, the !Kung San babies receive an amount of distal communication (looking, smiling, and vocalizing) similar to that received by American infants. In general, Konner notes that the trend is for infants in technological societies to have less proximal communications, such as physical contact, than infants in nonindustrialized societies do.

Japan

Ainu. Munroe and Munroe (1975) report on the Ainu of Japan. The Ainu neonate is given small doses of an herbal extract for a few days and then is breast-fed. From the age of 1 month, the infant is tied to a cradle suspended from the ceiling of the hut, and no attention is paid to his or her crying. When outdoors, the infant is transported by means of a tumpline, or carrying strap. The period of infancy is called *shointek* or *poishispe*, which means a lump of dung or dung-covered. This label reflects a cultural perception of the infant as a passive, unintelligent organism. However, the Ainu pattern of infant care appears to provide close mother-infant contact, with the infant sleeping with the mother.

Urban Japanese. Caudill and his associates (Caudill & Frost, 1972; Caudill & Plath, 1966; Caudill & Schooler, 1973; Caudill & Weinstein, 1969) were among the first to conduct systematic observational studies of mother–infant interaction from a cross-cultural perspective. Caudill started his work in the early 1960s by comparing childrearing in Japan and America, and a number of his studies are summarized here. Regrettably, he passed away before he could fully complete his longitudinal study.

Studies by Caudill and Weinstein (1969) and Caudill (1972) showed that American mothers engaged in more lively chatting with their babies than did Japanese mothers; as a result, the American infants had a generally higher level of vocalization and particularly responded with greater amounts of happy vocalization and gross motor activity. The Japanese mothers, on the other hand, did more vocal lulling, carrying, and rocking of their babies;

as a result, the Japanese babies were more physically passive. In addition, Japanese babies had a greater amount of unhappy vocalization because their mothers took longer to respond to such signals for attention.

Caudill (1972) has termed these vocalizations between mother and infant "tiny dramas," which he has further explored with sequential analysis. Basically, Caudill has found that the pace of the American mother is livelier: First, she is in and out of the room more and thus provides more naturally occurring opportunities to speak to her baby and for the baby to respond vocally as she comes to provide care. Second, the American mother generally responds more quickly to her baby's vocalizations, regardless of whether they are happy or unhappy. Third, she responds more quickly to unhappy vocalizations than to happy ones, thus teaching the infant to make a more discriminating use of his or her voice. Finally, the American mother has more vocal interactions with her baby, especially by chatting at the same time that the infant is happily vocal. Caudill suggests that this added vocal stimulation and encouragement by the mother carries over to the times when she is silent but the baby is happily vocalizing probably in anticipation of a response from the mother.

In contrast, the Japanese mother's pace is more leisurely, and her caretaking periods are fewer and longer in duration. She holds her baby until he or she falls asleep and then puts the child down, to which the infant responds with unhappy vocalization. (This situation accounts, in part, for the greater amount of unhappy vocalization among Japanese infants.) Also, the Japanese mother physically checks her sleeping baby by, for example, wiping sweat from his or her forehead or adjusting the covers. These practices sometimes awaken the sleeping baby and increase the unhappy vocalizations. The American mother, on the other hand, visually checks her sleeping baby.

According to Caudill (1972), childrearing practices in these two cultural settings vary because of differing perceptions of the child. The American mother views her baby as a separate and autonomous person. By responding to the infant's vocal communications, she therefore teaches the baby to express needs and wants. The Japanese mother, on the other hand, views her baby as an extension of herself and places great emphasis on attachment.

South Pacific Islands

Fias.   Sostek et al. (1981) coded ethnographic films of mother–infant interactions among a population in the United States and among the people of Fias Island, a small isolated island in the Pacific Ocean and bordering the Philippine Sea. In this Micronesian culture, the investigators were exploring the social contexts in which mother–infant interactions occur. The most common dyadic interaction among Fias occurred with the infant's head facing outward (i.e., the child would be on the mother's lap, not facing the mother but rather with his back to her, with both looking in the same direction). Face-to-face interaction was the most commonly found style in the films on American babies.

In addition, the social context varied between these two cultures. The American mother tended to be alone and indoors with her baby, while the Fias mother tended to be in social groups and outdoors when interacting with her baby. The presence of others changed the mother–infant interactions in both cultures; however, interactions were affected differently in each. For example, among Fias, when the mother and infant were alone, face-to-face interaction occurred more often than did other forms of interaction (such as that taking place in a facing-outward posture). In the presence of one to three other people, however, the infant walked or ran and the caregiver made more play faces and grimaces and held the infant less. when more than three persons were present, the caregiver reverted to holding the infant but did not engage in face-to-face positions. In America, when the dyad was alone, the infant's walking or running increased, but when there were one to three others present, the American mother's face-to-face interaction decreased. American mother–infant interactions in groups larger than three was so infrequent that it was omitted from the coding.

Marquesans. Martini and Kirkpatrick (1981) also studied Micronesian culture through parent interviews, ethnographic observations, and film study. They studied mother–infant interaction on UaPou, one of the high volcanic islands of the Marquesas in French Polynesia. These investigators found results similar to those of Sostek et al. (1981): "[Infants] were rarely held in a face-to-face position (25% of the time); they were faced outward 43% of the time and in a half-outward position 32% of the time" (p. 199).

The Marquesan caregivers spent much of their time calling their babies' names, directing them to look and wave at others, prompting them to perform motor skills, and directing 3- to 6-year-old siblings to play with them. The mother's function was to set up complex interactions involving three or more people, with the baby as focus. According to Martini and Kirkpatrick (1981), unlike American mothers, who have dyadic interactions with reciprocal turn-taking dialogues,

> the Marquesans did not engage in pseudo-dialogues in which caregivers act as if infants controlled the detailed turn-taking rules of conversation. Instead they had infants "recognize" others, even before they seemed capable of distinguishing the many people mentioned. (p. 208)

The Marquesan infants are remarkably quiet and particularly attentive to the surrounding social and object worlds from the first month onward. The infant is treated on the assumption that he or she has individual will and motivation, which often run counter to those of the adults. Unlike Japanese childrearing, Marquesan practices accentuate infant separateness. Japanese mothers perceive infants to be willful, but extensions of themselves, and rear them to be obedient and dependent on adults. Marquesan mothers perceive their babies to be willful and demanding but consider them to be separate individuals.

These two research reports again illustrate that the way infants are reared is based on how they are perceived by the adults around them. They further illustrate that face-to-face interaction, adult turn-taking dialogue, baby talk, and reciprocal social games, which are considered normal mother-infant interactions in Western cultures, are not universal patterns existing in all cultures. These studies demonstrate as well the impact of ecological variables (such as social density and childrearing taking place primarily out-of-doors) on the quantity and quality of all interactions.

Latin America

Colombians.   Super et al. (1981) studied infant-caregiver interaction in Bogota, Colombia, using interventional strategies that affected mother-infant interactions in this culture. The intent of this project was to evaluate the effects of two different kinds of interventions (namely, nutritional supplementation and maternal education) on the development of infants known to be at risk for early malnutrition. It was found that nutritional supplementation increased infants' levels of positive social and nonsocial activity. Maternal education influenced maternal beliefs about infant development, which in turn altered mother-infant interaction.

Guatemalans.   Klein, Lasky, Yarbrough, Habicht, and Sellers (1977) undertook an exploratory study in Guatemala to investigate mother-infant interaction and its relationship to malnutrition and cognitive development. They found that mothers spent a large part of their time at some distance from their infants and that the level of caretaker vocalization was low. High levels of physical contact were present, but relatively little of this contact involved active social play. The strongest relations between infant-caretaker interaction and variables and indices of nutritional status were in infant verbal behavior. In a different study, Lester and Brazelton (1982) reported that Guatemalan neonates had a stressful perinatal environment resulting in underdemanding infants who were poor elicitors of maternal responses.

Mexicans.   Brazelton (1977) also describes the Zinacanteco infants of southeastern Mexico. The Zinacanteco infants, unlike the Guatemalan infants, were considered very mature because they could control their temperature while quietly lying naked for as long as 30 minutes after birth. No jerky startle movements were found in Zinacanteco infants. (Brazelton reports that an American baby, when born, does have such jerky startle movements, and would have cried and shivered to regulate his or her temperature.)

Following a psychobiological model in this research, Brazelton noted that Zinacanteco mothers do not play with or talk to infants and that infants are fed 30 to 40 times a day, in each case before they cry from hunger. The Zinacanteco value quiet conformity with low-grade peaks of excitement; their socialization from infancy may result in a personality that is in conformity with these cultural goals.

Summary and Conclusions

The empirical research reviewed here generally indicates that three cross-cultural characteristics have an impact on mother-infant interaction: household structures and composition, feeding practices, and mothers' attitudes and beliefs.

Household structures and composition. There is wide variation in household arrangements in different cultures. Whiting and Whiting (1960) examined 565 societies representing a sample of world cultures. Only slightly more than a quarter of these societies were found to have monogamous nuclear family households. Most of the cultures reported on had extended family households. This high social density in turn affected mother–infant interactions.

The prevalence of multiple caregivers in a society and their impact on infant development are apparent, particularly in regard to attachment behavior and stranger anxiety. Siblings often assume a caregiving role, and their role as playmates and models may facilitate infants' social and cognitive development. Having these siblings learn parenting skills at an early age is of additional value.

The pattern of mother and infant sleeping together is a very common practice in many societies. Whiting, Kluckhohn, and Anthony (1958) have supported this perception. These investigators reported that only five out of their sample of 56 world societies had sleeping arrangements similar to those of Americans, where the mother and father share a bed and the baby sleeps alone. Thus the practice of having infants sleep in a crib or cradle of their own is a rare one, prevalent in fewer than 10% of the world's societies whose ethnographies they surveyed. Even when infants have a cradle or cot of their own, it is generally placed near the mother's bed within easy reach. Only in Western societies, notably in the middle class of the United States, do infants have bedrooms of their own.

Feeding practices. Breast-feeding on demand and continuously seems to be the traditional pattern in non-Westernized and nonindustrialized countries. Ainsworth (1977b) has described the easier integration of attachment behavior with consistent breast-feeding on demand for long periods of time, thus challenging Western feeding practices. Konner's (1977a) description of human milk as being more appropriate for continuous feeding is also provocative in this respect.

Many cultures offer breast-feeding as a soothing method for comforting a distressed child. Harlow and Harlow's (1966) experiments on the value of physical contact in neutralizing stress suggest the benefits in offering the breast as a comforter. In addition, many traditional cultures prolong breast-feeding and delay weaning until the birth of the next infant. Tremendous variation exists in methods and severity of weaning.

Finally, feeding practices are related to health practices, which in turn are related to superstitions. One such superstition, prevalent in many cultures, is the mother's belief in the "evil eye," or the ability of someone to cause harm to the vulnerable infant by looking at the child. Therefore, the mother may restrict strangers from interacting with and complimenting the infant (Lester & Brazelton, 1982; Whiting, 1963).

Mothers' attitudes and beliefs. Mother–infant interaction is dependent on the mother's culturally prescribed perception of the infant and her expectations for the child's performance and development. Many cultures view infants as passive and incapable of communicating their needs or having mastery over their environment. Such cultures act upon a child instead of interacting with the child. In such settings, mothers see their role as that of caregiver rather than facilitator of the infant's total development, with the result that they pay more attention to the child's physiological needs than they do to the child's cognitive and language development. Therefore, in many of the cultures reported on in the research, the mother has been found to do little or no talking to her infant.

In spite of the perceptions of caregivers who view infants as passive, infants do modify their caregivers' interaction. For example, the infant's health, responsiveness, and overall temperament shape adult expectations, perception, and affect (Brazelton, 1977; Klein et al., 1977).

RECOMMENDATIONS

Comparative child development research is itself in the stage of infancy. It is highly advisable that Western and Third World scientists undertake collaborative efforts to open up new frontiers in this field. The field of comparative child development also needs to attract professionals from various allied disciplines to actively participate in international research. This commitment to multinational and multidisciplinary ventures would provide a great impetus for the growth of knowledge in child development. It is hoped that the recent establishment of child development research units in universities in the Third World will provide the milieu for the exchange of scholars and for this type of research effort.

The bulk of Western research on child development at present does not generally address issues of importance to Third World nations, nor does it offer relevant solutions to problems confronted in these countries. Research done in universities in the Third World and studies undertaken by various international development agencies need to confront aspects of infant care such as health, nutrition, and caregiver–child interaction. In addition, such efforts should attempt to assess the interrelationships between these aspects and to gauge their effect on the infant's total development. Specifically, research might be designed to investigate the following five areas of concern:

1. The Existing Infant-Rearing Practices Within Given Cultural Contexts and Their Impact on Caregiver–Infant Interaction

Initial exploratory or pilot studies need to gather more data on the typical patterns of mother–infant interaction in the larger ecological and social-cultural context. Since Triandis's model (see Figure 2) indicates that ecology affects both individual and social-cultural factors, which in turn affect social interaction, it could be helpful in delineating specific variables for study.

Research described earlier in this discussion has indicated that social density, an ecological variable, modifies mother–infant interaction (Sostek et al., 1981; Martini & Kirkpatrick, 1981). Climate is another ecological variable that influences mother-infant interactions. In the tropical Micronesian culture, for example, most mother–infant interactions take place outdoors (Sostek et al., 1981; Martini & Kirkpatrick, 1981). Zinacanteco neonates have mild hypoxia due to high altitude, a condition that makes the infants alert but quiet. This behavior in turn shapes the infants' nurturing environment in the direction of passive caretaking practices (Lester & Brazelton, 1982). Hazardous ecological environments have also been found to influence mother–infant interactions (LeVine, 1977).

Norms, beliefs, and values are sociocultural variables influencing mother–infant interaction (see Figure 2). The review of empirical research presented earlier has indicated that the Japanese value restraint in infant-rearing while Americans value independence (Caudill, 1972). The Zinacantecos (Lester & Brazelton, 1982) and Ainu (Munroe & Munroe, 1975) value passivity and conformity. Micronesians value social interaction between siblings and infants (Martini & Kirkpatrick, 1981). Each of these differing value systems shapes the mother's interaction with her infant.

Research needs to unravel many more such specific ecological and sociocultural factors shaping mother–infant interactions. Dawson's model (see Figure 3) could also be helpful in identifying the interactions between specific biological and sociocultural variables having an impact on mothers and infants in the Third World. Specifically, Dawson's "biological variables" include such factors as malnutrition, disease, and parasitic infection. These influences, along with Dawson's "sociocultural variables" (factors such as socialization practices, ecology, and overcrowding), influence the individual's "psychological processes" and development. (Triandis's and Dawson's theoretical models are particularly recommended here because as yet they have not been used to design empirical research on mother-infant interactions.)

2. The Interactions and Relationships of all Potential Caregivers within the Child-Care System

Since multiple caregiving seems to be a common phenomenon in most Third World cultures, future research needs to be broadened in scope to include all potential auxiliary caregivers in addition to the primary caregiver (i.e., the mother). More systematic studies need to be undertaken to compare the similarities and differences between primary caregiver–infant interactions and auxiliary caregiver–infant interactions. It is also vital to compare the interactions between adult caregiver and infant with those occurring between child caregiver and infant. (In this review of research, only Leiderman et al., 1977, have addressed this issue directly.) Even among child caregivers, age and experience vary. Research is needed to investigate how these variables affect the child caregiver's interactions with the infant. Finally, studies are needed to explore the consequences of multiple caregiving on infant development.

3. The Relationship between Economic Resources and Mother–Infant Interactions

The availability of economic resources or the lack of them does have an impact on mother–infant interaction (Leiderman et al., 1977). Many urban Third World women of the lower middle class may choose to work outside the home due to financial necessity. This in turn may affect their interactions with their infants, perhaps resulting in a reduction of continuous physical contact or a shift from breast- to bottle-feeding. Future research needs to explore the impact of work outside the home on mothers' interactions with their infants. The choice of substitute infant care to replace the mother will also be partly affected by the availability of economic resources.

Research could also compare mother–infant interactions in various socioeconomic groups within the same culture. Third World women of the upper socioeconomic class often hire women of the lower socioeconomic class to raise their children. Very often, a completely different set of value systems and childrearing practices exist in the upper and lower socioeconomic classes.

Research is needed to investigate the impact these differing childrearing practices have on the infant. The mother's direct influence on the infant, as well as her indirect influence as mediated through hired help, also need to be explicitly delineated and stated.

In addition, research should help in identifying the different needs and options women have regarding infant care arrangements, as based on their economic resources. Suitable services could then be provided. For example, in India, poor women work on urban construction sites, and they bring their infants with them since they have no other caregiving arrangements. Mobile creches on some construction sites in India have now been provided so that these infants can be cared for in close proximity while their mothers are at work.

4. The Relationship between Women's Workloads and Mother–Infant Interactions

Western women have access to commercial baby food, disposable diapers, and ready-made infant garments, all of which make infant care less of a chore. These conveniences are largely unavailable to Third World women. Besides caring for infants, women in nonindustrial societies also have many labor-intensive household and agricultural tasks. Cumulatively, such women's roles and responsibilities are many and are bound to have an effect on the quality and quantity of interactions with their infants. Comparative child development research on mother–infant interactions has sorely neglected to study the effect of workload on the mother's interactions with her infant. Future research designs need to incorporate the variable of the mother's varying workload, keeping in mind its ecological setting. Research reviewed earlier has indicated that mothers in Third World countries seem to spend more time in caregiving activities and less time in social, playful, and language interactions with their infants. Lack of these interactions may be a result of heavy workload.

Brown (1973) reports that all tribal and peasant women work in nonindustrialized societies. These women are able to contribute substantially to their households' incomes because their major subsistence activities are such that the dictates of childrearing can be easily accommodated. She further explains that full-time motherhood is a rarity in the nonindustrialized societies — but that equally as rare is full-time work requiring as many hours, as inflexible a schedule, and as great a spatial separation from the child as is required by maternal employment in Western technological societies. Brown therefore recommends that research be conducted on how women in nonindustrialized societies juggle both work and childrearing. Such research may suggest ingenious solutions to maternal employment and childrearing problems in the United States.

5. The Relationship between Mother–Infant Interactions and Modernity, Change, and Acculturation

Introduction of Western goods, commodities, services, media, and ideas is bound to have an impact on existing traditional mother–infant interactions. Some of these variables may adversely affect infant-rearing practices. For example, Leiderman et al. (1977) reported that the fact that more female children in East Africa enrolled in school disrupted the existing infant-care system.

In addition, Western women are reverting to breast-feeding, while Third World women are discovering the convenience of bottle-feeding. Ainsworth (1977b) clearly advocates the advantages of breast-feeding, noting that it facilitates the infant's organization and integration of attachment behavior. Harlow and Harlow (1966) stress the value of physical contact between mother and infant. Slings are being sold in Western markets, and many Western mothers are reverting to their use. On the other hand, Ainsworth (1977b) has reported that acculturated Ganda women have abandoned the traditional use of slings and have been sold on cribs and carriages, for they provide the convenience of leaving the baby unsupervised. Konner (1977a) has also expressed concern about the long-term consequences of the shift from traditional to modern infant-rearing practices.

Also to be considered is the fact that many rural men in Third World countries are emigrating to the cities looking for jobs, leaving the family in rural areas. This in turn is bound to affect women's roles and responsibilities, which in turn would affect their interactions with their infants. In addition, the trend in Africa, Asia, Latin America, and the Middle East is for more women to be educated formally. The amount of education women are now receiving has also increased. LeVine (1982) has reviewed four studies reporting the impact of women's education on the maternal behavior of different groups of women: Yoruba (Nigeria), Gusii (Kenya), Philippino, and Mexican-American. From the research reviewed, LeVine has generalized that

> women's schooling is often associated with low fertility, lower infant and child mortality, and a style of maternal behavior toward young children that is more pedagogical and conversational than the styles indigenous to many Third World cultures. (p. 307)

Although LeVine has also noted that "none of these generalizations can be claimed as universal or uniform across regions, levels of schooling, or age cohorts" (p. 307), the need is clear for more research on the acculturation of Western ideas and on the attitudinal shifts women undergo in various cultures as a result of education. Such investigations might also focus on the impact of such schooling on infant-rearing practices.

In conclusion, the types of research recommended here have large ramifications, for they may provide direction to social policy makers. Researchers might recommend the development of appropriate support systems for women and their families undergoing rapid change in the Third World. Such recommendations might involve the development of infant creches, the provision of family life education in the context of women's literacy programs, or the staffing of maternal health clinics with child development specialists. It is hoped that suitable social intervention programs will be developed — and that these programs will be designed to respect the cultural fabric and integrity of the societies in which they are implemented.

REFERENCES

Ainsworth, M.D.S. (1967). *Infancy in Uganda: Infant care and the growth of love.* Baltimore: Johns Hopkins University Press.

Ainsworth, M.D.S. (1977a). Attachment theory and its utility in cross-cultural research. In P. Leiderman, S. Tulkin, & A. Rosenfeld (Eds.), *Culture and infancy* (pp. 49-67). New York: Academic Press.

Ainsworth, M.D.S. (1977b). Infant development and mother-infant interaction among Ganda and American families. In P. Leiderman, S. Tulkin, & A. Rosenfeld (Eds.), *Culture and infancy* (pp. 119-149). New York: Academic Press.

Bowlby, J. (1958). The nature of the child's tie to his mother. *International Journal of Psychoanalysis, 39,* 350-373.

Brazelton, T.B. (1977). Implications of infant development among the Mayan Indians of Mexico. In P. Leiderman, S. Tulkin, & A. Rosenfeld (Eds.), *Culture and infancy* (pp. 157-187). New York: Academic Press.

Brislin, R., Lonner, W., & Thorndike, R.M. (1973). *Cross-cultural research methods.* New York: Wiley.

Bronfenbrenner, U. (1979). *The ecology of human development.* Cambridge, MA: Harvard University Press.

Brown, J. (1973). The subsistence activities of women and the socialization of children. *Ethos, 1,* 413-423.

Caudill, W. (1972). Tiny dramas: Vocal communication between mother and infant in Japanese and American families. In W.P. Lebra (Ed.), *Youth, socialization and mental health: Mental health research in Asia and the Pacific* (Vol. 2, pp. 25-48). Honolulu: East-West Center Press.

Caudill, W., & Frost, L.A. (1972). A comparison of maternal care and infant behavior in Japanese-American, American, and Japanese families. In W.P. Lebra (Ed.), *Youth, socialization and mental health: Mental health research in Asia and the Pacific* (Vol. 2, pp. 3-15). Honolulu: East-West Center Press.

Caudill, W., & Plath, D. (1966). Who sleeps by whom? Parent-child involvement in urban Japanese families. *Psychiatry, 29,* 344-366.

Caudill, W., & Schooler, C. (1973). Child behavior and child rearing in Japan and the United States: An interim report. *Journal of Nervous and Mental Disease, 157,* 320-338.

Caudill, W., & Weinstein, H. (1969). Maternal care and infant behavior in Japan and America. *Psychiatry, 32,* 12-43.

Dawson, J.L.M. (1967). Traditional versus Western attitudes in West Africa: The construction, validation and application of a measuring device. *British Journal of Social and Clinical Psychology, 6,* 81-96.

Dawson, J.L.M. (1969a). Attitude change and conflict among Australian Aborigines. *Australian Journal of Psychology, 21,* 101–116.

Dawson, J.L.M. (1969b). Theoretical and research base of bio-social psychology. *University of Hong Kong: Supplement to the Gazette, 16,* 1–10.

Dawson, J.L.M., & Ng, W. (1972). Effects of parental attitudes and modern exposure on Chinese traditional-modern attitude formation. *Journal of Cross-Cultural Psychology, 3,* 201–207.

Dixon, S., Tronick, E., Keefer, C., & Brazelton, T.B. (1981). Mother-infant interaction among the Gusii of Kenya. In T.M. Field, A.M. Sostek, P. Vietze, & P.H. Leiderman (Eds.), *Culture and early interactions* (pp. 149–168). Hillsdale, NJ: Erlbaum.

Field, T.M., Sostek, A.M., Vietze, P., & Leiderman, P.H. (Eds.). (1981). *Culture and early interactions.* Hillsdale, NJ: Erlbaum.

Frijda, N., & Jahoda, G. (1966). On the scope and methods of cross-cultural research. *International Journal of Psychology, 58,* 67–89.

Geber, M. (1958). Psychomotor development in African children: The effect of social class and the need for improved tests. *Bulletin of the World Health Organization, 18,* 471–476.

Geber, M., & Dean, R.F.A. (1957). The state of development of newborn African children. *Lancet, 1,* 1216–1219.

Goldberg, S. (1977). Infant development and mother-infant interaction in urban Zambia. In P. Leiderman, S. Tulkin, & A. Rosenfeld (Eds.), *Culture and infancy* (pp. 211–243). New York: Academic Press.

Harlow, H.F., & Harlow, M.K. (1966). Learning to love. *American Scientist, 54* (3), 244–272.

Hull, C.L. (1943). *Principles of behavior.* New York: Appleton Century.

Klein, R.E., Lasky, R.E., Yarbrough, C., Habicht, J.P., & Sellers, M.J. (1977). Relationship of infant/caretaker interaction, social class and nutritional status to developmental test performance among Guatemalan infants. In P. Leiderman, S.Tulkin, & A. Rosenfeld (Eds.), *Culture and infancy* (pp. 385–403). New York: Academic Press.

Konner, M. (1977a). Evolution of human behavior development. In P. Leiderman, S. Tulkin, & A. Rosenfeld (Eds.), *Culture and infancy* (pp. 69–109). New York: Academic Press.

Konner, M. (1977b). Infancy among the Kalahari Desert San. In P. Leiderman, S. Tulkin, & A. Rosenfeld (Eds.), *Culture and infancy* (pp. 287–328). New York: Academic Press.

Kuhn, T.S. (1970). *The structure of scientific revolutions* (2nd ed.). Chicago: The University of Chicago Press.

Leiderman, P.H., & Leiderman, G. (1977). Economic change and infant care in an East African agricultural community. In P. Leiderman, S. Tulkin, & A. Rosenfeld (Eds.), *Culture and infancy* (pp. 405–438). New York: Academic Press.

Leiderman, P.H., Tulkin, S., & Rosenfeld, A. (1977). Overview of cultural influences in infancy. In P. Leiderman, S. Tulkin, & A. Rosenfeld (Eds.), *Culture and infancy* (pp. 3–11). New York: Academic Press.

Lester, B.M., & Brazelton, T.B. (1982). Cross cultural assessment of neonatal behavior. In D.A. Wagner & H.W. Stevenson (Eds.), *Cultural perspectives on child development.* San Francisco: W.H. Freeman.

LeVine, R.A. (1977). Child rearing as cultural adaptation. In P. Leiderman, S. Tulkin, & A. Rosenfeld (Eds.), *Culture and infancy* (pp. 15–27). New York: Academic Press.

LeVine, R.A. (1982). Influences of women's schooling on maternal behavior in the Third World. In G. Kelly & C. Elliott (Eds.), *Women's education in the Third World: Comparative perspectives* (pp. 283–310). Albany, NY: State University of New York Press.

Lewin, K.L. (1935). *A dynamic theory of personality.* New York: McGraw Hill.

Lozoff, B. (1977, March). The sensitive period: An anthropological view. Paper presented at the Biennial Meeting of the Society for Research in Child Development, New Orleans.

Martini, M., & Kirkpatrick, J. (1981). Early interactions in the Marquesas Islands. In T.M.

Field, A.M. Sostek, P. Vietze, & P.H. Leiderman (Eds.), *Culture and early interactions* (pp. 189–213). Hillsdale, NJ: Erlbaum.

Miller, N., & Dollard, J. (1941). *Social learning and imitation.* New Haven, CT: Yale University Press.

Minturn, L., & Lambert, W. (1964). *Mothers of six cultures.* New York: Wiley.

Munroe, R.L., & Munroe, R.H. (1975). *Cross-cultural human development.* Belmont, CA: Wadsworth.

Murray, H. (1949). *Exploration in personality.* New York: Oxford University Press.

Mussen, P.H., Conger, J.J., & Kagan, J. (1979). *Child development and personality* (5th ed.). New York: Harper and Row.

Osofsky, J.D., & Connors, K. (1979). Mother-infant interaction: An integrative view of a complex system. In J.D. Osofsky (Ed.), *Handbook of infant development* (pp. 519–548). New York: Wiley.

Piaget, J. (1975). *The construction of reality.* New York: Ballantine.

Sostek, A.M., Vietze, P., Zaslow, M., Kreiss, L., Waals, F.V., & Rubinstein, D. (1981). Social context in caregiver-infant interaction: A film study of Fias and the United States. In T.M. Field, A.M. Sostek, P. Vietze, & P.H. Leiderman, *Culture and early interactions* (pp. 21–37). Hillsdale, NJ: Erlbaum.

Stone, L.J., & Church, J. (1973). *Childhood and adolescence* (3rd ed.). New York: Random House.

Super, C.M., Clement, J., Vauri, L., Christiansen, N., Mora, J.O., & Herrera, G.M. (1981). Infant and caretaker behavior as mediators of nutritional and social intervention in the barrios of Bogota. In T.M. Field, A.M. Sostek, P. Vietze, & P.H. Leiderman, *Culture and early interactions* (pp. 171–188). Hillsdale, NJ: Erlbaum.

Super, C.M., & Harkness, S. (1982). The development of affect in infancy and early childhood. In D.A. Wagner & H.W. Stevenson (Eds.), *Cultural perspectives on child development* (pp. 1–19). San Francisco: W.H. Freeman.

Thomas, A., & Chess, S. (1977). *Temperament and development.* New York: Brunner/Mazel.

Triandis, H.C. (1979). Cross-cultural psychology, In M.E. Meyer (Ed.), *Foundations of contemporary psychology* (pp. 544–579). New York: Oxford Press.

Werner, E.E. (1979). *Cross-cultural child development.* Belmont, CA: Wadsworth.

White, B. (1975). *The first three years of life.* Englewood Cliffs, NJ: Prentice-Hall.

Whiting, B.B. (Ed.). (1963). *Six cultures: Studies of child-rearing.* New York: Wiley.

Whiting, J.W.M. (1977). A model of psychocultural research. In P. Leiderman, S. Tulkin, & A. Rosenfeld (Eds.), *Culture and infancy* (pp. 29–48). New York: Academic Press.

Whiting, J.W.M., Kluckhohn, F., & Anthony, A.S. (1958). The function of male initiation ceremonies at puberty. In E.E. Maccoby, T. Newcomb, & E. Hartley (Eds.), *Readings in social psychology* (pp. 359–370). New York: Holt.

Whiting, J.W.M., & Whiting, B.B. (1960). Contributions of anthropology to the methods of studying child-rearing. In P. Mussen (Ed.), *Handbook of research methods in child development* (pp. 918–944). New York: Wiley.

Whiting, J.W.M., & Whiting, B.B. (1975). *Children of six cultures: A psycho-cultural analysis.* Cambridge, MA: Harvard University Press.

Wolff, P.H. (1971). Mother-infant relations at birth. In I.J.G. Howels (Ed.), *Modern perspectives in international psychiatry* (pp. 80–97). New York: Brunner/Mazel.

2

The Role of Adults in Infant Development: Implications for Early Childhood Educators*

Alan Fogel

Purdue University

INTRODUCTION

Parenting, and its effect, has been the major subject of research related to the adult's role in early human development. As society's need for child care shifts to accommodate the needs of infants and toddlers, perspectives of the early childhood educator have been similarly broadened. The result is the expansion of the field of early childhood education to include children under the age of 3. Although some might label infant and toddler programs as day care, and mother-infant programs as caregiving, rather than educational, the traditional concerns of the professional early education specialist do not vanish by this semantic magic.

Infants are more closely allied with, and protected by, the home environment than are their elementary-school-age counterparts. Infants have a greater need for externally imposed controls and guidance when outside the home than do older children. This chapter presents a review and summary of recent research findings related to the adult's role in infant development. The selection of issues and findings presented here has been based on the following assumptions about infant development:

1. Adults are critical factors in the development and maintenance of cognitive, social, and emotional growth in infants and young children.
2. Parents and caregivers/educators can share in the infant's developmental progress. After the first year of life, infants can maintain quali-

---

*I would like to thank Thomas Hannan for his thoughtful comments on this paper.

tatively different relationships with each of the adults with whom they have regular contact.

3. During the first 3 years of life, more so than at any other age, educators must be aware of the specific nature of their own contributions and must comprehend how these contributions relate to those of other significant adults in the infant's life.

4. During the child's infancy, early childhood educators can serve an important role as educators of both parents and their infants. Therefore, knowledge of developmental processes in normal infants, particularly in the realm of social and emotional development, is essential.

In the first section of this chapter research on the parent–infant relationship will be discussed. Some of the classic concepts of infant development, such as bonding and fear of strangers, will be examined critically. The next section examines the role of nonfamilial caregivers, specifically in relation to group-care contexts and their impact on the infant and on the parent–infant relationship. Finally, issues related to the lasting effects of the infant's early experience with adults will be considered.

THE PARENT–INFANT INTERACTION

Recent research on the importance of parents in infants' lives has addressed several questions: At what age do infants recognize their parents? How important is early contact? and, How does the parent–infant relationship change with age?

One of the most important aspects of the parent–infant relationship is the infant's attachment to the parent, and vice versa. When does this attachment begin? Some have thought that the infant becomes attuned to the sound of the mother's heartbeat during prenatal development, although there is little concrete evidence for such a position (Detterman, 1978; Salk, 1978). More research has focused on the moments immediately following birth, hypothesizing that the amount of physical contact between parent and infant during that period will determine the course of their later relationship. The quality of the parent–infant relationship has been termed "bonding."

Bonding and Early Contact

Bonding has a number of definitions. Some use the word to signify the relationship of attachment between infant and parent. In this regard, one might hear someone speak of a relationship as being "bonded" or "not bonded." Bonding also has been used to refer to the events that take place during the first few hours after the birth of an infant, when parent and infant are placed alone together and in skin-to-skin contact, although this is more properly called "early contact." Finally, some people refer to bonding as the process that translates the latter experience into the former. These individuals hypothesize that skin-to-skin contact in the first hours after birth will predispose the parent–infant pair to a closer, more affectionate, and warmer relationship later on. In the research literature, however, bonding refers only to the parent's attachment to the child.

The current concerns about early contact and bonding grew out of the pioneering work of Marshall Klaus and John Kennell of Case Western Reserve University. Their first reports detailed an apparently universal pattern of behavior seen in mothers presented with their naked newborn immediately after birth. The mothers in their study first touched the neonate's fingers and toes for 4 to 8 minutes, then touched the infant's limbs, ending with an encompassing palm contact to the infant's abdomen accompanied by massaging movements (Klaus, Kennell, Plumb, & Zuehlke, 1970). In the same study, it was found that right after birth, mothers of premature infants progressed through the same phases, but they took a longer time exploring the baby's body than did the mothers of full-term infants.

Since then, studies reflecting this pattern of adult behavior at first contact have been replicated on many occasions and in a wide variety of settings. It also has been shown that fathers, when given the same opportunity to lie next to their newborn infants, progress through the same sequence of activity (McDonald, 1978; Rodholm & Larsson, 1979).

Though no one doubts the validity of the first-contact behavior pattern, a controversy has arisen over the relative importance of this behavior, or the lack of it, for the infant's development. Not long after these initial findings had been published, Klaus and colleagues conducted a study showing that mothers who had early contact with their infants in the newborn period were likely to spend more time holding their 1-month-old infants in an *en-face* position, in which the adult holds the infant so that each has a full view of the other's face (Klaus, Jerauld, Kreger, McAlpine, Steffa, & Kennell, 1972). In this study, the subjects were 28 low-income primiparous (first-time) mothers who did not plan to breast-feed. Compared with a control group of mothers who received routine hospital care, the experimental group had 1 hour of extra contact with their naked infants at birth and another 5 hours of extra contact each afternoon while in the hospital. The subjects were randomly assigned to experimental versus control groups, and the observers at one month were not aware of the group identity of the mothers.

Another study employed a sample of middle-class Caucasian infants from Canada who had normal deliveries (Kontos, 1978). The experimental group had 1 hour of extra contact beginning 45 minutes after birth. In follow-up observations at 1 and 3 months, the extra-contact group mothers did more smiling and singing, held their babies more in the *en face* position, and played more without the use of a toy than did the control group. This study used procedures of random assignment to experimental versus control groups similar to those of Klaus et al. (1972). The study was somewhat flawed, however, since only one of the two observers at the 1- and 3-month sessions was blind to the mother's group identity. We thus have no way of knowing in what way the informed observer might have influenced the naive observer.

In a well-controlled study done in Sweden, Schaller, Carlsson, & Larsson (1979) found evidence of higher levels of proximal contact (rubs, pats, kisses, and touches) in extended-contact mothers at 2 and 4 days, but no differences at 42 days. As in other studies, Schaller et al. compared a limited-contact group, who were allowed to hold their babies for only 5 minutes immediately following birth, with an extended-contact group, who held their naked infants for 1 hour after birth. A replication study by the same group of investigators (Carlsson et al., 1979) yielded similar findings: differences in the first few days but no differences 1 month later.

Another Swedish study gave extra-contact mothers skin-to-skin contact with their babies for the 15 minutes following birth that control-group babies were being weighed, washed, and dressed (DeChateau, 1980). This investigator reported some differences between extended-contact and control groups at 36 hours, but only in the position in which the mothers sat to hold their infants while feeding. In a 3-year follow-up, no differences were reported.

Finally, Svejda, Campos, and Emde (1980) had a similar experimental design, but took further precautions with their American middle-income sample. They made sure that each of the study mother's roommates received the same procedure and that there was only one study mother on the maternity ward at any time. By thus eliminating comparisons with other mothers, the mothers in the study were prevented from feeling special or different from other mothers in the hospital. Svejda et al. found no differences between experimental and control groups in mother–infant interaction at 36 hours after birth.

Although it is impossible to prove that early contact has no long-term effects, these studies, done in different countries and under many different conditions, seem to suggest that any differences due to extended or early contact are at best transitory, lasting no more than a few days or months. All of these studies have focused on maternal attachment or changes in maternal behavior following the experience of early contact. There is currently no evidence indicating that any of these manipulations has any effect on the baby's future attachment to the mother or on future cognitive and linguistic proficiency, in spite of news media claims to the contrary.

There is some evidence that early contact has effects on mothers from low-income groups, or on mothers who are at risk for attachment problems (Klaus et al., 1972). In these cases, the additional contact seems to act as an important boost to get the parent–infant system started. In ordinary cases, however, the parent–infant relationship has enough alternative resources to maintain its course without the benefit of additional early contact.

In general, the implication of this research is that parents who do not have the opportunity for extra early contact need not worry about the well-being of their infants. Indeed, there are many situations in which extra contact is impossible, as is the case for some premature infants, sick infants, sick mothers, or infants put up for adoption. In these cases, it is especially important for the family not to be beset by worries about what may have been lost, but rather to devote their energies to developing their relationships with the infant and to developing the family strengths necessary to cope with a high-risk infant.

None of this discussion is meant to deny the fact that it may be more satisfying for both parents to have the opportunity for early contact with their baby than to be isolated artificially by hospital rules and regulations. It therefore may be more convincing to argue for early and extended contact on the grounds of ensuring that each family gets the fullest possible enjoyment out of the childbirth experience, rather than on the grounds of preventing any lasting detrimental impact arising from the lack of that early contact.

The Early Relationship between Parent and Infant

Even though there is little evidence for the long-term impact of early extended contact, infants do learn to recognize their caregivers at an early age. In fact, studies have shown that the infant prefers his or her mother's voice to the voice of an unfamiliar female in the first few days of life (DeCasper & Fifer, 1980), and that, by the age of 3 months, most infants prefer to look at their mothers than at unfamiliar women (Barrera & Maurer, 1981; Hayes & Watson, 1981).

However remarkable these findings may seem, they do not prove that lack of visual or auditory exposure to the parent is necessarily detrimental. Blind infants do quite well without this kind of stimulation; they learn to recognize their caregivers by sound and touch (Fraiberg, 1974). These results, taken together, suggest that parents and infants begin to adapt to each other from the beginning of life. However, there is considerable flexibility in the way this process occurs, leaving open a wide range of developmental variations that can be considered normal.

Sander (1962) has suggested that the first phase of the parent-infant relationship, lasting from birth until about 2 months of age, is concerned primarily with the establishment of regular patterns of sleeping, feeding, arousal and quieting. In this phase, the parent's job is to get to know the baby's rhythms and to help the baby adjust those rhythms to fit into the routine of the family.

Parents in this period create frames in which the infant can function.

Frames are structures that initiate, maintain, and support adaptive functioning in the infant (Kaye, 1982). In the feeding frame, for example, the parent provides not only the food, but also a setting in which the infant can take full advantage of the warmth and tactile and vestibular stimulation that is provided. Other frames mentioned by Kaye are the discourse frame, the feedback frame, the memory frame, the modeling frame, the nurturant frame, and the protective frame. The discourse frame, for example, is one in which the parent creates the conditions under which a meaningful dialogue may take place. A situation within the discourse frame might be a give-and-take game in which the adult offers toys and then takes them from the infant, punctuating the actions with vocalizations. At the outset, this dialogue is likely to be one-sided, with the baby merely receiving the toy from the adult. Gradually, however, the baby learns the game by adopting bits and pieces of the routine, perhaps making a tentative offer or tugging at the adult's hand.

This example also embodies some of the other frames described by Kaye. Specifically, in the process of creating the frame for the discourse, the adult serves as the infant's external memory by picking up the game the next time where it was left off, even if the baby does not remember this. In addition, the adult serves as a model of appropriate action routines and as a source of feedback by helping the infant execute action that is consonant with the rules of the game.

Early Forms of Self-Regulation

Very young infants, even newborns, have a remarkable array of sensory and motor abilities. They can attend visually to the environment, and they can hear, smell, feel, and taste (Fogel, 1984). Although to remain alive and to acquire nourishment and stimulation the infant is dependent upon the adult, babies are born with rudimentary self-protective and self-calming abilities. One such ability, habituation, is the ability to tune out stimulation that is too noisy or too bright. If a stimulus is too intense, the infant will gradually look or listen less. Babies are also born with a set of reflexes that serve self-protective functions, such as turning the head away from nasal occlusion.

Another form of self-regulation, sucking on a pacifier, or nonnutritive sucking, occurs in many forms throughout infancy. If we count any incidence of nonnutritive sucking—on pacifiers, toys, fingers and thumbs, an adult's fingers—about 60 to 90% of all infants engage in this practice. Nonnutritive sucking usually stops at the end of the first year of life. It may, however, continue to occur until 4 to 7 years of age if the child is hungry, tired, or unhappy. A small proportion of children suck their thumbs until adolescence. In infants, thumb sucking appears primarily during sleep after the age of 4 months (Kessen, Haith, & Salapatek, 1970).

Pacification is one reason infants may suck. Whether associated with nutritive intake or not, sucking is an activity that immediately induces a state of calm in the infant. Another reason for nonnutritive sucking may be that it feels good. Sucking may be related neurologically with pleasure, or the infant may learn the association between the sucking response and the pleasurable intake of nutrient. Regardless of the particular reason, nonnutritive sucking appears to be a spontaneous behavior that has some important benefits to the newborn and older infant.

An infant's sucking on a pacifier is perceived as negative by a number of individuals. One of the reasons for such a perception is that the practice is primarily self-stimulation, suggesting to some observers that the infant somehow is not dealing effectively with the environment. The argument presented here, contrary to this view, is that nonnutritive sucking, like habituation, allows infants an opportunity to use their own resources for self-regulation. Even though the infant acts unselfconsciously, these behaviors are important steps on the path toward individual autonomy.

Interaction at a Distance

As infants begin to refine their visual-perceptual abilities and to recognize familiar people in their environment, they learn to appreciate noncontact interactions such as face-to-face play, in which parents and infants exchange smiles, gazes, and coos. According to Sander (1962), the period from 4 to 6 months is one in which the parent and infant, based on their prior familiarity, learn better to coordinate their feeding, playing, and other mutual activities.

Since all of the young infant's behavior is nonverbal, how does the parent or caregiver know what the infant needs or wants? In general, the process of "reading" a baby's signals is one involving some trial and error. The caregiver must experiment with different techniques in order to find responses that best suit the needs of the infant. It is not unusual for parents initially to misunderstand the infant's needs.

Some of the baby's signals are obvious: crying or smiling, for example. But there are many things that infants do during face-to-face interaction that may not have a clear meaning to adults. The baby's turning away from the interaction is one example of this ambiguity. Such gaze aversion has been interpreted to mean that the infant needs a "time out" from the interaction (Brazelton, Koslowski, & Main, 1974; Stern, 1974). Field (1982) studied gaze aversion in relation to changes in the infant's heart rate and the mother's behavior, finding that both gaze aversion and the infant's average heart rate were higher when the mother was trying to get the infant's attention. But she also found that heart rate and gaze aversion were equally high when the mother was asked to assume a "still-faced" expression—sitting quietly and looking at the infant. Gaze aversion may be a rudimentary coping skill whereby the infant can regulate the amount of visual stimulation according to his or her own abilities to process it (Fogel, 1982; Stern, 1974).

Field's (1982) study suggests that infants will avert their gaze if the caregiver does too little or if he or she overstimulates the baby. Kaye and Fogel (1980) found that in order to get their infant's attention, mothers increased the amount of touching and bouncing when the infant was looking away. After the infant looked at them, they began to increase the amount of facial expressiveness they displayed to the baby. It was found that facial expressiveness was more likely to *maintain* the infant's attention, while vestibular-tactual stimulation was used to *attract* the infant's attention when the baby was looking away.

Adults can read the infant's readiness to interact from the brightness versus dullness of the infant's eyes, raised versus furrowed brows, or smiling versus frowning. The infant's body position is also meaningful: slumping over, actively turning away, back arching, and squirming usually mean the baby wants a change of activity.

But can an infant "read" the signals of the adult during interaction? There is very little evidence that infants under 4 months of age can do so. In general, the infant's behavior is rigid and repetitive. Although it seems as though the mother and infant are "with" each other as infant arousal builds to a peak and tapers off, the research suggests that infants have little control over the pattern and timing of their own behavior (Kaye, 1982). For example, during face-to-face play at this age, infants may emit a series of cooing vocalizations and their caregivers may respond to each with another vocalization. The result looks like a mutual exchange of vocal "turns." Microanalyses of the behavior sequences during this sort of interaction, however, have revealed that the parent is responsible almost entirely for this affect, which is accomplished by skillfully inserting an imitative coo in between each of the baby's sounds (Fogel, 1977; Kaye & Fogel, 1980).

The adult becomes adept at fitting his or her behavior into the infant's cycles of activity and nonactivity. This pattern has prompted one investigator to label the early parent–infant interaction a pseudo-dialogue (Newson, 1977). This label suggests that the parent acts as if the baby had all the social skills of an older child, treating the baby's automatic actions as though they had some meaning and as if they were part of a true social act directed toward the parent. Infants of this age can and do feel pleasure, distress, disappointment, and wariness (Sroufe, 1979); nevertheless, their ability to take social initiatives is rather limited.

The Beginnings of Infant Initiative

Starting at about 5 months of age, infants begin to take an increasingly active role in their social relationships (Kaye, 1982; Kaye & Fogel, 1980;

Sander, 1962). They can now initiate social exchanges, anticipate, and play their first genuinely participatory games. At this age we also see an end to the period in which the caregiver does most of the "mutual adjustment" work. Kaye (1982) has suggested that at this age infants can be thought of as apprentices. They can take some initiatives on their own, but they still need the guidance of the "master," who sets up more advanced kinds of frames for them. Thus, a baby can learn to hide his or her own face, or that of the mother, but only in the context of a peek-a-boo routine that the parent has modeled and created for the baby.

By the end of the first year, the infant's initiatives have become more akin to demands, and the baby enters the period of expressing a desire to be near the caregiver, a wariness of strange situations, and a more realistic awareness of other people in the environment. Since this is the age at which the infant becomes attuned to the presence of other people and begins to understand them to be physically and emotionally different from the mother and father, and the age at which the infant begins clearly to express different emotional reactions to different people, it is a period that early childhood educators must understand more fully. Recent research has shed considerable light on the nature of the 12-month old's fears and on how the baby can best cope with them.

Coping with an Expanding Awareness and New Emotions

In the realm of sensorimotor development, the infant at 12 months is trying out new means to reach goals (Piaget, 1952). The psychological experience associated with this motor behavior is a mental comparison of alternatives. This sort of appraisal means that the infant does not react immediately, in knee-jerk fashion, to a particular event but tries to evaluate the event's effect with respect to possible alternative responses. Because infants have only rudimentary intrinsic appraisal skills at this age, they sometimes cope with their feelings of uncertainty by turning to the people around them for help. They will look to see how those people react to events and then adjust their own feelings accordingly.

The social referencing implicit in such behavior has been investigated in situations provoking uncertainty and fear. In one study, a noisy, flashing robot approached a 1-year-old child who was sitting nearby. The child's mother was asked to make either a fearful face, a smiling face, or a neutral face. Infants were less likely to be upset by the toy when their mothers posed either the smile or the neutral face (Klinnert, 1981). Similar results were found even if the adult was a stranger to the infant.

Feelings of uncertainty become more common as the infant develops cognitively. Related emotions, surprise and fear, also do not appear before the eighth or ninth month of life (Piaget's Stage IV). Because infants now have the ability to plan and to anticipate, they can be surprised by unexpected turns of events (Charlesworth, 1969). If the event is unexpected and seems threatening, then the infant feels fear. By the end of the first year of life, infants experience the emotion of fear in a wide variety of situations.

Infants may become fearful of an otherwise benign situation because it reminds them of something they found stressful, frightening, or painful in the past. Such acquired fears can be said to arise from a conditioned association and are different from fear of heights or of looming objects, which may be universal. Acquired fears are learned; examples include fear of particular people, of doctors' offices, or of certain kinds of sounds, such as a dog's barking (Bronson, 1972).

Infants also may be afraid of unfamiliar settings or people. Although infants' reactions to strangers are usually different from their responses to their parents, infants are not always fearful of strangers. Babies show more positive reactions if the stranger approaches them slowly (Kaltenbach, Weinraub, & Fullard, 1980; Trause, 1977), if their mother is present when the stranger approaches (Eckerman & Whatley, 1975; Ricciuti, 1974; Trause, 1977), if they are with a familiar caregiver such as a babysitter or child-care provider (Fox, 1977; Ricciuti, 1974), if the stranger is a child as opposed to a normal adult or a midget (Brooks & Lewis, 1976), if the stranger does not tower over the infant (Weinraub & Putney, 1978), and if the infant is in an unfamiliar setting such as a laboratory as opposed to the home (Brookhart & Hock, 1976; Skarin, 1977).

A number of studies have shown that babies can engage in positive and rewarding social interaction soon after meeting a new person. If the stranger proves acceptable to the baby, the baby will often spend more time playing with this interesting visitor than with the mother (Klein & Durfee, 1976; Ross & Goldman, 1977).

On the other hand, if the stranger approaches too quickly, looms, towers, or otherwise violates the infant's personal space, fearful reactions can easily be evoked. But would an adult react any differently? In one study (Kaltenbach et al., 1980), mothers and their 8-month-old infants sat side-by-side as unfamiliar female adults approached them quickly. The mothers showed more quizzical looks, frown, and gaze aversions as the stranger got closer than did their infants! This finding suggests that "stranger fear" is not simply a stage of development that babies go through. Rather, it may represent a step toward becoming more adult — a growing awareness of situations that all humans fear. Hesitancy toward strangers, especially intrusive ones, is something that stays with us throughout our lives.

Also commonly expressed at this point in the infant's development are fears of separation. Being left alone is a terrible experience for most babies of 12 months. Developmentalists once thought that separation distress or fear came from the baby's sense of loss due to separation from the parent. Research has shown, however, that if parents leave their babies in the company of familiar caregivers there is little or no separation distress (Ricciuti, 1974; Stayton, Ainsworth, & Main, 1973; Suwalsky & Klein, 1980). In one study of children admitted to residential care, it was found that infants admitted with a sibling showed less separation distress than those admitted by themselves, even if the sibling was not old enough to take care of the infant (Heinicke & Westheimer, 1966). Another study found that infants left with a total stranger coped significantly better with separation than infants left completely alone (Ricciuti, 1974).

Infants respond more positively to separation from one parent if they are left with any other person, particularly a familiar one; if they are left with toys of any kind and can see or hear their parents in an adjoining room (Corter, 1977); and if they are left with their own blankets or pacifiers (Halonen & Passman, 1978; Hong & Townes, 1976). The parent's saying "bye-bye," or making some other parting gesture before leaving had no effect on the abilities of 1-year-olds to cope with separation (Corter, 1977). These parting gestures do seem to help older infants, however, and are discussed at greater length in the following section.

The Beginnings of Self-Assertion

By the middle of the second year, infants' initiative taking becomes more self-conscious. Babies become aware of themselves as actors who have an effect on the environment, who can deliberately produce change, and who can manipulate the environment in order to produce an intended change (Piaget, 1952; Sander, 1962).

This newfound sense of self- and personal agency requires major adjustments in the adult–infant relationship. Infants have to learn to contend with the growing awareness of separateness from the adult, not an easy developmental task. Adults have to learn to channel the creative aspects of the child's budding autonomy, at the same time that they seek the child's compliance with the demands of health, safety, and social decorum.

A good many new coping skills arise in the infant of this age. Instead of immediately becoming upset in stressful situations, infants can be seen to fight back tears (Sroufe, 1979) or to bite their lower lips to control their distress (Demos, 1982). Infants can now use language to communicate their feelings to others, to reassure themselves, or to resort to a kind of pretend security in play situations (Piaget, 1962).

It is at this age that children come to rely on their teddy bears and blankets to comfort themselves. In studies conducted by Passman (1977) and Passman and Weisberg (1975), mothers rated their 2-year-olds' blanket attachment on a 10-point scale ranging from no attachment (1) to strong attachment (10). The sample was divided into blanket-attached children (those who scored between 6 and 10 on the scale) and non-blanket-attached children (those scoring below 6). The results showed that blanket-attached children with their blankets were able to comfort themselves better in a stressful situation without their mothers than were either blanket-attached children without their blankets or non-blanket-attached children.

Some investigators have suggested that the infant's reliance on a blanket as a source of comfort comes at precisely the time when the child is becoming more aware of his or her physical and psychological separateness from the caregiver. Although this sense of self as an independent individual does not take hold fully until the third year of life, the end of the second year can be thought of as an important transitional phase in the growth of autonomy. The blanket and other such attachment objects have been called transitional objects (Mahler, Pine, & Bergman, 1975; Winnicott, 1971) because they seem to serve as a bridge between the child's total reliance and dependence on the parent and the development of individuation.

Not all children develop blanket attachments. In countries where there is relatively more physical contact between infants and caregivers, there is less likely to be blanket attachment (Super, 1981). In a study of Italian children (Gaddini, 1970) only 4.9% of rural children had transitional object attachments, while 31.1% of urban children in Rome had them. Hong and Townes (1976) found that Korean infants used transitional objects less than did a matched sample of American infants, and Caudill and Weinstein (1969) reported less sucking on fingers and pacifiers in the relatively more indulged (as compared with Americans) Japanese infants. It seems that in societies in which children have continued access to physical contact, there is little need for transitional objects. This finding does not imply that parents in the United States should opt for closer physical contact with their children; it merely suggests that the interaction between culture and childrearing is complex and that children from each culture will develop culture-specific coping skills in response to culture-specific demands (cf. Fogel, 1984).

By the end of the second year, infants are taking their own initiatives in separating from their parents. Ley and Keopke (1982) found that infants of this age, observed with their parents in a public park, were not afraid to wander off at some distance. The situation is different, however, when it is the parents who initiate a separation, an occurrence that could happen for many reasons. The parents might want to go out in the evening, or they may need to travel away from the child for several days. This is often the time when mothers go into the hospital to have a second child. Other occasions for separation include the father's or mother's business trips, out-of-home child care, and even brief hospitalizations for the child.

Research suggests that parent-initiated separation episodes are more tolerable to the 2-year-old infant if the parent prepares the child for them beforehand. In one study (Weinraub & Lewis, 1977), 2-year-old children were least upset during separation if the mother explained that she would be leaving and gave the child instructions on what to do in her absence. This situation was especially true for children who were more developmentally advanced and who could understand better the mother's instructions. It also seemed to help the child during the separation if the mother spent more time at a distance and less time in close physical contact with the infant in the minutes just prior to the departure.

One additional finding of the Weinraub and Lewis (1977) study should provide at least a small measure of comfort to both parents and caregivers. These researchers discovered that the infant's immediate response to the parent's departure was not correlated with anything the parent said or did. Only after this initial response, when the infant finally calmed down, did the baby's behavior begin to reflect the efforts of the parent's preparation. Indeed, it seems common for babies of this age to protest loudly during the actual departure of the parent. As soon as it is clear that these protests are ineffective, the 2-year-old is generally capable of quieting down and even enjoying the substitute caregiver.

Another important issue for caregivers of children at this age is how to get the child to comply with the adult's wishes. How can adults effect immediate or short-term compliance while at the same time setting the stage for longer-term effects on child compliance and moral behavior? Although there has been a considerable amount of research on parental discipline styles and compliance in older children (Baumrind, 1967; Becker, 1964; Hoffman, 1970), relatively little has been done with children before the age of 3 years. This fact is surprising, since it is during the second year of life that children begin to assert themselves against the will of the caregiver.

One study of 27-month-olds found that children complied in over one-half of the situations in which requests for their compliance were made (Minton, Kagan, & Levine, 1971). In children of this age, Lytton (1979) found that suggestions were more likely to be followed by compliance than were command-prohibitions. This investigator also found that suggestions were most frequently used in situations in which the child had little reason not to comply (i.e., nonconflict situations). Schaffer and Crook (1980), in a study of 2-year-olds, found that compliance was more likely if the child was already disposed toward the situation. Thus, children who were asked to touch and pick up objects were more likely to do so if they were already looking at the objects. Children who were asked to manipulate objects were more likely to do this if they were already looking at and touching the object.

Following this same line of research, Holden (1983) made unobtrusive observations of middle-class mothers and their 2-year-olds in a supermarket. Observers watched mothers respond to a set of "undesired behaviors" on the part of the child: asking for food, reaching for things, standing in the cart, and ignoring the mother's requests. One group of mothers used "contingent" responses — that is, they scolded or reprimanded the child after the transgression had occurred. The other group of mothers used "preventive" responses, such as talking to the child while shopping and giving the child something to eat. The latter group of mothers had children who showed fewer instances of undesired behavior.

Compliance, therefore, seems to arise as a natural result of the caregiver's attempt to fit into and anticipate the child's behavior. From the child's point of view, the result is an increased feeling of control over the social and physical environment. This may seem paradoxical at first, since compliance typically is viewed as bringing the child under the adult's control. These studies seem to suggest, on the contrary, that compliance is the more-or-less automatic response of a child who has been allowed to develop his or her own initiatives within a carefully constructed caregiving frame. Indeed, Martin (1981a, 1981b) has shown that the more a caregiver attempts to assert power, demand firmness, and create an adversary position, the more likely it will be that the child will try to gain control. The children between 10 and 42 months of age whom Martin studied responded to parental coercion with behavior such as tugging, interfering, nagging, demanding, whining, touching, holding, and questioning.

To summarize, these studies suggest that getting a young child to comply fits into a more general pattern of creating effective caregiving frames. In other words, infants are more likely to comply if the caregiver creates a situation in which the child has no reason not to comply or in which there is no reason for the child to display the undesired behavior in the first place. In general, once the undesired behavior has begun, power assertion is not particularly effective. This does not mean that strong words and forceful discipline should not be used. One suspects that more research might reveal situations in which such methods are effective, but clearly the use of power as a regular tactic is questionable. Preventing troublesome situations and sensitivity to the child's states and goals seem to be the most effective "disciplinary" techniques for children this age.

Summary of Findings on the Parent-Infant Interaction

Child-care philosophies are always in flux, dependent as they are upon family and cultural factors (Kagan, Kearsley, & Zelazo, 1978). It is only relatively recently in the history of child care that the scientific method has been trained upon problems in this area. For many caregivers, intuition is enough; the advice of experts is a needless headache of conflicting and personally dissonant views. As much as possible, this review attempts to focus on the results of scientific research while refraining from giving advice. Indeed, science is only a kind of mirror in which reality has been reflected back upon the viewers, and it is up to the viewers to clarify the image in their own terms. With this cautionary note, the following results concerning the caregiver–infant relationship are enumerated:

1. During the first year of life, caregiving is primarily one-sided, with the adult providing a series of interdependent frames that initiate, maintain, support, and encourage infant behavior and development. These frames must constantly shift and change to correspond to changes in the infant's abilities and in particular to allow infants an increasing sense of control over their participation in the dialogue.
2. Because of this one-sided relationship, infants readily will accept substitute caregivers, as long as those caregivers are willing to learn to fit themselves into the infant's regular patterns of behavior. At this age, infants are not likely to experience a psychological aversion toward strange people or places.
3. A baby's differentiation among people and wariness of strangers, occurring near the end of the first year of life, do not signal automatic rejection of others, but merely suggest that the infant is able to develop qualitatively distinct relationships with different individuals. The best rules for making friends with babies of this age seem to be no different from those for making friends with anyone else: courtesy, respect, and sensitivity to individual responses and desires.
4. Most babies are attracted in a positive way to new people.
5. The ability to cope with distress, separation, and uncertainty increases as the child becomes more verbal and more self-aware.

It is important to note that most of the advice in child-care manuals on discipline and on the role of the caregiver in infant development is not based on systematic research. Certainly, parents and other caregivers need to do their jobs, and they cannot wait for research to verify what they feel intuitively are the best approaches. Nevertheless, child-care providers need to be updated on research findings as they become available, as part of an ongoing process to dispel myths and outdated practices. The studies discussed have shown that infants have the potential to develop positive and rewarding relationships inside and outside the home. They do not tell us how infants fare in group-care situations, nor do they inform us about the long-term effects of caregiving practices. These will be discussed in the following.

THE EFFECTS OF GROUP CARE ON INFANTS

Almost all the research on infants in groups has been done in high-quality day care centers; thus, it speaks for only a small proportion of the total population of young children who spend time in group-care settings. This means, in short, that much of what can be concluded from this research may not necessarily be generalized to the entire population of children.

Parent-Infant Attachment and Group Care

One of the main concerns voiced about group care has been whether, since infants often are separated from their parents for up to 8 to 10 hours per day, such arrangements disrupt the parent-infant attachment relationship. The answer seems to be that they do not. Children tend to prefer their mothers in stressful situations in which both mother and caregiver are available as a source of comfort, but in situations where quality care is given, infants can rely on the caregiver during the day and still maintain a special and different relationship with their parents (Kagan, Kearsley, & Zelazo, 1978; Portnoy & Simmons, 1978; Ragozin, 1980).

There is some evidence to suggest that the child's relationship to the caregiver is affected by parameters of the day-care situation. The most important factors affecting parent–infant relationships are not the total number of caregivers but rather: (1) the ratio of caregivers to children (1 caregiver to 3 infants under 18 months is desirable); (2) the emotional and physical availability of caregivers (one or more must be available to the child at least part of the time); and (3) the introduction of unfamiliar caregivers (new staff should be introduced gradually into the group). These findings suggest that day care not meeting these standards may have deleterious effects on the parent–infant relationship (Anderson, Nagle, Roberts, & Smith, 1981; Slaughter, 1980; Wilcox, Staff, & Romaine, 1980).

Until only a few years ago, most developmentalists sided with Bowlby's (1969) position that the best social environment for young infants consisted of attachment to a single important person, preferably the mother. Bowlby felt that more than one relationship during the first year would interfere with the infant's ability to develop attachments in general and with the mother in particular. Although research of the kind cited on the effects of group care allows us to see that infants easily can develop multiple relationships, not enough work has been done on the link between the infant's various social partners. Thus, we have little understanding about how experience in group care affects the parent–infant relationship, and vice versa: We know that there is an effect, but we do not understand how it is mediated.

The Effects of Day Care on Cognitive Development

Aside from effects on parent–child relationships, researchers and parents have wondered if the day-care experience has any lasting impact on the child's cognitive development. Some studies of middle-income infants have shown that quality day care neither enhances, nor detracts from, normal patterns of cognitive development (Kagan, Kearsley, & Zelazo, 1978). A recent study by Clarke-Stewart (1982), done in both day-care centers and day-care homes, showed that there was a significant increase in cognitive and social scores for day-care versus at-home-care infants. These recent findings should be a source of satisfaction to those involved in caregiving and the education of infants, for they seem to suggest positive outcomes as a result of conscientious efforts on the part of child-care providers.

Infants from lower-income backgrounds seem to benefit more from group care than do other infants. A recent report reviewed the findings of many research studies done on lower-income children who as infants had been in day care and preschool programs such as Head Start (Lazar & Darlington, 1982). Subjects were followed up between the ages of 9 and 19 years, and several results were reported.

As compared with children who had not been in group care, group-care children were more likely to meet their school's basic requirements, and they were less likely to have been retained a grade or to be in special education classes. This was true regardless of the child's sex, ethnic group, or family background. Group-care children had higher scores on Stanford-Binet IQ and standardized achievement tests; in addition, they were likely to focus on their own achievements, at school or work, as a reason to be proud of themselves. Finally, the group-care children were more likely than others to be affected by their mothers' attitudes toward school performance and vocational aspirations.

The Lazar and Darlington study is somewhat limited because it combined children in day care with children in preschool programs, like Head Start, and with children in parent–infant programs. One study has shown that parent–child development center programs, in which the low-income mother is taught the basic principles of child development, caregiving techniques, nutrition, health, and personal development, had a significant impact on maternal responsiveness and on the child's IQ at age 4 (Andrews et al., 1982).

In a related study (Slaughter, 1983), a 2-year early intervention program for low-income black mothers and their children, ages 18 to 44 months, was assessed with respect to the match between the intervention program and the social and cultural background that the mothers brought into the program. Specifically, the Levenstein toy demonstration program was contrasted to the Auerbach-Badger mothers' discussion group program. At the time of final evaluation, the mothers who participated in the discussion group were significantly higher on the Loevinger Scale of Ego Development, on observational measures of maternal teaching styles exhibited with their children, and on both frequency and quality of interaction with their children. The children of discussion-group mothers also verbalized more often during play. Children from both intervention groups scored higher on verbal and IQ measures than did controls, who were not exposed to any interventions. The investigator felt that the discussion group was more culturally relevant since it relied on sharing of experiences among group members and thus may have modeled an extended-family concept.

It seems, therefore, that group care can take many forms, both in terms of program format and in terms of the identity of participants. The effectiveness of group care may depend on the capacity of that care to support and foster the parent–child relationship. Encouraging this relationship is done by providing substitute care that is of comparable or better quality than parental care and by adapting the specific program elements to the needs, beliefs, and values of the family's cultural and subcultural heritage. In the preceding section of this paper, it was concluded that caregivers must change their behavior to fit the child's, thus providing the child with a sense of personal control and self-efficacy. Slaughter's (1983) research suggests that group-care programs must fit the ongoing patterns of behavior within the family, thus giving the family a sense of control and a measure of respect for the strengths to be found within their own culture or traditional childrearing practices.

The Role of Other Children in Group Care Settings

A review of the effects of peer relationships on children in group care would take us beyond the scope of this chapter, the goal of which is primarily to review the role of adults in infant development. However, there is a type of relationship that is an important intermediary between peer partnership and adult–child partnership; such relationships occur when children interact in mixed-age groups. Children are rarely exposed to nonpeers in formal educational or group-care settings. This sort of nonpeer relationship is most common between siblings, and there is a growing body of research on sibling relationships that attests to their importance (cf. Fogel & Melson, 1985).

In order to bridge the gap between sibling relationships in the home and peer relationships in group-care settings, recently a new line of research has begun in which infants are brought together with unfamiliar preschool children (cf. Fogel & Melson, 1985). In one study (Melson & Fogel, 1982), preschool children aged 3 to 5 years and of both sexes were left in a "waiting-room" situation with a 6-month-old infant whose mother, reading a magazine in a corner, was instructed not to become involved with the child or infant. No sex differences were found in the preschoolers' interest in or willingness to interact with the infant; however, only about one-third of the total sample of 70 children actually attempted to interact with the baby. In a second study (Fogel, Melson, & Mistry, 1985), mothers of the infants were instructed to follow a script to encourage the child to interact with the baby. The results were striking. The majority of the sample of 50 children became involved with the infant and seemed to enjoy the experience as much as the babies did. Again, no sex differences were found in the preschoolers' responsiveness to the infants. It seems that a relatively brief intervention by an unfamiliar adult (sessions lasted only 10 minutes) was enough to encourage a child placed in an unfamiliar setting with an unfamiliar infant to show positive responsiveness to the baby. Furthermore, parent reports indicated that 75% of the children in the sample express spontaneous interest in babies at least several times per week. Parents also reported equal amounts of interest in babies on the part of both boys and girls. The infants, for their part, showed much higher levels of interest in the children than the children did in them, rarely looking at their mothers when there was a child in the room.

Clearly, such research merely scratches the surface of a phenomenon with possible implications for early childhood education. Another study along similar lines (Berman, Monda, & Myerscough, 1977) placed an infant in a preschool classroom, a procedure that elicited considerable interest on the part of the children in the room. Researchers and educators may wish to develop and explore models for bringing children of different ages together. Because the interest children and infants have in each other is so strong, one might expect to produce important educational benefits for both partners. Such educational benefits may occur especially in cultural contexts in which older children are expected to take a responsible role in the care of infants, such as that of black or Asian Americans, typically cultures having an extended family form of living arrangement (Whiting & Whiting, 1975).

LASTING EFFECTS OF EARLY EXPERIENCE

In addition to conducting research on the parent-infant interaction and the effects of group care, investigators have looked for long-term effects of variations in the physical and caregiving environments to which infants are exposed during their first few years of life. The studies on the effects of early group care suggest that long-term benefits are associated with some kinds of early experiences. However, there are qualifications to this finding, to be described in this section.

Infants at Risk

Newborn infants are susceptible to a wide range of perinatal problems, ranging from oxygen deprivation to low birth weight. For all infants, the period immediately following birth is a time of adjustment from intra- to extrauterine life. Infants who suffer from one or more risk factors in the perinatal period may be unable to cope with the normal stresses of the first months of life and may therefore fall behind in their developmental progress.

In general, the research has found that many perinatal problems can be alleviated by a supportive environment. In a multiracial, multiclass sample of 670 infants born on the Hawaiian island of Kauai, it was found that all groups of children—regardless of race, social class, or age of mother— suffered about the same proportion of perinatal complications (Werner, Bierman, & French, 1971). In this sample, 13% suffered moderate complications, while 3% of the complications were severe. However, group membership predicted how well the infant recovered from the complication. Children born into lower-income families were less likely to recover fully by age 2. By age 10, the effects of perinatal problems had all but disappeared for all the groups, but children from lower-income groups had lower scores on intelligence tests and were doing more poorly in school than were children from middle-income groups.

Other research in this area has supported these conclusions. In general, the more stressful the environment—the more that parents lack economic and social support systems—the more likely it will be that infants will not recover quickly from perinatal complications (Crockenberg, 1981; Sameroff & Chandler, 1975; Waters, Vaughn, & Egeland, 1980). On the other hand, if there are adequate economic resources, if the parents are not under psychosocial stress, and if the infant is born normal except for the perinatal complications, then the effects usually do not persist.

Important too is the fact that if infants are not at risk, their behavior in the perinatal period seems not to predict any later aspects of infant functioning. Bell, Weller, and Waldrop (1971) found virtually no perinatal behavior that predicted the behavior of children in the preschool years. Dunn (1975) found that the success (or lack of success) with which mother and infant adjusted to each other during early feedings was not predictive of later mother-infant interaction patterns. Bell et al. (1971) and Dunn (1975) argue that the newborn is buffered against difficulties of early adjustment. Sameroff and Chandler (1975) speak of the infant as having a self-righting ability: Given an appropriately responsive environment, perinatal complications do not create any lasting organismic deficits, nor does perinatal behavior predict later functioning.

It may be that if parents are not under stress and are predisposed to provide competent caregiving, the infant at risk will evoke more maternal attention and solicitude than will a normal infant (Bakeman & Brown, 1980; Beckwith & Cohen, 1978; Crawford, 1982). This increased solicitude may be a factor in alleviating the early deficits in the first year or two of life. Thus, in certain circumstances, the environment can compensate for a wide range of individual variation.

The Effects of the Physical Environment

The physical environment surrounding the infant has been conceptualized in a number of ways. Typical dimensions that have been measured are the amount and availability of visual and auditory, and kinesthetic and tactile stimulation; the variety of inanimate objects; the contingent responsiveness of inanimate objects; the amount of freedom the infant has to explore the home; and the amount of noise and confusion in the home.

Research has suggested that aspects of the child's physical environment may affect later development. For example, early exposure in the first year to a variety of inanimate objects and to contingently responsive inanimate objects has been shown to lead to greater skill in problem solving and exploratory play in the second year (Yarrow, Rubenstein, & Pedersen, 1975). Provision of age-appropriate play materials during the first 2 years strongly predicts the child's Stanford-Binet IQ score at 4½ years (Bradley & Caldwell, 1976) and elementary school achievement test scores between 5 and 9 years (VanDoorninck, Caldwell, Wright, & Frankenburg, 1981).

Wachs (1982) has confirmed these findings and has introduced the notion of environmental specificity. In a sample of over 100 infants from a wide range of income groups and home environments, Wachs found that some aspects of the physical environment were more effective than others in promoting certain kinds of cognitive skills. For example, the development of spatial relations and perspective taking could be predicted best by the avoidance of noise, confusion, and environmental overcrowding during the first 2 years. Exploratory play skills in the second and third year were best enhanced by providing responsive objects, and by offering a variety of objects, in the first year. These factors, plus a well-organized environment and the use of age-appropriate play materials, were the best predictors of the child's ability to invent new means and plan effective strategies (Wachs, 1981; Wachs & Gruen, 1982).

It is interesting to note that environmental stimulation is not uniformly beneficial for all infants. Some forms of environmental stimulation have been found more effective for promoting the cognitive development of girls as compared with boys (Wachs & Gruen, 1982). Specifically, females were helped most by long-term stimulus variety, but they were relatively unaffected by overcrowding and noise confusion. On the other hand, males were negatively affected by noise confusion and by overcrowding but were positively affected by opportunities for exploration. It therefore may be that males are more vulnerable to stresses occurring early in life.

Interaction with the Social Environment

A number of more recent studies have shown that social and cognitive competence in preschool children — defined as a cluster of high IQ, advanced language skills, sociability to strangers, social competence in the peer group, and sociability in interaction with the mother — is strongly related to the quality of the early mother-infant relationship at 1 year. In particular, such competence is associated with the mother's early positive and responsive interaction with, and verbal responsiveness to the infant (Clarke-Stewart, VanderStoep, & Killian, 1979) and with the security of attachment of the infant to the mother (Arend, Gove, & Sroufe, 1979; Pastor, 1981; Waters, Wippman, & Sroufe, 1979).

Just as environmental specificity operates upon the interaction between physical environment and organism, there is also evidence for specificity in the interaction between social environment and organism. For example, tactile and vestibular stimulation from physical contact with the caregiver enhances later cognitive development, but only for the first few months. Maternal vocalization, contingent responsiveness, and involvement become important between 6 and 24 months, after which a lack of restrictiveness and the provision of opportunities to interact with other people are the best predictors of cognitive and language development (Bradley, Caldwell, & Elardo, 1979; Carew, 1980; Feiring & Lewis, 1981; Wachs & Gruen, 1982).

Need for Improved Research

The studies reviewed thus far have several limitations. First of all, they are almost all longitudinal studies of naturally occurring processes. There is nothing inherently wrong with such investigations; in fact, our understanding of human development would be enhanced if a greater number of carefully planned longitudinal studies were carried out. The problem is, however, that never can something measured at an early stage be established as the sole factor responsible for an outcome measured at a later age. For example, although the availability of responsive toys during the first year predicts cognitive development in the second year, this effect may be due to the involvement of the caregiver. If responsive toys and involved caregivers always go together, then there is no way to tell which of these factors is more important. It could be that in the absence of toys, an involved caregiver would be sufficient to foster cognitive-developmental skills.

An experimental manipulation could sort out the relative contributions of these factors, but scientific ethics prevent us from manipulating people's lives in the manner that would be most instructive. Therefore, the methodological solution to this problem is to learn better ways to interpret the data from nonmanipulative longitudinal studies and to avoid being fooled by the mere appearance of causality.

The other major problem with the investigations discussed is that they are limited to studying what can be measured with a valid and stable assessment scale. Infant assessment is a skill not yet well learned. There are a great number of extremely important dimensions of individual variation for which no carefully validated assessment scale exists. Examples of such dimensions are emotional maturity, coping skills, and social competence. One of the challenges to a science of infant development is the development of behavioral assessment techniques that capture the subtleties of emotional expression, interpersonal communication, and social competence (Adamson & Bakeman, 1982).

Finally, there are a whole host of questions that are crucial to our understanding of child and adult development: Why do some people develop psychopathology while others do not? Why do some, but not all, children have nightmares? and, Why are some people shy while others are outgoing? There is research related to all of these questions and others like them, but it suffers from poor conceptualization, lack of adequate experimental and statistical controls, and lack of representative samples of subjects. These flaws are not unique to infancy research; rather, they speak to a general need to improve research methods in all aspects of the social sciences.

INFANTS AND ADULTS: SOME CONCLUSIONS

The research summarized here leads to several conclusions. First, the environment plays a crucial role in the direction that development takes. If there is a strong relationship between an organismic factor early in development and the same factor in later development, the research suggests that this is not because of some stability within the infant, but because of stability within the environment — stable parental behavior, usually — that elicits similar behavior from the child at different ages (Bradley & Caldwell, 1981). In the absence of a supportive home environment of this sort, institutional care may be a crucial factor in stabilizing the infant's continued development (for example, Head Start — see Lazar & Darlington, 1982).

Second, in certain situations, early education can have a major impact on improving the home-care environment. For example, the success of parent-child development centers might be mentioned (Andrews et al., 1982). Improvements in the home-care environment may be especially likely if the early intervention program is designed to fit the cultural context of the target population (Slaughter, 1983).

Finally, in the case of a healthy and supportive home environment, early infant education can extend, complement, and enhance developmental progress, as well as provide needed encouragement for the parent's job well done (see Clarke-Stewart, 1982). Early education programs that focus only on the child are not likely to be as successful as those that incorporate the family into their curriculum and the culture into their philosophy.

A supportive environment can enrich the infant's life, but the environmental quality must be sustained and continually modified to meet the changing needs of the child at each age. During the first 3 years, it is more appropriate to think of adults as "environmental scaffolds" than as sources of new information. As such, adults temporarily erect social contexts that give the child a sense of control and efficacy in a limited sphere of endeavor and gradually allow the context to be superseded by genuine self-control in the child. The role of information provider is consonant with the view of the teacher of somewhat older children, who have already developed to the point that they can profit by the direct input they obtain from other people.

As compared with older children, infants need a curriculum in which "educational" experiences are presented with due respect for the emotional and social-control limitations of the pupils. The infant care "curriculum" should not be fixed or standardized. There is no evidence that caregiver acceleration of infant learning is effective, nor can infants be expected to climb up an already-built developmental scaffold. Instead, caregivers should be encouraged to provide small challenges within a scaffolding structure that is responsive to the individual infant and to the infant's developmental changes. It is the ongoing elaboration and change in this framing, or scaffolding, network — combined with a vision that includes the infant's family and culture within that network — that seems to be the most effective guarantor of the lasting impact of infant educational programs.

REFERENCES

Adamson, L., & Bakeman, R. (1982). Affectivity and reference: Concepts, methods and techniques in the study of communication development of 6- to 18-month-old-infants. In T. Field and A. Fogel (Eds.), *Emotion and early interaction* (pp. 213–236). Hillsdale, NJ: Erlbaum.

Anderson, C.W., Nagle, R.J., Roberts, W.A., & Smith, J.W. (1981). Attachment to substitute caregivers as a function of center quality and caregiver involvement. *Child Development, 52,* 53–61.

Andrews, R.R., Blumenthal, J.B., Johnson, D.L., Kahn, A.J., Ferguson, C.J., Lasater, T.M., Malone, P.E., & Wallace, D.B. (1982). The skills of mothering: A study of parent-child development centers. *Monographs of the Society for Research in Child Development, 47* (Serial No. 198).

Arend, R., Gove, F.L., & Sroufe, L.A. (1979). Continuity of individual adaptation from infancy to kindergarten: A predictive study of ego-resiliency and curiosity in preschoolers. *Child Development, 50,* 950–959.

Bakeman, R., & Brown, J. (1980). Analyzing behavioral sequences: Differences between preterm and full-term infant-mother dyads during the first months of life. In D. Sawin (Ed.), *Exceptional infants* (Vol. 4, pp. 271–299). New York: Brunner/Mazel.

Barrera, M.E., & Maurer, D. (1981). Discrimination of strangers by the three-month-old. *Child Development, 52,* 558–563.

Baumrind, D. (1967). Child care practices anteceding three patterns of preschool behavior. *Genetic Psychology Monographs, 75,* 43–88.

Becker, W.C. (1964). Consequences of different kinds of parental discipline. In M.L. Hoffman & L.W. Hoffman (Eds.), *Review of child development research* (Vol. 1, pp. 169–208). New York: Russell Sage Foundation.

Beckwith, L., & Cohen, S.E. (1978). Preterm birth; Hazardous obstetrical and postnatal events as related to caregiver-infant behavior. *Infant Behavior and Development, 1,* 403–412.

Bell, R., Weller, G., & Waldrop, M. (1971). Newborn and preschooler: Organization of behavior and relations between periods. *Monographs of the Society for Research in Child Development, 36* (Serial No. 142).

Berman, P., Monda, C., & Myerscough, R. (1977). Sex differences in young children's responses to an infant: An observation within a day care setting. *Child Development, 48,* 711–715.

Bowlby, J. (1969). *Attachment and Loss: Vol. 1. Attachment.* London: Hogarth.

Bradley, R. H., & Caldwell, B.M. (1976). The relation of infants' home environment to mental test performance at fifty-four months: A follow-up study. *Child Development, 47,* 1172–1173.

Bradley, R.H., & Caldwell, B.M. (1981). The stability of the home environment and its relation to child development. Paper presented at the meeting of the International Society for the Study of Behavioral Development, Toronto.

Bradley, R.H., Caldwell, B.M., & Elardo, R. (1979). Home environment and cognitive development in the first two years: A cross-lagged panel analysis. *Developmental Psychology, 15,* 246–250.

Brazelton, T.E., Koslowski, B., & Main, M. (1974). The origins of reciprocity. In M. Lewis and L. Rosenblum (Eds.), *The effect of the infant on its caregiver* (pp. 49–76). New York: Wiley.

Bronson, G.W. (1972). Infants' reactions to unfamiliar persons and novel objects. *Monographs of the Society for Research in Child Development, 47* (Serial No. 148).

Brookhart, J., & Hock, E. (1976). The effects of experiment and experiential background on infants' behavior toward their mothers and a stranger. *Child Development, 47,* 333–340.

Brooks, J., & Lewis, M. (1976). Infants' responses to strangers: Midget, adult and child. *Child Development, 47, 323–332.*

Carew, J.V. (1980). Experience and the development of intelligence in young children at home and in day care. *Monographs of the Society for Research in Child Development, 45* (Serial No. 187).

Carlsson, S.G., Fagerberg, H., Horneman, G., Hwang, C., Larsson, K., Rodholm, M., Schaller, J., Danielsson, B., & Gundewall, C. (1979). Effects of various amounts of contact between mother and child on the mother's nursing behavior: A follow-up study. *Infant Behavior and Development, 2,* 209–214.

Caudill, W., & Weinstein, H. (1969). Maternal care and infant behavior in Japan and America. *Psychiatry, 32,* 12–43.

Charlesworth, W. (1969). The role of surprise in cognitive development. In D. Elkind & J. Flavell (Eds.), *Studies in cognitive development* (pp. 257–314). London: Oxford University Press.

Clarke-Stewart, A. (1982). *Day care.* Cambridge, MA: Harvard University Press.

Clarke-Stewart, A., VanderStoep, L.P., & Killian, G.A. (1979). Analysis and replication of mother–child relations at two years of age. *Child Development, 50,* 777–793.

Corter, C. (1977). Brief separation and communication between infant and mother. In T. Alloway, P. Pliner, & L. Krames (Eds.), *Attachment behavior* (pp. 81–108). New York: Plenum.

Crawford, J.W. (1982). Mother-infant interaction in premature and full-term infants. *Child Development, 53,* 957–962.

Crockenberg, S.B. (1981). Infant irritability, mother responsiveness, and social support influences on the security of infant-mother attachment. *Child Development, 52,* 857–865.

DeCasper, A., & Fifer, W.P. (1980). Of human bonding: Newborns prefer their mothers' voices. *Science, 208,* 1174–1176.

DeChateau, P. (1980). Early post-partum contact and later attitudes. *International Journal of Behavioral Development, 3,* 273–286.

Demos, V. (1982). Facial expressions in young children: A descriptive analysis. In T. Field & A. Fogel (Eds.), *Emotions and early interaction* (pp. 127–160). Hillsdale, NJ: Erlbaum.

Detterman, D. K. (1978). The effect of heartbeat sound on neonatal crying. *Infant Behavior & Development, 1*(1), 36–48.

Dunn, J. (1975). Consistency and change in styles of mothering. In *Ciba Foundation Symposium: Parent-infant interaction* (pp. 155–176). New York: Elsevier.

Eckerman, C., & Whatley, J.L. (1975). Infants' reactions to unfamiliar adults varying in novelty. *Developmental Psychology, 11,* 562–566.

Feiring, C., & Lewis, M. (1981). Middle class differences in the mother-child interaction and the child's cognitive development. In T. Field, A. Sostek, P. Vietze, & P. Leiderman (Eds.), *Culture and early interactions* (pp. 63–94). Hillsdale, NJ: Erlbaum.

Field, T.M. (1982). Affective and physiological changes during manipulated interactions of high-risk infants. In T. Field & A. Fogel (Eds.), *Emotion and early interaction* (pp. 101–126). Hillsdale, NJ: Erlbaum.

Fogel, A. (1977). Temporal organization in mother-infant, face-to-face interaction. In H.R. Schaffer (Ed.), *Studies in mother-infant interaction* (pp. 119–153). London: Academic Press.

Fogel, A. (1982). Affect dynamics in early infancy: Affective tolerance. In T. Field & A. Fogel (Eds.), *Emotion and early interaction* (pp. 25–56). Hillsdale, NJ: Erlbaum.

Fogel, A. (1984). *Infancy: Infant, family, and society.* St. Paul, MN: West.

Fogel, A., & Melson, G. (Eds.) (1986). *Origins of nurturance: Developmental biological and cultural perspectives on caregiving.* Hillsdale, NJ: Erlbaum.

Fogel, A., Melson, G., & Mistry, J. (1986). Conceptualizing the determinants of nurturance: A reconsideration of sex differences. In A. Fogel & G. Melson (Eds.), *Origins of nurturance.* Hillsdale, NJ: Erlbaum.

Fox, N. (1977). Attachment of kibbutz infants to mother and metapelet. *Child Development, 48,* 1228–1239.

Fraiberg, S. (1974). Gross motor development in infants blind from birth. *Child Development, 45,* 114–126.

Gaddini, R. (1970). Transitional objects are the process of individuation. *Journal of the American Academy of Child Psychiatry, 9,* 347–365.

Halonen, J.S., & Passman, R. (1978). Pacifiers' effects upon play and separations from the mother for the one-year-old in a novel environment. *Infant Behavior and Development, 1,* 70–78.

Hayes, L., & Watson, J. (1981). Facial orientation of parents and elicited smiling by infants. *Infant Behavior and Development, 4,* 333–340.

Heinicke, C., & Westheimer, I. (1966). *Brief separations.* New York: Academic Press.

Hoffman, M.L. (1970). Moral development. In P.H. Mussen (Ed.), *Carmichael's manual of child development* (Vol. 2, 3rd ed., pp. 261–360). New York: Wiley.

Holden, G.W. (1983). Avoiding conflict: Mothers as statisticians in the supermarket. *Child Development, 54,* 233–240.

Hong, K., & Townes, B. (1976). Infants' attachment to inanimate objects: A cross-cultural study. *Journal of the American Academy of Child Psychiatry, 15,* 49–61.

Kagan, J., Kearsley, R., & Zelazo, P. (1978). *Infancy: Its place in human development.* Cambridge, MA: Harvard University Press.

Kaltenbach, M., Weinraub, M., & Fullard, W. (1980). Infant wariness toward strangers reconsidered: Infants' and mothers' reactions to unfamiliar persons. *Child Development, 51,* 1197–1202.

Kaye, K. (1982). *The mental and social life of babies.* Chicago: University of Chicago Press.

Kaye, K., & Fogel, A. (1980). The temporal structure of face-to-face communication between mothers and infants. *Developmental Psychology, 16,* 454–464.

Kessen, W., Haith, M., & Salapatek, P. (1970). Human infancy: A bibliography and guide. In P.H. Mussen (Ed.), *Carmichael's manual of child psychology* (Vol. 1, 3rd ed., pp. 287–446). New York: Wiley.

Klaus, M.H., Jerauld, R., Kreger, N.C., McAlpine, W., Steffa, M., & Kennell, J.H. (1972). Maternal attachment importance of the first post partum days. *New England Journal of Medicine, 46,* 187–192.

Klaus, M.H., Kennell, J.H., Plumb, N., & Zuehlke, S. (1970). Human maternal behavior at the first contact with her young. *Pediatrics, 46* 187–192.

Klein, R.P., & Durfee, J.T. (1976). Infants' reactions to unfamiliar adults versus mothers. *Child Development, 47,* 1194–1196.

Klinnert, M.D. (1981, April). Infants' use of mothers' facial expressions for regulating their own behavior. Paper presented at the meeting of the Society for Research in Child Development, Boston.

Kontos, D. (1978). A study of the effects of extended mother-infant contact on maternal behavior at one and three months. *Birth and the Family Journal, 5,* 133–140.

Lazar, I., & Darlington, R.B. (1982). Lasting effects of early education. *Monographs of the Society for Research in Child Development, 47* (Serial No. 195).

Ley, R.G., & Koepke, J.E. (1982). Attachment behavior out of doors: Naturalistic observations of sex and age differences in the separation behavior of young children. *Infant Behavior and Development, 5,* 195–201.

Lytton, H. (1979). Disciplinary encounters between young boys and their mothers and fathers: Is there a contingency system? *Developmental Psychology, 15,* 256–268.

Mahler, M., Pine, F., & Bergman, A. (1975). *The psychological birth of the human infant.* New York: Basic Books.

Martin, J.A. (1981a, April). The impact of children's influence attempts on conflict in the family. Paper presented at the meeting of the Society for Research in Child Development, Boston. (ERIC Document Reproduction Service No. ED 202 588)

Martin, J.A. (1981b). A longitudinal study of the consequences of early mother-infant interaction: A microanalytic approach. *Monographs of the Society for Research in Child Development, 46* (Serial No. 190).

McDonald, D. (1978). Paternal behavior at first contact with the newborn in a birth environment without intrusions. *Birth and the Family Journal, 5,* 123–132.

Melson, G., & Fogel, A. (1982). Young children's interest in unfamiliar infants. *Child Development, 53,* 693–700.

Minton, D., Kagan, J., & Levine, J.A. (1971). Maternal control and obedience in the two-year-old. *Child Development, 42,* 1873–1894.

Newson, J. (1977). An intersubjective approach to the systematic description of the mother-infant interaction. In H.R. Schaffer (Ed.), *Studies in mother-infant interaction* (pp. 47–62). London: Academic Press.

Passman, R. (1977). Providing attachment objects to facilitate learning and reduce distress: Effects of mothers and security blankets. *Developmental Psychology, 13,* 25–28.

Passman, R.H., & Weisberg, P. (1975). Mothers and blankets as agents for promoting play and exploration by young children in a novel environment: The effects of social and non-social attachment objects. *Developmental Psychology, 11,* 170–177.

Pastor, D.L. (1981). The quality of mother-infant attachment and its relationship to toddlers' initial sociability with peers. *Developmental Psychology, 17,* 326–335.

Piaget, J. (1952). *The origins of intelligence in children.* New York: International Universities Press.

Piaget, J. (1962). *Play, dreams, and limitation in childhood.* New York: Norton.

Portnoy, A., & Simmons, C.H. (1978). Day care and attachment. *Child Development, 49,* 239–242.

Ragozin, A.S. (1980). Attachment behavior of day-care children: Naturalistic and laboratory observations. *Child Development, 51,* 409–415.

Ricciuti, H.N. (1974). Fear and the development of social attachments in the first year of life. In M. Lewis & L. Rosenblum (Eds.), *The origins of fear* (pp. 73–106). New York: Wiley.

Rodholm, M., & Larsson, K. (1979). Father-infant interaction at the first contact after delivery. *Early Human Development, 3,* 21–27.

Ross, H.S., & Goldman, B.D. (1977). Establishing new social relations in infancy. In T. Alloway, P. Pliner, & L. Krames (Eds.), *Attachment behavior* (pp. 61–80). New York: Plenum.

Salk, Lee (1978). Response to Douglas K. Detterman's "The effect of heartbeat sound on neonatal crying." *Infant Behavior and Development, 1*(1), 49–50.

Sameroff, A., & Chandler, M. (1975). Reproductive risk and the continuum caretaking casualty. In F. Horowitz (Ed.), *Review of child development research* (pp. 187–244). Chicago: University of Chicago Press.

Sander, I.W. (1962). Issues in early mother-child interaction. *Journal of the American Academy of Child Psychiatry, 1,* 141–166.

Schaffer, H.R., & Crook, C.K. (1980). Child compliance and maternal control techniques. *Developmental Psychology, 16,* 54–56.

Schaller, J., Carlsson, S.G., & Larsson, K. (1979). Effects of extended post-partum mother-child contact on the mother's behavior during nursing. *Infant Behavior and Development, 2,* 319–324.

Skarin, K. (1977). Cognitive and contextual determinants of stranger fear in six- and eleven-month-old infants. *Child Development, 48,* 537–544.

Slaughter, D.T. (1980). Social policy issues affecting infants. In B. Weissbourd & J. Musick (Eds.), *Infants: Their social environments* (pp. 185–203). Washington, DC: National Association for the Education of Young Children.

Slaughter, D. (1983). Early intervention and its effects on maternal and child development. *Monographs of the Society for Research in Child Development, 48* (Serial No. 202).

Sroufe, L.A. (1979). Socioemotional development. In J. Osofsky (Ed.), *Handbook of infant development* (pp. 462–518). New York: Wiley.

Stayton, D.J., Ainsworth, M.D.S., & Main, M.B. (1973). The development of separation behavior in the first year of life: Protest, following, greeting. *Developmental Psychology, 9,* 213–225.

Stern, D.N. (1974). Mother and infant at play: The dyadic interaction involving facial, vocal and gaze behaviors. In M. Lewis & L. Rosenblum (Eds.), *The effect of the infant on its caregiver* (pp. 187–214). New York: Wiley.

Super, C.M. (1981). Behavioral development in infancy. In R. Munroe, R. Munroe, & B. Whiting (Eds.), *Handbook of cross-cultural human development* (pp. 181–271). New York: Garland.

Suwalsky, J.T., & Klein, R.P. (1980). Effects of naturally-occurring nontraumatic separations from mother. *Infant Mental Health Journal, 1,* 196–201.

Svejda, M.J., Campos, J.J., & Emde, R.N. (1980). Mother-infant "bonding": Failure to generalize. *Child Development, 48,* 1657–1661.

VanDoorninck, W.J., Caldwell, B.M., Wright, C., & Frankenburg, W.K. (1981). The relationship between twelve-month home stimulation and school achievement. *Child Development, 52,* 1080–1083.

Wachs, T.D. (1982). Early experience and early cognitive development: The search for specificity. In I. Uzgiris & J. Hunt (Eds.), *Research with scales of psychological development in infancy.* Urbana, IL: University of Illinois Press.

Wachs, T.D., & Gruen, G.E. (1982). *Early experience and human development.* New York: Plenum Press.

Waters, E., Vaughn, B., & Egeland, B. (1980). Individual differences in infant-mother attachment relationships at age one: Antecedents in neonatal behavior in an urban, economically disadvantaged sample. *Child Development, 51,* 208–216.

Waters, E., Wippman, J., & Sroufe, L.A. (1979). Attachment, positive affects and competence in the peer group: Two studies in construct validation. *Child Development, 50,* 821–829.

Weinraub, M., & Lewis, M. (1977). The determinants of children's responses to separation. *Monographs of the Society for Research in Child Development, 42* (Serial No. 172).

Weinraub, M., & Putney, E. (1978). The effects of height on infants' social responses to unfamiliar persons. *Child Development, 49,* 598–603.

Werner, E., Bierman, J., & French, F. (1971). *The children of Kauai.* Honolulu, HI: University of Hawaii Press.

Whiting, B.B., & Whiting, J.W. (1975). *Children of six cultures: A psycho-cultural analysis.* Cambridge, MA: Harvard University Press.

Wilcox, B.M., Staff, P., & Romaine, M.F. (1980). A comparison of individual with multiple assignment of caregivers to infants in day care. *Merrill-Palmer Quarterly, 26,* 53–62.

Winnicott, D. (1971). *Playing and reality.* New York: Basic Books.

Yarrow, L.J., Rubenstein, J.L., & Pedersen, F.A. (1975). *Infant and environment: Early cognitive and motivational development.* Washington, DC: Hemisphere Publishing Co.

3

Children's Social Comparison and Goal Setting in Achievement Contexts

Dale H. Schunk

University of Houston

Social comparison and goal setting are important contextual influences on children's task motivation, self-evaluations, and skillful performance in achievement settings. Because children's use of socially comparative and goal information changes with development, it is important that individuals who work with young children view the social comparison and goal-setting processes from a developmental perspective. The purposes of this discussion are to examine some theoretical ideas and research findings relevant to social comparison and goal setting, and to discuss the implications of this evidence for educational practice and future research.

Social comparison refers to the process of comparing oneself with others, whereas goal setting involves establishing a standard or objective to serve as the aim of one's actions. Social comparison and goal setting can enhance task motivation. These motivational effects are important because instructional procedures alone cannot fully account for children's diverse achievement patterns (Schunk, 1984b). Social comparison and goal setting can also convey to children that they are capable of performing well. As children then work at a task and observe their progress, these self-evaluations of capabilities are substantiated and help to sustain motivation. Collectively, higher levels of motivation and capability self-evaluations promote skillful performance, which in turn can serve as the basis for further social comparison and goal setting.

At the same time, different goals or types of social comparison will not motivate children equally well or convey the same information about capabilities. In short, how the social comparison and goal-setting processes affect motivation, self-evaluations, and skillful performance in achievement settings depends on children's developmental level as well as on the characteristics of these processes.

SOCIAL COMPARISON

In everyday life, social comparison is an important source for learning about the appropriateness of many behaviors (Masters, 1971; Veroff, 1969) because absolute behavioral standards often are ambiguous or nonexistent. In such cases, acceptability of behavior is relative to what is practiced generally. For example, children who converse too loudly with one another in the school library are apt to be told by the teacher to work quietly. To convey acceptable behavior to the children, the teacher could point out other children in the library who are talking quietly or whispering.

The social comparison process also can help individuals learn how capable they are at a task. In many human endeavors, one's capabilities are defined relative to the accomplishments of others. Festinger (1954) has discussed this role of social comparison as follows: "To the extent that objective, nonsocial means are not available, people evaluate their opinions and abilities by comparison respectively with the opinions and abilities of others" (p. 118). Thus, a child who wins the school spelling bee is likely to feel quite competent in spelling. In this example, though, the child's spelling excellence is relative to the performances of other children in the school.

Although the present review will focus primarily on young children (i.e., elementary age), the social comparison process is hypothesized to operate throughout life. Readers interested in social comparison among other age groups should consult Suls and Sanders (1982) for an excellent review.

Development of Social Comparison

The social comparison process is employed regularly by adults in forming self-evaluations of capabilities (Suls & Miller, 1977), but how children utilize social comparative information for self-evaluation purposes is less well understood. Developmental evidence suggests that the ability to use comparative information effectively depends on higher levels of cognitive development and experience in making comparative evaluations (Veroff, 1969). One question that arises concerns the age at which the ability to compare oneself with others develops. Veroff (1969) contends that Festinger's (1954) hypothesis is not applicable to children younger than 5 or 6. Such children are characterized by what Piaget termed *centration,* or the tendency not to relate two or more elements in thought, and *egocentrism,* which refers to the "self" dominating one's cognitive focus and judgments (Flavell, 1963; Higgins, 1981). The presence of these cognitive characteristics does not mean that very young children cannot evaluate themselves relative to others, but rather suggests that they do not automatically do so. Children show increasing interest in comparative information in the early elementary school years and by the fourth grade utilize such information to help form self-evaluations of performance capabilities (Ruble, Boggiano, Feldman, & Loebl, 1980; Ruble, Feldman, & Boggiano, 1976). Other research shows that by the fourth grade, children's performances on both motor and learning tasks are influenced by the performances of peers, but that the behaviors of younger children are affected more by direct adult social evaluation, such as praise (e.g., "You're good at this") and criticism ("You could do better") (Spear & Armstrong, 1978).

Recent research suggests that although very young children engage in social comparison, the meaning and function of comparative information change with development and especially as a result of entering school. Preschool children actively compare at an overt physical level; for example, they frequently compare the rewards they receive with those of others (Masters, 1971; Ruble et al., 1980). Mosatche and Bragonier (1981) found that preschoolers' social comparisons with peers primarily involved instances of (a) establishing how one was similar to and different from others ("I'm 4½, you're 4; we both had a birthday"), and (b) competition that seemed to be based on a need or desire to be better than others but that did not involve self-evaluation ("I'm the general; that's higher than the captain"). Much less frequently, children engaged in comparative behaviors for the purpose of evaluating their own qualifications ("I can do it, too").

Ruble and her colleagues (Feldman & Ruble, 1977; Ruble, 1983; Ruble, Feldman, & Boggiano, 1976; Ruble & Frey, 1982; Ruble, Parsons, & Ross, 1976) discuss the development of social comparison in young children as a multistep process. The earliest comparisons primarily involve similarities and differences but then shift to a concern for how to perform a task. For example, Feldman and Ruble (1977) found that first graders engaged in much peer comparison during an achievement task but primarily did so to obtain correct answers. Providing comparative information to very young children (preschoolers and children in primary grades) may increase their motivation more for practical reasons—such as to obtain correct answers—than for acquiring information about personal capabilities (Ruble, Feldman, & Boggiano, 1976). Young children do not necessarily become more motivated by knowing that others are performing better. At the same time, telling young children who fail at a task that most other children also do poorly may not alleviate the negative impact of failure (Ruble, Parsons, & Ross, 1976). As mentioned above, young children seem more responsive to direct evaluation of their capabilities (e.g., "You're good at this," and "You could do better") than to comparisons with peers (Spear & Armstrong, 1978). After first grade, interest increases in determining how well peers are doing, and comparative information begins to be used more often to help form self-evaluations of performance capabilities.

Social Comparison and Achievement Outcomes

A useful framework for viewing how social comparison affects achievement outcomes is Bandura's theory of *self-efficacy* (Bandura, 1977a, 1981, 1982). According to this theory, different procedures change behavior in part through the common mechanism of strengthening perceived self-efficacy. Self-efficacy (i.e., self-perceptions of performance capabilities) refers to personal judgments of how well one can perform behaviors in specific situations that may contain novel, unpredictable, and possibly stressful elements.

Self-efficacy is hypothesized to influence choice of activities (Bandura, 1977a). Children who hold a low sense of efficacy for accomplishing a task may attempt to avoid it, whereas those who feel more efficacious should participate more eagerly. Self-efficacy also is hypothesized to affect effort expenditure and task persistence (Bandura, 1977a). Especially when facing obstacles, children who hold a higher sense of efficacy should work harder and persist longer than those who doubt their capabilities (Bandura & Schunk, 1981; Schunk, 1984b). Individuals learn about their capabilities through their own performances, socially comparative vicarious (observational) means, verbal persuasion, and physiological indexes.

In this conception, social comparison of one's performance with the performances of others constitutes a vicarious source of efficacy information (Bandura, 1981). There is evidence attesting to the idea that similar others, rather than those much higher or lower in ability, offer the best information for judging one's own performance capabilities (Bandura, 1981; Suls & Miller, 1977). Because it is not until around age 9 that children begin to form a distinct conception of ability (Nicholls, 1978; Suls & Sanders, 1982), once children begin to engage in social comparison for the purpose of self-evaluation, perceived similarity is based more on actual performances than on underlying constructs such as ability. Thus, telling children that similar others can perform a task (e.g., "See how well Shawn is doing") can promote a sense of efficacy for succeeding because children are likely to believe that if other similar children perform at a certain level they can as well. In contrast, comparing oneself with those either much better or worse offers less information about what one can do. It should be noted that, with development, perceived similarity may be most influential for behaviors that reflect underlying constructs such as ability, whereas universal behaviors (e.g., obeying traffic lights) may be promoted better through observation of experts (Davidson & Smith, 1982).

The hypothesized effects of social comparison in achievement contexts are portrayed in Figure 1. When children perceive a negative discrepancy between their present level of performance and what similar others do, they are

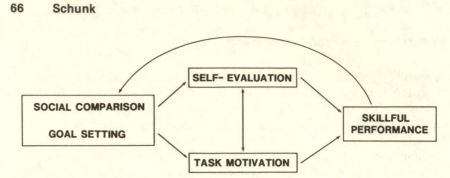

Figure 1: Hypothesized effects of social comparison and goal setting in achievement contexts.

apt to believe that they can perform as well and become motivated to attain the comparative level (Masters, 1971). As children work at the task, motivation and self-evaluation exert reciprocal effects. Motivation leads to progress toward the comparative level. When children observe that they are making progress, their initial capability self-evaluations are likely to be substantiated (Schunk, 1983a, 1984b). Enhanced self-evaluations help to sustain motivation. Collectively, these two processes can lead to a higher level of skillful performance over time. It might then be expected that this enhanced performance level would serve as the basis for future social comparison. These motivational and informational effects of social comparison are explored in greater depth below. (Goal setting, which is hypothesized to operate in similar fashion, will be covered later in this discussion.)

To illustrate, it is not unusual for young elementary school children to experience some anxiety and to doubt their capabilities to execute gymnastic movements such as cartwheels or somersaults. Such children may benefit from observing peers perform these exercises. Observation of peers may motivate children to try the exercises themselves and convey that children can learn the exercises. Then, as children actually perform cartwheels and somersaults, they ought to notice that they are improving and not injuring themselves. Such observations consequently help to sustain motivation. With skill improvement, children are apt to engage in further social comparison, such as that undertaken to determine how smooth their movements are as compared with those of others.

Motivational effects. There is research evidence indicating that social comparative information exerts strong motivational effects on children's performances by the fourth grade (Schunk, 1983a; Spear & Armstrong, 1978). Feldman and Ruble (1977) also found an enhanced level of motivation among second graders compared with younger children. Within this context, it might be asked what factors influence the likelihood and effectiveness of social comparison.

One theoretically relevant factor is an objective standard for evaluation (Festinger, 1954); there ought to be greater interest in social comparison in the absence of an objective criterion against which to evaluate one's performance. Among third graders, Pepitone (1972) found that the presence of a correct finished product (a jigsaw puzzle) reduced tendencies toward social comparison; however, among first and fourth graders, Feldman and Ruble (1977) obtained only a very weak effect on interest in social comparison due to the absence of an objective performance criterion (a time standard for the best performance). One possible interpretation of the latter finding is that even when an objective performance criterion is present, children still may be interested in social comparison to assess how their performance capabilities compare with those of others.

A second potentially important factor is the presence of competition. Social comparison theoretically should become more prevalent in a competitive setting. Although there are some exceptions, research studies generally have found increased comparative behaviors in more competitive as opposed to less competitive or noncompetitive settings (Feldman & Ruble, 1977; Mithaug, 1973; Pepitone, 1972; Ruble, Feldman, & Boggiano, 1976). For example, Feldman and Ruble (1977) found increased interest in social comparison when children knew that only the first child to finish puzzles would win a prize. In short, competition appears to increase children's motivation to compare themselves with others.

The effects of sex differences also have been explored. Ruble, Feldman, and Boggiano (1976) obtained evidence that, among children in kindergarten through second grade, boys showed greater interest in comparative information than did girls. Spear and Armstrong (1978) found that comparative information exerted motivational effects on boys' performances on easier tasks but not on difficult ones; no differences due to type of task were obtained for girls. Ruble, Feldman, and Boggiano (1976) suggest that among young children there may be more external (societal) pressure placed on boys than on girls to evaluate themselves relative to others.

Informational effects.   To the extent that children adopt comparative information as a standard of performance, they ought to evaluate their capabilities more highly as a result of working at a task and observing their progress toward the standard. Although research supports this proposition, the effects of comparative information on capability self-evaluations are not as strong as might be expected. For example, Schunk (1983a) provided comparative information on the typical progress of other similar children to fourth graders during a division competency development program. The comparative information enhanced task motivation in that children demonstrated a high rate of problem solving during the training program. Although comparative information also promoted children's self-efficacy for solving division problems, this effect was not particularly strong. Ruble, Parsons, and Ross (1976) worked with children ranging in age from 4 to 11 years on a matching familiar figures task (Zelniker, Jeffrey, Ault, & Parsons, 1972). The results showed that children's affective reactions toward the task and self-evaluations of ability were influenced more by task outcome information (whether children succeeded or failed) than by comparative information indicating the difficulty of the task (easy or hard). Schunk (1983b) found that directly telling fourth graders that they could work a given number of problems during a division training program (e.g., "You can work 25 problems") enhanced the children's sense of self-efficacy more than providing comparative information indicating that other similar children worked that many problems.

Ruble, Parsons, and Ross (1976) suggest that providing comparative information leads to high interest in self-evaluation; that is, children are apt to focus on how well they are doing relative to others. Results of the Schunk (1983a, 1983b) studies suggest that in the absence of comparative information children are likely to focus more on how their present performance attainments surpass their prior accomplishments, a process that ought to greatly enhance self-efficacy.

What social comparative information conveys to children about their level of competence is apt to depend on how the information is structured. When people compare themselves to similar others on ability-related attributes, they expect to perform at an equivalent level (Goethals & Darley, 1977). Even if their performance matches the comparative standard, they may not feel overly efficacious if they realize that their performance was only average (Schunk, 1983a). For most children, "similar others" are peers of average ability. Comparative information indicating average achievement motivates children to reach the standard but may not promote a strong sense of personal competence.

At the same time, comparative information indicating average accomplishments conveys the clearest information to children about their own capabilities. Information indicating an easy task (e.g., "All children can do this") conveys ambiguous information about one's capabilities (Goethals & Darley, 1977) because children who match the standard might nonetheless wonder how good they really are. Conversely, comparative information indicating a difficult task ("Few children can do this") could stifle motivation because many children will be reluctant to attempt the impossible. In this case, if children's subsequent performances were worse than the comparative level it would still be unclear how capable they really were. Of course, should children attain a high comparative standard, they probably would feel highly capable, although such a performance is unlikely.

The following situation may serve as an illustration: Children are assigned 20 spelling words on Monday, study each day, and are tested on Thursday.

Those who score 100% receive free time during Friday's spelling period, whereas others are retested on Friday. Children would learn little about their spelling capabilities if nearly everyone scored 100% on the Thursday tests because they probably would believe that the words were easy. On the other hand, few children would be motivated to put forth extra effort to study during the week if hardly anyone scored 100% on the Thursday tests. If about half of the class demonstrated mastery on Thursdays, children could derive the clearest information about their own capabilities because they readily could determine their relative standing (i.e., top or bottom half).

In short, comparative information indicating average performance is motivating for most children but may not constitute the most effective means of enhancing capability self-evaluations. Again, directly informing children about their capabilities ("You can do this") may motivate them equally well but better enhance self-efficacy (Schunk, 1983a). Once children work at a task, their actual performance successes and failures become more important influences on self-evaluations than do peer comparisons (Ruble, Parsons, & Ross, 1976).

It should be noted that how information about similar others affects self-evaluations may depend somewhat on the ability level of the child. It would seem that providing high achievers information about other high achievers could promote a high sense of self-efficacy if children were able to perform at the comparative level.

Reference Groups

In school, teachers often provide young children with comparative information ("See how well Kevin is working"), yet children also acquire much on their own. An interesting question concerns the others with whom children naturally choose to compare themselves. One suggestion is that children exercise considerable freedom in selecting comparative referents and may choose different referents for different types of comparisons (Rosenberg, 1968). To test this idea, Strang, Smith, and Rogers (1978) assessed the self-concepts of two groups of academically handicapped children ranging in age from 6 to 11 years: those who were mainstreamed for half a day and those who were not mainstreamed. The results showed that mainstreaming promoted children's self-concepts as assessed by the Piers-Harris Children's Self-Concept Scale (Piers, 1969). It is possible that the half-day mainstreaming was viewed by children as a sign of academic progress. To the extent that they continued to use children in their special class, as opposed to children in the regular class, as a basis for making academic self-evaluations, they probably felt more competent. The study thus shows that grouping practices can affect children's self-evaluations. Given the prevalence of grouping practices in elementary schools, this issue deserves further investigation. Such research ought to address how grouping affects nonhandicapped children as well.

GOAL SETTING

Goal setting involves comparing one's present level of performance with some desired standard (Bandura, 1977b). When individuals make self-satisfaction contingent on attaining the standard, they are likely to sustain their efforts until they achieve their goals (Bandura, 1977b).

A goal reflects one's purpose or intent and generally refers to quantity, quality, or rate of performance; however, goals also may be cast as deadlines, quotas, or budgets (Locke, Shaw, Saari, & Latham, 1981). People can set their own goals, or goals can be established for them by others such as teachers, parents, and supervisors. Quite often, social comparative information indicating a given level of performance becomes adopted as a goal, as when people strive to perform a task as well as or better than others.

As shown in Figure 1, the effects of goal setting bear much theoretical similarity to those of social comparison. Goal setting can motivate behavior and inform people about their capabilities. When children are given or select a goal, they may experience a sense of self-efficacy for attaining it. As children pursue their goals, they are apt to engage in appropriate activities, attend to instruction, persist at the task, and expend effort toward goal accomplishment. These motivational effects result in more on-task behavior (Schunk & Gaa, 1981). Children's initial sense of self-efficacy should be substantiated as they work at the task and observe their progress toward the goal because the perception of progress conveys that they are becoming more capable. In turn, heightened capability self-evaluations help sustain task motivation. Collectively, enhanced motivation and perceived competence lead to a higher level of skill development over time (see Figure 1). New goals may be adopted when children master their present ones.

To illustrate this process, in many elementary schools supplementary readers that parallel the vocabulary of basal readers are assigned to children to read at home. If a teacher assigns his or her third graders a goal of finishing three supplementary readers during the first 6-week grading period, the goal is apt to motivate children and result in an initial sense of competence for succeeding. This sense of competence is validated as children notice their progress toward the goal, and such self-perceptions help to sustain motivation. Collectively, higher self-evaluations and motivation could lead children to accomplish the goal in less than 6 weeks and to request a higher goal (e.g., four books) during the next grading period. It also should be noted that children could gain comparative capability information if the teacher maintains a progress chart allowing them to assess their progress relative to that of others.

This view of goal setting incorporates some elements of developmental perspectives on intrinsic motivation in children. According to Piaget, for example, children are intrinsically motivated to resolve the disequilibrium that results when new experiences conflict with established cognitive structures (Flavell, 1963). Such disequilibrium motivates children to bring experiences and structures into harmony. In a similar vein, White (1959) has suggested that behaviors such as curiosity, exploration, and mastery reflect a general effectance motive that leads children to attempt to deal competently with their environment.

Both of these positions view goal-oriented behavior as basically undifferentiated. Such generalized motivation may explain mastery attempts in infants and toddlers, but an undifferentiated motive cannot account for the fact that, with development, children become more selective in the goals they pursue. Some children seek mastery in mathematics, others in drawing, and still others in baseball. A general mastery orientation would imply that children, as well as adults, continually strive for competence in all aspects of their environment (Bandura, 1977b). Thus, a general motive contradicts everyday observations and lacks predictive power. Educational researchers and practitioners seek knowledge of how to enhance children's goal-directed behaviors. As Harter (1981) suggests, we need to specify the components (structure and content) of the child's motive system and to establish how these components change with development. Readers interested in children's mastery motivation should consult Harter (1981, 1982).

Goals by themselves do not automatically enhance achievement outcomes. Rather, certain properties of goals, when internalized as conscious intentions, serve as incentives for action (Latham & Yukl, 1975; Locke, 1968). In this regard, the effects of goal specificity, difficulty level, and proximity are particularly important.

Goal Specificity

Goals that incorporate specific standards of performance are more likely to increase motivation and to activate self-evaluative reactions than are general goals, such as "Do your best" (Locke, 1968; Locke et al., 1981). Specific goals boost task performance through their greater specification of the amount of effort required for success and through the self-satisfaction anticipated when accomplished (Bandura, 1977b). Specific goals can also promote self-evaluations of capabilities because progress toward an explicit goal is easy to gauge.

Much research attests to the effectiveness of specific goals in raising task performance (Bryan & Locke, 1967a; Locke, 1967; Locke & Bryan, 1966a, 1966b, 1967). This result has been demonstrated among adults performing a variety of cognitive and motor tasks. Because adults can more easily comprehend goal instructions, one might question whether these findings can be generalized to children; however, specific goals have been shown to promote task performance and capability self-evaluations among young children (Bandura & Schunk, 1981; Rosswork, 1977; Schunk, 1983a, 1983b).

Goal Difficulty Level

Goal difficulty refers to the level of task proficiency required as assessed against an external standard (Locke et al., 1981). How much effort people expend to attain a goal is likely to depend on the level at which it is set. People tend to expend greater effort to attain a more difficult goal than they do when the standard is lower. There is much evidence showing a positive relationship between difficulty level and task performance (Bryan & Locke, 1967b; Locke & Bryan, 1966b, 1967; Mento, Cartledge, & Locke, 1980). That difficult goals enhance children's performances and self-evaluations has also been demonstrated. Using sixth graders as subjects, Rosswork (1977) found that goal difficulty increased the rate that students composed sentences using vocabulary words. Schunk (1983b) gave children (mean age = 10 years) lacking division skills goals for solving a given number of problems during training sessions. Children who received more difficult goals (i.e., more problems) completed significantly more problems than did children given easier goals.

It should be noted that difficulty level and task performance do not bear an unlimited positive relationship to each other. Positive effects due to goal difficulty depend on the individuals having sufficient ability to reach the goal. Difficult goals do not enhance performance in the absence of requisite ability (Locke et al., 1981). When people believe that they do not possess the ability to attain a goal, they are apt to hold low expectations for success, a situation that does not foster goal acceptance (Locke et al., 1981; Mento et al., 1980). The effectiveness of any goal derives from making a commitment to attain it (Locke, 1968).

Goal Proximity

Goals also can be distinguished by how far they project into the future. Proximal goals, which are close at hand and can be achieved quickly, result in greater motivation directed toward attainment than more temporally distant goals (Bandura, 1977b; Bandura & Simon, 1977). From a developmental perspective, proximal goals ought to be especially influential with young children, who have short time frames of reference and who may not be fully capable of representing distant outcomes in thought (Schunk & Gaa, 1981). Proximal goals seem to fit in well with normal lesson planning. Elementary classrooms are activity-oriented: Teachers plan activities around blocks of time. Especially with young children, these activities tend to be short-term.

Pursuing proximal goals also conveys reliable information about one's capabilities. As children observe their progress toward a proximal goal, they are apt to develop a higher sense of self-efficacy; higher self-efficacy helps to sustain task motivation (Schunk, 1984b). Because progress toward a distal goal is more difficult to gauge, children receive less-clear information about their capabilities, even if they perform well.

Comparing the effects of proximal goals to those of more distant goals is difficult because, when given a long-term objective, adults tend to subdivide it into a series of short-range goals. Such subdivision does not necessarily occur among young children, whose developmental status may limit their ability to fractionate distant goals.

To test the idea that proximal goals constitute an important contextual influence on children's achievement outcomes, third-grade children engaged in a competency development program for subtraction (Bandura & Schunk, 1981). Children were given a written packet consisting of seven sets of materials and were told they would work on the materials over seven sessions. Some children pursued a proximal goal of completing one set each session, a second group pursued a distal goal of completing the entire packet by the end of the last session, and a third group was given only a general goal of working productively. The proximal and distal goals represented the same amount of work; however, because children could not yet divide, the distal subjects were not able to subdivide their goal.

Consistent with predictions, proximal goals heightened task motivation; subjects given these goals demonstrated the highest rate of problem solving during training. Proximal goals also led to the highest self-efficacy and subtraction skill. In contrast, the distal goal resulted in no benefits over those obtained from the general goal.

Gaa (1973, 1979) investigated the effects of proximal goals in the context of classroom goal-setting conferences. In one study (Gaa, 1973), first and second graders were assigned to one of three conditions: conferences with goal setting, conferences without goal setting, or no conferences. All children received the same in-class reading instruction. Children in the goal-conference condition met with the experimenter once a week for 4 weeks in sessions where they received a list of reading skills and selected those that they would attempt to accomplish the following week. They also received feedback on their previous week's goal accomplishments. Children who participated in conferences without setting goals met with the experimenter for the same amount of time but received only general information about material covered previously and about what would be covered the following week. During the last week of training, all subjects set performance goals to assess the effects of treatments on the goal-setting process.

The results showed that goal setting exerted both motivational and informational effects. Compared with children in the other two groups, children who participated in goal-setting conferences attained a higher level of reading achievement. During the last week of training, they also set fewer goals and showed a smaller discrepancy between goals set and mastered. In short, participation in proximal goal setting resulted in more accurate perceptions of capabilities.

This latter finding has implications for the classroom. Being able to estimate one's capabilities accurately is important. When children who overestimate their capabilities attempt tasks that are too difficult, the resulting failures can prove demoralizing. Children who underestimate what they can do may shun tasks within their means and thereby preclude opportunities for skill development (Schunk, 1984b). Teachers initially may have to assist children in setting realistic performance goals. At the same time, teachers need to ensure that children receive clear feedback on progress toward their goal attainment if beneficial effects of goal setting on children's self-appraisals are to be obtained.

Influences on Goal Effectiveness

In addition to goal properties, other factors influence how goals affect children's achievement outcomes.

Feedback. Self-evaluation of capabilities requires both a performance standard and knowledge of one's own performance (Bandura & Cervone, 1983). Simply pursuing a goal without knowing how well one is doing does not boost task performance (Locke, 1968); individuals gain little information about their capabilities because they have no way to gauge their progress.

Young children can acquire performance feedback on their own with certain types of tasks, such as when their goal is to complete a given number of workbook pages. It is probably fair to say that, for many tasks, children cannot adequately assess how well they are doing. As mentioned above, teachers may need to provide children with explicit feedback on their progress toward goals if goals are to foster achievement outcomes.

Rewards. That rewards are powerful motivators of behavior is well known (Bandura, 1977b; Lepper & Greene, 1978). With respect to goal setting, there is evidence that offering rewards can strengthen goal commitment (Locke et al., 1981), a finding that suggests that combining rewards with goals might exert especially beneficial effects on children's achievement outcomes. This combination often is found in schools, as when children work at a task and accrue points needed for extra free time.

Working with middle-school students during a 9-week English unit, Slavin (1980) evaluated the effects on student achievement of an evaluation-reward system in which students earned points based on how much their weekly quiz scores, as adjusted for previous quiz scores, exceeded their pretest scores. Compared with children who received the same instruction but no reward points or goal of exceeding their previous scores, the experimental subjects performed better. Rosswork (1977) assigned sixth graders goals on a writing task and offered students different levels of reward. The results showed that difficult goals enhanced performance across all reward conditions but that performance did not vary as a function of different rewards.

A recent study assessed the effects of rewards and goals during a division skill-development program with fourth graders who lacked division skills (Schunk, 1984a). Some children (rewards only) earned points based on the number of problems they completed during training, which they later exchanged for tangible rewards (e.g., magic markers, erasable pens, stickers). Others (goals only) pursued proximal performance goals of completing a given number of problems each training session. Children in a third condition (rewards plus goals) received both rewards and goals. The results showed that rewards only, goals only, and rewards plus goals enhanced motivation equally well; these groups did not differ in their rate of problem solving during training. Combining rewards with goals led to the highest self-efficacy and division skill as measured on the posttest. The rewards-only and goals-only conditions did not differ on these measures. Regardless of condition, children who judged self-efficacy higher subsequently demonstrated higher division skill.

On a measure of expectancy of goal attainment collected at the beginning of training, children who received rewards plus goals judged themselves more certain of attaining their goals than goals-only children. This result suggests that combining rewards with goals can strengthen goal commitment, which in turn ought to promote self-efficacy and skill. The implication here is that teachers who normally offer children tangible rewards might be well advised to link them to specific performance goals. Teachers who wish to avoid using tangible rewards may need to provide children with explicit information indicating that goals are attainable. Such information seems most important during the early stages of learning a particular skill, when children lack both task experience and knowledge of what they are capable of doing.

The preceding discussion is not intended as a recommendation that teachers dispense tangible rewards to children for their goal progress. There is evidence that such rewards can decrease task interest when children are given tangible rewards for merely working at a task that they otherwise enjoy (Deci, 1975; Lepper & Greene, 1978). Rewards are apt to exert beneficial effects on children's motivation, self-efficacy, and skills when they are delivered commensurate with progress, rather than simply for task participation (Bandura, 1977b; Schunk, 1984b). Of course, there are other means of conveying progress to children — for example, with charts, social rewards such as praise (e.g., "You're doing well"), and verbal comparisons of present with prior performance (e.g., "You're doing much better than before").

Ability to set realistic goals.   To enhance motivation and self-efficacy, goals need to be set at challenging but attainable levels (Bandura, 1977b). When children are allowed input into the selection of goals, they might be unrealistic concerning what they can accomplish given the time allotted, the difficulty of the task, or the skills required to succeed (Schunk & Gaa, 1981). Children with learning disabilities especially may be prone to unrealistic goal setting (Tollefson, Tracy, Johnsen, Farmer, & Buenning, 1984). Children initially may require training by teachers on how to set challenging but reasonable goals (Sagotsky, Patterson, & Lepper, 1978). For example, through the use of goal-setting conferences (Gaa, 1973, 1979), teachers and students can mutually agree on both long- and short-term goals. Frequent conferences would allow teachers to apprise students of their goal progress, and goals could be modified as necessary. The focus of the first few conferences could be more on helping students become aware of what they realistically can accomplish than on evaluation of work they produce.

Another way of teaching goal-setting strategies is through modeling. Modeling represents a vicarious (observational) means of learning and can motivate children to perform in a fashion similar to the model (Bandura, 1981). In a recent study, third-grade children observed a peer model play a game and choose either easy or difficult goals, whereas other children did not observe a model (Sagotsky & Lepper, 1982). Immediately afterward, subjects played the game themselves. Children who had observed a model choosing difficult goals chose more difficult goals than did children who viewed a model choosing easier goals or children not exposed to a model. Further, goal-choice preferences generalized to a spelling task 3 weeks later. It should be noted that observing peer models conveys social comparative information, which in this study influenced both immediate and delayed task performance.

Participation in goal setting.   Intuitively, participation in goal setting seems desirable, but research is inconclusive on whether self-set goals promote performance better than assigned goals (Locke et al., 1981). One potential benefit of self-set goals is that they may foster goal commitment better than assigned goals, and commitment is necessary if goals are to enhance performance outcomes (Locke et al., 1981).

A recent experiment tested this hypothesis (Schunk, in press). Subjects were sixth graders who previously had been classified as learning disabled in mathematics. Children received subtraction training that included instruction and practice opportunities over several sessions. Some children set proximal performance goals (i.e., number of pages of problems to complete) each session, while others had comparable goals assigned to them. Children in a third condition received the training but no goals. To mitigate potentially unrealistic goal setting, children were given feedback at the end of each session on how many pages they completed, and this number was compared with their goal. Although the self-set and assigned-goals groups completed more problems during training than the no-goals groups, the self-set group demonstrated the highest self-efficacy and skill on the posttest. Participation in goal setting, as opposed to the assignment of goals, also led to a higher initial expectancy of goal attainment.

Goal attainment information. Goals will not promote achievement outcomes if children are not committed to attaining them. Children are not likely to commit themselves to a goal if they perceive it to be overly difficult. This situation becomes a real possibility in skill development contexts, where performance goals initially are beyond children's skills but as a result of receiving instruction and practice opportunities children acquire the needed skills. In such instances, providing information indicating that the goal is attainable may foster motivation, skillful performance, and capability self-evaluations.

This idea was explored in a recent study (Schunk, 1983a). Fourth-grade children who lacked division skills received instruction in division and practice opportunities over two sessions. Half of the children worked under conditions involving a goal of completing a given number of problems each session, where the goal was of intermediate difficulty. The other half did not receive goals. Within each of these conditions, half of the subjects received social comparative information indicating the average number of problems solved by other similar children, whereas the other half did not receive comparative information. The goals and comparative information indicated the same number of problems.

Combining goals with comparative information yielded the greatest benefits. Children in this group worked more problems during training—a measure of motivation—than did children who received only goals or those who were given neither goals nor comparative information. Combined-treatment children also demonstrated higher division skill than did the children working under other conditions and higher self-efficacy than the children receiving only comparative information and those given neither goals nor comparative information.

Division is a difficult subject to master, and it is likely that children given goals viewed them as difficult. It was felt that combining goals with comparative information would convey that the goals were attainable. Although this combination led to higher motivation and skill development than did goals alone, the goals-only condition was equally effective in promoting self-efficacy. Goals-only children may have been overly swayed by their modest training successes, and it is even possible that they mistakenly assumed that goal attainment was synonymous with task mastery, an assumption that would have inflated self-efficacy.

A follow-up study explored the effects of different levels of goal difficulty and types of attainment information (Schunk, 1983b). During a division skill development program with fourth graders, children pursued goals of completing a given number of problems each session. Half of the children received difficult but attainable goals, whereas the other half were given easier goals. Within each of these conditions, half of the subjects received comparative information indicating that other similar children were able to complete that many problems. The other half were told directly that they could attain the goal (i.e., "You can work 25 problems,") but received no comparative information. Direct attainment information is a persuasive source of efficacy information because it conveys to children that they are capable of performing well and attaining the goal.

As expected, difficult goals were highly motivating and enhanced children's rates of problem solving during training. Children given difficult goals and direct attainment information judged self-efficacy higher than did children in both conditions receiving comparative information. In addition, they exhibited higher division skills than did subjects receiving the combination of easier goals and direct information. Regardless of treatment, higher self-efficacy was associated with greater subsequent skillful performance.

This study shows that the motivational effects of difficult goals did not automatically translate into high self-efficacy and skill-test performance. Children given difficult goals and comparative information knew that other similar children could attain the goals; thus, they would have had no reason to feel overly competent. In contrast, the direct attainment information conveyed nothing about other children's accomplishments. Such information can foster goal commitment and lead children to focus on their progress, in turn promoting strong perceptions of capabilities (Schunk, 1984b). These results suggest that, when tasks may appear difficult to children, direct attainment information might exert more beneficial effects on achievement outcomes than would comparative information. Once children work at the task, how well they do will affect their task motivation and self-evaluations.

SUMMARY

Social comparison and goal setting are viewed as important contextual influences on young children's task motivation, capability self-evaluations, and skillful performances. Both processes provide a performance standard against which children can compare their present performance levels. Children may experience an initial sense of self-efficacy for attaining the standard, and this perception can motivate them to expend effort at the task and persevere. As children observe their task progress, their initial capability self-perceptions are substantiated. These self-perceptions then help to sustain motivation. Collectively, enhanced motivation and self-evaluation lead to a higher level of performance. Once performance matches the goal or socially comparative level, children may engage in further goal setting or social comparison.

Young children's social comparisons with peers focus on practical concerns such as similarities and differences, equitable shares of rewards, and securing correct answers. By the fourth grade, children regularly seek out and use social comparative information to help form self-evaluations of capabilities. Knowledge about the accomplishments of similar others is especially informative about what one is capable of doing. Although comparative information enhances children's task motivation, it may not exert strong effects on their capability self-perceptions; children may be more strongly influenced by direct teacher evaluations of their capabilities and by their actual task performances.

The effects of goals depend on their properties: specificity, proximity, and difficulty level. Proximal goals are especially influential with young children, who may not be fully capable of representing distant outcomes in thought. Goals will not promote performance in the absence of goal commitment. Ways of fostering commitment include providing attainment information (direct or comparative), offering rewards for goal attainment, and, possibly, allowing children to set their own goals. Unrealistic goal setting may be a problem with young children, who may not be completely aware of what the task demands or the level of competence required to attain the goal. Teachers can help to foster realistic goal setting by initially assisting children in setting goals, giving clear performance feedback, and providing peer models.

FUTURE DIRECTIONS

This section presents suggestions for future research. Results of these endeavors would not only expand our knowledge of social comparison and goal-setting processes but also have important implications for educational practitioners.

Integration of Capability Information

An important research issue concerns how children cognitively process different pieces of information in forming and modifying self-evaluations of their capabilities to perform given tasks. Within this context, research ought also to address how cognitive processing changes with development. Little is known about how children combine capability information from various sources (Bandura, 1981). In school, children routinely acquire capability information in several ways. For example, as children solve arithmetic problems they gain capability information through their own work. Specifically, children's self-perceptions ought to differ depending on whether they do well or poorly. While working at the task, children may also observe one another. Whether similar others do well or poorly conveys information to children about their own capabilities. Further, teachers periodically monitor children's seatwork and give verbal feedback (e.g., "You're doing well," "You can do this," or "You could do better"). The information from these three sources may not be consistent. For example, a child may do poorly but be told "You can do this" and observe peers perform well. Questions that research might address are, How do children resolve such discrepancies? Do some sources "count" more heavily than others? and, Is there a developmental pattern in the weights that children give to different sources?

The practical implications of such research are important for teachers, who need to know how best to enhance children's motivation and self-evaluations of their capabilities. In the example above, a teacher has several options available to use alone or in combination with one another. In particular, the teacher may: (a) work individually with the child until the child experiences success; (b) point out similar children who are performing well (e.g., "See how well Gavin and Scott are doing?"); or (c) provide persuasive attainment information (e.g., "I know you can do well on this"). Because instructional procedures alone cannot fully explain children's achievement behaviors (Schunk, 1984b), it is important for teachers to know which strategies are likely to prove effective given the child's developmental status.

Peer Models and Self-Evaluation

Peer models can influence children's goal choices (Sagotsky & Lepper, 1982), and there is a vast body of literature demonstrating that children can learn new skills from models (Bandura, 1977b). An important issue still to be addressed is how peer models influence observers' capability self-perceptions. A situation is possible in which children who lack a particular skill observe a peer model successfully learn the skill. Research should explore whether this type of social comparative information promotes the observer's sense of self-efficacy for being able to learn the skill.

Research on peer models would have important implications for classroom practice. Although children can learn skills from observing teachers model them, children do not view teachers as similar in competence; therefore, children's self-evaluations of their capabilities may not be enhanced much through observing teachers. If research shows that peer models exert stronger effects on children's self-evaluations, then teachers would be advised to incorporate child models into their instructional planning. In arithmetic, for example, once a teacher has explained a particular operation, a child could model its application to some problems. In this regard, research should also explore how peer tutoring and cooperative learning groups affect children's self-evaluations (Slavin, 1983; Webb, 1982).

Classroom Research

Although most of the research summarized in this discussion has used school tasks (e.g., arithmetic and writing), many of these studies were not conducted in classrooms. As a consequence, the ways that social comparison and goal setting can be incorporated effectively into regular instructional practices have not been thoroughly explored. As has been suggested, to adequately investigate the interrelationship among learning, motivation, and self-evaluations it seems necessary to conduct research using existing instructional vehicles such as teachers, computers, and textbooks (Corno & Mandinach, 1983). By implication, more research needs to be conducted in classrooms.

A second recommendation is to work directly with classroom teachers in studying the effects of social comparison and goal setting. This type of research strategy would involve training teachers to administer social comparison and goal-setting treatments and to assess their effects. Once trained, these teachers can become active collaborators with researchers. In short, although a basic understanding of the social comparison and goal setting processes among children exists, we need to better explore the operation of these processes in classrooms to determine how they can be systematically employed to enhance children's task mastery and sense of personal competence.

REFERENCES

Bandura, A. (1977a). Self-efficacy: Toward a unifying theory of behavioral change. *Psychological Review, 84,* 191–215.

Bandura, A. (1977b). *Social learning theory.* Englewood Cliffs, NJ: Prentice-Hall.

Bandura, A. (1981). Self-referent thought: A developmental analysis of self-efficacy. In J.H. Flavell & L. Ross (Eds.), *Social cognitive development: Frontiers and possible futures* (pp. 200–239). Cambridge, England: Cambridge University Press.

Bandura, A. (1982). Self-efficacy mechanism in human agency. *American Psychologist, 37,* 122–147.

Bandura, A., & Cervone, D. (1983). Self-evaluative and self-efficacy mechanisms governing the motivational effects of goal systems. *Journal of Personality and Social Psychology, 45,* 1017–1028.

Bandura, A., & Schunk, D.H. (1981). Cultivating competence, self-efficacy, and intrinsic interest through proximal self-motivation. *Journal of Personality and Social Psychology, 41,* 586–598.

Bandura, A., & Simon, K.M. (1977). The role of proximal intentions in self-regulation of refractory behavior. *Cognitive Therapy and Research, 1,* 177–193.

Bryan, J.F., & Locke, E.A. (1967a). Goal setting as a means of increasing motivation. *Journal of Applied Psychology, 51,* 274–277.

Bryan, J.F., & Locke, E.A. (1967b). Parkinson's law as a goal-setting phenomenon. *Organizational Behavior and Human Performance, 2,* 258-275.

Corno, L., & Mandinach, E.B. (1983). The role of cognitive engagement in classroom learning and motivation. *Educational Psychologist, 18,* 88-108.

Davidson, E.S., & Smith, W.P. (1982). Imitation, social comparison, and self-reward. *Child Development, 53,* 928-932.

Deci, E.L. (1975). *Intrinsic motivation.* New York: Plenum Press.

Feldman, N.S., & Ruble, D.N. (1977). Awareness of social comparison interest and motivations: A developmental study. *Journal of Educational Psychology, 69,* 579-585.

Festinger, L. (1954). A theory of social comparison. *Human Relations, 7,* 117-140.

Flavell, J.H. (1963). *The developmental psychology of Jean Piaget.* New York: D. Van Nostrand.

Gaa, J.P. (1973). Effects of individual goal-setting conferences on achievement, attitudes, and goal-setting behavior. *Journal of Experimental Education, 42,* 22-28.

Gaa, J.P. (1979). The effects of individual goal-setting conferences on academic achievement and modification of locus of control orientation. *Psychology in the Schools, 16,* 591-597.

Goethals, G.R., & Darley, J.M. (1977). Social comparison theory: An attributional approach. In J.M. Suls & R.L. Miller (Eds.), *Social comparison processes: Theoretical and empirical perspectives* (pp. 259-278). Washington, DC: Hemisphere.

Harter, S. (1981). A model of mastery motivation in children: Individual differences and developmental change. In W.A. Collins (Ed.), *Aspects of the development of competence: The Minnesota Symposia on Child Psychology* (Vol. 14, pp. 215-255). Hillsdale, NJ: Erlbaum.

Harter, S. (1982). A developmental perspective on some parameters of self-regulation in children. In P. Karoly & F.H. Kanfer (Eds.), *Self-management and behavior change: From theory to practice* (pp. 165-204). Elmsford, NY: Pergamon Press.

Higgins, E.T. (1981). Role taking and social judgment: Alternative developmental perspectives and processes. In J.H. Flavell & L. Ross (Eds.), *Social cognitive development: Frontiers and possible futures* (pp. 119-153). Cambridge, England: Cambridge University Press.

Latham, G.P., & Yukl, G.A. (1975). A review of research on the application of goal setting in organizations. *Academy of Management Journal, 18,* 824-845.

Lepper, M.R., & Greene, D. (1978). *The hidden costs of reward: New perspectives on the psychology of human motivation.* Hillsdale, NJ: Erlbaum.

Locke, E.A. (1967). Motivational effects of knowledge of results: Knowledge or goal setting? *Journal of Applied Psychology, 51,* 324-329.

Locke, E.A. (1968). Toward a theory of task motivation and incentives. *Organizational Behavior and Human Performance, 3,* 157-189.

Locke, E.A., & Bryan, J.F. (1966a). Cognitive aspects of psychomotor performance: The effects of performance goals on level of performance. *Journal of Applied Psychology, 50,* 286-291.

Locke, E.A., & Bryan, J.F. (1966b). The effects of goal-setting, rule-learning, and knowledge of score on performance. *American Journal of Psychology, 79,* 451-457.

Locke, E.A., & Bryan, J.F. (1967). Performance goals as determinants of level of performance and boredom. *Journal of Applied Psychology, 51,* 120-130.

Locke, E.A., Shaw, K.N., Saari, L.M., & Latham, G.P. (1981). Goal setting and task performance: 1969-1980. *Psychological Bulletin, 90,* 125-152.

Masters, J.C. (1971). Social comparison by young children. *Young Children, 27,* 37-60.

Mento, A.J., Cartledge, N.D., & Locke, E.A. (1980). Maryland vs Michigan vs Minneosta: Another look at the relationship of expectancy and goal difficulty to task performance. *Organizational Behavior and Human Performance, 25,* 419-440.

Mithaug, D. (1973). The development of procedures for identifying competitive behavior in children. *Journal of Experimental Child Psychology, 16,* 76-90.

Mosatche, H.S., & Bragonier, P. (1981). An observational study of social comparison in preschoolers. *Child Development, 52,* 376–378.

Nicholls, J.G. (1978). The development of the concepts of effort and ability, perception of academic attainment, and the understanding that difficult tasks require more ability. *Child Development, 49,* 800–814.

Pepitone, E.A. (1972). Comparison behavior in elementary school children. *American Educational Research Journal, 9,* 45–63.

Piers, E.V. (1969). *Manual for the Piers-Harris Children's Self-Concept Scale.* Nashville, TN: Counselor Recordings and Tests.

Rosenberg, M. (1968). Psychological selectivity in self-esteem formation. In C. Gordon & K.J. Gergen (Eds.), *The self in social interaction* (Vol. 1, pp. 339–346). New York: Wiley.

Rosswork, S.G. (1977). Goal setting: The effects on an academic task with varying magnitudes of incentive. *Journal of Educational Psychology, 69,* 710–715.

Ruble, D.N. (1983). The development of social-comparison processes and their role in achievement-related self-socialization. In E.T. Higgins, D.N. Ruble, & W.W. Hartup (Eds.), *Social cognition and social development* (pp. 134–157). New York: Cambridge University Press.

Ruble, D.N., Boggiano, A.K. Feldman, N.S., & Loebl, J.H. (1980). Developmental analysis of the role of social comparison in self-evaluation. *Developmental Psychology, 16,* 105–115.

Ruble, D.N., Feldman, N.S., & Boggiano, A.K. (1976). Social comparison between young children in achievement situations. *Developmental Psychology, 12,* 191–197.

Ruble, D.N., & Frey, K.S. (1982, March). *Self-evaluation and social comparison in the classroom: A naturalistic study of peer interaction.* Paper presented at the meeting of the American Educational Research Association, New York.

Ruble, D.N., Parsons, J.E., & Ross, J. (1976). Self-evaluative responses of children in an achievement setting. *Child Development, 47,* 990–997.

Sagotsky, G., & Lepper, M.R. (1982). Generalization of changes in children's preferences for easy or difficult goals induced through peer modeling. *Child Development, 53,* 372–375.

Sagotsky, G., Patterson, C.J., & Lepper, M.R. (1978). Training children's self-control: A field experiment in self-monitoring and goal-setting in the classroom. *Journal of Experimental Child Psychology, 25,* 242–253.

Schunk, D.H. (1983a). Developing children's self-efficacy and skills: The roles of social comparative information and goal setting. *Contemporary Educational Psychology, 8,* 76–86.

Schunk, D.H. (1983b). Goal difficulty and attainment information: Effects on children's achievement behaviors. *Human Learning, 2,* 107–117.

Schunk, D.H. (1984a). Enhancing self-efficacy and achievement through rewards and goals: Motivational and informational effects. *Journal of Educational Research, 78,* 29–34.

Schunk, D.H. (1984b). Self-efficacy perspective on achievement behavior. *Educational Psychologist, 19,* 48–58.

Schunk, D.H. (in press). Participation in goal setting: Effects on learning disabled children's self-efficacy and skills. *Journal of Special Education.*

Schunk, D.H., & Gaa, J.P. (1981). Goal-setting influence on learning and self-evaluation. *Journal of Classroom Interaction, 16*(2), 38–44.

Slavin, R.E. (1980). Effects of individual learning expectations on student achievement. *Journal of Educational Psychology, 72,* 520–524.

Slavin, R.E. (1983). *Cooperative learning.* New York: Longman.

Spear, P.S., & Armstrong, S. (1978). Effects of performance expectancies created by peer comparison as related to social reinforcement, task difficulty, and age of child. *Journal of Experimental Child Psychology, 25,* 254–266.

Strang, L., Smith, M.D., & Rogers, C.M. (1978). Social comparison, multiple reference groups, and the self-concepts of academically handicapped children before and after mainstreaming. *Journal of Educational Psychology, 70,* 487-497.

Suls, J.M., & Miller, R.C. (1977). *Social comparison processes: Theoretical and empirical perspectives.* Washington, DC: Hemisphere.

Suls, J., & Sanders, G.S. (1982). Self-evaluation through social comparison: A developmental analysis. In L. Wheeler (Ed.), *Review of personality and social psychology* (Vol. 3, pp. 171-197). Beverly Hills, CA: Sage Publications.

Tollefson, N., Tracy, D.B., Johnsen, E.P., Farmer, A.W., & Buenning, M. (1984). Goal setting and personal responsibility training for LD adolescents. *Psychology in the Schools, 21,* 224-233.

Veroff, J. (1969). Social comparison and the development of achievement motivation. In C.P. Smith (Ed.), *Achievement-related motives in children* (pp. 46-101). New York: Russell Sage Foundation.

Webb, N.M. (1982). Student interaction and learning in small groups. *Review of Educational Research, 52,* 421-445.

White, R. (1959). Motivation reconsidered: The concept of competence. *Psychological Review, 66,* 297-323.

Zelniker, T., Jeffrey, W.E., Ault, R., & Parsons, J. (1972). Analysis and modification of search strategies of impulsive and reflective children on the Matching Familiar Figures Test. *Child Development, 43,* 321-337.

4

Parent Involvement: A Review of Research and Principles of Successful Practice

Rhoda McShane Becher

University of Illinois

INTRODUCTION

The involvement of parents in the development and education of their children has become a topic of intense interest to educators, researchers, politicians, and parents. Recognition has been given to the crucial role parents play in establishing the educability of their children, facilitating their development and achievement, and remedying educational and developmental problems. In addition, the rights and responsibilities of parents to influence educational programs have been emphasized. Programs of parent involvement and parent education continue to grow, and there is now an extensive and convincing body of research to support and guide these efforts.

The purpose of this discussion is to present a review of the research on parent involvement in order to serve as a basis for developing policies, programs, and practices. Specifically, the review concerns: (a) the role of parents/family/home in determining children's intelligence, competence, and achievement; (b) the effects of parent education programs on cognitive development and school achievement, and the characteristics of effective parent education programs; (c) parental practices that promote reading readiness and receptivity to reading instruction, and intervention efforts to enhance these effects; and (d) the effects of parent participation and involvement in child care/educational programs, the means for bringing about those efforts, and the means for improving parent-teacher relationships and communication. Attention is also given to research regarding the attitudes of parents, teachers, and administrators toward this involvement and to the problems encountered in parent involvement efforts.

In addition, a set of basic principles characterizing successful parent involvement programs is presented. These principles address implementation aspects not yet empirically established. They are, therefore, intended to serve as guidelines, and not prescriptions, for establishing successful parent involvement programs. They also serve to illustrate the skills teachers need for effective program development.

Finally, some serious cautions are discussed which should be considered when developing parent involvement policies and programs. Despite these cautions, however, the current state of knowledge about parent involvement, described in the discussion to follow, provides an extremely strong basis for the continued encouragement of these efforts. It also generates considerable optimism regarding the improvement of education and educational opportunities for children.

RESEARCH BACKGROUNDS

Parent Involvement and Achievement, Intelligence, and Competence

The role of parents in the development of intelligence, achievement, and cognitive and social/behavioral competence in their children is an area that has been the focus of extensive research. A variety of standardized tests and other measures, including observational systems, have been used to determine levels of development and performance. Efforts have been made to identify and understand the nature of the family characteristics, home conditions, and parent-child interactions that influence these. In addition, there have been numerous parent education intervention programs assessing the degree to which parents can be educated or trained to more positively affect their children's intelligence, cognitive development, and school-related achievement.

The important and, in fact, crucial role of the parents, family, and home in determining children's cognitive development and achievement has been documented in numerous studies. In addition, it has been shown that such factors are far more influential than school factors for such development (Coleman, 1966; Jencks, 1972; Mayeske, 1973; Mosteller & Moynihan, 1972).

Socioeconomic status, as defined by educational, occupational, and income levels, has been the most frequently studied family characteristic and one that has been consistently related to achievement (Fotheringham & Creal, 1980; Jencks, 1972; Keeves, 1972; Vernon, 1979). While significant and interesting, this research does not really explain how the effects are mediated to the child (Fotheringham & Creal, 1980).

Family process variables and parent behaviors.   In an effort to understand the mediating aspects of family and home environments, a second line of research has examined the relationships between specific family process variables and parent behaviors, and the development of intelligence, competence, and achievement in children. A number of major factors have been found to be significantly related.

First, children with higher scores on measures of achievement, competence, and intelligence had parents who held higher educational expectations and aspirations for them than did parents of children who did not score as high. Parents of the former children also exerted more pressure for achievement, provided more academic guidance, and exhibited a higher level of general interest in their children (Boocock, 1972; Entwisle & Hayduk, 1978; Gordon, 1978; Hess, Holloway, Price, & Dickson, 1979; Keeves, 1975; Parsons, 1981; Schaefer, 1972, 1973; Seginer, 1983).

Second, parents of children with higher scores had considerably more interactions that were *responsive* to children or contingent upon their responses than did parents whose children did not score as high (Bradley, Caldwell, & Elrado, 1977; Gordon, 1978; Ladd, Lange, & Kienapple, 1981).

Third, children with higher scores had parents whose perceptions of themselves as "teachers" of their children were stronger than those of parents with lower-scoring children. The former group of parents also used teaching modes and strategies considered to be more appropriate and effective (Brophy, 1970; Gordon, 1978; Hess & Shipman, 1965; Nottleman, 1978).

Fourth, parents of higher-scoring children used more advanced levels and styles of thought and language in interactions with their children than did parents of children who did not score as high. These advanced levels and styles of thought and language included the use of more advanced organizing information, more detailed instruction, and more verbal variety. In addition, the parents of higher-scoring children provided more explanations and reasons when correcting their children's behavior or performance. Furthermore, they provided better problem-solving strategies for their children and more assistance in the development of problem-solving strategies by their children (Gordon, 1978; Hess & Shipman, 1965; Olmsted & Jester, 1972).

Fifth, children with higher scores had parents who acted as stronger models of learning and achievement for their children than did parents of children who did not score as high (*Home and School Institute Report,* 1983; Seginer, 1983).

And, finally, higher-scoring children came from homes in which there was considerably more reinforcement of school behavior than there was in homes of children who did not score as high (see Atkinson & Forehand, 1979; Barth, 1979).

Effects of Parent Education Programs.   In addition to the research investigating naturally occurring behaviors of parents and aspects of the home environment associated with the development of competence, intelligence, and achievement in children, there is a large body of research assessing the effects of parent education programs on such development. Most of the empirical work in this area began in the mid- to late 1960s and extended through the mid-1970s. It centered on federally funded compensatory education program efforts to train low-income parents in how to teach their children in order to prevent or remediate basic cognitive and school achievement deficiencies.

There is considerable evidence indicating that parent education programs are effective in improving the intellectual functioning of children, as measured primarily by standardized intelligence tests (Gordon, 1969, 1972, 1973; Gordon, Olmsted, Rubin, & True, 1979; Grantham-McGregor & Desai, 1975; Gray & Klaus, 1970; Guinagh & Gordon, 1976; Johnson et al., 1974; Karnes, Studley, Wright, & Hodgins, 1968; Karnes, Teska, Hodgins, & Badger, 1970; Lambie, Bond, & Weikart, 1973, 1974; Lasater, 1974; Lasater, Briggs, Malone, Gillim, & Weisberg, 1975; Leler, Johnson, Kahn, & Brandt, 1974; Levenstein, 1970, 1971, 1972; Madden, Levenstein, & Levenstein, 1976; Radin, 1969, 1972; Sprigle, 1974, Weikart, 1971, 1973; Weikart, Deloria, Lawser, & Wiegerink, 1970; Weikart, Rogers, & Adcock, 1970; Wittes & Radin, 1969, 1971).[1] There is also evidence that the gains achieved have been sustained for at least 1 year, and in several cases for 3, 4, and 5 years following completion of the program (Gordon, 1972; Gordon & Guinagh, 1974; Gray & Klaus, 1970; Lasater, 1974; Levenstein, 1974; Radin, 1972; Sprigle, 1974).

Furthermore, there is substantial evidence that parent education programs are effective in improving children's language performance (Andrews, Blumenthal, Bache, & Weiner, 1975; Henderson & Garcia, 1973; Lasater et al., 1975; Mann, 1970; Sprigle, 1974); their performance on standardized achievement tests (Gray & Klaus, 1970; Sprigle, 1974; Weikart, 1971, 1973); and their general school behavior (Levenstein, 1974; Sprigle, 1974; Weikart, 1971, 1973).

In addition, parent education programs have produced significant positive changes in: (a) parents' teaching styles; (b) their interactions with their children; and (c) their provision of more stimulating home learning environments (Andrews et al., 1982; Gordon, 1970; Gordon & Guinagh, 1974; Gray & Klaus, 1970; Kogan & Gordon, 1975; Lambie et al., 1973; Lasater, 1974;

---

[1] Other studies indicating that parent education programs are effective in improving children's intellectual functioning, as measured by standardized intelligence tests, include Adkins and Crowell, 1969; Adkins and O'Malley, 1971; Alford and Hines, 1972; Andrews et al., 1975; Barbrack, 1970; Barbrack and Horton, 1970a, 1970b; Bertram, Hines, and Macdonald, 1971; Boger, Richter, Paolucci, and Whitmer, 1978; Boger, Kuipers and Berry, 1969; Boger, Kuipers, Wilson, and Andrews, 1973; *Final Report,* 1969; Gilmer and Gray, 1970; Mann, 1970; and Waters, 1972.

Lasater et al., 1975; Leler et al., 1974; Sandler, Dokecki, Stewart, Britton, & Horton, 1973; Weikart, 1971, 1973).[2]

Characteristics of effective parent education programs. While the evidence regarding the effectiveness of parent education programs in reaching their goals is convincing, few attempts have been made to systematically relate specific characteristics of effective programs to their outcomes. Some indications can be drawn, however, from the program analysis works of Goodson and Hess (1975, 1976), Stevens (1978), and Becher (1982). First, these analyses cautiously suggest that home visits, either alone or in combination with preschool classes, are apparently more effective than parent meetings, classes, or workshops in bringing about cognitive gains in children. Second, programs that place a high emphasis on encouraging parental teaching of children produce more stable long-term gains in children than programs that place only slight emphasis on this component. Third, no one type of program content (e.g., language development, sensorimotor development, cognitive development, child development principles, etc.) has been shown to be more effective than another in bringing about increased achievement. Fourth, a one-to-one parent-teacher relationship produces greater effects than a group instructional relationship. Fifth, highly structured, prescriptive, concrete tasks for parents produce more stable gains than less structured programs. Sixth, there is no difference in the effectiveness of programs that instruct parents in specific teaching techniques versus programs that encourage a general style of interaction. Seventh, programs that are most effective in producing considerable changes in both children and parents involve long-term consultation for a minimum of 18 to 24 months. And finally, effective programs are both prescriptive (attempting to achieve quality control through clearly specified goals, objectives, and activities, and careful monitoring) and personalized (emphasizing the modification of content so that a "proper fit" for each parent-child dyad is achieved).

In conclusion, although program analyses provide guidance for program development, there is a great deal more to be learned about the specific aspects of parent education programs contributing to effectiveness. It can be said with confidence, however, that parent education programs are effective in helping parents, particularly low-income parents, teach their children in order to prevent or remediate basic cognitive and school achievement deficiencies.

---

[2] Further evidence of the effects of parent education programs can be found in the following studies: Adkins and Crowell, 1969; Adkins and O'Malley, 1971; Andrews et al., 1975; Barbrack, 1970; Barbrack and Horton, 1970a, 1970b; Boger et al., 1973; Champagne and Goldman, 1970; and Mann, 1970.

Parent Involvement and Reading

The development of reading competence in children is perhaps the highest-ranking educational objective of teachers, parents, and the general public. There is an intense interest in the development of capable readers, and stringent criticisms are leveled against education for its failure to bring all children to an acceptable literacy level. As a consequence, a number of research investigations have been conducted to assess the critical roles parents play, in both the home and school environments, in promoting increased reading achievement.

Parental practices at home. One line of research has examined what parents do with their children at home to promote reading readiness and receptivity to reading instruction. Research repeatedly has indicated a significant positive relationship between the availability and range of reading materials in the home environment and children's attitudes toward and achievement in reading (Davie, Butler, & Goldstein, 1972; Douglas, 1964; Durkin, 1966; Lamme & Olmsted, 1977; Sheldon & Carrillo, 1952; Smith, 1971). Additional research has established a number of parental interactive practices that are significantly associated with the development of a positive attitude toward reading and increased reading achievement. Many of these practices may, in fact, mediate the influence of material availability (Wigfield & Asher, in press).

Reading to the child is one practice that has been shown to be significantly related to children's reading development. Specifically, this practice has been shown to improve children's: (a) receptive and expressive vocabularies; (b) literal and inferential comprehension skills; (c) sentence length; (d) letter and symbol recognition; (e) basic conceptual development, extension, and expansion; and (f) general interest in books (Brezinski, 1964; Burroughs, 1970; Dix, 1976; Green, 1981; Hansen, 1969; McCormick, 1981; McKay, 1981; Romotowski & Trepanier, 1977; Teale, 1978). Reading to the child is also important because it promotes a bond between children and parents, and establishes reading as a valued personal activity, exposes and develops shared topics of interest, promotes positive social-emotional interactions among family members, familiarizes children with a variety of language patterns and an expanded vocabulary, and serves as a source of data from which children construct knowledge about rules that govern the reading process (Dix, 1976; Durkin, 1966; Green, 1981; Hansen, 1969; Ransbury, 1973; Schickedanz, 1978; Siders & Sledjeski, 1978).

A very limited amount of research has examined specific aspects of the "reading to the child" practice. One area that has received some attention is the question of how much time parents should spend reading to their children. In a study of styles of parenting among parents of young gifted children, Karnes, Shwedel, and Steinberg (1982) found that parents of young children of average intelligence read to their children an average of 7 to 8 minutes a day, whereas parents of young gifted children spent an average of 21 minutes a day reading to their children. Hoskins (1976) found that prekindergarten children of parents who read to them at least 60 minutes a week, or an average of 8 to 9 minutes a day, for the 3 months prior to entering kindergarten showed significant increases in readiness abilities and more positive attitudes towards reading. In addition, they scored significantly higher on tests of reading achievement than did children in the control group, whose parents had not been asked to read to their children on a regular basis. Romotowski and Trepanier (1977) found that the reading achievement scores of young children whose parents read to them from four to seven times a week were significantly higher than the scores of children whose parents did not read to them that often. Henry (1975) found significant gains in reading readiness abilities among boys whose fathers read to them on a daily basis during the 6 months before entering kindergarten as compared with a similar group of boys whose fathers did not read to them.

Results of these studies, while not definitive, suggest that a regular pattern of reading to children 4 to 7 days a week for at least 8 minutes at a time is associated with more positive attitudes and more advanced abilities in reading. There is also a cautious suggestion that the more time children are read to, the higher their achievement level.

In addition to time devoted to reading to children, investigators have looked at some of the specific practices parents engage in while reading to their children. In examining parental styles of reading and their children's performance on reading-related tasks, Flood (1977) identified five factors significantly related to performance. First, children who talked more about the story during the reading process scored higher than children who did not talk during the story. Second, children who asked more questions during the story had higher performance scores on reading tasks than children who did not ask as many questions. Third, children who answered more questions about the story scored higher than children who did not answer as many questions. Fourth, children whose parents used "warm-up" questions before beginning reading performed better on reading tasks than children whose parents did not ask such questions. And finally, children whose parents used follow-up questions after completing the story received higher reading achievement scores than children whose parents did not use follow-up questions. Teale (1978) repeatedly found that the quality of interaction between the parent and child during the reading activity was associated with learning to read. Specifically, it was found that children who were more successful in learning to read had reading experiences with their parents that were more positive, more task-oriented, and more verbally stimulating than those of children who were less successful in learning to read. Furthermore, Smith

(1971) found that children whose parents discussed with them their various experiences and the books that they read exhibited greater reading abilities and more highly developed and expanded concepts than children whose parents did not engage in such discussions.

Although research is limited on the nature and effects of specific practices utilized while reading to the child, it can be concluded that the "engagement" of both the parent and child in the process of reading to and being read to is important in furthering reading development in children. The more that both the parents and the children became involved in the activity, the higher the children's reading achievement. These findings support the view that reading to the child is a cognitive or "thinking" activity rather than a "listening" activity; they also provide suggestions for parent education/intervention studies.

In addition to the important practice of reading to the child, a number of other practices engaged in by parents in the home environment have been shown to be related to the development of positive reading attitudes and increased achievement in reading. First, it has been found that children with more positive attitudes toward reading and higher achievement have parents who themselves read more and model the reading process more than the parents of children with less positive attitudes toward and lower achievement in reading (Dix, 1976; Hansen, 1969; Siders & Sledjeski, 1978). Second, children who have more positive attitudes and higher achievement scores have parents who provide more encouragement to read; who provide guidance in reading (including assisting in the setting of goals, selecting and discussing books, and looking things up); and who help with homework (Hansen, 1969; Wells, 1978). Third, children whose parents listen to them read on a regular basis have higher achievement scores and more positive attitudes toward reading than children whose parents don't (Hewison & Tizard, 1980). Fourth, children with higher achievement levels and more positive attitudes toward reading have parents who have actively coached or instructed them in the mechanics of reading. In addition, these parents have also provided materials useful in reading subskill development (Clegg, 1971; Hess et al., 1979; Hewison & Tizard, 1980; Teale, 1978). Fifth, children who exhibit higher achievement levels in reading have parents who have pressed for or expected this achievement (Hess et al., 1979). And sixth, children with more positive attitudes and higher achievement levels in reading have parents who have rewarded that achievement through extensive praise and reading-related activities. These rewarding activities include trips to the library, the purchase of additional books, and the selection of books of high interest to the child (Wells, 1978).

Some parental practices have been found to have negative effects on attitudes and achievement in reading. Children whose parents put excessive stress and emphasis on reading achievement, who push children to the point of frustration, and who punish their children for not reading or not reading well have less positive attitudes and lower achievement levels in reading than children whose parents do not engage in these practices (Wells, 1978).

The effects of parent involvement education efforts.   A second line of research has been interventionist in nature. Parents have been asked or trained to engage in a variety of additional, expanded, or altered experiences or practices in order to improve the reading attitudes and achievement of their children. Several approaches have been found to be successful. One approach has been to train parents in the teaching of reading and the development and use of reading materials. This has been done by holding parent meetings and workshops (Burgess, 1981; Raim, 1980; Swift, 1970; Vukelich, 1978; Wood, Barnard, & TeSelle, 1974); developing parent guides, handbooks, and information packets (Siders & Sledjeski, 1978); and using a combination of strategies including; (a) training sessions, information packets, and contingency management (Niedermeyer, 1970); and (b) training sessions, information packets, and meetings (McConnell, 1974). A second approach has been to specifically ask parents to read to their children for specified amounts of time (Henry, 1975; Hoskins, 1976). A third approach has been to increase the information parents have about the school reading program as well as to increase the communication parents receive from their child's reading teacher regarding their child's progress in reading. This practice enables the parents to better encourage, assist, and reinforce the reading process at home (Criscuolo, 1979; Grimmett & McCoy, 1980; McLaren, 1965; Rupley & Blair, 1975).

Although there are still many unanswered questions regarding the ways in which parents affect their children's attitudes and achievement in reading and concerning the best ways of maximizing their positive influence, the research to date does indicate that the parent's role is critical. In addition, it suggests that parents who assume, whether on their own or as a result of intervention efforts, an active, participating, "engaged" positive interactive strategy with their children regarding the reading process have children who exhibit higher reading achievement levels and more positive attitudes toward reading than the children of parents who assume more passive roles.

Parent Involvement and Schools

Improving parent-teacher-school relationships and expanding the roles parents play in child care and educational programs have received increasing emphasis during the past 15 years. Interest in such efforts has grown steadily as social, political, economic, educational, theoretical, empirical, and legislative forces have converged in response to difficult social and educational problems and changing cultural and societal norms. Several factors have refocused attention on the rights, responsibilities, and impact of parents who wish to influence educational programs. These factors include declining achievement scores, rising education costs, distrust of bureaucratic institutions, feelings of alienation, recognition of cultural and ethnic differences, and renewed interest in the basic American concept of participatory democracy. In addition, accumulating evidence indicates that parent involvement is critical in both preventing and remedying educational and developmental problems and in facilitating children's development and achievement. The consequence of these events is that, at present, vast numbers of people are being either strongly encouraged or required to participate in parent involvement efforts. Additional momentum has been added to this trend by the widely cited document *A Nation at Risk: The Imperative for Educational Reform* (National Commission on Excellence in Education, 1983) and by the call it issued to parents to assume an even more active role in ensuring excellence in the education of their children. As more and more parents and more schools and programs respond to the call, the need for research-based practices increases.

Effects of involvement. At present, there is accumulating research regarding the positive effects of parent participation and involvement in child care and educational programs, the means for bringing about those effects, and the means for improving parent-teacher relationships and communication. In addition, research exists that indicates some of the problems encountered in parent involvement efforts and that describes the attitudes of parents, teachers, and administrators toward such involvement.

Positive effects of parent involvement have been established for parents, teachers, and children on a number of different variables. Research has indicated that parents involved in educational programs have developed more positive attitudes about school and school personnel and that they have exhibited more positive attitudes than parents who did not become involved (Armer, Yeargen, & Hannah, 1977; Clarizio, 1968; Evans, 1973; Filipczak, 1973; Greenwood, Breivogel, & Bessent, 1972; Herman & Yeh, 1980; Rempson, 1967; Wenig & Brown, 1975; Young, 1975). Second, after having become involved in child care and educational programs, these parents have helped gather community support for the programs (Armer et al., 1977; Bowles, 1979; Filipczak, 1973). Third, parents who became involved have also become more actively involved in community activities than they had been before (Gordon, 1978; MIDCO Educational Associates, Inc., 1972). A fourth effect is that parents who have become involved in programs have developed more positive attitudes about themselves, increased their self-confidence, and enrolled in programs to enhance their own personal development (Boren, 1973; Donofrio, 1976; Gordon, 1878; Hereford, 1963; Herman & Yeh, 1980; Lane, Elzey, & Lewis, 1971; Radin, 1972; Rose, 1974; Strom & Johnson, 1974). A fifth effect of parent involvement is that the relationship between the parent and the child has improved and the frequency of the parent's involvement in the child's activities has increased (Rempson, 1967; Schaefer, 1972; Young, 1975). Parents were also found to have increased the amount of contact they made with the school (Herman & Yeh, 1980; Young, 1975) and their understanding of their child's development and the educational process also increased (Lane et al., 1971; Rempson, 1967). In addition, parents have become better teachers of their children at home and have used more positive forms of reinforcement (Andrews et al., 1982; Olmsted, 1977; Risley, 1968).

Furthermore, it has been shown that teachers, when associated with parent-involvement efforts, have become more proficient in their instructional and professional activities, allocated more of their own time to the instructional function, become more involved with the curriculum, and tended to experiment more. In addition, they have developed more student-oriented rather than text-oriented curricular activities (Benyon, 1968; Hedges, 1972).

And finally, there is substantial evidence indicating that children have significantly increased their academic achievement and cognitive development (Andrews et al., 1975; Beller, 1969; Brookover, 1965, 1967; Eash et al., 1980; Gordon, Olmstead, Rubin, & True, 1978; Henderson, 1981; Herman & Yeh, 1980; Irvine, 1979; Mowry, 1972; Olmsted, 1977; Wagenaar, 1977).

Successful approaches. Although no research was located that specifically compared the differential effects of the various forms of parent involvement, an examination of successful studies has indicated that a variety of approaches to parent involvement have been used. A number of studies reporting positive effects of parent involvement have used parent meetings and workshops as the means for educating parents and stimulating more participation in the education and development of children (Esterson, Feldman, Krigsman, & Warshaw, 1975; Evans, 1973; Gage, Crawford, Stallings, Corno, & Stayrook, 1978; Greenwood et al., 1972; Herman & Yeh, 1980; Irvine, 1979; Lane et al., 1971; McLaren, 1965; Meighan, 1981; Rempson, 1967). A second successful approach has been to use parent-teacher conferences as an opportunity to describe and encourage ways in which parents could become more actively involved in the child care or education program (Brooks, 1981; Herman & Yeh, 1980; Meighan, 1981; Rotter & Robinson, 1982). Third, increasing the amount and specificity of information parents receive about the school program and their child's performance in the program through more written and personal communication has also been used in programs reporting positive effects of parent involvement (Evans, 1973; Greenwood et al., 1972; Herman & Yeh, 1980; Seginer, 1983; Young, 1975). Fourth, successful programs have encouraged frequent visits to the center, school, or classroom and have directly involved parents in teaching activities (Brooks, 1981; Cramer, 1972; Goodson & Hess, 1975; Herman & Yeh, 1980; Irvine, 1979; Meighan, 1981; Risley, 1968; Young, 1975). And finally, the inclusion and encouraged participation of parents in decision-making and evaluation activities is another approach to parent involvement that has been used in programs reporting positive effects (Armer et al., 1977; Ferguson, 1977; Filipczak, 1973; Herman & Yeh, 1980; Middleton, 1975; *Project Unique*, 1969).

In addition, studies by McKinney (1978, 1980) and Maraschiello (1981) have assessed the most popular areas of parent participation in educational programs. These investigators also assessed the percentage of parents participating and the amount of time parents participated in each of these areas. Results indicated that classroom participation had the largest number of volunteer hours, and was the most popular form of involvement. Parent meetings and policy planning sessions were next, while social and fund-raising activities drew the least number of participants. Workshops and parent meetings were viewed by parents as important components of the programs, with parents exhibiting the most interest in meetings dealing with educational concerns, followed by those emphasizing personal growth and development. Topics dealing with careers, job training, and social services were of least interest.

As evidenced in the work reviewed here and as indicated in earlier reviews of parent involvement efforts (Gordon et al., 1978; Henderson, 1981), all forms of parent involvement strategies seem to be useful. However, those that are well-planned and more comprehensive in nature, offer more types of roles for parents to play, and occur over an extended period of time appear to be most effective.

Parent-teacher relationships. Several recent studies have examined some of the factors associated with positive parent-teacher relationships and effective communication. Mager (1980) studied the conditions that influence the teacher in initiating contacts with parents. One of the important findings of this study was that teachers reported considerably more contact with parents than had been reported in earlier studies. This may reflect the emphasis placed on such contacts in recent educational literature. Among the conditions influencing parent-teacher relationships, Mager found that teachers of upper middle class backgrounds reported a higher frequency of contacts with parents than did teachers of middle or lower middle class backgrounds. Teachers with a high frequency of contact reported significantly more reasons for making such contact and significantly more positive reasons than did teachers with a lower rate of contact. Teachers with high contact saw themselves as more responsible for initiating contacts and reported greater comfort in meeting the expectations of parents. These teachers did not see parents as placing unrealistic demands on them and felt that parents understood their efforts and limitations as teachers. Another finding was that, as teacher-initiated contacts increased, parent-initiated contacts increased as well.

Powell (1980) reported a synthesis of his work on parent-teacher relationships. He found that, with increases in parent-teacher interaction, there was a corresponding increase in the diversity of topics discussed and the complexity of the discussions. In addition, it was found that, as communication increased, parents used the staff members as primary information sources about education and development and decreased their use of more informal sources. Powell also found that increased communication was related to parents and teachers forming and sustaining a consistent, stable relationship — and in some cases, friendships developed.

Rotter and Robinson (1982) reviewed the research on effective communication and conferencing characteristics and skills in parent-teacher relationships, as well as the research concerned with effects of training teachers to implement these characteristics and skills. From their review, they concluded that the characteristics of effective communication included (a) concreteness, (b) genuineness, (c) immediacy, and (d) confrontation. The required skills included (a) listening, (b) attending, (c) perceiving, and (d) responding. Results of studies concerning the training of teachers included: (a) improved school climate; (b) improved teacher-parent, teacher-student, and teacher-teacher communication; (c) decreased discipline problems; (d) improved student self-concepts; and (e) increased student achievement. In addition, teachers' self-concepts were shown to improve; they reported increased satisfaction with their skills in the classroom and were judged by parents and evaluators to be more effective.

Since parent involvement in educational programs has been shown to be so effective, and since interpersonal relationships and communication are the heart of such contacts, it is encouraging that some of the conditions associated with effective contacts have been identified. It is also of importance that many of these characteristics and skills can be developed.

Theoretical versus actual commitment.   Extensive research has substantiated the effects of parent involvement, and numerous descriptive or testimonial articles have extolled the benefits to be gained (for an extensive bibliography on parent involvement, see Henniger, 1979). In addition, strong policy-level commitments and federal laws (e.g., Public Law 94-142, Elementary Secondary Education Act [ESEA] Title I and Title IV; federal interagency day care requirements) have mandated the return of more responsibility and control of educational programs to the parents of children who are served by them. However, it must also be recognized that a number of problems concerning parent involvement have been reported, and there is considerable evidence that many parental "commitments" are not being fully reflected in practice. For example, in studying the effects of parent involvement programs in ESEA Title I programs, McLaughlin (1975) indicated that he was unable to locate even one Title I evaluation report in which the parent advisory council was functioning as intended by law. Even more distressing, both Hightower (1978) and Kaplan and Forgione (1978) reported numerous instances of only "paper" advisory councils. Burns (1982) found, in a recent large-scale study of mandated parent involvement in federally funded ESEA Title I, ESEA Title VII Bilingual, Follow Through, and Emergency School Aid Act programs, that while communication between the projects and the home was indicated as the second most common form of involvement (following advisory councils), there was actually very little effort expended. Reports indicated that frequently only a single meeting was held to communicate with parents or to "train" them to assist in the instructional process.

Further evidence of the disparity between commitment and practice can be obtained from *The 13th Annual Gallup Poll of the Public's Attitudes toward Public Schools* (Gallup, 1981). Results indicated that respondents believe more parent involvement and better parent-teacher relationships are necessary for the improvement of schools. However, the respondents also indicated that a major problem facing the schools is a lack of interest on the part of both parents and teachers in parent involvement. In addition, Jackson and Stretch (1976), Hegenbart (1980), and Langenbrunner and Thornburg (1980) report survey results indicating that parents, teachers, and administrators all believe that there is significantly less actual parent involvement than is preferred or desired.

As to the reasons for this disparity, administrators indicate that while they believe in parent participation, it is one of their hardest tasks because parents refuse to participate (Duea & Bishop, 1980; Goldhammer, 1971; Hightower, 1978). Furthermore, although no data are available for elementary teachers, secondary teachers report parent relationships to be one of the most bothersome types of problems (Cruckshank, Kennedy, & Meyers, 1974), while preschool teachers report parent relationships to be not only bothersome but also their most frequently occurring type of problem (Wolfgang, Bratl, & Peck, 1977).

On the other hand, in many cases both parents (Gallup, 1981) and outside evaluators (Goodlad & Klein, 1970; Kaplan & Forgione, 1978; Levin, 1967) indicate that it is not the parents but the teachers and administrators who are apathetic about parent involvement. Levin (1967) found, for example, that when teachers asked parents for help, they responded readily, but teacher requests were not very common. Goodlad and Klein (1970) found that while teachers sincerely believed that they were encouraging parents to be involved in school programs, direct observations of teacher behaviors by trained observers indicated that teachers in fact did little to encourage involvement. Similarly, Tudor (1977) found that the more positive the attitudes of the teachers toward parent involvement, as expressed on an attitudinal survey, the more parent involvement occurred. In addition, research by Langenbrunner and Thornburg (1980), Hegenbart (1980), Jackson and Stretch

(1976), and Gallup (1981) suggests that parents are very willing to become involved. Related research indicates, however, that in many cases teachers initiate contact with parents only when a problem or crisis has developed (Carew & Lightfoot, 1979; Lortie, 1975; McPherson, 1972; Mager, 1980).

Related to this point, recent research by Guttman (1982) indicates that there are significant differences in parents' and teachers' causal attributions of problem behavior at school. More specifically, it was found that when a problem behavior occurred, teachers tended to attribute causes to the child first and the parents second. In addition, they tended to play down or dismiss any reasons associated with themselves. Parents, on the other hand, tended to attribute responsibility almost equally to the child, the teacher, and themselves. As Guttman pointed out, the differences in attributional patterns and external/internal locus of control orientations may account for much of the difficulty parents and teachers have in dealing with problem behaviors and arriving at constructive, mutually agreeable solutions.

Problems in initiating parent participation.   Research to determine some of the specific factors that impede the initiation and establishment of parental participation have indicated a number of important concerns. First, teachers report that they feel uncertain about how to involve parents and still maintain their role as specialized experts (Warren, 1973). Second, teachers indicate that they are uncertain about how to balance their concern for the group of children against a more personalized concern for each individual child, which they feel would be expected if parents were more involved (McPherson, 1972). Further, a report by the National Education Association (1972) indicates that teachers believe planning for parent involvement activities takes too much time. This report also states that teachers express concern that parents will try to take over teaching responsibilities and that they won't follow the teacher's instructions and school regulations. They are also concerned that parents will cause confusion and disrupt the classroom because they don't know how to work productively with children and that parents may use nonstandard English or demonstrate other characteristics teachers do not want introduced into the classroom. Other concerns teachers expressed were that parents would not keep their commitments, would discuss confidential information with their friends, and would be too critical and therefore make teachers uncomfortable. In contrast, research by Corwin and Wagenaar (1976) indicates that, according to parents, it is the bureaucratization of schools that keeps many of them from becoming involved and from bringing their concerns, complaints, and demands to the schools.

In summary, it is clear from these and other studies that parent involvement efforts encounter numerous difficulties in carrying commitments into practice. Yet, despite the difficulties, the accumulating research on the positive effects of parent participation in educational programs has caused interest in parent involvement to continue to grow. In addition, federal, state, and local requirements for greater parent involvement are expected to expand and to affect all teachers, not just those concerned with handicapped children and federally funded programs. The challenge that faces those of us who are committed to the importance of parent involvement is to decrease the disparity between commitment and practice, and to facilitate the establishment of effective programs.

PRINCIPLES OF SUCCESSFUL PRACTICE

As indicated by the preceding review, extensive, accumulating, and convincing research exists about the benefits and effects of parent involvement and about some of the specific practices found to be most effective. This research provides excellent support for the establishment of parent involvement programs and a sound basis for the selection and implementation of program components. However, additional implementation aspects not empirically established, need to be considered. From extensive teaching and consultation work with parents, teachers, and administrators in developing successful parent involvement programs, and from personal research and program analysis efforts (Becher, 1978, 1982, 1983), a set of basic principles characterizing successful[3] parent involvement programs or seemingly differentiating between successful and less successful programs has been identified. These principles fall into two groups. The first includes principles related to perspectives programs hold about parents. The second group includes implementation principles. Together, these two groups of principles provide a basis for planning and analyzing program development, implementation, and evaluation efforts, and they illustrate the skills teachers need for establishing successful parent involvement programs. They are intended to serve as guidelines, not prescriptions, for successful parent involvement program development.

Perspectives about Parents

1. Parents already make important contributions. The first principle apparent in successful parent involvement programs is that these programs recognize and value the important contributions parents already make to their children's development and education, regardless of the parents' educational and economic backgrounds. From the literature, as well as experience, evidence indicates that a great many parents are either unaware or uncertain

---

[3] For the purposes of this discussion, "successful" parent involvement programs are defined as those that are effective in reaching their goals, whatever their goals may be.

about the positive influences and impact they have on their children and about their importance in their child's development and education. Furthermore, even parents who are aware of their important role indicate that reinforcement from teachers is appreciated. Successful programs emphasize the strengths of parents and let them know that these strengths are valued. The consequence of this approach is that parents feel good about themselves and the program, and are more willing to become actively involved.

A practical example may illustrate this point: One group of teachers began to listen more carefully to the various things children said they did with their parents at home that reflected a positive relationship as well as sound learning experiences. When, for example, a child would say something like, "My mom let me help make chocolate chip cookies last night. She let me measure some of the things. We made 56 cookies!" the teacher would write a brief note home stating specifically what the parent had done that the child thought was important and that had made an impact. In addition, the teacher would indicate to the parent the educationally relevant aspects of the experience. The responses from parents were: (a) pleasure that the teacher took the time to let them know that they were doing things with their children that were enjoyed, appreciated, and important; (b) surprise, in many instances, that the child had valued and/or learned from so many small activities; (c) an increase in the activities they engaged in with their children; and (d) increased positive contact with the teachers.

2. Parents can make additional contributions. A second principle that emerges from examining successful programs is that these programs recognize that all parents can make additional contributions to their child's school or center program or to their child's education and development. Parents, however, may not realize what those potential contributions are. Successful programs help parents to identify what new things parents are capable of doing. In one school, for example, the first-grade teachers had written notes to the parents inviting them to participate in a unit on early America. The parents were asked to share some of their hobbies and engage in or demonstrate cooking or craft activities with the children. Initially, there was little response from the parents. The response increased considerably after personal contact by the teacher focused on helping the parents realize they did have skills to share. As one parent stated, "I know how to knit, but I didn't think I was good enough to teach anybody else." (In fact, the children were 6 years old, and the teacher really only intended for demonstrations to occur, not instruction.)

Another example occurred in a parent cooperative preschool. After watching one mother conduct an activity with the children, a graduate student assistant recording the interactions commented to the mother about the rich, varied, and excellent interactive teaching behaviors the mother had engaged in and complimented her on the range and depth of the concepts she developed. The graduate student then asked where the mother had received her training as a teacher. The mother looked at the student with disbelief and said, "I didn't know I was *teaching* the children anything; I just thought I was *talking* to them."

3. Parents can learn new parenting techniques. A third principle of successful parent involvement programs is that they incorporate the belief that parents have the capacity for and interest in learning developmental and educational techniques but that a positive approach is necessary. Techniques are presented as "new," "additional," or "alternative" techniques rather than as "better" ones. This perspective does not imply a criticism of existing parental practices. Instead, it suggests that parents have both the ability and interest to expand their parenting strategies and techniques. Although the specific parenting techniques shared (such as ways of correcting a child's errors in learning) may be the same in both successful and less successful programs, the more positive nature of this approach produces more enthusiastic responses from parents.

4. Parents have important perspectives on their children. Successful programs recognize that the perspectives parents have about their children are important and useful to teachers. For example, parents can provide information about their children's relationships, interests, and experiences outside of the school or center environment as well as describe how they learn in those contexts. This information enhances the teacher's understanding of the children and contributes to more effective teaching. It also establishes an important partnership relationship between parents and teachers that facilitates further involvement and learning.

5. Parent–child relationships are different from teacher-child relationships. Another principle of successful parent involvement programs is that they recognize the special nature of parent-child relationships. They also recognize that this relationship is quite different from the one between teacher and child.

Katz (1980) has discussed some of the significant distinctions between mothering and teaching, noting that parents and teachers necessarily differ in their relationships with children. The relationships parents have with their children are personal, subjective, and occur over a long period of time. In addition, parents see their children as members of a family, and they relate in the context of daily living. Teachers' relationships with children, on the other hand, need to be objective, impersonal, and short-term. Teachers see children as individuals in a group of similar-age children, and their relationship occurs in the context of a specifically designed educational environment. The distinctions in these relationships reflect differences in roles, goals, and values that may be complementary but are not interchangeable. Successful programs recognize and use these differences. A common mistake teachers make in less successful programs is to automatically suggest activities for parents to do with their children that they themselves have used successfully at school. Sometimes these activities work, but often they don't. When they don't, it is often because the suggestions do not take into account the different relationships and learning environments that exist at home. The effect of such suggestions is that parents either become frustrated with their child because they're "not paying attention" or "not learning," or become frustrated with the teacher because the activities are "stupid." Teachers, on the other hand, become frustrated because parents "aren't doing the activities I suggested." Successful programs suggest activities for parents to undertake with their children at home that make use of family situations in reaching goals. Furthermore, successful programs consult with parents when selecting and developing activities for use at home.

6. Parents' perspectives about involvement are important. In successful parent involvement programs, the process, efforts, and activities are viewed from the perspective of the parents rather than from those of the staff. In doing this, parents' views, feelings, and understandings about parent involvement are sought and not assumed.

In one low-income school, ESEA Title I kindergarten teachers had been attempting to involve parents and had experienced mixed success. As they put it, "We never get any response from the parents of children we really need to work with." While doing a "favorite recipe" cooking project, one of the teachers met one of the parents at the grocery store. This parent's child was one who had not brought in a recipe despite a number of notes sent home. When the teacher asked the parent to please remember to send in a recipe, the parent replied, "I don't have any cookbooks or use recipes since I can't read or write." The teacher was startled and realized that up until that time she had been blaming the parents for their lack of interest and nonresponsiveness to her notes when in fact the parent (and other parents, she came to find out) hadn't been able to read the notes and were embarrassed to say so.

Another example concerns a middle-income day care center where the director was getting very little input for board meetings despite the fact that every newsletter asked parents to bring concerns to the board. The director was feeling frustrated and saying that the parents "just weren't interested" in what happened at the center. In an effort to open up communication, it was suggested that she make some phone calls to some of the parents and discuss the problem. What she discovered was that a number of the parents hadn't been reading the newsletter, which was very long. They said that they usually put it aside "until later." When they did find time to read it, it seemed to have disappeared or they only skimmed it since it was "now so out of date." Most parents indicated that they weren't even aware of the board meetings or who was on the board. The director had assumed that since "it was in the newsletter," everyone knew and that they just weren't interested. After talking with the parents, she found a number who had good ideas to share and who also were interested in serving on the board. At the suggestion of the parents, she decided to send out shorter but more frequent newsletters so that they were more likely to be read.

7. Most parents really care about their children.   Another principle of successful parent involvement programs is that they hold and express a sincere belief that most parents really care about their children. This is in many ways related to the point concerning respect for parents' perspectives. When the point of view of the parent rather than the program is considered, and when the belief is held that most parents really care about their children, it sometimes happens that it may be in the best interest of the child that the parent *not* participate in an activity. This point emerged in a survey of parents' reasons for nonparticipation (Becher, 1983). Working parents indicated that, since there is so little time at home with their children, they often prefer to spend time as a family rather than attend activities that they consider not very interesting. They felt that the time they spent with their child was more important than the time spent listening to discussions often only somewhat related to their child. Thus, their nonparticipation was not an indication of a lack of interest but rather of a strong desire to be with their child. Another related and frequently stated point was that often the "time press" to get home, prepare dinner, get the children bathed, and get to a meeting created so much tension and conflict in the family that it just didn't seem worth it. These parents cared about their children, and from their perspective it was more important to have good relationships and time with their children than it was to attend an activity someone else thought was important for them. To further underscore this point, ample evidence suggests that parents will turn out in large numbers when their children are participants in a program or activity.

8. Parents have many reasons for their involvement.   Successful programs keep in mind the reasons for involvement when responding to "inappropriate" behavior by parents. One of the frequent concerns of teachers when beginning parent participation programs, whether at home or school, is that the parents will often undertake the activity for the child rather than help the child to accomplish it. Successful programs keep in mind that when parents do this their intentions are good but they often lack an understanding of how to help. When this occurs, successful programs extend additional efforts to make it clear what the purposes are for parent participation and how parents might work best with their child. Furthermore, even in cases in which parents don't seem to be responding to suggestions for "helping" rather than "doing," a successful program focuses on the good feelings generated in the parents and the positive relationships provided for the child and consider in effect that the purposes of parent involvement have been achieved. Because of this perspective, successful programs operate in such a way that if an activity must be done only by the child, in a very particular way, then it is not an activity to use for parent participation.

Program Goals, Activities, and Practices

1. Goals, purposes, and activities are matched. Parent involvement programs have many purposes. These include, for example, providing support for families, increasing children's achievement, meeting federal requirements, and keeping parents informed. There are also many "good," "interesting," and "fun" activities. While it seems obvious that the activities chosen should match or meet the goals and purposes of the programs, in many situations this is not the case. As a consequence, these programs are not very successful. As a case in point, one school district in Illinois established a parent involvement program in order to "have better relationships with the parents" and to "help improve children's achievement." Initially, there was excellent response on the part of the parents, but the enthusiasm soon diminished. The activities that parents were asked to do focused primarily on clerical tasks, particularly running dittoes "in the closet down the hall" and making bulletin boards, but in classes other than their children's classrooms. The parents became frustrated. They felt isolated and as though they were being used, not involved. It soon became clear that the tasks did not match the stated goals and in fact were counterproductive. After receiving numerous complaints from parents, the district reassessed the situation and established activities that involved parents in ways directly related to improving children's achievement and furthering more positive relationships.

2. Staff skills and available resources are considered. Staff members vary in the skills they possess and the resources available to them. Successful programs look at the staff's development and choose to do what is reasonable and productive rather than trying to "do it all." As the staff gains experience, programs are expanded. The emphasis is on producing success, however small, rather than orchestrating elaborate failures.

An example of a failed effort is an inner-city school that had no parent involvement program but decided to initiate a program in which all parents would share their hobbies, interests, or jobs with the children. Intensive efforts were made to ensure that every single parent returned the survey indicating what he or she would share. A number of weeks passed before all the forms were returned. It was now parent-teacher conference time at the school, and teachers were involved in preparing report cards and planning for the conference. Teachers then began the task of trying to sort through and schedule every parent. Since many parents had several children in the school, as well as limitations on availability, the mechanics of organizing the program soon became troublesome. Further frustration developed when parents' schedules changed and adjustments to the participation schedule were needed. Many parents became angry because it appeared they were not being chosen to participate after being pressured to return the survey. The school's interest in involving all the parents was commendable, but their inexperience, as well as that of the parents, made their first efforts unrealistic and unattainable.

As a counter example, a small group of kindergarten and first-grade teachers planned a single workshop for parents focusing on things to do with their children over the Christmas vacation. A wide variety of ideas and activities were shared, and parents were involved in making materials. The workshop was considered very successful, and parents requested several additional workshops through the year. In addition, parents began making more contacts with teachers about ideas they had that other parents might like to try.

3. Variations in parents' skills are recognized. Successful programs reflect the realization that there are many ways for parents to be involved and that all parents do not need to be involved in the same ways. They also recognize that the ways in which particular parents are involved can grow and change over time. These programs think about the involvement of Mr. Jones, Mrs. Smith, and Ms. Brown, rather than the involvement of "the parents" as a group. These programs also view even minor interest by the parents as contributing to the development of a basis for later, more active involvement. Simply beginning to change basic attitudes makes the efforts of the teacher the following year easier. Parent involvement is therefore viewed as a developing process rather than an all-or-none, now-and-forever situation.

4. Program activities are flexible and creative. Another principle of successful parent involvement programs is that the activities they develop are flexible and creative in order to be appropriate for and responsive to the particular needs of the parents. This is especially important when the majority of parents are working.

In one school district, which served mostly children of factory workers, the district superintendent contacted the major employing companies to arrange for time off, without loss of pay, for the parents (mainly fathers) of children in the school system so that they could occasionally participate in school activities. A great deal of publicity was given to those companies who supported the schools, and the program was considered to be very successful.

As one parent reported, "The companies probably more than made up the few half days they gave up because of the good will engendered in the employees, which in turn probably affected their overall productivity."

As another example, several day care programs combined potluck dinners with parent meetings. In these programs, parents brought a dish in the morning when they brought their children, and the staff arranged the meal at the end of the day so that parents could come straight from work, have dinner together, hold the parents' meeting (while the children were supervised in another area) and be home by 7:00 or 7:30 p.m. This avoided the problems of hurrying home to fix dinner, clean up, bathe the children, and generate enough energy to go out to a meeting. Positive responses to this approach have been extremely high.

5. Expectations, roles, and responsibilities are communicated. Successful parent involvement programs have clear task expectations, roles, and responsibilities, all of which are communicated to parents. One of the major areas of unease and conflict in parent involvement concerns who does what, when, where, and how. In many cases, there is no "right" or "wrong" way to do certain things, but the teacher may have preferred ways of operating because of her teaching style, philosophy, or goals. As long as parents are informed, the incidence of problems is minimal, and the program functions successfully. Parents are usually grateful to know what to do and how the teacher wants it done; it is much more reassuring to know what is expected than to feel uneasy at trying to guess and perhaps guess wrong.

6. Parents are involved in decision making, and administrative decisions are explained. In successful parent involvement programs, there is a strong emphasis on the communication of information. Such communication is important and relevant in allowing parents to participate in decision making and in understanding administrative decisions. These administrative decisions may concern policies and/or practices regarding both the school or center and parent involvement efforts.

One cause of parent-school conflict is the "announcement" of decisions with little or no information provided about how and why those decisions were reached; emphasis is placed more on "selling" than on explaining. On the other hand, in successful parent involvement programs, parents are given information that allows them to make and respond to decisions on a rational as opposed to an emotional basis. When parents lack information, they cannot participate freely in the decision-making process, and they can only respond emotionally to decisions that may be surprising or that appear threatening or arbitrary. When parents are provided with information describing the advantages and disadvantages of various positions, they can more effectively participate in the decision-making process and rational exchanges can occur.

7. Problems are expected but solutions are emphasized. In successful parent involvement programs, there is an expectation and an anticipation of problems. As a result, policies and procedures for dealing with them are developed and communicated to the parents. Furthermore, successful programs focus on finding solutions to problems rather than on the fact that they have problems.

There are always going to be some problems when a parent involvement program is established, just as there are always problems when any program is established. The difference between successful and less successful programs is that problems are expected and are therefore not considered to be alarming. Furthermore, in looking for solutions to problems, successful parent involvement programs look at problems or "failures" as the result of program goals, objectives, activities, tasks, or roles, rather than finding fault with the parents.

For example, when an activity is not effective, rather than blaming the parent for a lack of interest, successful programs consider the possibilities that the activities are not seen as relevant by the parent, that they are not scheduled at a convenient time, that the parents have unmet child care or transportation needs, that parents don't know what is expected, that parents lack information to respond appropriately, and so forth. In looking for these types of reasons, successful programs focus on areas that are changeable — thus, the problems are considered solvable. Blaming the parents is limiting and self-defeating. (If the parents are at fault, one can do little if anything about it, so why try?) Such an attitude suggests to the parents that there is no real interest in facilitating their involvement.

8. Optimum versus maximum involvement is sought. Successful parent involvement programs are programs in which there is optimum rather than maximum involvement so that all those involved enjoy rather than resent their involvement. If a program undertakes too much, it is unlikely to be successful. Parent involvement takes time, effort, and energy. If staff and parents become overextended, they may feel drained and resentful. If the efforts are optimal, involvement is invigorating.

Helping Teachers Develop More Effective Parent Involvement Skills

Several things need to be done in working with teachers to develop the skills suggested by the principles of successful parent involvement programs. First, teachers need to be helped to realize that they already possess a number of the skills necessary for establishing successful programs. Many of the skills needed are characteristic of good teachers — for example, caring, relating, individualizing, personalizing, selecting appropriate activities, reinforcing, teaching, explaining, reteaching, and evaluating. For the majority of teachers, it is a lack of awareness, priorities, and attention, rather than inability that hinders the development of successful involvement programs. Once teachers develop a commitment to parent involvement, they can begin to more systematically use the skills they already possess in achieving optimum and successful involvement.

Second, teachers need support for their efforts, particularly when things don't work. One way to help them in this regard is to establish a system of counseling by colleagues. Talking with others who are actively working at parent involvement efforts helps to renew one's energy as well as to solve problems.

Third, teachers need help in identifying their own feelings about various aspects of parent involvement. It is only when teachers become aware of their own fears, concerns, and negative feelings that they are able to rationally eliminate them and to develop more effective strategies.

Fourth, teachers need help in developing conflict resolution rather than conflict avoidance strategies. Many teachers express a fear that some conflict with a parent may arise if parents are actively involved. Therefore, to avoid having to deal with the conflict, they avoid parent involvement. Many models of assertiveness training and conflict resolution are available; choosing one and learning to use it provides the confidence and skills necessary to prevent the practice of avoiding problems by not doing anything.

Fifth, teachers need help in decentering their perspectives about parent involvement so that they begin to see the process from the perspective of the parents rather than solely from their own viewpoint. In order to do this, they need to begin really talking with and seeking advice from parents regarding the development of involvement strategies, selection of involvement activities, and establishment of appropriate role relationships.

Sixth, teachers need to be reminded or helped to select activities for parent involvement in terms of the goals and purposes of the program rather than because the activities look interesting or useful. The development of this skill is facilitated first by encouraging teachers to think about their goals and purposes when selecting activities and second by asking them to solicit specific feedback from parents as the programs progress.

Finally, teachers need to be reminded to bring into play the skills they use in making friends when reaching out to parents. Teachers possess these skills already. It's a matter of perspective to begin to think about parents as potential friends when beginning to relate to them. Once this occurs, the rest of the program can move forward effectively.

CONCLUSIONS, CAUTIONS, CONCERNS

In summarizing the research on parent involvement, it becomes clear that extensive, substantial, and convincing evidence suggests that parents play a crucial role in both the home and school environments with respect to facilitating the development of intelligence, achievement, and competence in their children. In addition, considerable evidence indicates that intervention programs designed to train or encourage parents to engage in a variety of additional, expanded, or altered experiences or practices with their children are effective in improving children's cognitive development and achievement. Further, while only a limited number of research studies have systematically examined the relationship of specific characteristics of effective programs to their outcomes or have evaluated the effectiveness of specific aspects of various parental teaching and involvement practices, there are some indications regarding the best ways of maximizing potential influence and positive impact. The proposed principles of successful practice provide an additional basis for analyzing and implementing program planning, action, and evaluation efforts, as well as for illustrating the skills teachers need to establish effective parent involvement programs. The current state of knowledge about parent involvement provides extremely strong support for the continued encouragement of such efforts. It also generates considerable optimism regarding the improvement of education and educational opportunities for children.

There are, however, some serious cautions and concerns that need to be addressed when developing parent involvement policies and programs. One caution concerns the degree to which continuous and increased emphasis on the crucial role of parents in facilitating intelligence, achievement, and educability places excessive pressure and responsibility on them. As Schlossman (1978) has said in a critical analysis of parent education and its politics,

> These programs . . . view poverty mothers — rather than professional educators — as the critical agents in developing their child's intellectual potential . . . Parent education programs thereby shift the burden of accountability for failure from . . . professional education to the poverty parent . . . Parent education not only tends to blame the victim, it places an inordinate share of blame on women alone. (pp. 790, 796)

A second closely related concern is the degree to which the now popular phrases describing parents as "the child's first teacher" or even "the child's best teacher" suggest that parents stand in loco magisterio (i.e., in place of teachers [Katz, 1980]). This view may in fact shift the focus of educational responsibilities and accountability sufficiently so that schools, programs, and teachers will fail to examine more critically the ways in which they might change to more fully enhance children's development, education, and achievement. An example of this phenomena is the interesting fact that when the work of Coleman (1966, 1975), Jencks (1972), and other similar studies documented that parents, families, and homes were far more influential than school factors in determining children's cognitive development and achievement, major emphasis was placed on training parents—and in many cases training them to be like teachers. Very little—if any—attention was given to considering the ways in which schools and teachers might become more like homes and parents in their work with children. About this point, Fotheringham and Creal (1980) have said,

> It is important to look at what differences between the learning environment of the home versus the school account for the homes' paramount influence. The home is an individual or small group learning situation that provides contact over time with a few caring adults, whereas the school is a large group environment generally teaching to the mean of existing children by a changing series of adults over time whose styles, values, and levels of commitments vary. If there are crucial differences in relation to achievement, then modifications of public schooling would require techniques to provide more individualized instruction in an environment that more consistently transmits its styles and attitudes towards learning than presently exist. (pp. 316–317)

While, as documented by this review, there has been considerable success in training parents to increase the achievement of their children, success in this area does not reduce the need for schools to continually explore alternative methods to increase effectiveness.

A further related concern is that as more and more parent involvement efforts become encouraged or required through policy commitments and legislated mandates, a number of teachers not personally disposed to establishing strong parent-teacher relationships will be asked to take a more active role. Since a number of teachers already feel that they assume more responsibilities than should be expected for activities beyond the direct instructional role, there is a danger that tension between teachers and parents will be created. Without specific training in parent involvement techniques and strategies, and without considerable help and guidance, it is unlikely that efforts can be successful. And, given the fact that there is no research indicating that teachers not disposed to establishing parent involvement programs and relationships can be successfully trained to do so, blanket expectations create risks, as well as promises unlikely to be fulfilled.

What is more, although the principles of successful practice can serve as guidelines for the establishment and implementation of parent involvement programs, since many of the connections between positive program outcomes and specific program components and practices have not been empirically established, program developers still must operate with a degree of uncertainty. While one can expect that additional research will continue to address this problem, optimism about the impact of such research efforts must be guarded. One reason for such reservation is the report of the decade-long, multimillion dollar Parent-Child Development Center Project (Andrews et al., 1982). This project, which was specifically designed to address substantial research issues in parent education and which represented one of the few attempts to mount a carefully controlled field experiment, was unable to respond successfully to many concerns. In explaining some of the major hindrances to success, Andrews et al. (1982) state that

> a good program must be able to respond both to changing participant needs and staff perceptions and to changing external circumstances. However, in order to fulfill the condition of being the independent variable, they must meet the opposite requirement: to change as little as possible and ideally not at all. (p. 76)

Another concern regarding program development and effective practices is that very little attention has been given to the role of the father. The increase in the number of employed mothers, and particularly of employed mothers of young children, means that fathers have more responsibilities for their children and that these responsibilities begin when the child is at an early age. As Parke's (1981) review of this research on fathers has indicated, fathers as well as mothers play very influential roles in facilitating cognitive development, but these roles are distinctive in nature. Mothers and fathers differ in how they organize the environment, in their encouragement of different behaviors, in their expectations of their children, and in the nature of their interactive relationships. What impact the participation of fathers in parent involvement programs will have on program structures, relationships with teachers and schools, roles ascribed to parents, and the effects of such programs on children's development and achievement remains to be assessed.

An additional related factor regarding the increasing rate of employment of mothers may also impinge directly on parent involvement efforts. This factor concerns the changing nature of mother-child relationships and the models of behavior working mothers present. Parke (1981) cites a study by Blanchard and Biller (1971) indicating that the role fathers play as models of perseverance, achievement motivation, and successful functioning in the outside world is significantly associated with the intellectual development and achievement of their sons. Research is needed exploring these relationships for mothers, who are now also serving as these same types of models. Recent research cited in the *Home and School Institute Report* (1983) regarding the effects of maternal employment on school achievement tentatively suggests that those roles may be operating positively for mothers as well. Again, how changing roles and relationships will affect parent involvement efforts and parent-teacher relationships remains to be established. Developing an awareness of the possible impact of the changing roles and relationships of fathers and mothers is essential if policies and practices are to be appropriately adapted to changing social and parental norms.

In conclusion, it is important to reiterate the fact that there is extensive, substantial, and convincing evidence regarding the crucial role of parents in the development and education of their children. There is also considerable evidence indicating that parents can be trained to engage in a variety of practices that positively affect their children's development and education. In addition, there is limited but growing research regarding the effectiveness of specific parental and program practices. Again, while cautions and concerns exist that must not be ignored when encouraging parent involvement, these are not barriers. Responsiveness to the issues may ensure that the increasing optimism regarding the improvement of educational opportunities for children through parent involvement will be justified.

REFERENCES

Adkins, D.C., & Crowell, D.C. (1969). *Final report on the development of a preschool language-oriented curriculum with a structured parent education program.* Honolulu, HI: University of Hawaii, Head Start Evaluation and Research Center.

Adkins, D.C., & O'Malley, J. (1971). *Final report on the continuation of programmatic research on curricular modules for early childhood education and parent participation.* Honolulu, HI: University of Hawaii, Center for Research in Early Childhood Education.

Alford, R.W., & Hines, B.W. (1972). *Demonstration of a home-oriented early childhood education program. Final report.* Charleston, WV: Appalachian Educational Laboratory, Inc.

Andrews, S.R., Blumenthal, J.M., Bache, W.L., & Weiner, S. (1975, April). *The New Orleans model: Parents as early childhood educators.* Paper presented at the biennial meeting of the Society for Research in Child Development, Denver.

Andrews, S.R., Blumenthal, J.B., Johnson, D.L., Kahn, A.J., Ferguson, C.J., Lasater, T.M., Malone, P.E., & Wallace, D.B. (1982). The skills of mothering: A study of parent-child development centers. *Monographs of the Society for Research in Child Development, 47,* (6, Serial No. 198).

Armer, B., Yeargen, C., & Hannah, M.E. (1977). Community polarization over educational programs can be avoided. *Psychology in the Schools, 14,* 54–61.

Atkinson, B.M., & Forehand, R. (1979). Home-based reinforcement programs designed to modify classroom behavior: A review and a methodological evaluation. *Psychological Bulletin, 86,* 1298–1308.

Barbrack, C.R. (1970). *The effects of three home visiting strategies upon measures of children's academic and maternal teaching behavior* (DARCEE Papers and Reports, Vol. 4, No. 1). Nashville, TN: George Peabody College for Teachers.

Barbrack, C.R., & Horton, D.M. (1970a). *Educational intervention in the home and paraprofessional career development: A first generation mother study* (DARCEE Papers and Reports, Vol. 4, No. 3). Nashville, TN: George Peabody College for Teachers.

Barbrack, C.R., & Horton, D.M. (1970b). *Educational intervention in the home and paraprofessional career development: A second generation mother study with an emphasis on costs and benefits. Final report* (DARCEE Papers and Reports, Vol. 4, No. 4). Nashville, TN: George Peabody College for Teachers.

Barth, R. (1979). Home-based reinforcement of school behavior: A review and analysis. *Review of Educational Research, 49,* 436–458.

Becher, R.M. (1978, January). *Parent involvement in education? A review of research and the state of the field.* Paper presented at the H.L. Smith Conference on Research in Education, Indiana University, Bloomington.

Becher, R.M. (1982). Parent education. In *Encyclopedia of Educational Research* (5th ed., pp. 1379–1382). New York: Macmillan and Free Press.

Becher, R.M. (1983). *Problems and practices of parent-teacher school relationships and parent involvement.* Unpublished manuscript, University of Illinois, Urbana.

Beller, E. (1969). The evaluation of effects of early educational intervention on intellectual and social development of lower-class disadvantaged children. In E. Grotberg (Ed.), *Critical Issues in Research Related to Disadvantaged Children* (pp. 1–40). Princeton, NJ: Educational Testing Service.

Benyon, M. (1968, October 25). Parents in classrooms: Hope for the future. *The Times Educational Supplement, 2788,* p. 897.

Bertram, C., Hines, B., & Macdonald, R. (1971). *Summative evaluation of the home-oriented preschool education program. Summary report.* Charleston, WV: Appalachia Educational Laboratory, Division of Research and Evaluation.

Blanchard, R.W., & Biller, H.B. (1971). Father availability and academic performance among third grade boys. *Developmental Psychology, 4,* 301–305.

Boger, R., Richter, R., Paolucci, B., & Whitmer, S. (1978). *Parents as teacher: Perspective of function and context.* (ERIC Document Reproduction Service No. ED 175 576)

Boger, R., Kuipers, J., & Berry, M. (1969). *Parents as primary change agents in an experimental Head Start program of language intervention.* East Lansing, MI: Michigan State University, Head Start Evaluation and Research Center.

Boger, R., Kuipers, J., Wilson, N., & Andrews, M. (1973). *Parents are teachers too: A curriculum module for increasing positive parent-child, parent-teacher, and parent-school interaction. Final report* (Vols. 1 & 2). East Lansing, MI: Michigan State University, Institute for Family and Child Study, College of Human Ecology.

Boocock, S.P. (1972). *An introduction to the sociology of learning.* Boston: Houghton Mifflin Co.

Boren, J. (1973, December). *A family program: Analysis and difficulties in implementation.* Paper presented at the meeting of the Association for Advancement of Therapy, Miami, FL.

Bowles, B.D. (1979, Fall). Little things make a difference, at least in community relations. *Wisconsin R and D Center News,* pp. 1–3.

Bradley, R., Caldwell, B.M., & Elrado, R. (1977). Home environment, social status, and mental test performance. *Journal of Educational Psychology, 69,* 697–701.

Brezinski, J.E. (1964). Beginning reading in Denver. *The Reading Teacher, 18,* 16–21.

Brookover, W.B. (1965). *Self-concept of ability and school achievement II.* East Lansing, MI: Michigan State University, Bureau of Educational Research Services.

Brookover, W.B. (1967). *Self-concept of ability and school achievement III.* East Lansing, MI: Michigan State University, Bureau of Educational Research Services.

Brooks, C. (1981). Parents in class. *New Society, 58,* 281–296.

Brophy, J. (1970). Mothers as teachers of their own preschool children: The influence of socioeconomic status and task structure on teaching specificity. *Child Development, 41,* 79–94.

Burgess, J.C. (1982). The effects of a training program for parents of preschoolers on the children's school readiness. *Reading Improvement, 19,* 313–319.

Burns, J. (1982). *The study of parental involvement in four federal education programs: Executive summary.* Washington, DC: Department of Education, Office of Planning, Budget and Education.

Burroughs, M.C. (1970). The stimulation of verbal behavior in culturally disadvantaged three-year-olds. Unpublished doctoral dissertation, Michigan State University, East Lansing.

Carew, J., & Lightfoot, S. (1979). *Beyond bias.* Cambridge, MA: Harvard University Press.

Champagne, D., & Goldman, R. (1970). *Development of a training program to increase the use of reinforcement in informal teaching by mothers of educationally disadvantaged children.* (ERIC Document Reproduction Service No. ED 047 034)

Clarizio, H. (1968). Maternal attitude change associated with involvement in Project Head Start. *Journal of Negro Education, 37,* 106–113.

Clegg, B. (1971). *The effectiveness of learning games used by economically disadvantage parents to increase reading achievement of their children.* Unpublished doctoral dissertation, University of Washington, Seattle.

Coleman, J. (1966). *Equality of educational opportunity.* Washington, DC: United States Office of Education. (ERIC Document Reproduction Service No. ED 172 339)

Coleman, J. (1975). Methods and results in the IEA studies of effects of school on learning. *Review of Educational Research, 4*(3), 335–86.

Corwin, R.G., & Wagenaar, T.C. (1976). Boundary interactions between service organizations and their publics: A study of teacher-parent relationships. *Social Forces, 55,* 471–491.

Cramer, W. (1972). My mom can teach reading too! *Elementary School Journal, 72,* 72–75.

Criscuolo, N.P. (1979). Activities that help involve parents in reading. *The Reading Teacher, 32,* 417–419.

Cruckshank, D.R., Kennedy, J., & Meyers, B. (1974). Perceived problems of secondary school teachers. *Journal of Educational Research, 68,* 154–159.

Davie, R., Butler, N., & Goldstein, H. (1972). *From birth to seven: A report of the National Child Development Study.* London: Longman.

Dix, M. (1976). *Are reading habits of parents related to reading performance of their children?* (ERIC Document Reproduction Service No. ED 133 693)

Donofrio, A.F. (1976). Parent education versus child psychotherapy. *Psychology in the Schools, 13,* 176–180.

Douglas, J.W.B. (1964). *The home and the school.* London: MacGibbon and Kee.

Duea, J., & Bishop, W.L. (1980). The PROBE results: Important differences in public and professional perceptions of the schools. *Phi Delta Kappan, 62,* 50–52.

Durkin, D.R. (1966). *Children who read early.* New York: Teachers College Press.

Eash, M.J., Haertel, G.D., Pascarella, E.T., Conrad, K.J., Iverson, B.K., & Vispoel, W.P. (1980, April). *Assessment of multiple outcomes: An evaluation research study of a compensatory early childhood program (Child-Parent Centers and Child-Parent Expansion Program).* Paper presented at the annual meeting of the American Educational Research Association, Boston. (ERIC Document Reproduction Service No. ED 189 176)

Entwisle, D.R., & Hayduk, L.A. (1978). *Too great expectations: The academic outlook for young children.* Baltimore: Johns Hopkins University Press.

Esterson, H., Feldman, C., Krigsman, N., & Warshaw, S. (1975). Time-limited group counseling with parents of pre-adolescent underachievers: A pilot program. *Psychology in the Schools, 12,* 79–84.

Evans, E. (1973). Orienting junior high parents. *Personnel and Guidance, 51,* 729–732.

Ferguson, D. (1977). Can your school survive a parent evaluation? *National Elementary Principal, 56,* 71–73.

Filipczak, J. (1973, August). *Press and community response to behavior modification in the public school.* Paper presented at the meeting of the American Psychological Association, Montreal.

Final report of the supplementary kindergarten intervention program, Cohort 2. (1969). Ann Arbor, MI: Ypsilanti Public Schools and University of Michigan School of Social Work.

Flood, J.E. (1977). Parental styles in reading episodes with young children. *The Reading Teacher, 30,* 864–867.

Fotheringham, J.B., & Creal, D. (1980). Family socioeconomic and educational-emotional characteristics as predictors of school achievement. *Journal of Educational Research, 76,* 311–317.

Gage, N., Crawford, J., Stallings, J., Corno, L., & Stayrook, N. (1978). *An experiment on teacher effectiveness and parent-assisted instruction in the third grade.* Stanford, CA: Stanford University Center for Research. (ERIC Document Reproduction Service No. ED 160 648)

Gallup, G.H. (1981). The 13th annual Gallup poll of the public's attitude toward the public schools. *Phi Delta Kappan, 63,* 33–47.

Gilmer, B.R., & Gray, S. (1970). *Intervention with mothers and young children: A study of intra-family effects* (DARCEE Papers and Reports, Vol. 4, No. 11). Nashville, TN: George Peabody College for Teachers.

Goldhammer, K. (1971). *Elementary principals and their schools: Beacons of brilliance and potholes of pestilence.* Eugene, OR: University of Oregon, Center for the Advanced Study of Educational Administration.

Goodlad, J., & Klein, J. (1970). *Behind the classroom door.* Worthington, OH: Jones Publishing Co.

Goodson, B.D., & Hess, R.D. (1975). *Parents as teachers of young children: An evaluative review of some contemporary concepts and programs. (ERIC Document Reproduction Service No. ED 136 967)*

Goodson, B.D., & Hess, R.D. (1976). The effects of parent training programs on child performance and parent behaviors. (ERIC Document Reproduction Service No. ED 136 912)

Gordon, I.J. (1969). *Early child stimulation through parent education.* Gainesville, FL: University of Florida, Institute for Development of Human Resources.

Gordon, I.J. (1970). Reaching the young child through parent education. *Childhood Education, 46,* 247–249.

Gordon, I.J. (1972). *A home learning center approach to early stimulation.* Gainesville, FL: University of Florida, Institute for Development of Human Resources.

Gordon, I.J. (1973). *The Florida parent education early intervention projects: A longitudinal look.* Gainesville, FL: University of Florida, Institute for Development of Human Resources.

Gordon, I.J. (1978, March). *What does research say about the effects of parent involvement for supervision and curriculum development?* Paper presented at the meeting of the Association for Supervision and Curriculum Development, San Francisco.

Gordon, I.J., & Guinagh, B.J. (1974). *A home learning center approach to early stimulation. Final report.* (ERIC Document Reproduction Service No. ED 115 388)

Gordon, I.J., Olmstead, P., Rubin, R., & True, J. (1978). *Continuity between home and school: Aspects of parent involvement in Follow Through.* Chapel Hill: University of North Carolina.

Gordon, I.J., Olmstead, P., Rubin, R., & True, J. (1979). *Aspects of parent involvement in the parent education Follow Through program.* (ERIC Document Reproduction Service No. ED 170 024)

Grantham-McGregor, S.M., & Desai, P. (1975). A home visiting intervention programme with Jamaican mothers and children. *Developmental Medicine and Child Neurology, 17,* 605–613.

Gray, S., & Klaus, R. (1970). The early training project: A seventh year report. *Child Development, 41,* 909–924.

Green, C. (1981). *Product evaluation of the elementary and middle school reading and communication skills component of the Detroit desegregation court order.* (ERIC Document Reproduction Service No. ED 208 113)

Greenwood, G.E., Breivogel, W.F., & Bessent, H. (1972). Some promising approaches to parent involvement. *Theory into Practice, 11,* 183–189.

Grimmett, S.A., & McCoy, M. (1980). Effects of parental communication on reading performance of third grade children. *The Reading Teacher, 3* 303–308.

Guinagh, B.J., & Gordon, I.J. (1976). *School performance as a function of early stimulation.
Final report.* Washington, DC: Office of Child Development (DHEW). (ERIC Document Reproduction Service No. ED 135 469)

Guttman, J. (1982). Pupils', teachers' and parents' causal attributions for problem behavior at
school. *Journal of Educational Research, 76,* 14–21.

Hansen, H.S. (1969). The impact of the home literary environment on reading attitude. *Elementary English, 46,* 17–24.

Hedges, H. (1972). *Volunteer parental assistance in elementary schools.* Unpublished manuscript, Ontario Institute for Studies in Education, Toronto.

Hegenbart, G.L. (1980). *How teachers and parents perceive parental involvement in elementary
schools.* Unpublished doctoral dissertation, University of Illinois, Urbana.

Henderson, H. (Ed.). (1981). *Parent participation – student achievement: The evidence grows.
Occasional paper.* Columbia, MD: National Committee for Citizens in Education.
(ERIC Document Reproduction Service No. ED 209 754)

Henderson, R.W., & Garcia, A.B. (1973). The effects of a parent training program on question-
asking behavior of Mexican-American children. *American Educational Research Journal, 10,* 193–201.

Henniger, M. (1979). *Parent involvement in education: A bibliography.* Urbana, IL: (ERIC
Document Reproduction Service No. ED 174 352)

Henry, B. (1975). Father to son reading: Its effect on boys' reading achievement. *Dissertation
Abstracts International, 36,* 41A–45A. (University Microfilms No. 75-13, 990)

Hereford, C. (1963). *Changing parental attitude through group discussion.* Austin: University
of Texas Press.

Herman, J.L., & Yeh, J.P. (1980, April). *Some effects of parent involvement in schools.* Paper
presented at the annual meeting of the American Educational Resarch Association, Boston. (ERIC Document Reproduction Service No. ED 206 963)

Hess, R.O., Holloway, S., Price, G.E., & Dickson, W.P. (1979). *Family environments and acquisition of reading skills: Toward a more precise analysis.* Paper presented at the conference "The Family as a Learning Environment," Educational Testing Service, Princeton,
NJ.

Hess, R.D., & Shipman, V.C. (1965). Early experience and the socialization of cognitive modes
in children. *Child Development, 36,* 369–386.

Hewison, J., & Tizard, A.J. (1980). Parent involvement and reading attainment. *British Journal
of Educational Psychology, 50*(3), 209–215.

Hightower, H.J. (1978, March). *Educational decision-making: The involvement of parents –
myth or reality?* Paper presented at the annual conference of the American Educational
Research Association, Toronto. (ERIC Document Reproduction Service No. ED
154 086)

Home and School Institute report. (1983). Washington, DC: Times Washington Bureau.

Hoskins, K.F. (1976). Effects of home reading experiences on academic readiness for kindergarten children. Unpublished doctoral dissertation, University of Missouri, Columbia.

Irvine, D.J. (1979). *Effects of parent involvement in a prekindergarten program on children's
cognitive performance.* Albany, NY: University of New York. (ERIC Document Reproduction Service No. ED 176 888)

Jackson, R.K., & Stretch, H.A. (1976). Perceptions of parents, teachers, and administrators to
parent involvement in early childhood programs. *The Alberta Journal of Educational
Research, 22,* 154–159.

Jencks, C. (1972). *Inequality: A reassessment of the effect of family and schools in America.*
New York: Basic Books.

Johnson, D., Leler, H., Rios, L., Brandt, L., Kahn, A., Mazeika, E., Frede, M., & Bissett, B.

(1974). The Houston Parent-Child Development Center: A parent education program for Mexican-American families. *American Journal of Orthopsychiatry, 44*(1), 121–128.

Kaplan, B.A., & Forgione, P.D. (1978, March). *Parent involvement in compensatory educational programs: Problems and potential strategies across 32 school districts.* Paper presented at the annual conference of the American Educational Research Association, Toronto. (ERIC Document Reproduction Service No. ED 155 242)

Karnes, M.B., Shwedel, A.M., & Steinberg, D. (1982). *Styles of parenting among parents of young gifted children.* Urbana, IL: University of Illinois, Institute for Child Behavior and Development.

Karnes, M.B., Studley, W.N., Wright, W.R., & Hodgins, A. (1968). An approach for working with mothers of disadvantaged preschool children. *Merrill Palmer Quarterly, 14*(2), 174–184.

Karnes, M.B., Teska, J., Hodgins, A., & Badger, E. (1970). Educational intervention at home by mothers of disadvantaged infants. *Child Development, 41,* 925–935.

Katz, L.G. (1980). Mothering and teaching: Some significant distinctions. In L.G. Katz (Ed.) *Current topics in early childhood education* (Vol. 3, pp. 47–64). Norwood, NJ: Ablex.

Keeves, J.P. (1972). *Educational environment and student achievement.* Melbourne: Australian Council for Educational Research.

Keeves, J.P. (1975). The home, the school, and achievement in mathematics and science. *Science Education, 59*(4), 439–460.

Kogan, K.L., & Gordon, B.N. (1975). A mother-instruction program documenting change in mother-child interactions. *Child Psychiatry and Human Development, 5,* 189–200.

Ladd, G.W., Lange, G., & Kienapple, K. (1981, April). Parents, teachers and competent children. Paper presented at the annual meeting of the Southern Association for Children Under Six, Biloxi, MS. (ERIC Document Reproduction Service No. ED 220 174)

Lambie, D.Z., Bond, J., & Weikart, D. (1973). *Ypsilanti-Carnegie infant education project. Infants, mothers and teaching: A study of infant education and home visits. Final report.* Ypsilanti, MI: High/Scope Educational Research Foundation.

Lambie, D.Z., Bond, J., & Weikart, D. (1974). *Home teaching with mothers and infants.* Ypsilanti, MI: High/Scope Educational Research Foundation.

Lamme, L., & Olmsted, D. (1977, May). Family reading habits and children's progress in reading. Paper presented at the annual meeting of the International Reading Association, Miami Beach. (ERIC Document Reproduction Service No. ED 138 963)

Lane, M., Elzey, E.F., & Lewis, M.S. (1971). *Nurseries in Cross Cultural Education (NICE). Final report.* San Francisco: San Francisco State College.

Langenbrunner, M.R., & Thornburg, K.R. (1980). Attitude of preschool directors, teachers, and parents toward parent involvement in the schools. *Reading Improvement, 17,* 286–91.

Lasater, T.M. (1974). *Birmingham Parent-child Development Center program report.* (ERIC Document Reproduction Service No. ED 211 236)

Lasater, T.M., Briggs, J., Maline, D., Gillim, C.F., & Weisberg, P. (1975, April). *The Birmingham model for parent education.* Paper presented at the biennial meeting of the Society for Research in Child Development, Denver, CO.

Leler, H., Johnson, D., Kahn, A., & Brandt, L. (1974). *Research report of the Houston Parent-Child Developmental Center.* Houston, TX: University of Houston.

Levenstein, P. (1970). Cognitive growth in preschoolers through verbal interaction with mothers. *American Journal of Orthopsychiatry, 40*(3), 426–432.

Levenstein, P. (1971). *Verbal Interaction Project: Aiding cognitive growth in disadvantaged preschoolers through the mother-child home program: July 1, 1967–Aaugust 31, 1970. Final report.* Freeport, NY: Family Service Association of Nassau County, Inc., Mother-Child Home Program.

Levenstein, P. (1972). *Verbal Interaction Project: Research plan, September 1973–August 1978, first year: September 1973–August 1974.* Freeport, NY: Family Service Association of Nassau County, Inc., Mother-Child Home Program.

Levenstein, P. (1974). *A message from home: A home-based intervention method for low income preschoolers.* (ERIC Document Reproduction Service No. ED 095 992)

Levin, T. (1967). Preschool education and the communities of the poor. In J. Hellmuth (Ed.), *Disadvantaged child* (Vol. 1, pp. 351–403). Seattle, WA: Special Child Publications.

Lortie, D.C. (1975). *School-teacher: A sociological study.* Chicago: University of Chicago Press.

Madden, J., Levenstein, P., & Levenstein, S. (1976). Longitudinal IQ outcomes of the Mother-Child Home Program, 1967–1973. *Child Development, 47,* 1015–1025.

Mager, G.M. (1980). The conditions which influence teachers in initiating contacts with parents. *Journal of Educational Research, 73,* 276–282.

Mann, M. (1970). *The effects of a preschool language program on two-year-old children and their mothers.* Tempe, AZ: Arizona State University.

Maraschiellio R. (1981). *Evaluation of the prekindergarten Head Start program 1979–1980* (Technical Summary Report No. 8132). Philadelphia, PA: Philadelphia School District, Office of Research and Evaluation. (ERIC Document Reproduction Service No. ED 206 637)

Mayeske, G.W. (1973). *A study of the achievement of our nation's students.* Washington, DC: United States Government Printing Office.

McConnell, B. (1974). *Bilingual mini-school tutoring project: Evaluation and progress report 3.* Olympia, WA: Washington Office of the State Superintendent of Instruction. (ERIC Document Reproduction Service No. ED 116 874)

McCormick, S. (1981, January). *Reading aloud to pre-schoolers ages 3–6: A review of the research.* Paper presented at the annual meeting of the Southwest Regional Conference of the International Reading Association, San Antonio, TX. (ERIC Document Reproduction Service No. ED 199 657)

McKay, D. (1981, January). *Introducing pre-school children to reading through parent involvement.* Paper presented at the annual meeting of the Parents and Reading Conference, New York. (ERIC Document Reproduction Service No. ED 206 406)

McKinney, J. (1978). *Study of parent involvement in early childhood programs.* Philadelphia: Philadelphia School Disrict, Office of Research and Evaluation. (ERIC Document Reproduction Service No. ED 164 134)

McKinney, J. (1980). *Evaluation of parent involvement in early childhood programs 1979–1980.* (Technical Summary, Report No. 8130). Philadelphia: Philadelphia School District, Office of Research and Evaluation. (ERIC Document Reproduction Service No. ED 204 388)

McLaren, F. (1965). *The effect of a parent information program upon deciding achievement in first grade.* Unpublished doctoral dissertation, University of Oklahoma, Norman.

McLaughlin, M. (1975). *The effects of Title I, ESEA: An exploratory study* (DHEW Contract No. OEC-0-70-5049). Cambridge, MA: Harvard University, Center for Educational Policy Research.

McPherson, G.H. (1972). *Small town teacher.* Cambridge, MA: Harvard University Press.

Meighan, R. (1981). A new teaching force? Some issues raised by seeing parents as educators and the implications for teacher education. *Educational Review, 33,* 133–142.

MIDCO Educational Associates, Inc. (1972). *Perspective on parent participation in Head Start: An analysis and critique.* Washington, DC: Office of Child Development, United States Department of Health, Education and Welfare.

Middleton, M. (1975). *An evaluation of the family life education course at Eric Harbor Secondary School.* Vancouver, British Columbia, Canada: Vancouver Educational Services

Group. (ERIC Document Reproduction Service No. ED 132 186)

Mosteller, F., & Moynihan, O.P. (Eds.). (1972). *On equality of educational opportunity.* New York: Random House.

Mowry, C. (1972). *Investigation of the effects of parent participation in Head Start: Nontechnical report.* Washington, DC: Office of Child Development, United States Department of Health, Education and Welfare.

National Education Association. (1972). *Parent involvement: A key to better schools.* Washington, DC: Author.

National Commission on Excellence in Education. (1983). *A nation at risk: the imperative for educational reform.* Washington, DC: United States Department of Education. (ERIC Document Reproduction Service No. ED 226 006)

Niedermeyer, F.C. (1970). Effects of school-to-home feedback and parent accountability on kindergarten reading performance, parent participation and pupil attitude. *Dissertation Abstracts International 30,* 3198A. (University Microfilms No. 70-2240)

Nottleman, E.D. (1978). *Parent-child interaction and children's achievement-related behavior.* Unpublished doctoral dissertation, University of Illinois, Urbana.

Olmsted, P. (1977). *The relationship of program participation and parental teaching behavior with children's standardized achievement measures in two program sites.* Unpublished doctoral dissertation, University of Florida, Gainesville.

Olmstead, P., & Jester, R.E. (1972). Mother-child interaction in a teaching situation. *Theory into Practice, 11,* 163–170.

Parke, R.D. (1981). *Fathers.* Cambridge, MA: Harvard University Press.

Parsons, J.E. (1981). *The development of achievement motivation* (Report No. 117). Ann Arbor, MI: University of Michigan Developmental Psychology Program.

Powell, D.R. (1980). Toward a sociological perspective of relations between parents and child care programs. In S. Kilmer (Ed.), *Advances in early education and day care* (pp. 203–226). Greenwich, CT: JAI Press.

Project Unique. (1969). New York: Center for Urban Education.

Radin, N. (1969). The impact of a kindergarten home counseling program. *Exceptional Children, 36,* 251–256.

Radin, N. (1972). Three degrees of maternal involvement in a preschool program: Impact on mothers and children. *Child Development, 43,* 1355–1364.

Raim, J. (1980). Who learns when parents teach children? *The Reading Teacher, 32,* 152–155.

Ransbury, M.K. (1973). An assessment of reading attitudes. *Journal of Reading, 17,* 25–28.

Rempson, J. (1967). *School-parent programs in depressed urban neighborhoods.* New York: Praeger.

Risley, T. (1968). Learning and lollipops. *Psychology Today, 1* (8), 28–31, 62–65.

Romotowski, J.A., & Trepanier, M.L. (1977). *Examining and influencing the home reading behaviors of young children.* (ERIC Document Reproduction Service No. ED 195 938)

Rose, S. (1974). Group training of parents as behavior modifiers. *Social Work, 19,* 156–162.

Rotter, J.C., & Robinson, E.H. III. (1982). *Parent-teacher conferencing: What research says to the teacher.* Washington, DC: National Education Association (ERIC Document Reproduction Service No. ED 222 487)

Rupley, W.H., & Blair, T.R. (1975). Early reading: Teachers and parents. *The Reading Teacher, 28,* 716–717.

Sandler, H.M., Dokecki, P., Stewart, L., Britton, V., & Horton, D. (1973). The valuation of a home-based educational intervention for preschoolers and their mothers. *Journal of Community Psychology, 1,* 372–374.

Schaefer, E. (1972). Parents as educators: Evidence from cross-sectional, longitudinal, and intervention research. *Young Children, 28,* 227–239.

Schaefer, E. (1973, February). *Child development research and education revolution: The child, the family, and the education profession.* Paper presented at the annual meeting of the American Educational Research Association, New Orleans.

Schickedanz, J.A. (1978). Please read that story again. *Young Children, 33*(5), 48–55.

Schlossman, S. (1978). The parent-teacher education game: The politics of child psychology in the 1970s. *Teachers College Record, 79*(4), 788–809.

Seginer, R. (1983). Parents' educational expectations and children's academic achievements: A literature review. *Merrill-Palmer Quarterly, 29,* 1–23.

Sheldon, W.D., & Carrillo, R. (1952). Relation of parent, home and certain developmental characteristics to children's reading ability. *Elementary School Journal, 52,* 262–270.

Siders, M., & Sledjeski, S. (1978). *How to grow a happy reader: Report on a study of parental involvement as it relates to a child's attitude and achievement in the acquisition of reading skills.* (ERIC Document Reproduction Service No. ED 214 124)

Smith, C.B. (1971). The effect of environment on learning to read. In Smith, C.B. (Ed.), *Parents and reading* (pp. 10–22). Newark, DE: International Reading Association.

Sprigle, H.A. (1974). *The learning to learn teacher education program.* Jacksonville, FL: Learning to Learn School.

Stevens, J.H., Jr. (1978). Parent education programs. *Young Children,* (4), 59–65.

Strom, R., & Johnson, A. (1974). The parent as teacher. *Education, 95,* 40–43.

Swift, M.S. (1970). Training poverty mothers in communication skills. *The Reading Teacher, 23,* 360–367.

Teale, W.H. (1978). Positive environments for learning to read: What studies of early readers tell us. *Language Arts, 55,* 922–931.

Tudor, K. (1977). An exploratory study of teacher attitude and behavior toward parent education and involvement. *Educational Research Quarterly, 2*(3), 22–28.

Vernon, P.E. (1979). *Intelligence: Heredity and environment.* San Francisco: W.H. Freeman.

Vukelich, C. (1978). Parents are teachers: A beginning reading program. *The Reading Teacher, 31,* 524–527.

Wagenaar, T.C. (1977, September). *School achievement level vis-à-vis community involvement and support: An empirical assessment.* Paper presented at the annual meeting of the American Sociological Association, Ohio State University, Columbus. (ERIC Document Reproduction Service No. ED 146 111)

Warren, R.L. (1973). The classroom as a sanctuary for teachers: Discontinuities in social control. *American Anthropologist, 75,* 280–291.

Waters, J.J. (1972). *Preschool program: Narrative evaluation report 1971–1972, state preschool program.* Oakland, CA: Oakland Unified School District, Research Department.

Weikart, D. (1971). *Ypsilanti preschool curriculum demonstration project, 1968–1971.* Ypsilanti, MI: High/Scope Educational Research Foundation.

Weikart, D. (1973). *Development of effective preschool programs: A report on the results of the High/Scope-Ypsilanti Preschool Projects.* Ypsilanti, MI: High/Scope Research Foundation.

Weikart, D., Deloria, D., Lawser, S., & Wiegerink, R. (1970). *Longitudinal results of the Ypsilanti Perry Preschool Project. Final report.* (Vol. 2). Ypsilanti, MI: High/Scope Educational Research Foundation.

Weikart, D., Rogers, L., & Adcock, C. (1970). *The cognitively-oriented curriculum: A framework for preschool teachers. Final report* (Vol. 1). Ypsilanti, MI: High/Scope Educational Research Foundation.

Wells, R. (1978). Parents and reading: What fifth graders report. *Journal of Research and Development in Education, 11,* 20–25.

Wenig, M., & Brown, M. (1975). School effects and parent/teacher communication = happy young children. *Young Children, 30,* 373–377.

Wigfield, A., & Asher, S.R. (in press). Social and motivational influences on reading. In P.D.

Pearson, R. Barr, M.L. Kamil, & P.B. Mosenthal (Eds.), *Handbook of reading research*. New York: Longman.

Wittes, G., & Radin, N. (1969). *Helping your child to learn: The nurturance approach*. San Rafael, CA: Dimensions Publishing.

Wittes, G., & Radin, N. (1971). Two approaches to group work with parents in a compensatory preschool program. *Social Work, 16*(1), 42–50.

Wolfgang, C.H., Bratl, H., & Peck, M. (1977). *Perceived problems of preschool-day-care teachers*. Unpublished manuscript, Ohio State University, Columbus.

Woods, C., Barnard, D.P., & TeSelle, E. (1974). *The effect of the parent involvement program on reading readiness scores*. Mesa, AZ: Mesa Public Schools. (ERIC Document Reproduction Service No. ED 104 527)

Young, C. (1975). *Parents as liaison workers: An evaluative study of Title VII programs*. Unpublished doctoral dissertation, University of Illinois, Urbana.

5

Perspectives on Teacher Education: Some Relations Between Theory and Practice

Elizabeth Jones

Pacific Oaks College
Pasadena, California

As a teacher of young children turned teacher of adults, I have found it consistently useful to refer back to what I know about teaching children as I try to teach adults well. I do so because I'm a good teacher of children and I want to build on that competence — and because early childhood is really the only level of education that has taken developmental principles seriously and developed criteria and procedures for active learning. So I have asked myself repeatedly, What are the equivalents, in a college classroom, of the blocks, climbing structures, sand and water, and paints of the preschool classroom? How can I trust adult learners to grow in the way I have always trusted children to grow? How can I offer them choices in a rich environment? and, How can I empower them as self-directed learners?

As a teacher of children, I come from the tradition Franklin and Biber (1977), writing in the first volume of this series, call *developmental-interaction* — a tradition in which both affective and cognitive development are taken seriously. Pacific Oaks, like Bank Street, has been a source and sustainer of this tradition, and this is the approach I have sought to implement in teacher education.

Both the title and the organization of this article have been adapted from Franklin and Biber (1977). These investigators identify three theoretical approaches in early childhood education: behavioristic-learning, cognitive-developmental, and developmental-interaction. The behavioristic-learning and cognitive-developmental approaches, as they indicate, are based quite explicitly on two divergent psychological perspectives. Developmental-interaction theory "represents an integration of cognitive-developmental stage concepts and ego psychology formulations and has roots in the progressive education ideology of the John Dewey period" (Franklin & Biber, 1977, p. 3). This approach emphasizes intuition, feeling, and imagination as well as goal-directed thinking, and demands teacher behavior that is responsive to the situation rather than standardized.

As Katz (1977) has suggested, these approaches, despite their basis in psychological theory, function as ideologies when applied to education. Behaviorists start from a different set of premises about human nature and learning than developmentalists do, and their methods and measures are accordingly different.

Teachers, who must make continual decisions about their own and their students' behavior, do so on the basis of their ideologies, hidden or expressed. They cannot be objective in the way an observer can. I believe it is useful to take a stand on our ideologies in order both to clarify our own thinking and to make it accessible to argument by others with different perspectives.

This is, therefore, a position paper, written from my own experiences as a teacher educator. By design, it is less scholarly and more personal than its prototype, though I am following Franklin and Biber's example in making my own position clear. There is no need for me to repeat their excellent theoretical review. Instead, I want to be as concrete as I can, to give illustrations from practice rather than abstractions from theory, and to draw a parallel between these approaches in early childhood education and in teacher education. I make the assumption that teachers are more likely to teach as they were taught than as they were taught to teach (E. Jones, 1975, 1981; Wasserman, 1973). Thus, a behaviorist approach in teacher education is appropriate if we wish to prepare behaviorist teachers of young children.

My impression is that the behaviorist approach dominates teacher education, even though I doubt that many of its practitioners intend to have their students transfer it whole into programs for young children. Perhaps the often-remarked gap between the ivory tower of the college and the real world of schools and day care centers can be directly attributed not so much to the unreality of the content taught as to the reality of the way in which it is taught. It seems likely that college students, like children, quickly learn what really counts; they *do,* and they understand. (They hear, and they forget [Nuffield Mathematics Project, 1967].)

THE BEHAVIORISTIC-LEARNING APPROACH

The aim of behavior modification is to achieve measurable changes in observable behavior. Reinforcers, positive and negative, are employed to produce the behaviors that someone has defined as desirable or appropriate.

While this theory is not often directly credited for prevailing practice in higher education, it is certainly consistent with it. Course content and learning behaviors are defined by the experts—individual teachers and departmental committees. Reinforcers are agreed upon by the system as a whole, and strenuous efforts are made to keep them consistent (to avoid grade inflation, for example).

In most college classes, appropriate behavior is operationally defined as marking correct answers on examinations. Behaviorists do not acknowledge Piaget's distinction between logical knowledge, which must be constructed by the knower, and social knowledge, which is learned by rote, but believe any concept may be taught verbally (Engelmann, 1971; Kamii & Derman, 1971). Correct verbal learning is reinforced, both positively and negatively, by letter grades; the most appropriately behaving students receive A's, while the altogether recalcitrant get F's. The system is straightforward, and the rules of the game are clear to teachers and students alike. Like good behaviorists, college instructors rarely try to distinguish between what a student *does*—his or her behavior on the exam—and what a student *knows*. The latter question is vague and not really relevant. (We are, after all, scientists; we do not waste our time posing unanswerable questions.)

Teacher education, striving to be a respectable discipline in colleges and universities, has generally conformed to this system. We make a point of teaching the theories underlying practice and requiring students to learn verbal abstractions as well as practical methods. Many teacher educators agree that there is an unfortunate division between academic classes and practical work, and call for more bridge building and more direct experience with children (Spodek, 1974). Several have emphasized the importance of using the same approaches with students that we expect them to use with children (Katz, 1974; Ward, 1974). However, few have come to terms with the radical restructuring of academic classes that would be necessary to make such classes consistent with students' experience with children. My purpose in this discussion is to suggest the forms that restructuring might take.

Because the behaviorist approach is familiar to all of us who have been to school, I need not describe it in more detail here.[1] The other approaches, much less familiar in college teaching, are described in greater detail.

THE COGNITIVE-DEVELOPMENTAL APPROACH

I believe that the behaviorist approach, which offers preselected closed tasks and contingent reinforcement, can be expected to produce teacher-technicians. In contrast, the cognitive-developmental approach, which of-

---

[1] For further reference on behaviorism, see Ackerman (1972) and Skinner (1971).

fers opportunities for cognitive action, produces problem-solving teachers focused on the content of children's learning. This approach is based on the theories of Jean Piaget.[2] Knowledge, according to Piaget, is acquired as the outcome of the interaction betwen the learner and the environment. Through active exploration of the physical world, children acquire direct sensory awareness of the things around them. Gradually, through discovering patterns, and creating relationships and reflecting upon them, children construct logico-mathematical theories about the world and how it works. Interaction with peers is an essential part of the process of learning about the physical as well as the social world.

Cognitive development is an orderly process; each stage serves as a necessary foundation for the next. Young children encounter the world directly through their actions, without mediation or representation through symbols. As they mature, they are able to organize their experience symbolically. Eventually, in the formal operations stage, they will be able to reason symbolically, without needing the presence of the concrete object to reinforce and check out their understanding.

It is important to recognize that Piaget's stages describe a sequence in learning, not a predictable age-stage relationship. Thus, while adolescents and adults have the capacity for formal operations, "The results [of a number of research studies] are unequivocal. A significantly and surprisingly large number of high school and college students appear to be operating at less than an optimal level" (Schwebel, 1976, p. 4). Furth (1973), interpreting Piaget's work, emphasizes that attainment of formal operations is the most variable stage in the developmental sequence:

> There is ample evidence that all healthy persons in all societies reach the stage of concrete operations. A like assertion cannot be made with equal confidence for formal thinking . . . The closer a person is to adulthood the more likely is it that individual and particularly also sociocultural preferences and opportunities have a decisive influence on the content and manner in which a person's intelligence is used. (p. 67)

A community college teacher has described her experiences with her students as follows:

> Many of [the students], I have observed, have not progressed intellectually past concrete operations in many areas – and some seem to be still preoperational! For example, I did a math workshop and had a lot of materials requiring seriation, classification, etc. Many students were very hesitant to try things out. In desperation I applied a little adult authority and led one of the students over

---

[2] For summaries of Piaget's theories, see Kamii and DeVries (1977), Labinowicz (1980), and Pulaski (1971).

to a table of different leaves to be classified. I was amazed to discover that this student could not shift to a different category beyond her first one. I knew that her teaching philosophy was strongly authoritarian, limiting children to closed experiences. Suddenly I understood why she could not entertain notions of educational programs that were other than authority-centered, imitative, rigid "right-answer" ones! (Hanson, 1983, p. 60)

David Hawkins (1970), teaching university students, comments:

I have long suspected that my students' difficulties with the intellectual process come not from the complexity of college work itself, but mainly from their home background and the first years of their formal education. A student who cannot seem to understand the workings of the Ptolemaic astronomy, for example, turns out to have no evident acquaintance with the simple and "obvious" relativity of motion, or the simple geometrical relations of light and shadow. Sometimes for these students a style of laboratory work which might be called "Kindergarten Revisited" has dramatically liberated their intellectual powers. Turn on your heel with your head back until you *see* the ceiling—turn the other way—and don't fall over! (p. 37)

If we take Piaget seriously, in teacher education as in early childhood education, it seems evident that experiential or laboratory or workshop instruction needs to precede, or at least be concurrent with, any teaching of general principles. To understand, we must manipulate, combine and recombine —or, in the words of Kenneth Grahame's Water Rat, simply "mess about" (Hawkins, 1970). Teacher education needs "to provide students with opportunities to construct their own conceptual maps of the logic of the terrain of teaching" (Soltis, 1973, p. 7). This takes time, and it takes direct experience.

Straightforward lecture, the typical mode of college teaching, is an appropriate way (a) to present social knowledge or (b) to sum up the logical knowledge that formally operating students already possess on the basis of their personal experience. Piaget explains social knowledge as the conventions of one's culture—the names of things and the rules for behavior. Because these things are arbitrary, they can only be taught directly, by telling or showing. In contrast, logical knowledge about the ways the world works (in both physical and interpersonal terms) is constructed by the learner, who generalizes from repeated experiences (Kamii & DeVries, 1977, p. 368).

Students not yet formal-operating often take in logically constructed knowledge as social knowledge only. For example, they may be taught that positive redirection is a useful principle in dealing with children's inappropriate behavior: Instead of saying "No," help the child find an acceptable alternative. If this technique is taught directly as a rule for teacher behavior, some students will apply it with children because they have been told to. However, this is a logical principle generated by teacher experimentation with alternative ways of managing children's behavior. Students will understand the logic of the principle more fully if they have opportunities to observe, to experiment, and to discuss their experiences with one another.

Students who have learned such principles by rote (memorized them as social knowledge) may be perfectly capable of stating them in an examination. In a behaviorist framework, rote learning demonstrates competence as well as logical learning does. But rote learning is difficult to apply in practice; it doesn't generalize with any flexibility to new situations. In a culture teeming with new situations, it would seem much more to the point to provide learners of any age with the concrete experiences, and the opportunities to talk about them with peers, that Piaget describes as essential for the establishment of formal operations in any area. The cognitive-developmental approach implies such active learning.

There is no shortcut to understanding, in Piaget's view:

> Without a doubt it is necessary to reach abstraction . . . but abstraction is only a sort of trickery and deflection of the mind if it doesn't constitute the crowning stage of a series of previously uninterrupted concrete actions. The true cause of failures in formal education is therefore essentially the fact that one begins with language . . . instead of beginning with real and material action. (Piaget, 1973, pp. 103–104)

Whether or not adults are formal-operating, they need to engage actively with the material. Capacity for formal operations means simply that action and interaction can be carried on at a symbolic level; argument about ideas replaces argument about objects. All adult students have the potential for reflecting on and generalizing from their experiences through thinking, writing, and discussion.

A helpful guide to the design of active learning experiences for adults is *Contexts for Learning* (Finkel & Monk, 1978). Its authors, a psychologist and a mathematician, tackle head-on the issue of providing students with direct experience about the questions of a discipline. Their methods enable students *"to go through experiences similar to those that excited the teacher"* in the first place (p. 1, emphasis in the original). Generously detailed examples and a lucid analysis of the process of designing such experiences are provided. To select conceptual goals for students' learning, the authors advise, "work backwards from the products of a discipline toward the intellectual experiences that lead to these products" (p. 53).

Our goal as teachers is to help students engage in mental activities that generate knowledge as they enter an unfamiliar learning environment. The student begins understanding new material in the only way possible — in terms of his or her preexisting ideas:

[The student] applies his own conceptual framework to it. A more intellectually adequate framework can only be developed through a modification and refinement of the student's initial framework. . . . The primary means of inducing a person to alter his intellectual framework is to get him to use it in varied, challenging, and specific ways. Under the strain of active use, inadequacies in the ideas, poor and absent connections between ideas, and any overall unsuitability will become manifest. (Finkel & Monk, 1978, pp. 53–55)

Course planning in this framework has two stages, based on answers to the following questions: (a) What are the concepts that will contribute to students' understanding of the subject? and (b) What experiences will help students to develop understanding of the concepts? Stating conceptual goals for a course, in Finkel and Monk's words,

is a task that can be performed only by the teacher responsible for that course. We and our collaborators have found that this task necessitates a rethinking of one's own discipline, a process that in itself is deeply satisfying. (p. 57)

Engaging in this process myself one day, I listed the following concepts as basic to an understanding of child development: (a) There are basic needs common to all human beings. (b) Development (physical, social, emotional, intellectual) occurs in stages and in a predictable sequence. (c) Normal development includes broad individual variations. (d) Observing children is a good way to learn about them. (e) Children learn through play. (f) Because children are dependent on adults, it is important to examine the roles, attitudes and culture of adult caregivers. (g) Because assumptions and biases affect any adult's understanding of children, it is important to examine one's own.

Engaging in a similar process, Elizabeth Prescott, a member of the faculty of Pacific Oaks, came up with single- or few-word concepts rather than sentences: object permanence, attachment, separation, autonomy, initiative, learning about rules and fairness, industry (accomplishment and failure), and sense of the future (Prescott, personal communication, September 1982).

Given these or another list of concepts, the next question to ask is, How might such concepts be learned through workshop experiences or laboratory investigations? The laboratory available to the teacher of child development comes in two parts, as I see it. The first includes those experiences with people — children and adults — that students have had and are having outside the classroom and that can be discussed in the classroom. These experiences may be assigned by the teacher ("Observe a child under two in interaction with his mother . . .") or drawn from a common human past ("Describe a memorable childhood passion. What did you care about very much as a child?" "Describe a time when you experienced a sense of failure. Did you ever achieve mastery later?").

The second set of laboratory experiences is found in the human relations in the college classroom itself. What kinds of thought-provoking experiences can the teacher structure for the students during class time, in interaction with each other, either in the room or in the community together? ("Go out of the room and come back in on a small child's level. What do you notice?" "Try first to print your name and then to cut with scissors using your left hand, if you're right-handed, or vice versa. Can you do it? How does it make you feel?" "Lead a blindfolded partner outdoors, keeping her safe while providing a variety of sensory experiences.") These are examples of relatively simple activities; others may be more complex. If instructions are given in writing on a worksheet available to students as they enter the class, students can work independently; they need not wait for the teacher's initiative to begin the action.

In this structure, the teacher takes on some new roles, becoming an asker of questions, a provider of materials, a laboratory participant, a class chairperson and secretary, and a discussion leader (Renner & Lawson, 1973). The teacher calls the students together, takes note of the data they have gathered, and encourages discussion of the data. In addition, it is the teacher's role to suggest names for what the students have discovered, thus relating the data to concepts, and to decide when and how to move on to exploration of the next concept. As Renner and Lawson observe,

> this teacher is not a teller, he is a director of learning. Traditional teaching methods embrace the notions that (a) teaching is telling, (b) memorization is learning, and (c) being able to repeat something on an examination is evidence of understanding — those points are the antithesis of inquiry. (p. 276)

The goal of this structure is student-centered intellectual activity, with the teacher out of center stage. There are many opportunities for small-group work, for interactions among students. In Piaget's (1973) words:

> No real intellectual activity could be carried on in the form of experimental actions and spontaneous investigations without free collaboration among individuals — that is to say, among the students themselves, and not only between the teacher and the student. Using the intelligence assumes not only continual mutual stimulation, but also and more importantly mutual control and exercise of the critical spirit, which alone can lead the individual to objectivity and to a need for conclusive evidence. The workings of logic are, in effect, always "cooperations" . . . The active school presupposes working in common, alternating between individual work and work in groups, since collective living has been shown to be essential to the full development of the personality in all its facets — even the more intellectual. (pp. 107–109)

The traditional teaching model is two-person, teacher-to-student, in spite of the presence of all those other people. In contrast, the workshop approach, in Finkel and Monk's words, "breaks the iron grip of the two-person model." (1978, p. 103) Most teachers are strongly inclined to identify themselves with the subject they teach and to assume that they must be present as intermediary between students and subject matter. In so doing, they fuse their role as knower and their role as helper in the learning process.

In a workshop approach, the two roles are separated in time and place. The teacher plans the workshop on the basis of his or her knowledge, formulating ideas in a worksheet that serves to initiate students' action, typically in small groups. Because the teacher is not the center of this action, he or she is free to observe, to evaluate the effectiveness of prior planning, to engage students' thinking and interaction. The teacher is free to intervene with a group or an individual, becoming a helper in a variety of ways and discovering which ways are most effective and most enjoyable.

To quote Finkel and Monk (1978) once more on the subject:

> Perhaps the most liberating change of all: [the teacher] no longer has to supply the energy of the class. The students are already interacting with the worksheet when he enters to help. He may now question, probe, hint, support, provoke, facilitate, argue, emote, in ways that he may always have wanted to, but never could, because the presentation of the subject matter always took precedence. He will also receive responses to these ways of expressing himself, quite separate from the intellectual responses to the worksheet. Thus, he can distinguish between reactions to his style as a teacher and reactions to his way of presenting material. . . . There is a true dialectic between writing worksheets and running workshops based on them. They represent two modes of sharing one's subject with students. (pp. 103–106)

The worksheet, as thus described, sounds to me a good deal like the blocks and paints and sand of the preschool classroom. It serves to get active learning started. The instructor, like the preschool teacher, watches to see what will happen, intervening as he or she chooses.

THE DEVELOPMENTAL-INTERACTION APPROACH

As Franklin and Biber (1977) have pointed out, there is a large measure of common ground between early childhood programs based on a cognitive-developmental approach and those programs that they call developmental-interaction. A cognitive-developmental approach to teacher education, as described in the previous section, may be expected to produce problem-solving teachers focused on the content of children's learning. A developmental-interaction approach, which offers opportunities for both cognitive and affective action, produces problem-solving teachers concerned with both the content and the process of children's learning. Workshop-style teaching may concentrate on the cognitive, or it may make a point of incorporating affective experience as well. Finkel and Monk (1978, pp. 87–88) comment that some affective learning is inevitable as students help each other, enjoy one another's company, and discover how they function in groups. The developmental-interaction teacher educator plans consciously for these and other affective goals:

> It is a premise of the developmental-interaction view here under discussion that the separation of these major developmental sequences—the cognitive-intellectual and the affective-social—has important heuristic value but that, in utilizing these formulations in connection with educational planning, it is essential to be continuously cognizant of their interdependence in the way children and people actually function. (Franklin and Biber, 1977, p. 18)

Like behaviorists, developmental-interactionists are actively concerned with motivation. Behaviorists concentrate on extrinsic sources of motivation, assuming that all behavior occurs because it is reinforced. Developmentalists concentrate on intrinsic motivation of the sort described by White (1959) and Hunt (1971); they believe that human beings are naturally curious and stimulus-seeking, and that motivation is inherent in doing. White calls this attribute *competence motivation*—a need to bring about an effect by acting on the environment.

Psychodynamic theorists have emphasized the ways in which anxiety may interfere with this natural curiosity. Spontaneous growth will occur only in an environment that minimizes anxiety and maximizes the delights of growth (Maslow, 1962). In a learning environment, the teacher who offers students "unconditional positive regard" (Rogers, 1951, 1969) supports them in taking the risks inherent in new learning.

Relatively few college teachers concern themselves directly with their students' affective-social development. Some may do so on an informal basis, making themselves available to students outside of class and being sympathetic to their personal concerns. But it is rare to find interpersonal dynamics taken into account as part of the content of a course—even courses in human development and education. College teachers tend to ignore or minimize the risks involved in learning—especially learning in emotionally laden subject areas.

Dugger (1983) quotes a community college student as saying, "When I was in seventh grade, I asked a question, and the teacher told me it was a dumb question. I never asked another question in school" (p. 58). Students who learn not to ask questions give up behaving intelligently in the classroom; a whole source of energy for learning is cut off. And so my first concern, as a college teacher in this mode, is to reduce students' anxiety about learning. I try to provide a psychologically safe space—to be a teacher who demonstrates qualities of warmth, empathy, and respect, and thus can be trusted. Trust is an essential climate for learning (Meade, 1975). And I share power with students, encouraging them to take responsibility for choosing their own learning activities and evaluating their efforts, rather than asking them to play "please-the-teacher."

Teachers at Pacific Oaks have written about working in this mode with a 4-year-old: "What we are trying to do is to give him the power to do whatever he wants to do—to make an impact on his world, to be able to exert genuine choice. This is our goal for all children" (Rabiroff & Prescott, 1978, p. 133). Power is thus shared, not abdicated. As teacher I retain responsibility for defining the parameters of the course, selecting basic concepts, providing a workable learning structure—even stating process objectives in behavioral terms (E. Jones, 1983). But I give students real choices among a wide range of options and expect them to evaluate their own learning. For example, instead of assigning a textbook I ask students to make their own choices from a reading list. I ask them to write their personal reactions to their reading, to questions raised in class, to the class structure and how it is working for them. I want all students to read and write, talk and listen, observe and reflect—these are my behavioral objectives. But because they are individuals, I expect students to do different things, rather than perform a single task on which I could rank their relative success. I value their differences rather than evaluate them.

Faced with such power of choice, students are often excited. They are often also uncertain of their ability to handle the situation, and the learning that comes out of this dilemma may well be the most important thing that happens for them. As one teacher education student wrote in her self-evaluation:

> Throughout my years of schooling I have always been guided. To suddenly be expected to do and discover on my own has been very difficult for me to adjust to. This semester has been one of self-exploration, and I still am not sure as to where all the scattered pieces of myself fit in. . . . I am left to depend on myself. I realize that my teaching will be a lot like this. When I am faced with a problem, I will have to look inside and discover an answer for myself. . . . I am only now beginning to put together, in a sense, my life as a teacher. (Stephanie Feeney, personal communication, August 1981)

My second concern, after reduction of anxiety, is to plan cognitive learning experiences that take feelings into account. Feelings serve as the context that determines students' ability to learn; feelings are therefore considered directly in planning for the learning process. Franklin and Biber (1977) cite

Dewey in this respect: "Learning experiences designed to further cognitive facility are weighed in terms of the simultaneous learning that is going on with respect to self-image, attitudes toward others, work patterns, or general behavioral modes" (p. 20).

My class activities are designed to promote the following goals:

1. Introduce students to the resources available (readings, places to observe, me, and one another) and help them get started in making choices among these resources for their learning.
2. Establish a communication network. When learning activities are individualized, it is crucial that everyone be accountable on a continuing basis, in writing as well as orally.
3. Cover the content through action, interaction, and reflection on experience.
4. Deal with students' feelings about the content and the people in the group (other students and the teacher).

Whenever possible, I combine two or more of these purposes in one activity. For example, I might ask students to get acquainted in a child development class by sharing an early childhood experience with each other. Paired conversation helps reduce anxiety about not knowing anyone in the group and introduces students to one another's experiences. We might then build on this basis by generating developmental themes out of the kinds of experiences the students chose to relate ("Did any of your experiences have to do with separation? Autonomy? Being competent? Does the introduction of these abstract concepts help you to put your personal, concrete experienes in broader perspective?").

Teachers who make a clear distinction between "therapy" and "education" may feel that it is inappropriate to encourage college students to express their feelings and explore their past emotional experiences. However, affectively-oriented teaching differs from therapy in that the setting is educational, the student has come to learn about something, and the teacher's goal is to teach. There is a consistent reality base, beyond the individual's concern with self, underscored by the questions, What are you learning about? and, What do you want to do? Personal search undertaken in an educational rather than a therapy setting has an instrumental quality that tends to move it beyond egocentrism; that is, the individual is exploring self in order to understand others better and to become a more competent professional.

However, teachers who restructure relationships in their classrooms, thereby raising such questions, may be suspect. Writing about survival in an open-classroom situation, Beukema (1978) remarks on the response of others to such restructuring:

> One of the criticisms leveled at me, both by students and by friends and colleagues, was that I was running group therapy or sensitivity sessions. "I am not," I protested, wondering why people talking to each other should be seen as therapeutic. Later I realized that people were being human with each other in a context where humanness doesn't usually happen. Students speaking to each other about "course content" may be an acceptable classroom behavior, but students speaking about themselves is generally not. (p. 145)

Given the opportunity, people are likely to share with one another not only intellectual ideas, but also personal anxieties and dilemmas and feelings of all sorts. Classrooms are simpler, tidier places without these things. In a traditional classroom, students can maintain a protective anonymity by listening, taking notes, and staying quiet – and, from a developmental-interaction point of view, not learning very much. Learning is an active process, involving both cognition and affect.

Essentially, I find that combining these two aspects of learning requires me to slow down in my teaching. Whenever my anxiety over covering course content takes precedence, it triggers student anxiety, which is what I want to reduce. Traditionally, anxiety is an appropriate motivator in schools. (If you don't use assignments, due dates, and grades, how can you ever get students to work?) But I choose instead to trust myself, my students, and the learning process, recognizing that any content is potentially infinite; it cannot possibly be "covered." Duckworth (1972) quotes David Hawkins on curriculum development: "You don't want to cover a subject; you want to uncover it" (p. 226). This is what we try to do by identifying the critical concepts in a field; they serve as rallying points, not boundaries. It is teachers and curriculum planners who for their own convenience set arbitrary, manageable boundaries to subject areas. Students, given the opportunity, will continually make unpredicted connections relevant to their own learning. I may sometimes, as a teacher, help an individual or group focus by defining something as "off the subject," but that's an arbitrary, best-guess pedagogical decision on my part; it has nothing to do with the structure of knowledge.

PUTTING IT INTO PRACTICE: SOME HAZARDS

As I indicated at the beginning of this discussion, a developmental-interaction approach is uncommon in teacher education in spite of its broad-based theoretical justification. Why? Franklin and Biber (1977) have commented that

> the teacher carries a complex role in the implementation of this ideology. . . .
> The lack of standardization, like the requirements for awareness and respons-

ivity, makes the teacher's role challenging but often very difficult. Perhaps more than in other programs, successful realization of educational goals depends upon the teacher's ability to take genuine initiative in translating basic precepts into a productive learning environment. The unusually complex requirements of the teacher's role constitute a challenge to teacher education not readily met within the framework of most teacher education programs. (p. 24)

The challenge, in fact, comes in two parts: (a) to teacher educators' own awareness and responsivity to their students and their ability to take genuine initiative in designing and implementing learning experiences, and (b) to their readiness to trust their students' potential for becoming teachers who can take genuine initiative. As a colleague said to me, in defense of the prepared curriculum she was giving to students to use with children: "But what do you do about the mediocre teachers?" Assuming some teachers will be mediocre, she saw it as necessary to treat them as technicians and provide them with "teacher-proof" curricula. Some teacher educators who have great faith in children's potential for growth have given up on adults, who they feel have lost the unspoiled qualities of childhood. For my part, I believe strongly in self-fulfilling prophecies, and I find that if I trust my college students to be competent, they are more likely to behave competently and caringly than if I do not.

College teachers who choose to do so can become more aware and responsive, and they can learn to design active learning experiences. They may not, of course, get recognition from their colleagues for doing so (J. Jones, 1983); the model professor is an expert, reasonably entertaining lecturer who maintains a suitable distance from students. To trust learners is suspect, unless they are little children, and it was easier to trust little children as learners in the era in which preschool "didn't count." As the early years have been taken more seriously, "traditional" (developmental-interaction) preschools have been criticized as laissez-faire by the advocates of more "rational," often behaviorist models ("Let's shape these kids up—they don't have time to play" [Bereiter & Engelmann, 1966]).

Traditional preschool education derived from leisurely, detailed attention to what children are like. It doesn't hurry children; it respects their pace and recognizes the importance of redundancy in learning. So did Piaget—a most leisurely, detailed observer. However, in his name all sorts of hurry-them-up curricula have been devised (see Lavatelli, 1970; Weikart, Rogers, Adcock, & McClelland, 1971).[3] (Piaget himself, of course, referred to the concern for speeding up development as "the American question.") As Engelmann (1971)

---

[3] Constance Kamii, discussing this issue, states that she now regards her earlier efforts to improve children's performances on Piagetian tasks as a misapplication of Piaget's theory to education (Kamii & DeVries, 1977, p. 390).

makes clear, Piaget's primary interest was development, not instruction, and an authentic "Piagetian" curriculum might be expected to retain this emphasis (cf. Franklin & Biber, 1977, pp. 13–15; Kamii & DeVries, 1977, pp. 366–367). Likewise, in a developmental-interaction framework the most important teacher skill is observation: Wait, watch, pay attention—intervene when you are needed (Dewey, 1943/1902, 1963/1938). The college teaching equivalent of this style has been described earlier in this discussion.

Teacher education, unlike preschool education, does "count," or wants to, especially in universities where it is competing for academic status. We must be sure to pour in all that content so our students will know everything a teacher must know. But we can't do that except by teaching as if it all were social knowledge—words to be memorized; in hardly any program is enough time allowed to learn it all by doing. Perhaps, then, it won't all be learned before a teacher begins to teach. Accepting that fact seems to me to be the preferable alternative to pouring it in. Learning to teach is like the young child's learning—the slow, untidy attempt to gain understanding of all the parts and pieces of a whole new world. It can't be hurried, nor can it be detached from the person. I do care that teachers know, but I care much more about who they are (see Feeney, Christensen, & Moravcik, 1983). And I care that they have opportunities, as part of their professional learning, to get in touch with parts of their experience that may have been split off from their awareness and that may give them trouble later in their encounters with children and parents. Students will be unable to be good to children or to recognize their prejudices when they are on their own in the classroom if no one has been good to them (Hilliard, 1974). But it is hard, in an academic setting, to justify self-understanding as the primary content of teacher education, as Paul Goodman and others have proposed that it be (Dennison, 1969, p. 257).

It is also hard to risk, as college teachers, teaching who we are and not just what we know. But if we are asking students to be fully present in their learning, we are obligated to *be there* as persons in our teaching. This is risky. When we try new ways and they don't work, we are more vulnerable than if we had stuck properly to lecturing (J. Jones, 1983). The most effective way I have discovered for defusing my anxiety is to acknowledge it rationally: "You know, I thought that discussion would work, and it bombed. Has that ever happened to you? What do you do when your plans don't work? How could we make it better next time?" By doing this I am modeling for students, making it clear to them that teaching is a learning process and that learning isn't always full steam ahead; there's a lot of slippage. We can turn our failures into learning experiences if we can detach ourselves a bit from them and analyze what happened. If my students become teachers themselves, I think they will find this piece of information useful (E. Jones, 1981).

Effective socialization into a profession demands laboratory experience. I want students to get a first-hand sense of what it's like to be a teacher, and so I ask them to engage, in my classroom, in teacher-type behaviors: planning, giving information, responding to others, evaluating. Too often students are asked to engage only in student-type behaviors, which serve primarily to screen them for minimum academic competence, not for teaching potential (Katz, 1974).

TEACHING ALL OUR STUDENTS

In American society, as Green (1968) and Herndon (1971) have pointed out, we depend on the schools and colleges to sort out people for the economic system — to decide who will be winners and who will be losers. There are few other routes to success. This is why Illich (1971) has described the educational system as the 20th century replacement for the medieval church; it monopolizes access to social status.

The students know this; that's why they're in school. They don't expect college to be any more exciting than public school was. It's just something you have to do to get ahead in the world. If you want a particular career, like teaching, you have to go to college, even if that means you don't get to try teaching a real child for years. And besides, what else is there to do after high school? As Shor (1980) has noted, our system has a vested interest in keeping young adults out of the labor force as long as possible.

Many of the students in teacher education programs have experienced only indifferent success, or worse, in previous schooling. They are unlikely to have high opinions of themselves as learners. In addition, students who think they'd like to work with people are more likely to have intuitive and interpersonal competence than the logical/abstract competence that colleges value most highly.

Of course, teachers need theory, but working teachers build theory out of their experience; they don't just quote others' theory. They don't act as they do because Piaget said so; they do it because *they* say so — because they have observed and experienced and know that this is appropriate. (If they can also cite Piaget, they are in a stronger position to communicate with others and be confident in themselves.) Dugger (1983), teaching teacher aides,

> pointed out to them that each of them had a theory about children; the only difference was that they had never written theirs down and gotten famous. So [they] were going to learn about the famous theories written about in the book, and then each person could add to or change their theory as they observed children and saw how it checked out with the others. Or write theirs and become famous. (p. 53)

This approach does not, in my view, trivialize theory; it does demystify it, giving students an accurate view of its sources in experience. Like Dugger, I want the people whom I teach to gain more power over their lives. I want to subvert students who are accustomed to being mere game-players — to enable them to find out what they really want to do, develop the skills and discipline to do it, and discover learning as exciting and themselves as competent.

What students need to learn in school is that they *can* learn, that learning is exciting and that it's something you can do for yourself. Prospective teachers, more than anyone else, need to learn this. Rote learning is very poor preparation for teaching. Teachers need to have developed independence and reciprocity in both the intellectual and moral spheres. Independence means that you feel confident in asking your own questions and finding your own answers. Reciprocity means that you can listen to other people and have a well-developed capacity for putting yourself in their shoes. These essential qualities are developed through active learning, not through passive learning (E. Jones, 1978).

In Piaget's words (1973), the intellectual and moral spheres constitute an "indissoluble whole." He states that

> it is not possible to create independent personalities in the ethical area if the individual is also subjected to intellectual constraint to such an extent that he must restrict himself to learning by rote without discovering the truth for himself. If he is intellectually passive, he will not know how to be free ethically. Conversely, if his ethics consist exclusively in submission to adult authority, and if the only social exchanges that make up the life of the class are those that bind each student individually to a master holding all power, he will not know how to be intellectually active. (p. 107)

Only by giving students problems to solve — not facts to memorize — as starters for their thinking, will we get quality teaching in early childhood education. Only by trusting teachers to be effective problem solvers will we go beyond mediocrity in the classroom. Only as teachers and parents raise questions about the quality of children's lives will we accomplish necessary educational and social change.

This is not a scientific statement; it is a political one, an ideology. With Katz (1977), I recognize that I adopt a point of view in education not because I know it to be fact but because I believe it to be true on the basis of my own experience, feelings, and values. Teacher educators cannot be neutral. My point in this discussion is that we choose our theoretical positions in early childhood education, and, having done so, we have an obligation to make our teacher education consistent with them.

REFERENCES

Ackerman, J.M. (1972). *Operant conditioning techniques for the classroom.* Glenview, IL: Scott Foresman.

Bereiter, C., & Engelmann, S. (1966). *Teaching disadvantaged children in the preschool.* Englewood Cliffs, NJ: Prentice-Hall.

Beukema, S. (1978). Surviving in an open classroom: Fight, flight, or freeze? Unpublished master's thesis, Pacific Oaks College, Pasadena, CA. Abridged version in E. Jones (Ed.) (1983), *On the growing edge: Notes from college teachers making changes* (pp. 3-14). Pasadena, CA: Pacific Oaks College.

Dennison, G. (1969). *The lives of children.* New York: Vintage.

Dewey, J. (1943). *The child and the curriculum: The school and society.* Chicago: University of Chicago. (Original work published 1902)

Dewey, J. (1963). *Experience and education.* New York: Macmillan. (Original work published 1938)

Duckworth, E. (1972). The having of wonderful ideas. *Harvard Education Review, 42,* 217-231.

Dugger, J. (1983). The new kid on the block. In E. Jones (Ed.), *On the growing edge: Notes from college teachers making changes* (pp. 51-58). Pasadena, CA: Pacific Oaks College.

Engelmann, S. (1971). Does the Piagetian approach imply instruction? In D.R. Green, M. Ford, & G. Flamer (Eds.), *Measurement and Piaget* (pp. 118-126). New York: McGraw-Hill.

Finkel, D.L., & Monk, G.S. (1978). *Contexts for learning: A teacher's guide to the design of intellectual experience.* Olympia, WA: The Evergreen State College.

Feeney, S., Christensen, D., & Moravcik, E. (1983). *Who am I in the lives of children? Instructor's manual.* Columbus, OH: Merrill.

Franklin, M., & Biber, B. (1977). Psychological perspectives and early childhood education: Some relations between theory and practice. In L. Katz (Ed.), *Current topics in early childhood education* (Vol. 1, pp. 1-32). Norwood, NJ: Ablex. (ERIC Document Reproduction Service No. ED 092 242)

Furth, H. (1973). Piaget, IQ, and the nature-nurture controversy. *Human Development, 16,* 61-73.

Green, T.H. (1968). *Work, leisure, and the American schools.* New York: Random House.

Hanson, A. (1983). Beginning where they are . . . and then what? In E. Jones (Ed.), *On the growing edge: Notes from college teachers making changes* (pp. 59-62). Pasadena, CA: Pacific Oaks College.

Hawkins, D. (1970). Messing about in science. In *The ESS reader* (pp. 37-44). Newton, MA: Education Development Center.

Herndon, J. (1971). *How to survive in your native land.* New York: Simon and Schuster.

Hilliard, A. (1974). Moving from abstract to functional teacher education. In B. Spodek, *Teacher education* (pp. 7-23). Washington, DC: National Association for the Education of Young Children.

Hunt, J.M. (1971). *Intelligence and experience.* New York: Ronald.

Illich, I. (1971). *Deschooling society.* New York: Harper.

Jones, E. (1975). Providing college-level role models for the socialization of elementary-level open classroom teachers. *California Journal of Teacher Education, 2,* 33-52.

Jones, E. (1978). Teacher education: Entertainment or interaction? *Young Children, 33,* 15-23.

Jones, E. (1981). Open structures for adult learning: A theoretical base. *Educational Perspectives, 20,* 4-7.

Jones, E. (1983). On the use of behavioral objectives in open education. In E. Jones (Ed.), *On the growing edge: Notes from college teachers making changes.* Pasadena, CA: Pacific Oaks College.

Jones J. (1983). Back to the basics: The whole person. In E. Jones (Ed.), *On the growing edge: Notes from college teachers making changes* (pp. 93-99). Pasadena, CA: Pacific Oaks College.

Kamii, C., & Derman, L. (1971). The Engelmann approach to teaching logical thinking: Findings from the administration of some Piagetian tasks. In D.R. Green, M. Ford, & G. Flamer, *Measurement and Piaget* (pp. 127-147). New York: McGraw-Hill.

Kamii, C., & DeVries, R. (1977). Piaget for early education. In M.C. Day & R. Parker (Eds.), *The preschool in action* (pp. 365–420). Boston: Allyn & Bacon.

Katz, L. (1974). Issues and problems in teacher education. In B. Spodek (Ed.), *Teacher education* (pp. 55–56). Washington, DC: National Association for the Education of Young Children.

Katz, L. (1977). Early childhood programs and ideological disputes. In L. Katz, *Talks with teachers* (pp. 69–74). Washington, DC: National Association for the Education of Young Children.

Labinowicz, E. (1980). *The Piaget primer.* Menlo Park, CA: Addison-Wesley.

Lavatelli, C. (1970). *Teacher's guide to accompany early childhood curriculum: A Piaget program.* Boston: American Science and Engineering.

Maslow, A. (1962). *Toward a psychology of being.* New York: Van Nostrand Reinhold.

Meade, E.J. (1975). *On training teachers: Trust in the classroom.* New York: Ford Foundation.

Nuffield Mathematics Project. (1967). *I do, and I understand.* London: John Murray.

Piaget, J. (1973). *To understand is to invent.* New York: Grossman.

Pulaski, M. (1971). *Understanding Piaget.* New York: Harper and Row.

Rabiroff, B., & Prescott, E. (1978). The invisible child: Challenge to teacher attentiveness. In E. Jones (Ed.), *Joys and risks in teaching young children* (pp. 123–133). Pasadena, CA: Pacific Oaks College.

Renner, J.W., & Lawson, A.E. (1973). Promoting intellectual development through science teaching. *Physics Teacher, 11,* 273–276.

Rogers, C. (1951). *Client-centered therapy.* Boston: Houghton Mifflin.

Rogers, C. (1969). *Freedom to learn.* Columbus, OH: Merrill.

Schwebel, M. (1976). The role of experience in cognitive development. In M.K. Poulson, J.F. Magary, & G.I. Lubin (Eds.), *Piagetian theory and the helping professions* (pp. 1–18). Los Angeles: University of Southern California.

Shor, I. (1980). *Critical teaching and everyday life.* Boston: South End Press.

Skinner, B.F. (1971). *Beyond freedom and dignity.* New York: Knopf.

Soltis, J.F. (1973). The passion to teach. *Theory into Practice, 12,* 5–12.

Spodek, B. (1974). *Teacher education.* Washington, DC: National Association for the Education of Young Children.

Ward, E. (1974). The making of a teacher: Many disciplines. In B. Spodek (Ed.), *Teacher education* (pp. 45–54). Washington, DC: National Association for the Education of Young Children.

Wasserman, S. (1973). The open classroom in teacher education; or, Putting your money where your mouth is. *Childhood Education, 49,* 295–301.

Weikart, D., Rogers, L., Adcock, C., & McClelland, D. (1971). *The cognitively oriented curriculum: A framework for preschool teachers.* Urbana, IL: University of Illinois.

White, R. (1959). Motivation reconsidered: The concept of competence. *Psychological Review, 66,* 297–333.

6

Trends in Early Childhood Education in The United Kingdom

Sheila M. Shinman

Brunel University
Uxbridge, Middlesex, England

INTRODUCTION

The purpose of this discussion is to provide an overview of major developments in preschool education in the United Kingdom from 1973 to 1983. Research emphasis will be on later studies, since ongoing work of the early 1970s has been comprehensively reviewed elsewhere (Tizard, 1975).

Interests have changed considerably over this period. The preoccupation with issues of compensatory education, with class-based studies of cognitive and linguistic programs, and with topics encouraged by anticipated expansion of preschooling gave way in the mid-1970s to a concern about the overall structure and efficacy of preschool policy and practice. Questions that latterly occupy the minds of researchers and practitioners include the following: What constitutes quality in the various preschool contexts? What is meant by parental involvement, and how can it be fostered? How can disadvantaged parents who do not come forward to use services be reached? and, How can parents be supported in bringing up their children? It is clear from these questions that the extension of interest from child and school to include parents and home, which is characteristic of the 1970s, also dictates that "preschool education" be interpreted here in its broadest sense and not be confined to formal preschool settings.

GENERAL OBSERVATIONS AND MAJOR TRENDS

Rapid Social Change

Heightened tension has been a feature of the 1970s and early 1980s. Ironically, improved living conditions—new towns, tower blocks, estates on city outskirts—have resulted in unforeseen problems, notably increased isolation, especially for mothers with young children (Brown & Harris, 1978; Gittis, 1976).

Emotional strain clearly underlies figures that show a dramatic increase in the dissolution of marriages (one in three currently end in divorce). One in eight families is likely to be headed by a single parent. Because many divorced parents remarry, an increasing number of children will be brought up by a stepfather or stepmother (Wicks & Rimmer, 1980). All this is not to say that happy adjustments cannot be made, but rather to suggest that the process leading to adjustment and the business of coping alone carry additional pressures and strains (Ferri, 1976; Ferri & Robinson, 1976).

Added to these changes in family structure are the contrast in conditions and values between urban and rural families (Centre for the Study of Rural Society, 1978); the changing patterns of women's employment; the economic and psychological pressures of high unemployment; the impact of technological change; and, over it all, the malaise of living in a nuclear age. Clearly, we have a rapidly changing environment conducive to tension, self-questioning, and political and family debate.

Low Priority Accorded to Preschooling

The 1970s began with high expectations. The Conservative government of the United Kingdom affirmed the importance of the family and its intention of making preschooling available for all children aged 3 and 4 whose parents wanted it. Provision was to be mainly in the form of part-time places in nursery classes. According to the Conservative administration, particular attention would be paid to disadvantaged families (Department of Education and Science, 1972).

However, doubts concerning formal education as a medium of social change, together with economic uncertainty and recent recession, have resulted in substantial cutbacks in government support for education and social services. A falling birthrate initially cushioned children under 5 from these effects, but since the upward turn in the birthrate in 1978, drastic and uneven pruning of much state provision has become increasingly evident.

Diversity: A Key Feature of Early Childhood Education

Preschooling is not compulsory in the United Kingdom. In theory, children under 5 (that is, those of preschool age) may stay at home or attend some form of external provision. *Nursery schools* are provided free by Local Education Authorities or offered on a fee-paying basis by private enterprise to meet the educational and other needs of children between 3 (sometimes 2) and 5 years of age.[1] There are normally two sessions each day, from 9:30 a.m. to 12 noon and/or from 1:00 p.m. to 3:30 p.m. Schools are open during term time only—about 40 weeks of the year. Attendance may be full or part-time. *Nursery classes* are similar to state-run nursery schools, but they are attached to a primary school. The majority of preschool places made available in the post-1972 period of expansion were in the first classes in *infant schools*—that is, in reception classes. Age of entry varies between 4 and 5½ years. All these types of provision generally conform to high standards. They are staffed by qualified teachers and by assistants who are nursery nurses. Increasingly, parents are made welcome.

Playgroups are another care alternative. They are usually set up outside the statutory provision by parents, by private enterprise, or by voluntary organizations to give 3- and 4-year-olds the opportunity to mix with others and to provide them with safe and satisfying play. While a small proportion of playgroups have extended hours to meet the needs of working mothers, the great majority offer only part-time facilities.

The main sources of income for most playgroups are still the charge they make to parents and fund raising. Fees vary considerably. About one-third of such groups receive minimal grant aid, mainly from the county or district council, which is also responsible for social services in the area—that is, the local authority (Pre-School Playgroups Association National Training Committee, 1982). Some groups have trained supervisors, and all playgroups are registered with a local authority social services department. Many playgroups are characterized by the extent to which they involve and support parents.

Children of working mothers may, if they or their parents fulfill certain criteria of need, attend *state-run day nurseries*. Parents are tested for means of support and are often referred by welfare services. Premises are open year-round from about 8:00 a.m. to 6:00 p.m. Most children attend full-time and are often cared for in family groups. Most staff are qualified nursery nurses, with some assistants without specific qualifications. Some *day nurseries* or *creches* are provided by private or voluntary organizations, as well as by employers. Such nurseries may be free or heavily subsidized, but all must register with the local authority social services department.

---

[1] A Local Education Authority (LEA) is part of the elected local authority—for example, a County or District Council. An LEA is responsible for the provision of education (in schools, colleges, and polytechnics, but not universities) in a given geographical area of the United Kingdom. The LEAs operate with considerable autonomy (through their education committee, education officers, advisers, etc.) but are always open to pressure from central government. The nearest equivalent in the United States would be a local school board or board of education (Rowntree, 1981). Responsibility for preschool services other than nursery schools and classes rests with the social services department of each local authority.

Otherwise, children of working mothers are cared for by relatives or by *childminders*. A childminder is defined, under the 1968 Health and Public Service Act, as any one who "for reward takes any child to whom they are not related into their homes and cares for him for two hours or more during the day" (Law Reports Statutes, Pt. 1, 1968, p. 1183). Childminders are normally, though not necessarily, women. They are required to register with the social services department of the local authority; it is the responsibility of the local authority to inspect homes and to ensure that they meet statutory health and safety regulations.

In general, the standard of staffing and equipment in state-run provision is high, but elsewhere a wide range of precept and practice is found. Proportions of children attending different forms of provision also vary greatly. Overall, approximately 30% of children receive no formal preschooling (Bone, 1977). The chart provided, representing day care for children under 5, shows that in national terms, childminders provide the majority of day care places. However, even more children are cared for by relatives (Central Statistical Office, 1983). Playgroups account for most part-time places.

The statistics shown in this chart fail to convey the considerable differences that exist in the availability of provision. For example, more than half

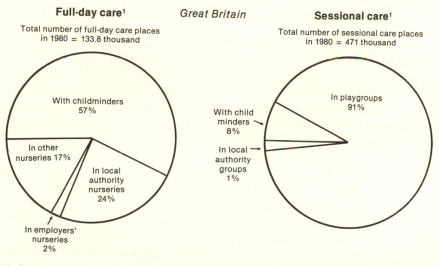

Full-day care[1]   *Great Britain*   **Sessional care[1]**

Total number of full-day care places in 1980 = 133.8 thousand

With childminders 57%

In other nurseries 17%

In local authority nurseries 24%

In employers' nurseries 2%

Total number of sessional care places in 1980 = 471 thousand

In playgroups 91%

With childminders 8%

In local authority groups 1%

[1]In Scotland all children cared for by childminders are counted as full-day care.

Source: Department of Health and Social Security: Social Work Services Group, Scottish Office; Welsh Office

Note. From *Social Trends, 12* (p. 229) by Central Statistical Office, 1982, London: Her Majesty's Stationery Office. Copyright 1982 by HMSO. Reprinted by permission.

Figure 1. Day Care for Children under 5: Places Available, 1980

the children living in rural areas attend no form of registered provision, as compared with 18% in the inner cities (Department of Education and Science, 1975). Similar wide regional variations are found within and among local authorities (Haystead, Howarth, & Strachan, 1980).

Further inconsistency stems from the division of responsibility for services between the Department of Education and Science, and the Department of Health and Social Security. Nursery schools and nursery classes are the responsibility of the former, while all other forms of provision fall under the aegis of the latter. Consequently, part-time and full-time provision are usually separate, both physically and administratively; there is a clear distinction between "education" and "care." Day nurseries, for example, are staffed by nursery nurses and not by qualified teachers. As a result, there is concern over a possible lack of educational input in that form of provision. Thus, even though it is widely held that there is very little difference among types of provision with respect to the way children spend their time (Tizard, 1975), children under 5 in the United Kingdom nevertheless may have widely different preschool experiences. The problem is compounded in inner-city areas characterized by cultural diversity. There the gap between home and school experience may be even more considerable (van der Eyken, Michell, & Grubb, 1979).

Children with Special Needs

The last decade has seen considerable progress in ensuring coherent and comprehensive provision for handicapped children and their families. Higher financial benefits have gone some way in alleviating everyday problems. Professionals have manifested greater awareness of the difficulties facing many such families and, more important, of the role parents can play in helping their children. The Court Report on Child Health Services (Committee on Child Health Services, 1976) underlined the support that professionals should give *all* parents: "We have found no better way to raise a child than to re-inforce the abilities of his parents to do so" (p. 2). The report of the Warnock Committee (Department of Education and Science, 1978) on the education of handicapped children (estimated nationally at 20% of pupils) spelled out the following message: "Unless parents are seen as equal partners in the educational process, the purpose of our report will be frustrated" (p. 150). In the light of the report, the Education Act of 1981 established a new framework requiring special educational provision for children whether in special or ordinary schools. Archaic terms like "educationally subnormal" have been replaced by the concept of special educational needs; this new concept embraces not only physical and mental disabilities but any kind of learning difficulty experienced by a child, providing it is significantly greater than that experienced by the majority of children the same age. This concept excludes difficulties that arise solely because the language of instruction is different from the language of the child's home. Parents have also been accorded new rights: for example, to information and consultation, to make their views known during formal assessment, and to a copy of all the evidence on which a decision has been made regarding a child's needs.

Significantly, the Act gives legislative backing to the principle of integration, whereby authorities have duties to provide for children with special educational needs in ordinary schools (Department of Education and Science, 1981a). While the 1981 Act does not go as far as legislation already in force in other countries (for example, the Education for All Handicapped Children Act in the United States), it nevertheless marks an important step toward a genuinely multidisciplinary and flexible approach, in which "shared care" is the keynote.

Day Care

Growing demand. As the 1970s progressed, it became clear that provision of part-time and nursery places as envisaged in the Education White Paper (Department of Education and Science, 1972) was inappropriate for a substantial proportion of children under 5 (Bone, 1977; Tizard, Moss, & Perry, 1976). This fact is hardly surprising given the dramatic changes in attitudes and lifestyles that gathered impetus in the 1970s. The postwar trend toward smaller families, of one or two children, has meant women spend less of their lives bearing and rearing children and feel more able to work outside the home (Wicks & Rimmer, 1980). Recession has forced many women into the labor market to supply or to supplement the family income. Many others are determined both to follow a career and to have a family. While data for 1978–80 suggest that the trend for married women ages 16 to 59 with dependent children to seek paid employment has leveled off at 54%, a substantial proportion (46%) remain at home (Office of Population Censuses and Surveys, 1982). The explanation for this situation may lie in an increase in the general fertility rate and in the effect of the recession on availability of jobs and day care rather than in any significant decrease in the numbers of mothers wishing to work outside the home.

Thus the persistent and ongoing lobby for more day care gained substantial ground during this period (Equal Opportunities Commission, 1978; Hughes, Mayall, Petrie, Moss, & Pinkerton, 1980). This lobby is identified largely with the view that the state should take increased responsibility for children, for they represent a major investment in the country's future. Day care in the form of day nurseries is perceived as being just one pressing aspect of adequate health, education, and social services. Others, however, have argued against any form of group day care for children under 5 (Leach, 1979), expressing the view that adequate benefits should be available for mothers who wish to stay at home with their young children (Pringle, 1979) and that no one should bring a child into the world without being prepared to devote 3 years to that child (Pringle, 1980).

Improved status of childminding. Also during this period, attitudes toward childminding changed. Childminders offer the nearest alternative to a child's own home, and there has been growing recognition on the part of central and local government that good childminders have a significant part to play in the total day care provision for children under 5. This trend is indicated by the appointment of specialist childminding support workers by local authority social services departments, a procedure that has become commonplace since the mid-1970s. It is notable too that the National Child-minding Association has received a large proportion of government funding for "new initiatives" by voluntary organizations in the preschool field.

Family centers. Emphasis has also shifted away from simple care provision for children of working mothers to the need to educate and support mothers deemed inadequate. Community-based projects called *family centers* have mushroomed. They range from quite large centers, which have day care as their core activity, to small neighborhood projects. Such schemes vary widely, but they are normally part of preventive social work and are generally committed to merging the lessons of community work with social work so that neighborhood becomes important and organizing groups becomes a regular activity (Birchall, 1982a; Warren & Adamson, 1982).

Combined nursery centers and children's centers. Attempts to combine day care and education in *nursery centers*, which offer a choice for mothers and a comprehensive form of provision, were initially disappointing. In spite of greater educational emphasis for children in day care, the distinction between care and education lingered in staff attitudes toward parents and children (Ferri, Birchall, Gingell, & Gipps, 1981). Nevertheless, ideas pursued in some pioneer *children's centers* — providing open access to all parents in a defined catchment area and encouraging parental involvement in management as well as in everyday activities — have made a considerable positive impact on practitioners and policy makers (Moss, Bax, & Plewis, 1979). Overall, findings have drawn attention to the need to reconsider the training and preparation of all who work with young children and their families.

Part-time Provision

Continuing demand. A comprehensive survey (Bone, 1977) supported by General Household Survey figures for 1982 suggested not so much an overwhelming demand for full-time work by women with children under 5 as their desire for progressively more part-time preschool provision as their children grow older (see Bone, 1977, p. 15, Table 3, 6). Indeed, between 1971 and 1981, the percentage of 3- and 4-year-olds attending nursery schools and classes (i.e., part-time provision) increased from 19 to 40% (Central Statistical Office, 1981), a reflection of demand as well as increased provision. The growth of the playgroup movement over the past two decades also testifies to demand for part-time provision. By 1982, there were 12,000 member playgroups belonging to the National Pre-School Playgroups Association and catering to 555,000 children (Pre-School Playgroups Association Research and Information Committee, 1983).

Consolidation and extension of the playgroup movement. It is a striking fact that playgroups have achieved such remarkable status and credibility. The Pre-School Playgroups Association is a mere 21 years old, with its roots in the determination of a few mothers to set up what was initially seen as stopgap provision against government inaction over nursery schooling. Yet the needs of the embryo association as defined in the 1974 address by the organization's president (Plowden, 1974) — for recognition by all local authorities as a valued service, for support by social services for volunteers and area organizers, for extension of courses, for research and documentation, and for funding for individual playgroups, especially in disadvantaged areas — have, to a marked degree, come about. It appears that a solid core of women are prepared to take considerable responsibility for their children's preschooling and show a high level of satisfaction both on their own behalf and on the behalf of their children (Gray & McMahon, 1982).

Activities among member groups have diversified over the past 10 years. In spite of doubts expressed about the ability of playgroups to meet the needs of some disadvantaged children and families (Ferri & Niblett, 1977), there has been an expansion of work in this field (Overton, 1981; Scottish Pre-School Playgroups Association Playgroups in Areas of Need Sub-Committee, 1977). This includes pioneer projects aimed at breaking down the isolation of childminders and the children in their care by setting up informal groups and courses along playgroup lines (Shinman, 1979). Increased work among ethnic minorities and involvement with families and children with special needs also followed the Warnock Report (Department of Education and Science, 1978) and the Education Act of 1981 (Ferri, 1982; Pre-School Playgroups Association Research and Information Committee, 1983).

Cooperation between secondary schools and playgroups followed the rise in the school-leaving age from 15 to 16 in 1972–73. Many schools were anxious to give pupils in child development courses practical experience and, with the dearth of state preschools, sought placement for them in playgroups. At this time, youngsters are also being placed in playgroups from a wide range of Further Education College courses and from government-funded projects designed to help unemployed school-leavers (Scottish Pre-School Playgroups Association Working Party, 1978). Overall, 54% of playgroups are involved in this work (Pre-School Playgroups Association Research and Information Committee, 1983). In consequence, playgroups now figure in the school-based examination Certificate of Secondary Education (CSE), taken by pupils around the age of 15 or 16 years and aimed at students of middle ability. Increasingly, a significant part of the Pre-School Playgroup Association's work has been provision of opportunities for adults wishing to learn more about preschool children. Comparison of figures for the years 1979–80 and 1980–81 shows dramatic growth. In 1 year, courses that aim to enhance parents' confidence in their ability to meet their children's needs increased from 1,700 to 2,300, and the number of students increased from 27,000 to 38,400 (Pre-School Playgroups Association National Training Committee, 1982).

Distance learning. The Open University was established at Milton Keynes in 1969 by royal charter. Its first aim was to provide university education for adults in their own homes through correspondence texts, radio, television, and a network of contacts and local tutors. During the latter part of the 1970s, however, it began to work in close collaboration with outside agencies, notably the Pre-School Playgroups Association and the Health Education Council, in an attempt to meet the needs of people who might be deterred by a conventional academic approach. Thus, Open University community education courses tend to be short, easily assimilated, and of practical relevance to people at all stages of life, including parents expecting their first baby or those bringing up a toddler or preschool-age child (Wolfson, 1982).

Rapid growth of mother and toddler clubs. During the 1970s, clubs for mothers with very young children at home also became widely recognized as a vital link in the network of family support, filling the gap between postnatal care and the child's introduction to nursery school or playgroup. Such clubs are started and supported by mothers themselves, by community workers, health visitors, or vicars, as well as by playgroup leaders (Hanton, 1977). Each club is independent and is not obliged to register with the local authority social services department. Consequently, there are no official figures to indicate the extent of growth. Nevertheless, in a survey of over 1,000 clubs carried out in 1977, 56% had been started since January of 1975 (Pre-School Playgroups Association Working Party, 1978), and growth appears to continue unabated (Pre-School Playgroups Association Research and Information Committee, 1983):

The "typical" club meets in a community or church hall for up to two hours one afternoon a week, except school holidays. Mothers sit and chat in the same room as the children and play with the children at activities which probably include some kind of "messy" play. There is probably no regular playleader, tho' there is an organizer who may include this among her roles. Fees are supplemented by fund-raising. Some, if not all, the mothers take some share in organizing the group and running the session. (Pre-School Playgroups Association Working Party, 1978, p. 1)

Summary

The foregoing discussion indicates the broad developments of early childhood education in the United Kingdom. Overall, emphasis lies in flexibility of approach and preference for local solutions to local needs rather than in the imposition of a national blueprint.

RESEARCH AND DEVELOPMENT

It is diversity of experience and our lack of knowledge about how to promote competence and skills in *all* preschool children that have formed the baseline for recent research and development. Following the 1972 Education White Paper, when major expansion in preschool care was anticipated, much research was commissioned by the Department of Education and Science, the Scottish Education Department, the Department of Health and Social Security, the Social Science Research Council, and the Schools Council (Department of Education and Science, 1981b). Research into the processes of early childhood education has been pursued in both institutional and home-based settings. Observational techniques were frequently employed, for the 1970s witnessed a turning away from experimental design.

The Institutional Setting

Play in nursery school, playgroup, and day nursery.   One common aim of all preschooling is to provide an environment that will stimulate and satisfy the child's developing needs. Yet doubts have been voiced as to how far all children in the preschool play to their best advantage (Bruner, 1980), given that there is little difference among types of provision in the way children spend their time (Cleave, Jowett, & Bate, 1982; Ferri et al., 1981; Hutt, 1979). Advocates of the traditional philosophy of nursery schools maintain that free play in a planned, prepared, and organized setting is all that is required. Ideally, the teacher will be aware of the child's activities and will respond in such a way as to encourage neglected occupations, prolong concentration, and foster language skill (Parry & Archer, 1975; Webb, 1975).

Even though belief has waned that highly structured compensatory programs can be successfully integrated into the English nursery school curriculum (see literature reviewed by Woodhead, 1976) several recent studies have noted that children too often seem to pass the time in occupations that do not demand imaginative or complex play (Tizard, Philips, & Plewis, 1975). About 10% of 3- and 4-year-olds spend their time "cruising" and drifting about aimlessly (Cleave et al., 1982; Ferri et al., 1981). One inference is that, when fostering skills involving thought rather than feeling or movement, a more structured approach is needed. The basis for this argument is that children benefit intellectually from activities when they choose their own goals; they know how far their efforts are successful because there is feedback and a consequent sense of achievement. In comparison, pretend games (such as play with dolls and cars) entail no commitment to a goal; these games are even used for "cover or just plain rest" (Sylva, Roy, & Painter, 1980, p. 64). Yet children undoubtedly benefit in other ways from relaxing activities that encourage talk among themselves or from physical exertion indulged in for the sheer pleasure of it. Indeed, it has been suggested that a sense of relaxation and ease is the necessary precondition for fantasy play (Hutt, 1979). But such occupations do not, it is argued, involve goals or planning – or consequently complex, elaborated play (Sylva et al., 1980).

In the study conducted by Sylva et al. (1980), observations of 120 children for a total of 4,800 minutes were carried out, focusing on the extent to which a child is enabled to concentrate and to elaborate play. A painstaking method of observing and recording the activities and language of one child (the "Target Child"), developed by Holmes and McMahon (1977), was used. Attention was divided between boys and girls ages 3½ to 4½ and 4½ to 5½ enrolled in three kinds of part-time preschool: nursery school, nursery class, and playgroup.

Activities were then examined to decide how "challenging" they were and how far they were likely to "stretch" a child. In rank order, high-yield activities included music (when not led by an adult), small-scale construction, art (where the child chose the medium), large-scale construction, and activity with structured materials. Moderate-yield activities were pretend play and manipulative play with all toys, while low-yield occupations were defined as nonplayful interaction, informal games, rule-bound games, and gross motor play. Least challenging of all were social play, "horsing around," and giggling. Two other indications of richness in play identified by the investigators were longer spans of concentration and the degree of absorption. These were manifest primarily in play with structured materials, pretend, small-scale construction and art, and adult-led groups such as singing or storytelling. Least absorbing activities were informal games and adult-directed art.

When a distinction was drawn between centers that required children to take part in at least two compulsory educational activities each session and those with no such patterning, it transpired that children in the structured programs had three times as much play with structured materials as those in entirely unstructured environments. An important finding was that much of this was in free play sessions, a situation indicating that children chose to persist with such activities.

An ecological perspective.   Another focus of research interest has been the effect of environmental factors on children's play and behavior. Such factors include, for example, group size, noise levels, playroom design, and the way the staff use resources.

In the study just described (Sylva et al., 1980), the advantage lay with small groups (most usually playgroups), which manifested greater contact between children and adults, a higher level of intellectual play, and more pretend play. More physical play was characteristic of larger centers, while small, secluded areas like the "home corner" encouraged rich dialogue.[2] Further evidence that smaller areas are associated with more educationally valuable activities accrue from a correlational study of staff and children in three types of preschool building: conversions of old buildings with fairly small rooms; open, airy buildings with high ceilings and rectangular playrooms; and open-plan designs with low ceilings and an irregularly shaped room. Findings suggest that more open settings are associated with higher noise levels, which interfere with activities of potentially high educational yield (like staff-child dialogue). In addition, those children who tend to wander aimlessly about are also those least likely to attract staff attention in open-plan units, while new children spend more time alone during the settling-in period (Neill, 1982).

Experimentally based studies largely support this "small is beautiful" thesis. For example, Smith and Connolly (1980) set up a playgroup in a church hall in a north country industrial city and employed three experienced staff members to run it. Two independent groups of socioeconomically mixed children attended two mornings a week. The environment was then manipulated by varying each of the available resources for up to 60 sessions and observing and recording individual children's behavior. Classes of 10, 20, and 30 children were varied in such a way that the same children could be compared in a large or small class. On balance, here too the advantage lay with smaller classes, through for reasons different from those in the previous

---

[2] The "home corner" is part of most preschool settings in the United Kingdom and provides an opportunity for rich and varied play. One section is arranged as a "living room" and "kitchen"; it may be divided from the "bedroom" by a curtain or screen.

studies cited. Specifically, in small groups children were more likely to make friends and to become involved in sociodramatic play. Shy, withdrawn children were found to be particularly vulnerable in large groups.

As the ratio of staff to children was increased from 1:4 to 1:14, so talk between children increased and that between adults and children became more prohibitive and one-sided in character. Further, the more outgoing, competent children tended to monopolize conversation with staff to the detriment of those who were shyer and more withdrawn (Smith & Connolly, 1980). Similarly, children with special needs placed in ordinary schools, as recommended by the Warnock Report, also tend to be those who stand ignored on the sidelines (Chazan, Laing, Shackleton-Bailey, & Jones, 1980; Clark, Robinson, & Browning, 1984).

The adult role in language development. Many studies (notably Tizard, 1979) have reported disappointingly low levels of conversation between adults and children in the prechool setting. Evidence from tapescripts of adult-child interaction take us a stage further. In their own classrooms or playgroups, a total of 24 nursery teachers and playgroup leaders each made ½-hour recordings designed to catch typical but varied segments of the day. Analysis of approximately 1,500 minutes of talk aimed to discover the effects of different "teaching styles" (Wood, McMahon, & Cranstoun, 1980).

In general, styles that involved shared experience and play with children — activities that in more structured programs encouraged elaborated play — were those least in evidence. Yet it was the adult who, to a great extent, had control over the ease and fluency of children's conversation. Two characteristics of children's talk with adults emerged as major obstacles in the development of sustained conversation: Children were inclined to jump into a conversation without preamble, and they tended to pick up a word from an ongoing conversation and go off at a tangent.

Adults tended to react in one of three ways. Some acknowledged and responded to every opening gambit or interjection (a style that manifestly did not prolong conversation). Others used a strategy that ignored the child and persisted with their own line of questioning. To the surprise of teachers participating in the study, this latter style of conversation was their most frequent type of response. A third type of response was also noted: Teachers asked a question aimed at stimulating the child to reply, then showed interest in a nondirective, relaxed way so as to leave room for the child to elaborate along lines of his or her own choosing. Tapescript evidence suggested that for the adult to then respond with another question was often to constrain the flow of conversation. A more constructive strategy was to recast what the child had been saying or make a noncommittal response. In probing further the question of control of conversation, analysis suggested that those children talking with adults with the least "controlling" style asked more questions, contributed more often, and went on to elaborate the subject. In contrast, adults who exerted most control appeared to inhibit prolonged and complex conversations.

Such conclusions have much in common with studies that emphasize the potential of adult-child dialogue in fostering language development (Clark et al., 1984; Donaldson, 1978; Tough, 1977; Turner, 1977). Sensitivity in the adult is crucial. Tough (1977) argues the need for the teacher to work in an informal situation, building on the individual child's innate curiosity and assuming that, if the child is helped to use language with meaning, he or she will progress naturally from the simple to the complex. Tough's pioneering studies focused on disadvantaged children, however, and were recorded under quasi-experimental conditions; she assumed that differences among children in the ways they used language were a reflection of differing kinds of talk they experienced with their parents.

Other challenging evidence has shown that even disadvantaged children have rich conversations with their mothers at home (Tizard, 1979). Few language differences were found to emerge between middle- and working-class children in a direct observational study of 165 children at home (Davie, Hutt, Vincent, & Mason, 1984). Further, Wells (1981) examined talk in the context of school and home in a broad-based and carefully controlled two-stage study of 129 children assessed between 15 and 42 months and again between 39 and 66 months. Each child was observed 10 times at 3-month intervals. In the home, this was achieved by a radio microphone on a lightweight harness under the child's top garment; the microphone transmitted continuously and did not hinder the child's movement. This "fly on the wall" technique revealed scant evidence of mismatch between home and school in the patterns of asking and answering questions. What differences there were concerned grammatical structures and speaking rights that, Wells argues, stem from different social relationships and different ratios of adults to children. Here again, it was suggested that it is the strategies that adults use to develop and extend children's language that count.

Impact of organization and structure on the quality of care. Several studies have shown that, in actuality, the amount of adult-child contact is disappointingly low in most care settings (Cleave et al., 1982; Ferri et al., 1981). In particular, staff in day nurseries tend to be less involved in children's activities than those in nursery schools and playgroups. Yet contact with adults (even as passive presences) has been associated with children's spending longer periods in concentrated play (Garland & White, 1980; Sylva et al., 1980; Tyler, Foy, & Hutt, 1979).

One question raised by this observation is how far organization and structure of the preschool affect the style of adult-child interaction and hence the quality of care (Bruner, 1980). These twin aspects — care provided for children and organizational patterns — were the focus of a study of nine day nurseries in London, three of which were recommended for good practice by local authority social services departments (Garland & White, 1980). Each day nursery was distinctive in its organization and ethos. Programs ranged from a specialist nursery staffed by trained teachers, who lay particular stress on language training for ethnic minority children, to an all-day playgroup in unprepossessing premises but with a friendly relaxing atmosphere; from a state day nursery designed and built for that purpose, which encouraged and achieved a high degree of parent participation, to a nursery based in a suburban hospital specifically for the children of nurses who worked there. The researchers were hoping to determine aspects of organization or structure that would promote a secure environment. They took emotional security to be paramount and a necessary basis on which cognitive skills could develop.

The range of care and organization observed was wide, yet certain related patterns were discernible. These patterns owed much to the objectives of the organization and to the philosophy of the person or group (both internal and external to the institution) responsible for policy and day-to-day decisions. Clearly, nurseries with roots embedded in child-centered progressive education will differ fundamentally from those in the "caregiving" tradition, which historically tends toward condescending and authoritarian attitudes. The existence of such differences underlines the importance of an explicit contract between staff and parents to make clear what both have in mind. The study further suggests that a collaborative relationship among staff members within the unit and among adults and children enhances the quality of children's play and conversational exchanges (Garland & White, 1980).

Transition and continuity in early childhood education. A somewhat different orientation to quality of care and to the effect of different styles of control and deployment of resources concerns transition from one type of setting to another. Starting school or moving from one setting to another is an important event in the child's life. It can be a traumatic experience for parents and children as they adjust to the emotional, social, and intellectual demands of a strange environment.

Two recent studies pinpoint problems of transition from home to preschool (Blatchford, Battle, & Mays, 1982) and from preschool to primary school (Cleave et al., 1982). The first focused on one geographical area and involved interviews with parents and with staff in nursery schools and playgroups, with the addition of an intensive study of a small sample of children from a few months before they started school until about 1 year into the nursery. Major sources of discontinuity were found by Blatchford et al. (1982) to be the wide range of settings, different ages of entry, and different levels of curriculum planning, together with parents' lack of knowledge regarding available services. A gentle, staggered introduction into preschool, with mothers present, eased the child's adjustment to the new environment and encouraged parents' later involvement.

Mothers experienced greater stress when their chilldren started school than had been anticipated, but they adapted over a period of about 10 weeks. Most children, however, did not show signs of stress and settled in within 3 weeks. Much of the first 4 weeks was spent in solitary play; from the third to ninth week, preschoolers engaged in contacting other children. There was relatively infrequent contact between adults and children. Popular activities included outside play with sand and water, play with constructional toys, and dramatic play, although, in terms of time spent, "just waiting and watching" predominated.

The second study (Cleave et al., 1982) followed the progress of 36 children in five different Local Education Authority areas through the transition period from preschool to primary school by means of direct observation and face-to-face interviews with parents and teachers. The study was both longitudinal (where children were concerned) and cross-sectional (across six types of provision).

Discontinuities were most marked for children coming to the infant school straight from home or from a childminder or small group. Such children had to adjust to a longer day, to larger numbers of adults and children, and to a very different curriculum with unfamiliar activities in a school setting that could be confusing in both design and layout. Physical education was identified as a particular source of anxiety; this activity called for very sensitive handling. As Ferri et al. (1981) reported in relation to experimental centers that combined nursery education and day care, large numbers of staff and children and many comings and goings tended to inhibit the development of confidence, independence, and sociability in new entrants.

Practical recommendations made by Cleave et al. (1982) to ease such problems include a very gradual introduction to the new setting and experiences (for example, postponement of school dinners for a week or two) and imaginative preparation for introductory visits to the infant school, in which familiar playthings like sand and water are made available. Finally, the importance of encouraging parental support is given particular prominence.

Parental involvement.   The influence parents can have in the achievement of their children is well documented (see reviews in Smith, 1980; Tizard, Mortimor, & Burchall, 1981), and exhortations to foster "parental involvement" to this end are commonplace. The value of such involvement to parents as opposed to children is less widely acknowledged. Despite all that has been written, considerable confusion and lack of consensus persist. A major task for research has been that of clarifying the issues and teasing out ideas underlying use of the term (Ferri & Niblett, 1977; Smith, 1980; van der Eyken, 1979).

The development of community nurseries in the 1970s illustrates one interpretation in which parental control is the crucial variable. These nurseries (of which there are now about 20, mainly in the London area) are set up by groups of parents or local people to serve the needs of their neighborhood. They aim to provide flexible, integrated services whereby parents assert their right to have a say in their children's education (Hughes et al., 1980; van der Eyken, 1979).

Another viewpoint commonly held in playgroups emphasizes shared responsibility. Playgroup philosophy holds that the "deepest involvement and shared responsibility often occur when all parents want to be involved in the decision-making process" (Pre-School Playgroups Association Working Party, 1980, p. 41). Most recent evidence suggests, however, that it is in parent-run playgroups where mothers help and are welcome at playgroup sessions, as compared with those where participation is solely at the management level, that mothers who worry about how they are bringing up their children appear to gain confidence in themselves (Gray & McMahon, 1982).

A further aspect of experiential thinking within the playgroup movement is the belief that involvement is essentially a learning process for parents and carries with it a core element of active responsibility at every stage (Pre-School Playgroups Association Working Party, 1980). Indeed, parents may derive benefit from involvement, gaining in confidence and self-esteem as parents (Smith, 1980), as well as developing skills in dealing with adults (Henderson, 1978). In contrast, the rationale for parental participation in the nursery school is based on benefits derived by the child. This approach tends to be child-centered and to expect a more passive role from the parents (Hughes et al., 1980).

This distinction between parent-centered and child-centered settings emerged clearly in an observational study concerned with the process of involvement in 15 Oxfordshire groups. Three nursery schools, four nursery classes, and eight playgroups were selected to provide a mix of rural and city-based provision, in which it was known that two-thirds had parents helping (Smith, 1980).

Five categories of parent participation were identified: (1) working with children on educational activities, with little apparent difference in the role between the professional teacher and the parent as a teacher; (2) working with groups but doing chores; (3) servicing a group, but not always working alongside children (e.g., fund raisng); (4) performing miscellaneous functions having to do with the openness and "welcomingness" of the group and shared experience (e.g., visiting before a child starts school, staying to settle the child in, dropping in casually); and (5) involvement in management. In the groups studied, participation in nursery schools was more likely to fall into categories 2, 3, or 4, whereas involvement in playgroups included categories 1 and 5. There was, of course, some overlap.

Two main patterns of parental involvement emerge from Smith's (1980) group-oriented analysis: an open/professional model and an open/partnership model. In both cases, the atmosphere is open, welcoming, and warm, but in the first instance professionals involve parents simply to provide continuity and information about home background, remaining somewhat directive and aloof themselves. By contrast, the second pattern is based on shared experiences and a partnership between parents and professionals involved in a collaborative process of educating children.

We do not yet know which model is more effective (Smith, 1980). But even where, in principle, there is acceptance and exploration of the partnership model, difficulties abound. Not all parents use pre-schooling, even when it is available for their children. Some parents are happy and confident in keeping their children at home (Shinman, 1981; Smith, 1980). Others are alienated from society and "authority"; characterized by negative attitudes, they too do not send their children to pre-school (Shinman, 1981). A major inhibiting factor is parents' lack of confidence (Haystead et al., 1980; Sandow & Clarke, 1978). Some parents also feel they lack power in the school setting. In addition, mothers working full-time and non-English-speaking parents present obvious problems in communication (Tizard et al., 1981).

What teachers expect from parents is not always the same as what parents expect from teachers; good communication between staff and parents is often lacking (Tizard et al., 1981). Nevertheless, there is general consensus that a substantial majority of parents whose children attend a preschool — including those from minority and disadvantaged groups — want to be involved (Clark & Cheyne, 1979; Haystead et al., 1980; Shinman, 1981; Smith, 1980; Tizard et al., 1981; van der Eyken, 1978; Watt, 1977).

Reported changes in parental behavior are not all that dramatic, however. A 1-year study of involvement in seven nursery schools suggested that passivity previously associated with working-class parents is giving way to more active and lasting concern for children's education (Tizard et al., 1981). Parents in this study were also more likely to allow "messy" play at home and to buy toys they had seen in the nursery. Supporting evidence (Haystead et al., 1980) suggested that parents became critical of children's activities in nursery units and playgroups on the grounds of lack of structure and direct teaching.

An approach through before-and-after experimental design (Clark & Cheyne, 1979), designed to test the efficacy of a 4-month program in which schools involved mothers of 3- and 4-year-old children, resulted in marked changes in behavior, notably in the amount of time mothers spent reading to their children. In general, however, even where considerable effort has gone into intensive programs involving parents in school-based activities, results have disappointed those who wanted to increase parental appreciation of what nursery schooling was about. Apparent increase in personal trust between parents and teachers, by itself, was not judged likely to achieve the aim of parent involvement programs (Tizard et al., 1981).

Undoubtedly, some of the most encouraging results have occurred in programs in which both strong motivation and step-by-step learning were combined. Outstanding examples concern the parents of handicapped children who have been involved with professionals in workshops and taught to help their children (Collins & Collins, 1976; Cunningham & Jeffree, 1975; Pugh & Russell, 1977). Nonetheless, a dispiriting aspect is that, since provision is inadequate to meet demand, many children whose parents would appreciate the opportunity of a workshop, nursery school, playgroup, or day nursery do not have that experience. Furthermore, there is a substantial minority of young, isolated, and depressed parents—often with large families—who are not only at a disadvantage in society, but also unlikely to seek or sustain the use of existing preschool facilities even when they are available (Shinman, 1981). In such subgroups (for example, families with handicapped children officially designated "in need of help"), as many as 60 out of 150 (40%) parents have been found unwilling to participate in a school-based program designed to meet their needs (Jeffree & McConkey, 1976).

Home-based Services and Support

The 1970s saw a dramatic expansion in family services and support outside the formal institutional setting. Specifically, such efforts include those in which the child is cared for in someone else's home, in which a service or support is provided in the child's home, and in which support is community-based.

Childminding. In the early 1970s, few people even in the field of early childhood education were aware of the existence of childminding, or home day care. Attention was focused on this issue by an alarming account of children who were kept in Dickensian conditions in some northern towns while their parents worked (Jackson, 1973). This revelation coincided with a generally increasing need for day care followed by cutbacks in education and social services. Home day care became a politically charged issue. Childminders were seen by some as offering low cost day care, to be encouraged; others saw childminding as provision on the cheap and consequently a second-class service (Department of Health and Social Security & Department of Education and Science, 1976).

Given insufficient day nursery places to meet demand, as outlined previously, many mothers are obliged to fall back on childminders. A total of 57% of children under 5 and 40% of children under 2 in day care are with childminders (Bone, 1977). Available evidence (Community Relations Commission, 1975; Jackson & Jackson, 1979; Gibson, Nandy, & Russell, 1977; National Educational Research and Development Trust, Childminding Research and Development Unit, 1974, 1975) suggests that in spite of statutory supervision, considerable variation exists in the quality of care offered by childminders; and there are marked differences too between local authorities as to the amount of supervision and support they provide.

Against this background, two influential studies were carried out. One was London-based and concerned "an unusually favored sample of 39 daily minders from four London Boroughs" (Mayall & Petrie, 1977, p. 63). The second (Bryant, Harris, & Newton, 1980) was a survey in Oxfordshire, a comparatively rural county, of 66 currently employed minders, 73 currently unemployed minders, and 26 ex-minders, together with a sample of 63 mothers of children in their care. Both investigations were concerned with the quality of care offered and aimed to analyze the strengths and weakneses of the service. Both were also particularly interested in the minder-child relationship, as compared with the mother-child relationship, since one of the alleged advantages of childminding was that the minder was a mother substitute.

Findings were remarkably congruent in spite of the fact that samples were drawn from urban and rural areas, respectively. Concern focused on the findings that: (1) Lack of communication existed between parents and minder; (2) two-thirds of the children tended to be withdrawn and passive at the minders'; (3) the minder-child relationship differed markedly from the mother-child relationship; and (4) minders "care" rather than "educate or stimulate" — in other words, they lack a sense of profession. A follow-up study carried out in 1977 (Mayall & Petrie, 1983) of 66 minded children under 2 found a very high turnover of children, also revealing that over a third of minders were reluctant to take ethnic minority children and babies, and that 70% were unwilling to take handicapped children. These findings prompted the conclusion that childminding could not be recommended — even that "the present practice of childminding will increase maladjustment in the generation exposed to it!" (Bruner, 1980, p. 127).

This research raised two fundamental questions: Is the assumption justified that children cared for by childminders are disadvantaged in their language and social skills by virtue of that care? and, Is an improvement in the skills of childminders possible? A verdict of insufficient available evidence on the first count (Raven & Robb, 1980) followed comparison of two groups of children who differed only in that one group had been minded and the other had not. As in Mayall and Petrie (1983), each group was given standardized tests of language and social ability. There was no appreciable difference between the two groups, but the performance of both was below the norm.

As to change, evaluation of a project in which 10 black women in a predominantly West Indian district of Inner London were paid to attend a crash course on childminding, child care, and play leadership was not encouraging (Jackson, 1976). All women found the experience highly enjoyable, but when reassessed after 6 months, changes in physical conditions and in quality of care at the minders were all of "near nil." In discussing findings, Brian Jackson, the principal investigator, drew attention to these mistakes: trying to do too much in a short time; using informal, heuristic methods with women who had always seen learning in authoritarian terms; and lack of an adequate support system for minders.

With these comments in mind, findings from an in-depth study of all 70 registered and active childminders in two separate priority areas of Inner London are relevant (Shinman, 1981). They afford a comprehensive picture of legitimate home day care and, more important, describe how it developed and improved over an 18-month period of increased support, informal training, and encouragement of self-help. Comprehensive assessment schedules incorporated measures used in the Jackson study (1976) with an Index of Maternal Alienation, which reflects degree of isolation and alienation in a mother or childminder together with differences in attitude and behavior toward the child and his or her perceived needs. This index had previously proved predictive of hard-to-reach families who make use of services irregularly or not at all (Shinman, 1978).

Initially, there were clear indications of problems reported in previous studies, of difficulties in communication, and of cultural barriers and lack of stimulating play for the children. However, findings failed to confirm a preponderance of passive children. Reassessment of minders after 18 months revealed striking change and development. Care and counsel in placing children with suitable minders dramatically reduced movement from one minder to another and substantially scaled down difficulties that stemmed from diverse cultures and languages. Other changes related to tolerance and encouragement of "messy play," to choice of toys, to how minders talked and listened to children both in the home and at drop-in centers, and to the way minders coped with problems inherent in looking after other people's children. Considerable antagonism gave way to willingness to follow training courses and to a distinctly professional attitude toward the job. Analysis also showed that reported instability among minders, a source of disquiet, was due on one hand to an influx of new and well-screened minders and on the other to the removal of the least satisfactory minders (20% of the sample). The residue of more responsible minders remained remarkably stable. Overall, given support and supervision for minders, there was a more hopeful prognosis for childminding than previous studies had suggested. A similar conclusion emerged from a study of a random sample of 69 active minders and parents of minded children in Staffordshire (Davie, in preparation). In this study, children were not characterized as being withdrawn and passive, minders manifested a professional attitude toward the job, and the major cause for concern was the attitude and behavior of some parents.

The studies discussed were small and localized, and, as with earlier studies (Mayall & Petrie, 1983; Bryant et al., 1980), one cannot generalize from them. However, the likelihood that they reflect a genuine and widespread trend finds support in subsequent developments. The National Childminding Association was started by a group of childminders, parents, and other interested people in 1977, during the first showing of a British Broadcasting Corporation television series for childminders entitled "Other People's Children" (see Jackson, Moseley, & Wheeler, 1976). By October of 1982, there were over 5,000 members in 208 local groups. Although members constitute a small proportion of the total number of registered childminders (approximately 9%), their existence as an organized group is a development that less than a decade ago was unthinkable. Other positive effects of the television series and its supporting material, evident from a nationally spread sample of 100 childminders, included improved physical surroundings for children and more time spent by minders playing with and listening to them (Department of Education and Science, 1981c). These effects were still apparent after 1 year.

One of the National Childminding Association's aims is to advance the education and training of minders. It is revealing that in 1978 it was not even thought appropriate in an association survey to ask whether a minder had attended any training or preparation course. Answers to that question, by 1981 considered to the point (Goddard & Smith, 1981), showed that 34% had attended a course. Of the remainder, 63% said they would like to. Subsequently, regional meetings held nationwide during 1981 testify to the ability and enthusiasm of a solid core of minders toward pursuing a vigorous training policy (Beckwith, 1982).

Diverse support schemes have mushroomed; these include an experiment in salaried childminding in which minders work together as a team and as paraprofessional staff attached to a day nursery (Willmott & Challiss, 1977), as well as drop-in centers, training schemes, phone-ins, and television and radio programs (Jackson & Jackson, 1979; London Council of Social Services, 1977; Shinman, 1979). Thus the decade has witnessed considerable change and development in this still controversial form of day care. Many issues still give grounds for concern. The crucial question, unanswered in research terms in the absence of a longitudinal study, is whether or how much children benefit from such developments.

One consequence of raising standards of childminding and creating an accountable and acceptable service is that unsatisfactory minders, who are usually mothers with young children of their own, are dissuaded or prevented from minding. Thereby, they often forego any form of supervision or support since they are not always known to social workers or health visitors. They drop below the horizon of the statutory body unless and until they become crisis cases (Shinman, 1981), joining the ranks of those whom other forms of home-based day care may reach.

Educational home visiting. Acceptance of the overriding importance of the mother and home in early childhood education, commitment to the need for early intervention, a structured approach in fostering cognitive development, and desire to reach the "hard-to-reach" family all feature in educational home visiting in the United Kingdom. The number of these schemes has grown rapidly during the 1970s, although there are no official figures of the numbers of mothers involved (Birchall, 1982b).

Early projects stressed the need to raise the morale of the mother and her ability to cope as well as the desirability of fostering the child's social, linguistic, and emotional development (Poulton & James, 1975). Initially, visitors were trained teachers who operated from nursery or infant schools. Typically, within a school catchment area, each week for about an hour they visited mothers with children between 18 months and 4 years of age. Some schemes involved all parents within the area, in order to avoid possible stigma attaching to the few parents deemed most in need of intervention. Workers in these programs took appropriate books, toys, and games and worked with the mother to develop specific skills.

Subsequently, schemes have developed that aim to reach multiproblem families who often do not participate in parent involvement schemes. Diversity is a key feature of home-based programs; these have grown up mostly to meet local needs and provide local solutions. The philosophy behind such schemes ranges from a concept in which people work together to solve their own problems to professional intervention with specific goals in mind (Aplin & Pugh, 1983).

The Portage Scheme is a particularly successful home-based model designed to help parents with handicapped children. Imported from the United States to Britain in 1976, its core components are direct teaching and a positive monitoring system. A peripatetic behavioral checklist helps parents identify a child's existing skills and pinpoint those they would like him or her to acquire. Portage cards provide specific teaching suggestions for each of approximately 700 teaching objectives on the checklist; activity charts contain clear directions to enable parents (or other direct contact people) to teach the handicapped child new skills and to record the results of their teaching efforts. There is a reported 80 to 95% success rate (Cameron, 1982). The model has been extended into settings other than the home; it now operates in hospitals, children's homes, schools, pediatric units, opportunity groups,[3] playgroups, and adult training centers.

Only a small proportion of early home visiting projects have been eval-

---

[3] Opportunity Groups are characterized by the bringing together in playgroups of handicapped and non-handicapped under-fives, and by a separate supportive program for parents of the handicapped children. Such groups developed out of concern felt by parents and professionals at the lack of statutory provision and support; they began in 1966 and have since proliferated.

uated. In general, children have shown only short-term gains and the tendency to settle better at school than their counterparts not involved in such projects (Jayne, 1976). The main effects have been on parental attitudes. Parents of 20 children who took part in the first Educational Priority Area action research project – the Red House experiment in the West Riding area of Yorkshire – were found, 5 years later, to have far more positive attitudes toward education than did a comparable group not taking part in the project (Armstrong & Brown, 1979). In the South East London Educational Home Visiting Scheme, again the most marked difference between participants and nonparticipants was that mothers who had taken part saw their role as "extremely" or "very" important (Anders & Costerton, 1979), whereas before they had rated their role as being of lesser importance.

Clearly, quantitative evaluation of such schemes is fraught with difficulty and is often even considered inappropriate (Pugh, 1981). Concentration on program aspects that can be measured may result in neglect of most important but elusive features: the development of a child's confidence and the improvement of a family's quality of life (Raven, 1979). Resources and/or research instruments to probe such areas are often lacking. Thus the accounts that follow serve merely to highlight stages in experience and thinking; they are not definitive, but rather raise fundamental questions.

The East Lothian Home Visiting Scheme is an exmaple of a program that uses mainly teachers or other professionals. The purpose of the project evaluation, conducted by Raven (1980), was to assess whether educational home visiting should be routinely available in the region. Attention focused on six trained teachers, five of whom were appointed to the staffs of five schools judged to be in areas of disadvantage; the sixth worked with handicapped children. All teachers were selected for their capacity to use professional skills without undermining mothers' confidence. Their job was to work with 2- and 3-year-olds in their parents' presence for about 1 hour a week over a period of about 9 months, so as to encourage the mothers to play a more active part in their children's development.

The usual practice was to take in some object to provide a focus for activities (sand, water, colored paper), but an underlying aim was to persuade mothers that they could use ordinary household materials to help their children learn. Visitors were given considerable latitude as to how they might tackle the job. In practice, some pursued a skills-training technique; others developed enabling or befriending styles (McCail, 1981). A total of 41 home-visited families, 200 families from the same disadvantaged area, and 80 families from a more well-to-do area were included in the sample. Participants were selected on the grounds that they were likely to benefit from the scheme. Disturbed families were excluded.

On the credit side, statistical evaluation showed that educational home visits had substantial impact on children's adjustment to school; specifically, children learned to adapt to a teacher-style, and mothers were more favorably disposed to the children doing schoolwork. As a result of the scheme, all five schools in the study established community activities involving groups of parents. Parents also felt able and justified to complain to the school when they were not satisfied. On balance, however, the scheme could not be recommended; its "long-term social implications gave grounds for unease" (Raven, 1980, p. 80).

Following observation and interviews, what emerged most clearly on the debit side was that educational home visiting had a major impact on what parents thought, but not, in the way that was hoped, on what they did. Parents attached greater importance to intellectual and academic abilities like thinking for oneself and reading, but books were seen as opportunities to "test" rather than to stimulate interest and enjoyment. Instead of helping parents to think of themselves as facilitators of development, visits led them to produce a climate unlikely to encourage interest and joint child-initiated activities. The message that the mother was the child's most important educator appeared to have been utterly undermined. Strikingly, better-off families were preoccupied with intellectual activities and with fostering independence in their children. These families taught by example, whereas "disadvantaged" families valued deference, obedience, and dependence. For them, teaching meant telling, and there was no evidence of change due to intervention.

Raven's (1980) appraisal looked beyond bald results to speculate on the possibility that home visitors, as experts, could lead parents to feel less confident in their own abilities and to entertain the idea that the mothering and teaching roles (that is, a facilitative versus a directive stance) were incompatible. What was undetermined was whether the active element in any success was befriending a mother and helping her establish social contacts or whether the mother and home visitor (in an extra-professional role) worked together to solve the mother's problems. Another relevant factor might be the frequency of visits and the associated style of interaction between visitor and parents (Sandow & Clarke, 1978). In a program of home-based intervention with two groups of severely subnormal preschool children and their parents, it was found that frequently visited children, after initial superiority over infrequently visited children, later showed deceleration in intellectual growth. Less frequently visited children conversely showed a later rise in performance. Explanations centered on the comparative lack of dependence on the visitor by parents in the latter group and on these parents' consequent ability to take more positive action in helping their children.

Community-based support and preparation for parenthood.   A 4-year evaluation of Home-Start, a community-based project of family support, affords some insights into the type of scheme that depends on volunteers (van der Eyken, 1982). This scheme began in 1973 in Leicestershire to offer support, friendship, and practical help for families with children under 5. On the basis of a one-to-one relationship, it encourages parental strengths and emotional well-being in the belief that these qualities are fundamental to children's development. In working toward increased confidence and independence of the family unit, volunteers who have undergone a special preparatory course encourage families to widen their network of relationships and to use community support and services effectively (Morehen, 1982).

Several features distinguish Home-Start and a number of similar schemes from purely "educational" home visiting schemes, though distinctions between the two types of intervention are in practice becoming increasingly blurred as insights are pooled. Specifically, these differences include the following points:

1. The scheme is based on the use of volunteers who are "ordinary mothers," not paraprofessionals or teachers.
2. Attention is focused on parents as people in their own right. Parents are not seen as "agents of change," nor is the mother perceived as being the child's first teacher.
3. Families are typically under stress, with many members living on low incomes in poor and overcrowded conditions. Mothers are often of low intelligence, in poor health, lonely, and isolated; all members of the family may suffer emotional or physical battering. Children lack stimuli and new experiences.
4. A self-selected volunteer is carefully prepared and matched to a family, whom she "befriends." This is a contractual relationship based on trust, reciprocal in that both volunteer and family members stand to benefit from the experience.
5. Volunteers maintain lines of commmunication with different levels of support within the community; with playgroups and toy libraries; and with the statutory services of health visiting, social work, and education — all within Home-Start's own multidisciplinary support network.

School-based education home visiting schemes have not been very successful with "hard-to-reach" and disadvantaged families (Raven, 1980). In terms of children at risk not actually being taken into care, and according to assessment by independent professional workers, the Home-Start type of intervention, however, has had a marked beneficial effect on a significant proportion of families referred to it, particularly those suffering from environmental stress (van der Eyken, 1982). Key elements brought out in the evaluation to account for observed changes include the following:

1. Volunteers are person-oriented; they have time and are committed to befriending the family, in comparison with social workers, who are

problem-oriented, maintain professional distance, and are often seen as authorities.

2. Volunteers and social workers, possessing different attributes, nevertheless work in tandem, complementing each other's skills.

3. Mothering is the crucial offering made by volunteers. Three stages of growth, having much in common with stages in Reality Therapy (Glasser, 1965; van der Eyken, 1982) are identified: the formation of a trusting relationship between volunteer and family; a corrective stage when unrealistic behavior, but not the family, is rejected; and active teaching of better ways to fulfill family needs.

Van der Eyken (1982) has argued that "loss of control" is a key point in description of families under stress from the environment and that Home-Start aimed to help a family gain control to the point where it could, perhaps for the first time, function as a healthy childrearing environment.

The nurturing of a sense of control is descriptive of many recent schemes designed to support parents in the community. Interest in preparation for parenthood has only recently intensified (Pugh, 1980). There has been only one study of fathering (Jackson, 1984). Schemes and services are embryonic and still thinly and unevenly spread across the country; the various approaches tend to be piecemeal and uncoordinated, and there is considerable confusion in aims and methodology (Pugh, 1982). Projects range from informal mother-toddler groups and formal classes in hospitals to post-experience courses promoted by the Open University for parents at every age and stage of life (Wolfson, 1982). There are also a few expanding, documented parent preparation schemes like the Community Education Centre in Coventry (Aplin & Pugh, 1983) and SCOPE in Southampton (Hevey, 1981; Poulton, 1982). The aim of this latter program is to help parents gain a greater sense of power and control over their lives. To this end, SCOPE promotes neighborhood groups where children and their parents — mothers and fathers with child management problems, marital tensions, or handicapped children — can get together. It provides creches, toy library facilities, and a family center that offers free short recuperative residential breaks for families under stress, as well as home visits and training courses emphasizing practical work with schools at primary and secondary levels.

SUMMARY AND CONCLUSIONS

Against the background of a decade of changing social values and economic constraint, this overview has tried to convey the diversity that characterizes early childhood education in the United Kingdom. It has also been the intention to highlight trends — in particular the increasing importance of the voluntary sector, the shift in focus from the child to the family and community, and the growing and unmet need for day care. The discussion has indicated the breadth and range of research and highlighted some particular examples of interest. These studies have reflected two major themes — the need to intro-duce a more structured approach into the peschool environment and the need for partnership between parents and professionals.

The argument for structuring the preschool environment, in the context of research reported here, rests on the efficacy of structure in promoting cogni-tive development. Observation of children, adults, and institutional organi-zation has clearly demonsrated how much more could be done to encourage children's concentration through complex, elaborated play and in general to improve the quality of care. "Partnership" between parents and professionals is a far more complex matter than the catchword suggests. Some headway has been made in defining what is meant by parental involvement and in clari-fying issues. Especially difficult problems relate to locus of control, differing values and cultural backgrounds of practitioners and parents, and confusion over the nature and requirements of teaching and parenting. Such diffi-culties extend beyond formal institutional settings to home day care and to community-based schemes.

Beginning to emerge is the need to recognize and build on the disposition of individual parents — to begin where they are. This is particularly important with those who are alienated and under stress from the environment. Such parents may not have enjoyed good mothering themselves and may need to experience something comparable — a committed relationship with a con-cerned worker — in order to reach a stage where they are able or want to begin to change and respond positively to other approaches.

Finally, it is now widely acknowledged that parenting skills are not always naturally acquired; parents benefit from professional guidance and support, provided it does not undermine their confidence in their own abilities. Schemes that have sprung up to meet local and specific needs reflect the de-termination of early childhood educators to make both services and support appropriate and acceptable to all families with young children.

Implications for Educators

Practical suggestions. Those concerned with young children will be helped by the wealth of practical advice implicit in much of the research. Variously, the research suggests that teachers may benefit if they incorporate the following suggestions: (1) Create situations in which children play in pairs. This not only helps in the acquisition of social skills but fosters children's language and powers of concentration. (2) Make the most of materials and activities that have a clear goal structure (e.g., constructive toys, drawing, puzzles). These are effective means whereby children progress to more elaborate self-directed play. (3) Balance the daily routine of free choice with prescribed educational tasks. (4) Plan use of physical resources in such a way as to minimize noise levels and facilitate play in small groups. (5) Cultivate a generally relaxed and collaborative style, and aim for fewer but longer chats with individual children. (One way to free staff and make this possible is by inviting parents in to help.)

In addition, the identification of underlying difficulties that inhibit parental involvement and over which teachers have control both implies the possibility of change and indicates parameters for action. The question is one of creating opportunities for parents and teachers to meet and talk about joint goals, of being willing to take time and listen. Equally important is the fostering of mutual respect and the development of new attitudes among professionals in which parental skills are recognized and valued. As has already been indicated, if a committed relationship akin to mothering is necessary to bring some parents to the point where they can accept and benefit from formal teaching, if a directive stance is counterproductive with some of the parents it is most hoped to influence, then recognition of the complementary roles of teaching and mothering is vital. The clearer understanding of respective skills that emerges from much action research may reassure professionals and volunteers that both roles are valuable in early childhood education, and may encourage new lines of communication.

The importance of training.   These ideas about parent involvement and collaboration between professionals and volunteers represent very different underlying attitudes from those prevalent when many practicing teachers were trained. Consequently it is of fundamental importance that the form, content, and ethos of initial and in-service training courses take account of such developments. There is a need, not always met, to make experience with families an integral part of training in order to develop sensitive awareness of and communication skills with adults of very different persuasions and backgrounds, as opposed to solely preparing individuals for work with young children.

The tools for self-observation and for child observation developed and modified by several researchers, notably Holmes and McMahon (1977) and Clark et al. (1984) have considerable practical relevance. Educators can benefit as never before from being able to assess their teaching styles and achievement more objectively; this may be of particular help in drawing attention to shy, withdrawn children, who it seems tend to be neglected, albeit unintentionally.

There is a more fundamental point, however: Reconsideration of the training and preparation of all who work with young children is an issue of crucial and immediate importance. Difficulties encountered in bringing together the two separate strands of "education" and "care" that characterize preschooling in the United Kingdom have largely occurred because of divisive philosophies, career structures, and conditions of work entrenched in training courses and associated with the respective types of institutions. Two major concerns exist: (1) the need for a comprehensive and unifying foundation course and in-service training to ensure a continuing supply of suitably prepared workers, and (2) the need to redress the present imbalance whereby there are too few experienced and qualified people working with young children. This problem is made particularly acute with the expansion of nursery places in the form of early entry into primary school reception classes, where neither physical arrangements nor teacher training are necssarily geared to the developmental needs of very young children.

Coordination and cooperation. Clearly, no service can meet all the needs of families with young children. A multidisciplinary approach needs structure and coordination. Consequently, a network of information is needed between local authority administration and other organizations and individuals working in the field. A national survey of coordination procedures (Bradley, 1982) revealed the existence of only a partial network. Here personal attitudes are crucial; the network has been found to be at its most successful where attitudes support variety and flexibility in meeting changing needs. But policies that encourage variety and flexibility can, without vigilance, lead to imbalance and to inequitable provision.

Balance and objectivity. Equilibrium is vital. All recommendations have to be tested against experience and seen in a wider context. Thus emphasis on strategies that develop children's cognitive abilities must not diminish attention to social and emotional factors — children's happiness, their sense of security, or what may be simply a need to "stand and stare." The new tools and techniques being developed to help workers assess themselves and the children in their care offer fresh but ony partial insights into precept and practice. There is therefore a need to extend, refine, and broaden the scope of such techniques to take account of other essentials of the preschool curriculum. Research has an obvious part to play. The need to develop more precise means for observing, recording, and evaluating different approaches in relation to individual families is emphasized by the fact that open access to, among other things, schools and shared experience between teachers and parents does not always bring about desired improvements.

In sum, the last decade has seen considerable progress in understanding the needs of families with young children and the ways to respond effectively to them. It has witnessed growing awareness of the part played by organization and structure in preschool services and the gaps that exist in the present provision. Implementation of policies that make use of what we know demand substantial resources. It remains to be seen where priorities for investment in our future will lie.

REFERENCES

Anders, T., & Costerton, J. (1979). *Education home visiting.* London: Joint Resource Centre of Frobisher Institute.

Aplin, G., & Pugh, G. (Eds.). (1983). *Perspectives on pre-school home visiting.* London: National Children's Bureau and Coventry Community Education Development Centre.

Armstrong, G., & Brown, F. (1979). *Five years on: A follow-up study of the long term effects on parents and children of an early learning programme in the home.* Oxford: Social Evaluation Unit, Department of Social and Administrative Studies.

Beckwith, J. (1982). *Training and support in childminding — a national response.* Available from author, National Childminding Association, 13 London Rd., Bromley, Kent BR1 1DE, England.

Birchall, D. (1982a). *Family centres* (Concern No. 43). London: National Children's Bureau.

Birchall, D. (1982b). *Home based services for the under fives: A review of research* (Highlight No. 54). London: National Children's Bureau.

Blatchford, P., Battle, S., & Mays, J. (1982). *The first transition: Home to pre-school.* Windsor, England: NFER-Nelson.

Bone, M. (1977). *Pre-school children and the need for day care.* London: Her Majesty's Stationery Office.

Bradley, M. (1982). *The co-ordination of services for children under five.* Windsor, England: NFER-Nelson.

Brown, G., & Harris, T. (1978). *The social origins of depression.* London: Tavistock.

Bruner, J. (1980). *Under fives in Britain.* London: Grant McIntyre.

Bryant, B., Harris, M., & Newton, D. (1980). *Children and minders.* London: Grant McIntyre.

Cameron, R.J. (Ed.). (1982). *Working together. Portage in the U.K.* Windsor, England: NFER-Nelson.

Central Statistical Office. (1982). *Social trends, 12.* London: Her Majesty's Stationery Office.

Central Statistical Office. (1983). *Social trends, 13.* London: Her Majesty's Stationery Office.

Centre for the Study of Rural Society. (1978). *The country child.* Lincoln, England: Bishop Grossteste College of Education.

Chazan, M., Laing, A.F., Shackleton-Bailey, M., & Jones, G.E. (1980). *Some of our children: The discovery, care and education of under fives with special needs.* London: Open Books.

Clark, M., & Cheyne, W.M. (Eds.). (1979). *Studies in pre-school education: Empirical studies in pre-school units in Scotland and their implications for educational practices.* London: Hodder and Stoughton.

Clark, M., Robinson, B., & Browning, M. (1984). *Pre-school education and children with special needs.* Available from author, Dept. of Educational Psychology, Faculty of Education, University of Birmingham, Birmingham B15 2TT, England.

Cleave, S., Jowett, S., & Bate, M. (1982). *And so to school.* Windsor, England: NFER-Nelson.

Committee on Child Health Services. (1976). *Fit for the future* (Court Report). London: Her Majesty's Stationery Office.

Community Relations Commission. (1975). *Who minds? A study of working mothers and childminding in ethnic minority communities.* Available from author, Reference and Technical Services Division, 15-16 Bedford St., London WC2, England.

Collins, M., & Collins, D. (1976). *Kith and kids.* London: Souvenir Press.

Cunningham, C., & Jeffree, D. (1975). The organisation and structure of workshops for parents of mentally handicapped children. *Bulletin of the British Psychological Society, 28,* 405–411.

Davie, C.E. (in preparation). *A study of childminding in non-inner city areas* (Department of Health and Social Security Report). Information available from author, Keele University, Staffordshire, England.

Davie, C.E., Hutt, J., Vincent, E., & Mason, M. (1984). *The young child at home.* Windsor: NFER-Nelson.

Department of Education and Science. (1972). *Education white paper: A framework for expansion.* London: Her Majesty's Stationery Office.

Department of Education and Science. (1975). *Pre-school education and care: Some topics requiring research or development projects.* Available from author, Elizabeth House, York Rd., London SE1 7PH, England.

Department of Education and Science. (1978). *Special educational needs* (Report of the Warnock Committee of Enquiry into the Education of Handicapped Children and Young People). London: Her Majesty's Stationery Office.

Department of Education and Science (1981a). *Education Act 1981.* Available from author, Elizbabeth House, York Rd., London SE1 7PH, England.

Department of Education and Science (1981b). *Circular No. 8/81.* Available from author, Elizabeth House, York Rd., London SE1, 7PH, England.

Department of Education and Science (1981c). *Under fives: A programme of research* (London Under Fives Research Dissemination Group). Available from author, Publications Despatch Centre, Honeypot Lane, Canons Park, Stanmore, Middlesex, England.

Department of Health and Social Security, & Department of Education and Science. (1976). *Low cost provision for the under-fives.* London: Her Majesty's Stationery Office.

Donaldson, M. (1978). *Children's minds.* Glasgow, Scotland: Fontana/Collins.

Equal Opportunities Commission. (1978). *I want to work . . . but what about the kids?* Day care for young children and opportunities for working parents. Available from author, Overseas House, Quay St., Manchester M3 3HN, England.

Ferri, E. (1976). *Growing up in a one-parent family.* Windsor, England; National Children's Bureau and National Foundation for Educational Research.

Ferri, E. (1982). *Opportunity groups – an expanding role?* (Concern No. 43). London: National Children's Bureau.

Ferri, E., Birchall, D., Gingell, V., & Gipps, B. (1981). *Combined nursery centres – a new approach to education and day care.* London: The MacMillan Press Ltd.

Ferri, E., & Niblett, R. (1977). *Disadvantaged families and playgroups.* Windsor, England: National Foundation for Educational Research.

Ferri, E., & Robinson, H. (1976). *Coping alone.* Windsor, England: National Children's Bureau and National Foundation for Educational Research.

Garland, C., & White, S. (1980). *Children and day nurseries.* London: Grant McIntyre.

Gibson, M., Nandy, L., & Russell, P. (1977). *Childminding in London: A study of support services for childminders.* London: London Council of Social Services.

Gittis, E. (1976). *Flats, families, and the under fives.* London: Routledge and Kegan Paul.

Glasser, W. (1965). *Reality therapy – a new approach to psychiatry.* New York: Harper and Row.

Goddard, A., & Smith, C. (1981). *Do childminders care?* Available from National Childminding Association, 13 London Rd., Bromley, Kent BR1 1DE, England.

Gray, M., & McMahon, L. (1982). *Families in playgroups.* London: Pre-School Playgroups Association.

Hanton, M. (1977). *Playgroups: A shared adventure.* London: Inner London Pre-School Playgroups Association.

Haystead, J., Howarth, V., & Strachan, A. (1980). *Pre-school education and care.* Sevenoaks, England: Hodder and Stoughton for the Scottish Council for Research in Education.

Henderson, M. (1978). *Cogs and spindles.* London: Pre-School Playgroups Association.

Hevey, D. (1981). *Report of the social science research council officer in three experimental under fives coordination schemes in Hampshire.* Southampton University, Department of Child Health, Southampton, England.

Holmes, A., & McMahon, L. (1977). *Teaching others to observe — a guide to using target child observation on playgroup courses.* Oxford, England: Oxford Pre-School Research Group.

Hughes, M., Mayall, B., Petrie, P., Moss, P., & Pinkerton, G. (1980). *Nurseries now: A fair deal for parents and children.* Harmondsworth, England: Penguin Books Ltd.

Hutt, C. (1979). Play in the under-fives: Form development and function. In J.G. Howell (Ed.), *Modern perspectives in the psychiatry of infancy* (pp. 95–141). The Hague, Netherlands: Bruner/Maazel.

Jackson, B. (1973). The childminders. *New Society, 26* (582), 521–523.

Jackson, B. (1976). *Changing childminders?* London: National Elfrida Rathbone Society.

Jackson, B. (1984). *Fatherhood.* London: Allen & Unwin.

Jackson, B., & Jackson, S. (1979). *Childminder: A study in action research.* London: Routledge and Kegan Paul.

Jackson, S., Moseley, J., & Wheeler, B. (1976). *Other people's children: A handbook for childminders.* London: British Broadcasting Corporation.

Jayne, E. (1976). *Deptford home visiting project* (Research Report ILEA (RS/645/76). London: Inner London Education Authority.

Jeffree, D.M., & McConkey, R. (1976). *Parental involvement in facilitating development of young mentally handicapped children.* Manchester, England, Manchester University, Hester Adrian Centre.

Law Reports Statutes, Pt. 1. (1968). Health Services and Public Health Act, London Council of Law Reporting, 3 Stone Buildings, Lincoln's Inn, London WC2, England.

Leach, P. (1979). *Who cares?* Harmondsworth, England: Penguin Books Ltd.

London Council of Social Services. (1977). Childminding in London, a study of support services for childminders. London: Author.

Mayall, B., & Petrie, P. (1977). *Minder, mother and child.* London: University of London, Institute of Education.

Mayall, B., & Petrie, P. (1983). *Childminding and day nurseries* (Studies in Education 13). London: Heinemann Educational Books for the University of London, Institute of Education.

McCail, G. (1981). *Mother start.* Edinburgh: The Scottish Council for Research in Education.

Morehen, M. (1982). Degrees of intervention: A view from the voluntary sector. In G. Pugh (Ed.), *Parenting papers No. 5: Working with families — services or support?* (pp. 23–28). London: National Children's Bureau.

Moss, P., Bax, M.C.O., & Plewis, I. (1979). *Pre-school families and services.* Unpublished report, Thomas Coram Research Unit, London University Institute of Education.

National Educational Research and Development Trust, Childminding Research and Development Unit. (1974). *Action register No. 2.* Available from author, 32 Trumpington St., Cambridge, England.

National Educational Research and Development Trust, Childminding Research and Development Unit. (1975). *Action register No. 3.* Available from author, 32 Trumpington St., Cambridge, England.

Neill, St. John, S. R. (1982). Pre-school design and child behavior. *Journal of Child Psychology and Psychiatry, 23* (3), 309–318.

Office of Population Censuses and Surveys. (1982). *General household survey 82/1* (Reference 9HS 82/1). London: Her Majesty's Stationery Office.

Overton, J. (1981). *Stepping stone projects. The first three years 1978–81.* Glasgow: Scottish Pre-School Playgroups Association.

Parry, M., & Archer, H. (1975). *Two to five: A handbook for students and teachers.* London: Schools Council and MacMillan Education.

Plowden, Lady B. (April, 1974). *The world of children.* Paper presented at the annual conference of the Pre-School Playgroups Association, Exeter, England. London: Preschool Playgroups Association.

Poulton, L. (1982). Support: Who gives it and when? In G. Pugh (Ed.), *Parenting papers No. 1: Parenthood education and support—a continuous process.* London: National Children's Bureau.

Poulton, G.A., & James, T. (1975). *Pre-school learning in the community: Strategies for change.* London: Routledge and Kegan Paul.

Pre-School Playgroups Association National Training Committee. (1982). *Course Statistics, July 1980-81.* London: Pre-School Playgroups Association.

Pre-School Playgroups Association Research and Information Committee. (1983). *Facts and figures.* London: Preschool Playgroups Association.

Pre-School Playgroups Association Working Party. (1978). *Report on mother and toddler groups.* London: Pre-School Playgroups Association.

Pre-School Playgroups Association Working Party. (1980). *Report on parental involvement in playgroups.* London: Pre-School Playgroups Association.

Pringle, M. (1979). *Putting children first* (Concern No. 33). London: National Children's Bureau.

Pringle, M. (Ed.). (1980). *A fairer future for children: Towards better parental and professional care.* London: The MacMillan Press Ltd.

Pugh, G. (1980). *Preparation for parenthood: Some current initiatives and thinking.* London: National Children's Bureau.

Pugh, G. (1981). *Parents as partners: Intervention schemes and group work with parents of handicapped children.* London: National Children's Bureau.

Pugh, G. (1982). *A job for life: Education and support for parents.* London: National Children's Bureau, National Children's Home, and National Marriage Guidance Council.

Pugh, G., & Russell, P. (1977). *Shared Care: Support services for families with handicapped children.* London: National Children's Bureau.

Raven, J. (1979, September). *Educational home visiting and the growth of competence and confidence in adults and children.* Paper presented at the annual conference of the British Educational Research Association, Shoredith College, Egham, England.

Raven, J. (1980). *Parents, teachers and children: A study of an educational home visiting scheme.* London: Hodder and Stoughton for the Scottish Council for Research in Education.

Raven, M., & Robb, B. (1980). Childminding: Implications for education. *Research in Education, 23,* 14–26.

Rowntree, D. (1981). *A dictionary of education.* London: Harper and Row.

Sandow, S., & Clarke, A.D.B. (1978). Home intervention with parents of severely sub-normal pre-school children: An interim report. *Child Care, Health, and Development, 4,* 29–39.

Scottish Pre-School Playgroups Association Playgroups in Areas of Need Sub-Committee. (1977). *Playgroups in areas of need.* Glasgow: Scottish Pre-School Playgroups Association.

Scottish Pre-School Playgroups Association Working Party. (1978). *Student placement in playgroups.* Glasgow: Author.

Shinman, S. (1978). *Pre-school facilities: Some factors affecting demand and utilisation.* Unpublished doctoral dissertation, Brunel University, Uxbridge, Middlesex, England. (British Lending Library No. D7783/78)

Shinman, S. (1979). *Focus on childminders—a profile of the first Bunbury drop-in centres.* London: Inner London Pre-School Playgroup Association.

Shinman, S. (1981). *A chance for every child? Access and response to pre-school provision.*

London: Tavistock.

Smith, T., & Connolly, K. (1980). *The ecology of pre-school behaviour.* Cambridge, England: Cambridge University Press.

Smith, P.K. (1980). *Parents and preschool.* London: Grant McIntyre.

Sylva, K., Roy, C., & Painter, M. (1980). *Childwatching at playgroup and nursery school.* London: Grant McIntyre.

Tizard, B. (1975). *Early childhood education: A review and discussion of research in Britain.* Slough, England: Social Science Research Council/National Foundation for Educational Research.

Tizard, B. (1979). Language at home and at school. In C.B. Cazden (Ed.), *Language and early childhood education* (pp. 17–26). Washington, DC: National Association for the Education of Young Children.

Tizard, B., Mortimor, J., & Burchall, B. (1981). *Involving parents in nursery and infant schools: A source book for teachers.* London: Grant McIntyre.

Tizard, B., Philips, J., & Plewis, I. (1975). Play in pre-school centres: Play measures and their relation to age, sex and I.Q. *Journal of Child Psychology and Psychiatry, 17,* 251–264.

Tizard, J., Moss, P., & Perry, J. (1976). *All our children: Pre-school services in a changing society.* London: Temple Smith/New Society.

Tough, J. (1977). *The development of meaning.* London: Allen and Unwin.

Turner, I. (1977). *Pre-school playgroups research and evaluation project: Final report to Northern Ireland Department of Health and Human Services.* Belfast: Queen's University, Department of Psychology.

Tyler, S., Foy, H., & Hutt, C. (1979). Attention and activity in the young child. *British Journal of Educational Psychology, 49* (2), 194–197.

van der Eyken, W. (1978). *Under five in Liverpool.* Unpublished commentary of a survey, directed by Dr. Martin Bradley, undertaken by the Liverpool Institute of Higher Education in conjunction with PRIORITY.

van der Eyken, W. (1979). Community nurseries. *Early Child Development and Care, 6* (1, 2), 61–72.

van der Eyken, W. (1982). *Home-Start: A four year evaluation.* Leicester, England: Home-Start Consultancy.

van der Eyken, W., Michell, L., & Grubb, J. (1979). *Pre-schooling in England, Scotland and Wales.* Bristol, England: University of Bristol, Department of Child Health.

Warren, C., & Adamson, J. (1982). What is a family centre? In G. Pugh (Ed.), *Parenting Papers No. 3: Supporting Parents in the Community* (pp. 16–22). London: National Children's Bureau.

Watt, J. (1977). *Co-operation in pre-school education.* London: Social Science Research Council.

Webb, L. (1975). *Purpose annd practice in nursery education.* Oxford, England: Blackwell.

Wells, G. (1981). *Learning through interaction: The study of language development.* Cambridge, England: Cambridge University Press.

Wicks, M., & Rimmer, L. (1980). *Happy families? A discussion paper on families in Britain.* London: Study Commission on the Family.

Willmott, P., & Challis, L. (1977). *The Groveway Project: An experiment in salaried childminding* (Lambeth Inner Area Study IAS/LA/17). London: Department of the Environment.

Wolfson, J. (1982). Tools for Teaching parenting skills. In G. Pugh (Ed.), *Parenting Papers No. 4: Can parenting skills be taught?* (pp. 21–29). London: National Children's Bureau.

Wood, D., McMahon, L., & Cranstoun, Y. (1980). *Working with under fives.* London: Grant McIntyre.

Woodhead, M. (1976). *Intervening in disadvantage – a challenge for nursery education.* Slough, England: National Foundation for Educational Research.

7

Cognitive Style and Children's Learning: Individual Variation in Cognitive Processes

Olivia N. Saracho

University of Maryland

Bernard Spodek

University of Illinois

Cognitive style is a psychological construct concerning the manner in which individuals differ from one another in intellectual functioning. Researchers in the area of cognitive style have amassed evidence that suggests that cognitive style affects the way students learn, the way teachers teach, and the way students and teachers interact with one another in the school context. The purpose of this discussion is to provide a brief overview of the field dependence/independence dimension of cognitive style, define that dimension, describe the most popular instruments used to measure cognitive style, discuss the advantages and disadvantages of cognitive flexibility, identify the relationship between cognitive style and intellectual functioning (including academic achievement), and describe students' learning styles and teachers' teaching styles. Implications for future research and practice are also drawn.

THEORETICAL PERSPECTIVES

Research on cognitive style was initiated in the early 1950s by Witkin and associates (Witkin, 1974; Witkin, Hertzman, Machover, Meissner, & Wapner, 1954/1972), who originally referred to the construct as "field dependence" versus "field independence." At present, some researchers prefer using the term "psychological differentiation" (Oltman, Goodenough, Witkin, Freedman, & Friedman, 1975; Witkin, Dyk, Faterson, Goodenough, & Karp, 1962/1974) rather than field dependence/independence; others favor using the term "field articulation" (global versus analytic) (Wallach, 1962). Regardless of the term used, the psychological construct characterizes individuals by distinguishing the ways in which they cope with complex and confusing circumstances as well as the manner in which they provide cognitive responses to different situations.

Field dependence/independence is a dimension of cognitive style that defines individual modes of perceiving, remembering, and thinking as well as individual ways of apprehending, storing, transforming, and processing information. The term "cognitive style" most frequently denotes consistencies in individual ways of functioning in a variety of behavioral situations. This psychological construct denotes a domain of observable behaviors. Such observability of behavior is one reason many researchers employ cognitive style to differentiate individuals in their modes of functioning, classifying them as having field dependent (global or undifferentiated) and field independent (analytic or differentiated) cognitive styles.

In the field dependent mode, individuals respond to the context as a whole. They react in an impulsive way without reflecting on and analyzing the situation. Field dependent persons tend to be sociable, are interested in people, exhibit a high reliance on the surrounding field, rely on authority, observe the faces of those around them for information, prefer to be with people, and experience their environment in a relatively global fashion by conforming to the effects of the prevailing field.

In the field independent mode, individuals separate the various components or features of circumstances from one another. They disregard any irrelevant characteristics in the situation, reflecting on the situation, analyzing it, and providing a conceptual response. Field independent persons tend to be analytic, autonomous, socially detached, removed, cold, distant, oriented toward active striving, and self-aware. They analyze and structure incoming information. Of course, these descriptions represent extremes; in reality, all individuals manifest some elements of both cognitive styles.

The modes of functioning in cognitive style are highly pervasive and consistent and are associated with educational factors. In tasks requiring incidental memory of social words (Fitzgibbons, Goldberger, & Eagle, 1965; Minard & Mooney, 1969) and the memory of faces (Messick & Damarin, 1964), field dependent subjects perform better than field independent subjects. In relation to school, field dependent students are favorably oriented to subject areas that relate most directly to people, such as the social sciences. Field independent students favor impersonal, abstract subjects such as mathematics and the physical sciences. Field dependent students learn better with material containing social content because they are attentive to social cues, which they utilize in learning (Witkin, 1974). They also rely on externally defined goals and reinforcements. Field independent students define their own goals and reinforcements, prefer impersonal and abstract material, and use mediators in learning as they abstract from their experiences. Field dependent teachers tend to make greater use of discussion and discovery strategies to enhance interpersonal relationships, whereas field independent teachers employ direct techniques that minimize interpersonal relationships, such as lecturing.

MEASURES

Field dependence/independence has been the most widely known and thoroughly researched dimension of cognitive style. Witkin and other experts in the area have developed reliable and valid instruments to assess cognitive styles. Saracho (1983a) describes the following measures as the most widely used:

Rod-and-Frame-Test (RFT)

The RFT is an apparatus with a luminous square that moves independently of a frame; both are pivoted at their centers to make the frame tilt to the left or to the right. Subjects are tested in a darkened room, where they are asked to adjust the rod to an upright position.

Tilting-Room Tilting Chair Test (TRTC)

The TRTC assesses an individual's visual and bodily perception in relation to the upright position. This apparatus conceives the body, rather than an external object, as the object to adjust. Subjects sit in a chair suspended into a small box-like room. The chair and room tilt clockwise or counterclockwise independently of each other. As subjects sit on the chair, the examiner tilts the chair and room. Subjects then are asked to adjust their body to an upright position.

Articulation of the Body-Concept Scale (ABC)

The ABC scale requires pictures of males and females to be drawn by the subject. The drawings are rated according to specified criteria to determine the subject's degree of field dependence or independence. A minimum of two judges independently rate each set of drawings.

Embedded Figures Test (EFT)

The EFT is a paper-and-pencil test that requires the subject to locate a simple figure within a complex figure. This standardized measure consists of a series of 24 complex figures.

These measures have been standardized, and their reliability has been widely investigated. Specifically, reliability for the various measures has been assessed as follows: the RFT ranges from .66 to .92 (Gardner, Jackson, & Messick, 1960); the TRTC ranges from .74 (Loeff, 1961) to .90 (Linton, 1952); the EFT ranges from .72 (Saracho, 1980) to .95 (Gardner et al., 1960); the Preschool EFT, a measure of cognitive style for young children, ranges from .74 to .91 (Coates, 1972); and the ABC Scale ranges from .72 to .92 (Saracho, 1982, 1983d).

Researchers have used all of these measures to study cognitive style. Witkin (1974) affirms that the different scores on these tests reflect the subjects' perceptual skills as well as their underlying thinking styles. Witkin, Goodenough, and Karp (1967) gathered substantial evidence to support a consistency of these measures when used with cross-sectional groups (ages 8 to 21). It is evident that consistency exists among groups and with respect to the relationship among the different instruments employed to study cognitive style. Therefore, researchers feel a high degree of confidence that cognitive style can be adequately assessed with the above-mentioned instruments.

Recently, another instrument assessing different dimensions of cognitive style has been developed. Thompson and Pitts (1981) have developed and validated the Children's Cognitive Style Assessment (CCSA) to measure several dimensions of cognitive style. They found this instrument reasonably valid, although the teachers who assessed the children's cognitive styles had difficulty distinguishing between two dimensions: breadth of categorization and field dependence/independence. However, the results strongly support the validity of the field dependence/independence dimension scale of the CCSA.

Measures of cognitive characteristics relating to intellectual abilities, information-processing skills, and subject-matter knowledge are necessary for evaluating educational theory and practice. Personality characteristics can also be classified as aptitude since they predict students' responses to instruction and the educational environment. Although some educators view personality characteristics as noncognitive, these characteristics do include cognitive attributes and can predict students' current and future achievement by providing information on learning ability (see Bloom, 1976; Cronbach & Snow, 1977; Linn & Swiney, 1981; Messick, 1982). Scores on cognitive measures also can be used to diagnose students' learning strengths and needs in order to plan their instructional programs (Messick, 1979).

COGNITIVE FLEXIBILITY

Some educators suggest that it is important not only to identify cognitive style but also to be able to modify it to help individuals employ the characteristics of both field dependence and field independence. Cognitive flexibility, the degree to which individuals are able to vary their information processing techniques in relation to specific activities, has been proposed as an educational goal by researchers (e.g., Battig, 1979; Davis & Cochran, 1982; Davis & Frank, 1979; MacLeod, 1979; Ramírez & Castañeda, 1974; Saracho & Spodek, 1981). However, it is uncertain whether such modification can be achieved.

Some researchers indicate that field independent persons have more flexibility in selecting effective strategies in a range of activities. Kogan (1971), for example, believes that field dependent individuals are more resistant to cognitive style modification than are field independent individuals. The difference between field dependent and field independent students could possibly relate to the wider range of alternative opportunities they receive, to their willingness to use a variety of techniques, and/or to their ability to become aware that a specific strategy is not effective. Information-processing systems may differ according to individuals' cognitive flexibility and depending on their ability to function using the characteristics of the cognitive style that is required for the particular task.

The issue of modifiability of cognitive style is important because of its implications for facilitating or stifling learning. It is possible for a specific style to be maladaptive in a particular instructional context but valuable in other contexts. For instance, a teacher may plan a mathematics lesson, considered to be a field independent activity, for a field dependent child. This child will have difficulty with formal instruction in mathematics and will probably learn the concept better through a social activity, such as dramatic play. In order for this child to be able to learn mathematics in an abstract mode, his or her cognitive style would need to be modified to ensure adequate functioning in a field independent way. On the other hand, the field independent child can easily perform cognitive problem-solving tasks but may be deficient in performing tasks involving social sensitivity, interpersonal harmony, and other important affective skills.

Kogan (1971) suggests a guiding question for those interested in modifying cognitive functioning: Will the change enhance the individual's cognitive flexibility? One desirable goal of such modification is to assist individuals to acquire the capacity to shift their cognitive approach based on changing task requirements. Individuals who have become "locked" into a customarily adaptive manner of cognition may find that their usual approach can be harmful when applied to certain tasks. In attempting to enhance anyone's cognitive flexibility, it is important to consider whether the modification will actually alter functioning in a way that will allow the individual to deliberately choose a style of cognition rather than be compelled to approach a given problem in a specific way. It is also important to consider whether, as a result of heredity, personal constitution, or early experiences, some styles are profoundly inherent in some persons and thus cannot be changed.

Ramírez and Castañeda (1974) have found that, depending on the activity, task, or specific atmosphere in which individuals are functioning, many adults and children manifest both field dependent and field independent cognitive styles, thus exhibiting "bicognitive development." In varying circumstances, individuals may cooperate or compete, solve problems using inductive or deductive reasoning, and react to or ignore the social milieu. These individuals possess a repertoire of techniques that may be employed in learning and problem-solving processes.

Further information has been provided by Saracho (1983b), who mapped children's cognitive styles to obtain profiles describing their thinking, learning, and performance. In brief, cognitive style mapping is a formalized set of self-descriptive statements. Based on the characteristics of field dependence and field independence and on descriptions included in the profiles, participating children were characterized according to cognitive style. The profiles suggested that subjects had characteristics of both cognitive styles. In analyzing the cognitive mapping, the investigator found that 5-year-olds relied on their own interpretation of symbols (a field independent characteristic). In addition, children inferred meaning by defining things in order to understand them (a field dependent characteristic), reasoned as they compared and contrasted characteristics or measurements (a field independent characteristic), and synthesized a number of dimensions or incidents into a unified meaning (a field independent characteristic). When children used cultural determinants to interpret symbols and their meaning, their own interpretations influenced their expression of symbol meaning (a field independent characteristic), but children were also influenced by members of their families or by close friends in their interpretations of the meanings of symbols (a field dependent characteristic).

Ramírez and Castañeda (1974) suggest that individuals can be taught to extend their repertoires beyond those characteristics and behaviors associated with their own cognitive styles. Experiences that match children's cognitive styles can be provided to make children feel comfortable and secure. Then teachers can gradually introduce activities that do not match the children's cognitive styles. A degree of such cognitive dissonance can assist children in making the transition. Saracho and Spodek (1981) suggest that field independent children can participate in activities such as chairing a committee or working with a group to make gifts for an ill classmate. Such activities require social sensitivity, a field dependent attribute. On the other hand, field dependent children can participate in activities that demand a field independent application of analytic skills, such as working alone to solve a problem relating to a building structure or mathematics task. In this way, individuals can respond more flexibly to a range of data sources in their interactions with ideas and people (Saracho & Spodek, 1981). Although both Ramírez and Castañeda (1974) and Saracho and Spodek (1981) suggest that persons can learn to function according to a cognitive style different from their preferred one, additional developmentally oriented research needs to be conducted on cognitive flexibility and on bicognitive development in individuals from different groups.

INTELLECTUAL FUNCTIONING

Studies in cognitive style (e.g., Coates, 1975; Goodenough & Karp, 1961; Linn & Kyllonen, 1981; Schimek, 1968; Sherman, 1967) have indicated a relationship between field dependence/independence and many other elements of intellectual functioning. Some research suggests that field dependent individuals may not perform as efficiently as field independent individuals on standardized intelligence tests. Conversely, a major concern in the testing for cognitive style is the impact that an individual's intelligence has on his or her performance on such tests. Some researchers (e.g., Bieri, Bradburn, & Galinsky, 1958; Spotts & Mackler, 1967) have found relationships between measures of intelligence and some tests of cognitive style. Goodenough and Karp (1961) have supported the hypotheses that some intellectual and perceptual tests have a common requirement for overcoming embedding contexts and that relationships obtained between field dependence/independence and standardized tests of intelligence are based on this common factor. Goodenough and Karp's (1961) study was part of a larger investigation conducted by Witkin et al. (1974), which found significant correlations between scores on field dependence/independence tests and on the Stanford-Binet and WISC tests of intelligence. However, Witkin et al. (1974) have denied the importance of intellectual factors in the field dependence/independence dimension. Rather, they suggest that parallels in the structure of subtests account for the significant relationships found between intelligence scores and perceptual scores of cognitive style and that, since the measures require the individual to overcome embedded contexts, these relationships should be anticipated.

Dubois and Cohen (1970) challenged the interpretation of Witkin et al. (1974) concerning the relationship between measures of field dependence/independence and intellectual functioning. The former investigators hypothesized that significant relationships can be found between measures of field dependence/independence and a number of measures of intellectual ability that do not require subjects to overcome embedded contexts. Their results indicate that the RFT may be less "contaminated" by intelligence than the EFT. All but two of these correlations (English/Art and Music) were low but statistically significant between field dependence/independence measures and past achievement measures, which ostensibly have little relationship to embedded contexts, spatial-perceptual skills, or nonverbal organization. All correlations were negative, and the correlations noted were similar to intercorrelations found among measures of intellectual achievement. Those who perceive field independence simply as a semi-specific factor of ability or intelligence may view such results as atypical; thus, it would seem that researchers who have found that field independent individuals also possess other ability and intelligence factors will probably not accept such results, regardless of the low correlations found.

Dubois and Cohen (1970) assume that field dependence/independence can be considered one factor of intelligence. If the acquired generality and stability of the external correlates of field dependence/independence assessments rely to some extent on their sizable correlations with indices of a more generalized intellectual ability, and if the intellectual factor is removed, field dependence/independence may not have enough power to generate differences on specific dimensions. Dubois and Cohen propose that researchers thoroughly investigate the relationship between ability measures and field dependent/independent measures.

Zigler (1963) and Vernon (1972) have assumed that knowledge of field dependence/independence is not enough to predict intelligence scores. Vernon has extensively reviewed the literature and has determined that the group paper-and-pencil tests of cognitive style fail to define a factor on intelligence tests.

Coates (1975) duplicated Goodenough and Karp's (1961) study with 4½-year-old children. The Preschool EFT loaded a common factor that also exists in the WPPSI Block Design and Geometric Design. This factor was concluded to be a perceptual analytic factor that Goodenough and Karp obtained with older children (ages 10 and 12).

Pedersen and Wender (1968) also examined field dependence/independence and personality in nursery school children between the ages of 2 and 6. Small and irregular correlations in the anticipated direction were found between four clusters and children's performance on the Preschool EFT, WISC performance (nonverbal), and Kagan's relational (but not analytic) scores.

LEARNING STYLES

Educators are continually examining ways to adapt instructional conditions and techniques to the characteristics of individual students. In making such adaptations, children's age, intelligence, and interests have been considered. Reiff (1982) concludes that academic performance can be enhanced by assessing the students' learning styles and planning, as well as by selecting appropriate materials and strategies.

Goodenough (1976) reviewed the literature on the relationship of field dependence/independence to learning and memory, concluding that field dependent and field independent individuals vary more consistently in the way they learn or memorize than they do in the effectiveness of either process. He proposed two hypotheses: (a) Field independent individuals are probably more advanced developmentally than field dependent individuals; and (b) assuming that field dependent and field independent individuals employ their cognitive processes differently, the efficiency of their performance will vary under some conditions.

Research on concept learning supports Goodenough's hypothesis that field dependent and field independent individuals utilize various learning processes without manifesting different performance; however, it has been found that field independent persons usually perform more efficiently. Since research indicates that cognitive style affects differences in cognitive activities, Hester and Tagatz (1971) concluded that cognitive style can be considered an inherent organismic variable. Therefore, field dependent and field independent cognitive styles are similar to conservative and commonality strategies regarding the degree of dependence on analysis in concept attainment tasks. Specifically, these researchers sought to determine which cognitive style would help students acquire concepts more effectively when they were instructed with techniques appropriate for their cognitive styles. Using a repeated measures design, they tested the relationships among the following variables: (a) cognitive style (analytic or global), (b) instruction (conservative or commonality), and (c) achievement on 10 concept attainment tasks. The investigators found that efficiency in concept attainment may depend on cognitive style. Field independent subjects psychologically grasped the nature of concept attainment tasks upon initial exposure to the tasks and determined the relevant elements within the stimulus field faster than did field dependent subjects. It was also found that individuals with a specific cognitive style attained concepts efficiently when they were taught with a solutional strategy appropriate to that style. Field independent individuals were able to perform effectively under either instructional treatment, whereas field dependent individuals performed as effectively as field independent subjects when instructed in a strategy consistent with their cognitive style. The learning performance of field dependent subjects decreased when they were taught with a technique inconsistent with their dominant cognitive style. All subjects received the same initial exposure to information processing.

Since both groups performed equally well with strategies devised for field dependent individuals, Hester and Tagatz (1971) concluded that, although initial exposure to information processing may be beneficial to subsequent performance on concept attainment tasks, more than exposure alone is needed to overcome the individual differences in cognitive functioning under different kinds of instructional techniques. Prior learning in concept attainment can influence cognitive style to facilitate learning; learning efficiency can be stifled if these requirements are not met. Field dependence/independence is a unique factor that affects a range of components integrated in learning and memory.

As noted earlier, Goodenough (1976) asserted that field dependent and field independent individuals differed more in their learning and memory processes than they did in how much they learned and remembered. Davis and Frank (1979) emphasized developmental differences between field dependent and field independent learners in the effectiveness of performance, noting that field independence increases with age (up to 16 years). Increase in field independence does not occur only as a result of experience but is to some extent a normal pattern of individual development. Specifically, these investigators found that memory performance (such as concept learning) of field dependent learners tends to be poorer than that of field independent learners if the task requires an increased amount of information to be processed in working memory. When interference occurs and when the information load is high, field independent students tend to be more effective than field dependent students in the recall of information stored in short-term memory. In contrast, if information is low and no interference occurs, field dependent and field independent students do not differ. The studies reviewed by these investigators suggest the need for further speculation and investigation of memory and developmental differences in field dependent and field independent learners.

Davis and Cochran (1982), in reviewing those research studies published after Goodenough's (1976) review, suggest that three stages of information processing characterize field dependent and field independent individuals. These stages include selective attention, encoding, and long-term memory processes.

Attention is an information processing paradigm including tasks of dichotic listening, signal detection, and visual search. The research studies reviewed by Davis and Cochran (1982) showed that field dependent persons have difficulty attending to relevant cues, especially when distracting cues are present.

Encoding has been related to attentional processes in tasks that require encoding specificity, digit span, and working memory tasks. Although field dependence is associated with differences in encoding processes, when a restricted amount of information is processed, few or no differences are found between field dependent and field independent students. In contrast, if a large degree of information is processed, field independent learners process information more effectively than do field dependent learners.

Long-term memory has been found in most recent research studies to relate to performance on associative learning and memory tasks, indicating that organizational processes affect memory differences in field dependent and field independent individuals. Field independent learners are better than field dependent individuals in selective attention, encoding, and long-term memory processes.

The stages described above indicate that there are differences in the information-processing attributes of field dependent and field independent persons. Davis and Cochran's (1982) review suggests that field independent persons are more effective than field dependent persons in concept attainment, selective attention, and long-term memory processes. The degree of field dependence/independence affects students' learning and techniques outcomes (e.g., field dependent students prefer material with social content, and field independent students prefer material with impersonal content). Thus, it is essential that students' cognitive styles be considered in planning educational programs.

TEACHING STYLES

The literature on teaching styles reflects findings varying to some degree. According to Saracho (1983c), several styles interact in educational settings, and a number of interactions between children and teachers take place in a classroom. Researchers have suggested matching achievement styles to instructional environments (Ross, 1980), matching students' cognitive responses to teaching skills (Winnie & Marx, 1980), and matching students' preferences to the teaching style (Reiff, 1982). Researchers usually examine teaching styles by exploring the teachers' and students' perceptions of each other. Witkin, Moore, Goodenough, and Cox (1977) reviewed the relationship of teaching style to teachers' cognitive style. Field dependent teachers favored a warm and personal learning milieu and involved students in establishing goals and guiding their learning. Conversely, field independent teachers strived to express the cognitive aspects of teaching and preferred to organize and direct the learning. While field dependent teachers tend to employ discussion methods, field independent teachers use more lecture methods. Wu (1968) supports the idea that field dependent teachers favor greater interaction with their students, whereas field independent teachers favor teaching situations that are impersonal in nature and oriented toward more abstract cognitive aspects of instruction.

In a study by Moore (1973), field dependent teachers employed questions primarily in evaluating pupils' learning and after the instructional phase was finished. Emmerich, Oltman, and McDonald (cited in Witkin et al., 1977) concluded that field dependent teachers favored class discussion over teacher lectures as a technique to enhance pupils' learning. In addition, as compared with field independent teachers, field dependent teachers more greatly favored high student involvement in structuring the learning activity as a teaching strategy. Field independent teachers employed questions as instructional tools more frequently than did field dependent teachers as they introduced new units and responded to students' answers. Reinforcement also varied based on the teachers' cognitive style. Field independent teachers were found to more greatly favor feedback indicating errors (negative assessment) and explaining the underlying error to promote learning.

Ekstrom (1976) examined the relationship between certain cognitive and attitudinal characteristics and the instructional mode of elementary school teachers. At both second- and fifth-grade levels, few of the teacher scores indicated a consistent relationship to any teaching behavior exhibited in either reading or mathematics instruction. Field dependent teachers were more concerned with behavioral control in the classroom than were field independent teachers. In addition, field dependent and field independent teachers viewed the requirements for the grades and subject areas differently. Teachers did not perceive training as a homogeneous task but chose different teaching styles based on their perceptions of the demands of the instructional task. Cognitive flexibility in teachers permits them to employ several organizational techniques (such as using aides, various groupings, etc.) to provide individual instruction.

Mahlios (1981) found that approaches used in classroom teaching relate to teachers' cognitive styles, although observations of teachers' approaches did not indicate the way teachers differ in meeting students' learning styles. Specifically, Mahlios investigated the differences in teaching preferences and instructional approaches between field dependent and field independent teachers observed under special research conditions, attempting to determine whether such differences are representative of cognitive style differences in actual classroom teaching. He examined (a) the frequency and context of instruction (whole groups versus small groups and individual students), (b) the function of questions teachers ask children, and (c) the frequency and kind of corrective feedback teachers use. Field dependent teachers interacted significantly more often with their pupils in small groups and individually, whereas field independent teachers initiated a significantly greater number of academic interactions with their pupils as a whole class.

Mahlios (1981) also found that field dependent teachers asked more factual questions, whereas field independent teachers asked more analytical questions. In addition, field independent teachers asked more academic questions than did their field dependent peers. Thus, field dependent teachers preferred to encourage pupils to apply principles. Field independent teachers also yielded more corrective feedback statements after pupils' failures and conceptually elaborated and extended their feedback after pupils' successful statements. Apparently, field dependent and field independent teachers vary in their academic interactions, in the context of their interactions with pupils, in the conceptual level of instructional activity, and in the type of feedback they give their students.

Coward, Davis, and Wichern (1978) investigated the variation of eleventh- and twelfth-grade students' perceptions of the "ideal" teacher. They examined the perceptions of field dependent and field independent pupils to determine whether these perceptions systematically reflect a preference for task-oriented or socially-oriented teacher characteristics. Students ranked five characteristics indicating a more social orientation to teaching and five other characteristics reflecting a greater task orientation to teaching. The more field independent students ranked three of the teacher characteristics in a way significantly different from that of their field dependent peers, ranking the trait "conducts informative lectures" highest. In comparison, field dependent students gave the highest rankings to two of the task-oriented traits ("well organized" and "clearly explains directions for assignments"). Coward et al. suggest that field dependent pupils who valued task-oriented teacher characteristics more highly than did field independent pupils may have been expressing a need for teachers who exhibit the characteristics they themselves lack.

Packer and Bain (1978) found that students' assessments of teachers were affected by the teachers' cognitive styles, with the more field dependent teachers receiving a greater number of positive ratings than the more field independent teachers. They found that, for field dependent pupils, field dependent teachers were superior to field independent teachers; likewise, for field independent students, field independent teachers were superior. Saracho and Spodek (1981) suggest that field independent students might best be assigned to field independent teachers. However, their data differ from Packer and Bain's in relation to the other assignments. They suggest, based on rankings of achievement scores, that for optimal academic success, placements might be prioritized as indicated in Figure 1. Frank and Davis (1982) suggest an assignment similar to Saracho and Spodek's (1981). The former researchers examined 64 dyads of students either matched or mismatched on field dependence/independence to see if they differed from each other regarding the effectiveness of their performance. They found that matched dyads with field independent students performed significantly better than matched dyads with field dependent students, with the mismatched dyads falling in between. Therefore, field independent students perform better than do field dependent students when placed with field dependent teachers.

In examining second- and fifth-grade teachers' perceptions of students based on cognitive style, Saracho (1980) found that field dependent teachers make more negative assessments than field independent teachers when evaluating field independent students, whereas field independent teachers make more positive assessments of field dependent students than do field dependent teachers. Saracho and Dayton (1980) found that field independent students assigned to field independent teachers achieved greater gains on a standardized achievement test than did field independent students with field dependent teachers.

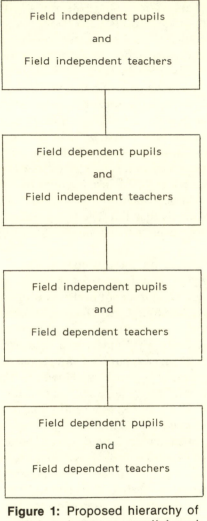

Figure 1: Proposed hierarchy of matches between pupils' and teachers' cognitive styles.

In a recent study with first- and third-grade children, Saracho (1983d) found significant relationships among cognitive style, sex, and age. With first-grade children, both field dependent and field independent teachers underestimated field dependent and field independent students; with third-grade children, field dependent teachers overestimated field dependent and field independent students. Field independent teachers' assessments of field dependent and field independent students' performances were similar to the children's scores on a standardized achievement test. Specifically, Saracho (1982) reported the following in relation to test scores:

1. Field dependent teachers underestimated their field dependent male and female students but underestimated their field dependent male students more.
2. Field dependent teachers overestimated their field independent female students but underestimated their field independent male students more than they underestimated their field dependent male and female students.
3. Field dependent teachers assessed their field independent female students' performance to be similar to that measured on the test.
4. Field independent teachers underestimated their field independent male students.
5. Field independent teachers overestimated their field dependent male students and underestimated their field dependent female students.

The inconsistency of these results with those of other studies suggests that relationships may be complex and that further research, studying a large number of factors and using different methodologies, needs to be conducted in this area.

The area of teachers' cognitive styles and instruction and the relationship of teachers' cognitive styles to students' characteristics and learning styles has not been greatly studied, yet it seems plausible to suggest that methods of instruction are related to students' cognitive styles. Field dependent students may learn more from a didactic mode of teaching in which rules and principles are explicitly stated instead of induced. However, educators may optimize the learning of subject matter at the price of never providing field dependent students with the opportunity to make a discovery during their school career. Educators cannot afford an exclusive preoccupation with mastery of subject matter; they need to consider the students' individual modes of thinking as well.

Much research still needs to be conducted, but the work already completed and in progress suggests that greater attention to variability in the cognitive styles of learners can help educators provide a better match between educational resources and the ability of students to utilize these resources. Thus, by responding more broadly to individual differences among children, educators can provide greater equality of educational opportunity to all.

REFERENCES

Battig, W.F. (1979). Are the important "individual differences" between or within individuals? *Journal of Research in Personality, 13,* 546–558.

Bieri, J., Bradburn, W.M., & Galinsky, M.D. (1958). Sex differences in perceptual behavior. *Journal of Personality, 26,* 1–12.

Bloom, B.S. (1976). *Human characteristics and school learning.* New York: McGraw-Hill.

Coates, S. (1972). *Preschool Embedded Figures Test.* Palo Alto, CA: Consulting Psychologists Press.

Coates, S. (1975). Field independence and intellectual functioning in preschool children. *Perceptual and Motor Skills, 41,* 251–254.

Coward, R.T., Davis, J.K., & Wichern, R.L. (1978). Cognitive style and perceptions of the ideal teacher. *Contemporary Educational Psychology, 3*(3), 232–238.

Cronbach, L.J., & Snow, R.E. (1977). *Aptitudes and instructional methods: A handbook for research on interaction.* New York: Irvington.

Davis, J.K., & Cochran, K.F. (1982, March). Toward an information processing analysis of field independence. In R.E. Schutz (Chair), *Trends in cognitive style research: Directions and dilemmas.* Symposium conducted at the meeting of the American Educational Research Association, New York.

Davis, J.K., & Frank, B.M. (1979). Learning and memory of field independent-dependent individuals. *Journal of Research in Personality, 13,* 469–479.

Dubois, T.E., & Cohen, W. (1970). Relationship between measures of psychological and intellectual ability. *Perceptual and Motor Skills, 31,* 411–416.

Ekstrom, R.B. (1976). Teacher aptitudes, knowledge, attitudes and cognitive style as predictors of teacher behavior. *Journal of Teacher Education, 27*(4), 329–331.

Fitzgibbons, D., Goldberger, L., & Eagle, M. (1965). Field dependence and memory for incidental material. *Perceptual and Motor Skills, 21,* 743–749.

Frank, B.M., & Davis, J.K. (1982). Effect of field-independence match or mismatch on a communication task. *Journal of Educational Psychology, 74,* 23–31.

Gardner, R.W., Jackson, D.N., & Messick, S.J. (1960). Personality organization in cognitive controls and intellectual abilities. *Psychological Issues, 2*(4, Serial No. 8).

Goodenough, D.R. (1976). The role of individual differences in field dependence as a factor in learning and memory. *Psychological Bulletin, 83,* 675–794.

Goodenough, D.R., & Karp, S.A. (1961). Field dependence and intellectual functioning. *Journal of Abnormal and Social Psychology, 63*(2), 241–246.

Hester, F.M.., & Tagatz, G.E. (1971). The effects of cognitive style and instructional strategy on concept attainment. *The Journal of Genetic Psychology, 85*(2), 229–237.

Kogan, N. (1971). Educational implications of cognitive styles. In G.S. Lesser (Ed.), *Psychology and educational practice* (pp. 242–292). Glenview, IL: Scott, Foresman.

Linn, M.C., & Kyllonen, P. (1981). The field dependence-independence construct. *Journal of Educational Psychology, 73*(2), 261–273.

Linn, M.C., & Swiney, J.F. (1981). Individual differences in formal thought: Role expectations and aptitudes. *Journal of Educational Psychology, 73*(2), 274–286.

Linton, H.B. (1952). *Relationships between mode of perception and tendency to conform.* Unpubliished doctoral dissertation, Yale University, New Haven, CT.

Loeff, R.G. (1961). *Embedding and distracting field contexts as related to the field dependence dimension.* Unpublished master's thesis, Brooklyn College, Brooklyn, NY.

MacLeod, C.M. (1979). Individual differences in learning and memory: A unitary information processing approach. *Journal of Research in Personality, 13,* 530–545.

Mahlios, M.C. (1981). Instructional design and cognitive styles of teachers in elementary schools. *Perceptual and Motor Skills, 52,* 335–338.

Messick, S. (1979). Potential uses of noncognitive measurement in education. *Journal of Educational Psychology, 71*(3), 281–292.

Messick, S. (1982). *Cognitive styles in educational practice* (Research Bulletin No. RR-8). Princeton, NJ: Educational Testing Service.

Messick, S., & Damarin, F. (1964). Cognitive styles and memory for faces. *Journal of Abnormal and Social Psychology, 69,* 313–318.

Minard, J.C., & Mooney, W. (1969). Psychological differentiation and perceptual defense: Studies of the separation of perception from emotion. *Journal of Abnormal Psychology, 74,* 131–139.

Moore, C.A. (1973). Styles of teacher behavior under simulated teaching conditions. *Dissertation Abstracts International, 34,* 3149A–3150A. (University Microfilms No. 73-30, 449)

Oltman, P.K., Goodenough, D.R., Witkin, H.A., & Friedman, F. (1975). Psychological differentiation as a factor in conflict resolution. *Journal of Personality and Social Psychology, 32,* 730–736.

Packer, J., & Bain, J.D. (1978). Cognitive style and teacher-student compatability. *Journal of Educational Psychology, 70*(5), 864–871.

Pedersen, F.A., & Wender, P.H. (1968). Early social correlates of cognitive functioning in six-year-old boys. *Child Development, 39,* 185–193.

Ramírez, M. III, & Castañeda, A. (1974). *Cultural democracy, bicognitive development, and education.* New York: Academic Press.

Reiff, J. (1982, April). *Identifying learning preferences of young children.* Paper presented at the meeting of the Association for Childhood Education International Conference, Atlanta, GA.

Ross, H.G. (1980). Matching achievement styles and instructional environments. *Contemporary Educational Psychology, 5*(3), 216–226.

Saracho, O.N. (1980). The relationship between teachers' cognitive styles and their perceptions of their students' academic achievement. *Educational Research Quarterly, 5,* 40–49.

Saracho, O.N. (1982, March). *The cognitive style of teachers and their perceptions of their matched and mismatched children's academic competence.* Paper presented at the annual meeting of the American Educational Research Association, New York.

Saracho, O.N. (1983a). Assessing individual differences in young children. *Studies in Educational Evaluation, 8,* 229–236.

Saracho, O.N. (1983b). Cognitive style and Mexican American children's perceptions of reading. In T.H. Escobedo (Ed.), *Early childhood education: A bilingual perspective* (pp. 201–221). New York: Teachers' College Press.

Saracho, O.N. (1983c). Cultural differencces in the cognitive style of Mexican American students. *Journal of the Association for the Study of Perception, 18*(1), 3–10.

Saracho, O.N., & Dayton, C.M. (1980). Relationship of teachers' cognitive styles to pupils' academic achievement gains. *Journal of Educational Psychology, 72,* 544–547.

Saracho, O.N., & Spodek, B. (1981). Teachers' cognitive styles and their educational implications. *Educational Forum, 45,* 153–159.

Schimek, J.G. (1968). Cognitive style and defenses: A longitudinal study of intellectualization and field independence. *Journal of Abnormal Psychology, 73*(6), 575–580.

Sherman, J.A. (1967). Problem of sex differences in space perception and aspects of intellectual functioning. *Psychological Review, 74*(4), 290–299.

Spotts, J.W., & Mackler, B. (1967). Relationship of field-dependent and field independent cognitive styles to creative test performance. *Perceptual and Motor Skills, 24,* 239–268.

Thompson, B., & Pitts, M.C. (1981). Validity of teachers' perceptions of children's cognitive styles. *Measurement and Evaluation, 14*(2), 90–95.

Vernon, P.E. (1972). The distinctiveness of field-independence. *Journal of Personality, 40,* 366–391.

Wallach, M.A. (1962). Commentary: Active-analytical vs. passive-global cognitive functioning. In S. Messick and J. Ross (Eds.), *Measurement in personality and cognition* (pp. 199–215). New York: Wiley.

Winnie, P.H., & Marx, R.W. (1980). Matching students' cognitive styles to teaching skills. *Jour-*

nal of Educational Psychology, 72(2), 257–264.

Witkin, H.A. (1974). Cognitive style perspective on evaluation and guidance. In *Proceedings of the 1973 Invitational Conference on Testing Problems — Measurement for self-understanding and personal development,* (pp. 21–27). Princeton, NJ: Educational Testing Service.

Witkin, H.A., Dyk, R.B., Faterson, H.F., Goodenough, D.R., & Karp, S.A. (1974). *Psychological differentiation.* Potomac, MD: Erlbaum. (Original work published 1962)

Witkin, H.A., Goodenough, D.R., & Karp, S.A. (1967). Stability of cognitive styles from childhood to young adulthood. *Journal of Personality and Social Psychology, 7,* 291–300.

Witkin, H.A., Hertzman, M., Machover, K., Meissner, P.B., & Wapner, S. (1972). *Personality through perception.* Westport, CT: Greenwood Press. (Original work published 1954)

Witkin, H.A., Moore, C.A., Goodenough, D.R., & Cox, P.W. (1977). Field-dependent and field-independent cognitive styles and their educational implications. *Review of Educational Research, 47,* 1–64.

Wu, J.J. (1968). Cognitive style and task performance — a study of student teachers. *Dissertation Abstracts International, 29,* 176A. (University Microfilms No. 68–7408)

Zigler, E. (1963). A measure in search of theory. *Contemporary Psychology, 8,* 133–135.

8

Montessori and Regular Preschools: A Comparison

J.A. Simons

Institute of Early Childhood Studies
Sydney, Australia

F.A. Simons

Labor Council of New South Wales
Sydney, Australia

INTRODUCTION

The revival of interest in Montessori education began in the 1960s and 1970s and continues in the 1980s. The expectation that children at Montessori schools would master academic skills at an earlier age, that they would learn independence and persistence, and that they would experience a disciplined learning environment, has led many teachers and parents to favor the Montessori approach to preschool education. Interest in regular preschools has also continued at a high level, with parents and teachers expecting that children would develop social skills, language skills, creativity, and preparedness for grade school from their preschool experiences.

In this discussion, "regular preschools" are taken to be those that are non-Montessorian and that take an eclectic approach to the education of young children. The term does not apply to specific programs, such as the Bereiter–Englemann Direct Instruction Program, but does encompass programs subscribing to cognitive enrichment and social-emotional goals, such as those found in nursery schools and many Head Start programs in the United States, and those found in most early childhood centers in Australia. An eclectic program may, of course, include practices that evolved from Montessori's contribution to early childhood education. Reviewing the Perry Preschool Program, Schweinhart and Weikart (1980) stated that preschool provides "a social and emotional adaptation as well as an academic and cognitive headstart" (p. 66). This statement characterizes the modern eclectic preschool, which will be referred to as the regular preschool throughout this discussion.

Parents, teachers, and other educators are interested in the Montessori debate. Are experiences provided at Montessori preschools better than those provided at regular preschools? Is the method of education advocated by Montessori in the early part of this century a better way to teach today's young children than the approaches advocated by more recent theorists and educators? This discussion seeks to compare the Montessori approach and the regular nursery school approach to preschool education. The comparison involves an investigation into general education objectives, the curriculum, children's activities, instructional approaches, and the teacher's role. Material for this comparison has been drawn from the literature (Koche, 1973; Montessori, 1914, 1964; Orem, 1974; Simons, 1980; Ward, 1913), from the authors' observations of Montessori and regular preschools in America and Australia, and from experience in early childhood teacher education in Australia. While there is some research on the performance of children in Montessori and regular preschools, there has been little documentation (other than from exponents of Montessori education) about the way Montessori education is implemented or about how this approach differs from regular preschool education.

The preparation of early childhood teachers for Montessori and for regular preschool will also be compared and discussed in relation to advances in knowledge of child development and modern educational theory and practice. Recent research is reviewed for comparisons of educational outcomes of Montessori and regular preschool education. The discussion will conclude with an evaluation of the relevance and usefulness of the Montessori approach within the field of preschool education and teacher education today.

THE SCHOOL CURRICULUM

The curriculum in preschool education is taken to mean the total of all activities and experiences that impinge upon children in relation to their enrollment in a preschool service. Therefore, discussed in this section will be general activities (structured and unstructured in classroom and playground), as well as activities related to subject disciplines (language, math, and music). The variety of instructional approaches and settings employed by teachers, the degree of parental involvement, grouping for instruction, approaches to discipline, and other teacher behaviors are each considered as components of the curriculum. Examination of the curriculum begins with a summary of the broad educational objectives of Montessori and regular preschools.

Objectives

Both Montessori and regular preschools seek to maximize young children's learning potential by laying the foundations for subsequent learning and social adjustment. However, they differ in the emphasis they give to the importance of various aspects of social, emotional, cognitive, physical, and moral/ethical/religious development.

Comparison of Objectives.   The objectives of the regular or "traditional" preschool have been summarized by Pitcher (1966). She writes:

> We want to have children get to know everyday phenomena in many firsthand, sensory ways, to question thoughtfully and think for themselves. They need to enjoy the satisfactions of problem solving and learning skills, lest they stop seeking. They also need to express their feelings and sense of self through dramatic play, dance, graphic art, literature. We want to help children to begin to symbolize ideas with pictures and signs as well as with spoken words. We want to cultivate in them a delight in language used playfully and imaginatively, in ways other than just labeling or demanding. We want them to have fun as they play, since play is a young child's natural way of working. (p. 491)

Such a summary of educational objectives may be contrasted with this recent statement issued by the American Montessori Institute — an affiliate of the Association Montessori Internationale (AMI) — in which a narrower range of objectives is presented:

> Dr. Montessori recognized that the only valid impulse to learning is the self motivation of the child. The director/directress prepares the environment, programmes the activity, functions as the reference person and exemplar, offers the child stimulations; but it is the child who learns, who is motivated through the work itself to persist in his or her chosen task. If the Montessori child is free to learn, it is because he has acquired from his exposure to both physical and mental order, an "inner discipline." This is the core of Dr. Montessori's educational philosophy. (Montessori Institute of Los Angeles, Inc., n.d.)

Montessori developed her educational theories by working first in the area of special education.[1] She demonstrated that, by good teaching, so-called idiot children could learn to read and write (Edmonson, 1966). Specifically, Montessori used three educational strategies to promote her pupils' learning achievement. The first was the use of structured material. Developing with great insight and intelligence the work of Itard and Séguin, she devised a didactic apparatus that was intrinsically motivating to young children, graded, and in many cases, self-correcting. She recognized that a great deal of sensory experience with concrete materials was a necessary prerequisite to

---

[1] For expansion on this subject, see Montessori (1914), and Phillips (1977), a discussion of Montessori's ideas, philosophical and pedagogical, from a historical perspective.

later academic learning. This method of assisting the child's learning has been fully accepted and incorporated in regular preschool practice.

The second strategy was the creation of a literate and numerate classroom environment. The mathematical and language-based activities available to the children encouraged them to take the initiative in exploring literacy and numeracy. This approach is used by preschool teachers today.

Her third strategy was to individualize instruction. Montessori was a brilliant analytical teacher and an acute observer of young children. She was one of the originators of the study of child development; today, preschool teachers reflect her influence when they use an individualized approach to young children's learning and employ individual development records as a basis for planning.

Montessori formulated many forward-looking educational objectives, one of the most important being the "liberty of the child" in the learning environment. In this, she was a great innovator, as Italian schools and indeed all schools at the turn of the century were formal, authoritarian, and prescriptive. On a visit to America in 1913, she lectured to vast audiences on the subject of children as eager learners who would take the initiative to learn if given an appropriate learning environment (Kornegay, 1981). Within the limits of materials available in the classroom, Montessori offered the child the opportunity to select learning tasks. This practice, a great innovation in its time, has been accepted in regular preschool practice today. Montessori believed that education should develop in children the personal characteristics of self-discipline, persistence, respect for the rights of others, self-confidence, and morality. It is probably true to say that most of these outcomes would also be sought by regular preschool teachers, and it is not in these general objectives that Montesorri and regular preschool educators differ. However, some educational objectives considered important today were not stressed by Montessori. While Montessori did not ignore physical development, social development, and creativity, she did give them a lower priority.

Physical development. By allowing children to move about freely within the classroom, Montessori offered more opportunity for physical activity than did the schools of her day. She advocated a daily period of gymnastics and used lines painted on the floor of the classroom for children to practice balanced walking, as on a tightrope, without the danger of falling. She recommended that a "gate" frame that children could hang from to strengthen their arms be positioned unobtrusively in the garden (Montessori, 1914). It may be conjectured that she would approve of the playground and indoor apparatus provided today in most regular preschools to stimulate gross motor activity and to help develop gross motor skills. However, Montessori preschools today, as observed by one of the present authors in both Australia and the United States, tend to have little apparatus for the development of motor skills.

Social development.   Social development could occur more easily in a Montessori school than in an Italian school of the 1900s simply because in the former, children were free to move about and interact during the course of the school day. Nowadays, regular preschools make explicit provision for social development by drawing children's attention to the need for care and consideration in social relationships with children and adults. In the Montessori preschool today, the teacher is expected to exhibit polite and considerate behavior in her relationships with children and adults. It is expected that children will copy such behavior. To the observer, the teacher's actions may often seem stilted.

Creativity.   Creativity (as expressed through fantasy and fairy tales, dramatic play, creative dance, and drama) had, and continues to have, little place in Montessori schools. A contemporary Montessori educator comments, "Montessori realized that a reality-bound school situation may prove more beneficial to the child in order to release his creative forces at a time when he is incapable of distinguishing fact from fantasy" (Rambusch, 1962, p. 93). This "realization" of Montessori's has not been validated by modern psychologists and educators, and the regular preschool curriculum includes many opportunities for the child to engage in dramatic play (in which the child takes a variety of social roles) and free play (in which the child uses certain objects symbolically or uses imaginary props for the play situation). Smilansky (1968) was the first of many to validate empirically the claim that dramatic fantasy play can enhance children's cognitive development. Elkind (1983), after discussing the value of play in children's cognitive and emotional development, has argued that it is time for Montessori educators to reevaluate their attitude toward such play in the education of young children. While Montessori failed to observe the learning potential in dramatic and symbolic play, she did understand that the aspect of fantasy represented in many of the rather macabre traditional fairy tales was inappropriate for very young children. Many modern educators would agree with her.

After reading the George (1912) translation of *The Montessori Method*, Simpson (1912), an Australian kindergarten teacher, made an interesting comparison between Montessori and regular preschool education in the early 1900s: "Dr. Montessori does not recognise the value of literature (myth, fairy tale, nursery rhyme, etc.) in the education of little children. The whole appeal of her educational method appears to be to the senses and intellect — imagination, sentiment and emotion are left out" (p. 7). This comment also characterizes the Montessori classroom today.

In short, the regular preschool has assimilated and incorporated many of the revolutionary educational goals of Montessori in such areas as freedom of choice of activity and physical expression. The regular preschool educator refers to modern developmental psychology for insight into the way children think and learn. The regular preschool curriculum includes further educational goals in the areas of social, emotional, and physical development. These goals are implemented through play, the encouragement of creativity, and the use of language.

To the extent, then, that present-day Montessori schools adhere to the original Montessori educational objectives, they may be inadequate learning environments for today's young children. This assertion will be elaborated in the following discussion.

Activities

Montessori centered the children's activities around learning domestic competencies, engaging in sensory discrimination, and mastering fine motor skills. These activities are the vehicle for a large part of the present-day Montessori curriculum. In a regular preschool, the range of activities is wider, including gross motor skills and indoor and outdoor play. The teacher encourages and stimulates these activities, frequently joining in the play.

Berk (1976) studied the activities undertaken by children in laboratory/demonstration schools which were regular preschools and in Montessori schools. Although the activities in Montessori schools were selected by children rather than their teachers, these activities realized teachers' goals, according to Berk. She found that children engaged in observably different activities according to the school program, attributing this phenomenon to the "well-defined philosophies and clear curricular rationales" (p. 80) of these two types of school program.

Of course, all teachers make activities available to their preschool classes. The Montessori activities are to be undertaken according to rules of procedure demonstrated by the teacher. Activities in the regular classroom may, in general, be undertaken by the child in any way he or she wishes.

Domestic competencies. In a Montessori school, activities to encourage domestic competencies are called "practical life" activities. These activities are offered to the child in order to increase his or her competence in the business of daily life. Practical life activities include sweeping, mopping, dusting, cleaning mirrors, polishing furniture or metal objects, pouring, spooning, measuring, buttoning, lacing, tying bows, and caring for plants and animals. Howells (1977) describes such activities in a Montessori school in Rome. As in Montessori's day, the children she observed were engaged in a variety of bona fide practical tasks. In the original Montessori schools, children performed all the necessary housekeeping tasks — sweeping, dusting, tidying, setting tables for meals, waiting at tables, clearing away afterward, and so forth. However, many modern Montessori preschools have attenuated these functions: The child is offered a toy broom with which to "sweep" the floor, while the teacher does the real sweeping up at the end of a session after the children have departed (Simons, 1980). This procedure directly contradicts Montessori's intention that the child, at an early age, become truly independent and competent in housekeeping and in personal management skills and suggests a conceptual confusion about the nature and role of these activities.

Many Montessori teachers nowadays feel free to devise additional practical life activities. Accordingly, children may be seen engaged in such activities as transferring liquid from one container to another by means of a small sponge or an eyedropper or transferring objects (dried beans or marbles) from one container to another by means of tweezers or sugar tongs. Such activities as these clearly do not occur in daily life, and any intrinsic value in such activities would be by way of fine motor skill development. However, ample opportunity for fine motor development is found in both regular preschool and Montessori classrooms, and it is suggestive of a conceptual woolliness that such activities are presented in Montessori preschools under the guise of practical life activities.

In regular preschools, a variety of "practical life" activities are usually undertaken by children as and when the actual need arises — sweeping the classroom floor at the end of a session, sweeping the surroundings of the sandbox, mopping up a spilled bucket of water or a paint-splashed floor, dusting the playhouse, picking up and laying out mats. Buttoning and bow tying are encouraged in the context of putting on and taking off clothes. In many centers, cooking and food preparation are regular events.

Sensory experiences. In a Montessori school, sensory experiences are gained by working with designated "sensorial" materials. Examples of Montessori sensorial materials are baric tablets, broad stair (a set of rectangular prisms graduated by size and mass), pink tower (a set of cubes graduated by size and mass to be assembled vertically), rough and smooth tablets, smelling bottles, and sound boxes. In a regular preschool, these materials would be categorized as discrimination aids — visual, auditory, tactile, olfactory. Some of these materials, as developed by Montessori, would be found in regular preschool classrooms today. In addition, variations, elaborations, and extensions of exercises in discrimination, often teacher-made (Farrow & Hill, 1975), would be found in regular preschools and in some present Montessori preschools, but in the more traditional Montessori preschools, no additional sensorial materials would be provided. Gitter (1970) gives precise directions for introducing sensorial materials to children.

The regular preschool teacher feels it necessary to offer discrimination materials that respond to pupils' interests and levels of understanding and that present the concepts in novel and attractive ways to lead the child to interact with the materials. In addition, the regular preschool teacher looks for opportunities to develop sensory awareness through the use of day-to-day occurrences involving environmental sounds, sights, and textures.[2] Montessori planned her materials to be attractive to children, and thus intrinsically motivating, but the pupils at the first Montessori schools (in the slums of Milan in the early 1900s) and the children of today (when even the majority of households below the poverty line have television sets) are not comparable populations. One of the present authors has observed that in most Montessori schools, the sensory materials available seem somewhat neglected by children, presumably because they are not now intrinsically interesting or are of limited interest.

Fine motor skills.   As mentioned earlier, both Montessori and regular preschool classrooms are rich in a supply of activities to promote the development of fine motor skills in children. One obvious observable difference is that the regular preschool tends to be stocked with a wider variety of materials — puzzles, games, toys, and constructional kits, either bought or teacher-made.

Gross motor skills.   The development of gross motor skills is relatively neglected in many of today's Montessori schools. On the basis of the present authors' observations, the teacher's daily program rarely makes provision for the acquisition of such skills. By contrast, teachers in regular preschools program for gross motor developmental activities and tend to keep developmental records that include the dimension of gross motor skills.

Play.   The opportunity for and encouragement of dramatic and symbolic play forms an important part of the activity of a regular preschool. However, as discussed earlier, Montessori saw little value in free, creative play. Consequently, these types of play are not generally permitted in a Montessori school. The regular preschool teacher provides suitable properties — clothing, hats, fabric, sand, boxes, water, tools, toys, models of real-life objects or the objects themselves (e.g., telephones or toy farmyard animals), blocks, and waste materials — with which children are encouraged to play. There is no set way for using these materials, and children are free to combine them as they desire or as their play requires. Children may thus build a house with empty cartons or blocks, dress up as a family, live in the

---

[2] See, for example, Almy (1975), *The Early Childhood Educator at Work,* pp. 22–26. Almy points out that the thrust of the regular early childhood educator's strategy is to respond flexibly — in terms of materials used and strategies employed — to children's interests.

house, and bring into it those objects they need to further their play. They may transform their house into a fire station or supermarket, and the teacher will help and encourage them, especially by stimulating language and thinking as problems arise.

Subject Disciplines

The curricula of regular and Montessori preschools are commonly planned to include activities within the following subject disciplines: language and literature, music, science, social studies, and mathematics. Montessori and regular preschool curricula differ in the amount of time allocated to these disciplines and in the way in which they are taught.

Language and literature. Montessori largely ruled out the use of language as the medium of instruction: "With normal children, the Montessori teacher limits her verbal contacts to a considerable extent. Deprived children will need more structured language lessons" (Pinho, 1967, p. 143). Montesori emphasized the role of didactic equipment over the role of language. The teacher was exhorted to silence whenever possible and instructed to use the fewest words that would serve on any particular occasion. Montessori was doubtless reacting to the classroom situation of her day, in which the teacher talked and the children did not. By requiring her teachers to talk little, she allowed the children to take the initiative. To this extent, she did in fact introduce child language into the classroom. However, the child's language development was not specifically encouraged and facilitated as it is in the modern regular preschool. Teachers in the modern Montessori classroom are still enjoined to use as few words as possible. As Edmonson (1966) observed of the Montessori teacher, "Her task is not to talk but to arrange a series of 'motives' in a special environment" (p. 72).

With respect to literacy education, Montessori was extremely innovative, creating materials that could assist children to teach themselves to read and write. Children also become facilitators for one another in the Montessori classroom where there is a mixed-age group (typically between 2½ or 3 to 6 years). Some Montessori literacy materials are used in the regular preschool, but these form only a small part of the total set of literacy materials and facilities available to the modern preschool child. Literacy materials available in the modern setting include an abundance of inexpensive and attractive picture and storybooks and a variety of audiovisual aids, including films, videotapes, slides, and audiotapes to accompany written materials. The Montessori literacy materials look unstimulating and limited by comparison. Elkind (1983) points out that Montessori's approach to reading instruction is based on identity decoding, appropriate for learning to read Italian, rather than on the equivalence decoding appropriate for learning to read English.

Once children have made a start in learning to read, Montessori schools introduce grammar, sentence structure, and formal composition along the lines laid down by Montessori. This part of the curriculum appears most inappropriate for schools of today, where language and literacy teaching reflect the principles of functional linguistics.

The regular preschool teacher accepts the view that mastery of one's language promotes cognitive growth and academic achievement. Thus, the teacher has a responsibility for initiating activities that directly contribute to children's language development. Examples of the way the regular teacher promotes such an environment include establishing the classroom as a literate environment, presenting children's literature, encouraging children to verbalize and record their activities, introducing new vocabulary (especially through social studies and mathematics), encouraging children to speak freely in the classroom and the playground, and promoting the daily use and enjoyment of books. Such a concentration of situational language is absent from a typical Montessori classroom. The present authors have observed that, in most, the use of books is not fostered and the library collection tends to be small. Children are usually not read to daily. As Evans (1975) has concluded, "Montessori's position on language development is not sufficiently comprehensive to satisfy modern criteria for a theory of language" (p. 284).

Music. Beginning with sensory exercises with sound boxes, Montessori pupils progress to using a set of bells also designed by Montessori. Bells are paired, as a sensory exercise, and then the tones and semitones are learned, named, and represented on staves with movable notes. These exercises, combined with the unaccompanied singing of children's songs, seem to form the Montessori music syllabus for young children. The material is useful as far as it goes, but the regular preschool music curriculum offers a great deal more, such as the use of tuned and untuned percussion instruments and integration of music and movement to develop an understanding of rhythm, pitch, duration, and timbre. On the basis of the authors' observations, it can also be noted that the regular preschool program usually has a daily group lesson in music but the Montessori preschool usually does not. As Faulman (1980) has pointed out, Montessori's inventiveness in her approach to music education for young children is undisputed; however, her didactic methods, which focus only on pitch matching, have been overtaken first by the instructional techniques of Dalcroze and later by those of Orff and Kodaly.

Science and social studies. Montessori developed simple didactic activities for children's use in science and social studies. Her topics seem developmentally inappropriate today, and the presentation methods as observed in use by strict Montessori teachers seem mechanical. The Montessori reliance on maps and mapping for the teaching of geography, for example, takes no account of the child's developmental understanding of the concept of "map." The regular preschool teacher, on the other hand, may use a variety of methods, including pictures, excursions, and block-play activities to introduce this concept. In *The Montessori Manual of Cultural Subjects: A Guide for Teachers,* Koche (1973) provides an overview of subjects such as botany, history, and geography. The approach is a narrow one and enshrines many old-fashioned concepts of systematics in science. These subjects can now be studied in situ as well as in the classroom.

Mathematics.   Montessori was brilliantly inventive in the area of mathematical apparatus. A perusal of the catalogue of the major commercial supplier of Montessori equipment (Niehuis Montessori) reveals a long list of items that are conceptually sound embodiments of mathematical principles in arithmetic, geometry, and algebra. However, it seems that Montessori had an almost mystical belief in the ability of a piece of structured apparatus to transfer the mathematical concepts it embodied to the mind of the child who worked with it. Reflecting on her training as a Montessori teacher, Rambusch (1978) wrote, "The materials were not discussed in terms of the concepts they encapsulated. They were offered as quasi-magical mechanisms, through which children would prehend sensorially what others struggled to comprehend cognitively" (p. 10).

The study of child development leads the modern preschool educator to believe that the origins of mathematical understanding lie in experience with concrete materials together with the use of language to describe, label, compare, and contrast. Thus, the child gradually comes to understand physical and mathematical concepts. The language aspect of mathematical development was not stressed by Montessori, nor is it stressed in the curriculum of today's Montessori schools. A certain amount of labeling in Montessori programs takes place (big/little, thick/thin, tall/short), but little occurs in the way of the real-life number use considered important in the regular preschool (for example, using cardinals and ordinals in sentences: Who's third in this line? How many children do I need to carry these four baskets?).

Instructional Approaches

It is clear to the observer that a Montessori classroom looks, sounds, and feels quite different from a regular preschool classroom. This section examines some of the dimensions where a difference is perceptible.

The classroom environment.   Modern Montessorians state that an important feature of their approach is that children work within a "prepared environment." There seems to be some suggestion that children in other approaches do not. "A classroom should not look like a supermarket," a Montessori teacher educator informed one of the present authors. It is true that no Montessori classroom looks like a supermarket, but there are some features of a supermarket that, even before supermarkets were invented, Montessori educators were using to achieve educational ends: a variety of choice, orderly presentation of like materials, attractiveness in display, and enticement.

Despite the implication that the regular preschool lacks an intentional structure, the regular preschool teacher uses the same principles to create a prepared environment. The difference arises because the Montessori teacher is limited in the number of new materials he or she may introduce, while the regular preschool teacher is not. As a result, the Montessori pupil enters a supermarket where the shelves are rather bare, physically and conceptually. The regular preschool pupil's supermarket is more fully stocked, offers a wider choice to the customer, and has a stock that changes in response to customer needs.

Wiley and Langford (1981) noted that in Melbourne, Australia, all of the five Montessori schools and four regular preschools they observed for a comparative study "contained the traditional [preschool] kindergarten activities of puzzles, painting, pasting, playdough" (p. 25). In this respect, the Montessori preschools created an environment similar to that of the regular preschools. Two important questions are raised here: Can Montessori schools that have environments significantly different from those Montessori specified really be called Montessori schools? and, How do these self-styled "Montessori schools" then differ from regular preschools?

Krogh (1982) argued that the Montessori type of prepared environment can be helpful to the handicapped child in an integrated classroom. She considered the ready availability of learning materials, their easy accessibility on the shelves, and the controlled level of stimulation achieved by restricting the number of items available at any one time to be features of a Montessori classroom that could assist the handicapped child to engage in self-directed learning and to avoid potentially rejecting group situations. She stated that "the mainstreamed child is less likely to feel rejected, a prime factor in the development of self-image" (p. 60). However, a "controlled level of stimulation" may be facilitative for an autistic child, or for one described as hyperactive, but may not be facilitative for a child with cerebral palsy or limited hearing. Thus, the nature of the handicap should be considered before this argument can be accepted. Furthermore, while the opportunity for individual work may indeed mean that the child is less likely to experience peer-group rejection, this fact does not mean that the child will necessarily feel more accepted by the peer group: There may be little meaningful peer group contact for acceptance to develop. Surely, acceptance is at least as important as nonrejection in the development of self-image.

Playground environment.   Since the Children's Houses established by Montessori herself apparently made little use of the outdoors as a teaching environment, modern Montessorians seem likewise to neglect its possibilities. The playground is used in the same way as in elementary schools – as a place to send the children for a "break" from the classroom.

By contrast, the regular preschool uses the playground as a second learning environment, finding it particularly suitable for large muscle development, consolidation of gross motor skills, social cooperation, and social play. In areas where the climate does not permit outdoor activities for part of the year, or where no outdoor area is available, the regular preschool establishes an indoor gymnasium to encourage gross motor activity.

Grouping for instruction.   Montessori individualized instruction for young children, a great innovation at the time. The individualized approach she demonstrated has been fully accepted as one appropriate method for teaching young children. Small group instruction and larger group instruction are also used in regular schools as considered appropriate. Learning in groups seems to have advantages for social and language learning, as well as being an economical use of the teacher's time. Observation by one of the present authors in Montessori classrooms suggests that unless a teacher has the assistance of a well-trained aide or aides, he or she is unable to offer instruction to even half the children in the classroom in each session. So, although children receive individual instruction, they do not receive it daily. A review of research by McGrath (1980) found that Montessori children had a lower rate of child/adult interaction than did children in a regular classroom. More research is needed to establish accurately the amount of small group, large group, and individual instruction that occurs in Montessori and regular preschools.

Parental involvement.   The regular preschool has always maintained a close working relationship with its children's parents and other caretakers. There are various ways in which parents, teachers, and children come more closely together. The most basic relationship is renewed daily as parents bring children to the center and pick them up at the end of each session. Ideally, the preschool teacher can spend a few moments with each parent each day since the arrival and dismissal procedures do not take place within the confines of a timetable. Arrivals may take place over a half hour (or longer in a day care center), and children may be picked up in a leisurely fashion at the end of a session when the teacher would be free to talk. Regular preschools believe that the child is assisted in assimilating and accommodating the change from home to school when schools take the initiative in establishing links with the home through parent involvement. The parents of newly enrolled children are encouraged to stay with the child in the classroom until the child has settled in. In recent years, parents of children in regular preschools have been invited to assist the teacher in the classroom if they have the time and interest, and many parent assistants have been helped to understand their children better by seeing them in relation to other children and through the eyes of the teacher, a professional trained in child development. Regular preschools are thus likely to have many adults in their classrooms and playgrounds, and children are encouraged to use these other adults as resources.

Montessori preschools, by contrast, generally allow parents and other adults into the classroom by appointment only, never more than two at a time, and for an observation period of 30 to 45 minutes only (Simons, 1980). The observer is placed on a low chair in an out-of-the-way corner and is prohibited from moving, from making eye contact with the children, or from interacting with the staff. In general, Montessori preschools limit parental involvement to fundraising and management activities.

The daily program and "the liberty of the child." In the contemporary Montessori classroom, the greater part of each session is available to the child for the pursuit of self-selected activities. In the regular preschool, the session is usually programmed to offer the child a substantial period of time for self-selected activities. The remainder of the session is devoted to group activities, which may include experiences with literature, music, language, math, science, social studies, or drama. These groups are usually not compulsory and are initiated in response to children's perceived interests.

The greater amount of teacher-directed time in a regular preschool program than in a Montessori preschool is taken as evidence, by Montessori educators, of the greater "liberty of the child" in the Montessori situation. However, evaluating the relative amount of "liberty" is difficult. The important issue is that the dimensions of liberty differ in the following ways: In a Montessori preschool, liberty resides in the notion that the child is free to select his or her own activity, whereas in the regular preschool, liberty resides in the notion that the child is free to use the activities in any way he or she chooses. For example, having chosen the pink tower, the child in the Montessori classroom may use it in one way only. If a child in a regular preschool were to select the pink tower, he or she would be free to make a train with it, to find a set of toy people to ride in the train, or to use it in other symbolic ways.

As has been mentioned, the child in an original Montessori school had far greater liberty than his or her contemporaries in Italian schools of the day. A school day in a Montessori setting in Italy lasted from 9:00 a.m. to 4:00 or 5:00 p.m., and the program could include clay modeling, design, care of plants and animals, gymnastics, games (directed), religion, conversation (i.e., children giving an account of the events of the day before), music, singing, housekeeping, brick-making and building, and potting (Montessori, 1964).

Almost all of these activities have disappeared from the curriculum of present-day Montessori preschools, leaving them as pale shadows of her rich vision. Further, as Montessori's son, Mario, Jr., states, "The school must be a cultural environment, so that children have the opportunity to become familiar with the basic aspects of their own culture" (Mario M. Montessori, 1976, p. 42). This dictum did not appear to be followed in any Montessori preschool visited by the authors of this discussion, nor was there evidence of teaching toward cultural pluralism.

Teacher behavior.   It is the teacher's behavior that most sharply differentiates the Montessori and the regular preschool. The Montessori teacher is enjoined to prepare the didactic environment (the teaching materials and the aesthetic appearance) before the child enters and then to step back and leave the child to interact with it. The teacher intervenes only: (a) on academic grounds, if a child seeks assistance, or if it is deemed that a child or group needs an introductory or continuation lesson in any area of the curriculum (whether the child or group has solicited the lesson or not); or (b) if a child is interfering with another child, misusing materials (using material in a way different from that demonstrated by the teacher), or being destructive toward material (Montessori, 1914, 1964; Orem, 1974; Rambusch, 1962, n.d.; Elkind, 1983; Beyer, 1966). The Montessori teacher does not, therefore, engage in such regular preschool teacher behaviors as making friendly overtures to any child within the classroom, engaging in conversation that is not directly related to the work at hand, commenting on the child's work by way of praise or encouragement, assisting the child to find a suitable occupation, positioning himself or herself in the classroom near an activity in order to stimulate the child's interest in it, joining in any ongoing activity in order to assist the child to achieve objectives more fully (such as illustrating a new way to join materials together during construction with waste materials), entering the child's conversation or initiating one in order to introduce appropriate vocabulary or concepts, modeling techniques (such as new ways to do finger painting), assisting the child to enter an ongoing social situation, or initiating an activity that adds an extra dimension to an ongoing activity (such as chant or song to accompany children's actions).

This range of teacher activities may occur during any work session in a regular preschool. The teacher acts, in short, to enrich the educational climate and environment. It is hard to believe that Montessori would have forbidden these activities out of hand since most of them maintain the child as the controller of his or her own learning. Indeed, she spoke often of the teacher's need to observe the child closely before making any intervention.

Montessori's injunction to the teacher to stand back was generated in response to the then-current behavior in which the teacher did the talking and the children listened. Montessori demonstrated that there were other ways of teaching than being the focal point in the classroom, and regular preschool teachers have accepted this "diffused" teaching style as one possible strategy. In the authors' view, modern Montessori teachers have accepted Montessori's ideas but have codified them to the point of limiting themselves to interacting with children within a narrow range of possibilities: "[In regular preschools] a strong teacher-pupil relationship is frequently viewed as the key to the child's successful learning. For Montessori, however, the critical relationship is between the child and his learning materials" (Evans, 1975, p. 266).

One aspect of the Montessori teacher's role is to act as guardian of the environment. The teacher should, therefore, keep an eye on all children so that they do not walk away from an activity before tidying up their work area and returning the activity to its rightful place. A regular preschool teacher encourages rather than requires this sort of behavior when an individual activity is selected, but many activities in the regular preschool are for use by groups, and the clearing up is undertaken by the group or by other children at the end of a work period. The regular preschool teacher sees this activity as a useful lesson in cooperation.

Montessori teachers may tend to take their responsibility for the environment to excessive lengths when they walk about the room straightening mats, trays, and materials that children are currently working on. The modeling of this behavior causes children to tend to act in the same way.[3]

For the Montessori teacher, the role of demonstrator is an important one. The teacher is to demonstrate to the child, either at the child's request or on the teacher's initiative, the way in which the classroom material is to be used. Caldwell, Yussen, and Peterson (1981), in a study of 17 Montessori teachers and 20 traditional teachers, showed that Montessori teachers were "more structured in their beliefs about the manner in which they should guide the child's use of instructional materials" (p. 43). This finding is not surprising. During training, the teacher will have compiled "albums" or notebooks, usually handwritten, often illustrated, on the exact method to be used in introducing each piece of material to the child. The quality of the teacher's presentation to the child is one criterion by which the Montessori teacher is judged. The presentation includes modeling the correct way to lay out the materials before they are used and illustrating the ideal sequence of actions to be taken in using the material. When the teacher withdraws, the child theoretically is free to operate upon the materials in any way he or she chooses. However, the child's behavior may pose a dilemma to the Montessori teacher as to whether intervention is desirable if the actions are too dissimilar from the ideal or if

---

[3] For an example of obsessive tidiness in a child, see Simons (1980), p. 12.

the behavior moves into fantasy play. If, for example, a block from the pink tower set is used as a racing car to race in and out of the other blocks, the teacher would tend to intervene, saying, "You are not using these things properly. Please put them away on the shelf."

Such an episode brings into focus basic differences in the behavior of the Montessori and the regular preschool teacher. The Montessori teacher is the custodian of the materials and a regulator of the behavior that may occur when the child uses them. In this respect, the role is an inhibitory one. In the same situation, a regular preschool teacher would have perhaps made no intervention or might have joined the child to encourage the addition of language to the action, modeling as necessary ("Your car is going fast; you are avoiding collisions"). The teacher might even have suggested that a bigger and better raceway could be constructed in the block corner, reflecting that this child was able to use an object (a pink block) symbolically and could be helped in the future with symbolic thinking. Thus, the regular preschool teacher's behavior tends both to be stimulatory and to include a wider range of possible responses than that of the Montessorian.

Discipline. On the question of discipline of the child, modern Montessorians have codified and limited a suggestion made by Montessori about the usefulness of isolating the wrongdoer and have ended up with a system of discipline that may appear to be harsh when compared with regular preschool practices. In the light of modern psychological insights, it may also be alienating to the child.

Montessori (1914) wrote with respect to the disciplining of a child who disturbed others that "we placed one of the little tables in a corner of the room, and in this way isolated the child, having him sit in a comfortable little armchair, so placed that he might see his companions at work, and giving him those games and toys to which he was most attracted. This isolation almost always succeeded in calming the child . . . The isolated child was always made the object of special care, almost as if he were ill" (p. 103).

Note that this solicitous treatment was meted out to children who disturbed others. Nowadays, the method may be applied to a wide variety of transgressions and consists of isolation without solace. The isolated child is required to be ignored by all, a practice that very often causes distress to classmates when, as one of the present authors has observed, the isolated one sits sobbing. Note also Montessori's mention of "toys." There are no "toys" in the Montessori classroom of today for anybody's consolation; all materials have a specific purpose, and playful manipulation or exploration, which characterizes a child's use of a toy, is not permitted.

The regular preschool teacher's approach to discipline may include a variety of strategies (see Almy, 1975). These may include verbal intervention (perhaps explaining, conciliating, helping children to negotiate frictions); direct verbal prohibition, if need be; or physical restraint of a child in an emergency. The teacher would be expected to think quickly before acting and to choose the most useful intervention to fit the situation. In cases of misbehavior in a group teaching situation, the offender might be asked to leave the group until such time as he or she were able to participate without disturbing others. Ideally, the child decides when to rejoin the group, thus taking responsibility for his or her own behavior.

One of the present authors has observed that, by contrast, the Montessori teacher seems to stand aloof as a situation develops and then moves to the offender to direct him or her to the isolation chair. Sometimes a caution is issued first. Thus, children miss valuable social learning experiences. Montessori children tend to experience an impersonal authority, though in many cases a private discussion of the misbehavior may follow at the end of the isolation period.

RESEARCH COMPARISONS

Research comparing Montessori preschool education with regular preschool and kindergarten education for middle class and economically disadvantaged children was surveyed by Miezitis (1971) and McGrath (1980). Miezitis reviewed 10 different studies, five of which involved middle class children and five of which involved disadvantaged children. The number of children across the 10 studies was approximately 350. In the five studies using middle class children, Miezitis found that the majority of comparisons revealed no significant differences between Montessori and other preschool and kindergarten programs on measures of ability assessed on the Illinois Test of Psycholinguistic Abilities (ITPA) and Piagetian conservation tasks. Preschool children in a structured cognitive program (Bereiter-Engelmann) were superior to Montessori children on measures of arithmetic, reading, and spelling.

On sociomotivational and cognitive style measures, there were few significant differences between Montessori and non-Montessori groups. However, Montessori groups showed significantly higher scores on measures of task persistence, reflective cognitive tempo, and self-reliance. The regular preschool group was superior on measures of nonverbal creativity and in the depiction of people (rather than geometric figures) in a free-drawing task. Miezitis suggests that for these middle class groups the similarities in home environment may be more influential than any differences in schooling.

In the five studies with disadvantaged children, Miezitis found that on cognitive ability and achievement measures Montessori preschool groups showed (a) greater gains than control groups without preschool education, (b) nonsignificant gains in comparison with regular preschool groups, and (c) lower gains in comparison with structured cognitive-oriented preschool programs of the Bereiter-Engelmann type.

In sociomotivational and learner style measures obtained in four studies, Miezitis found significantly higher scores for Montessori groups on measures of attentiveness, intentional learning ability, efficiency in structured problem solving, motor impulse control, field independence, task persistence, and test confidence. However, in a fifth study these differences were nonsignificant or favored non-Montessori groups.

In summary, Miezitis found that results from the 10 studies did not show strong differences in favor of Montessori groups. The clearest differences were found with disadvantaged groups of children in the cognitive area and appeared to reflect classroom structure, a high degree of structure apparently promoting cognitive gain. However, when Montessori groups were compared with groups that were even more highly structured, children in these latter groups outperformed Montessori children.

In McGrath's (1980) review of research, involving 11 separate studies, Montessori children were shown to spend more of their free time in social interaction, to have a lower rate of child-adult interaction than other children, and to show cognitive gains in direct proportion to number of years of Montessori education. Children were significantly advanced in the acquisition of seriation and classification skills but not in conversation skills (White, Yussen, & Docherty, 1976); in addition, they experienced more variety of activity per day than did children in other preschool programs (Berk, 1976). On the question of creativity, findings were equivocal. McGrath cited three studies that she interpreted as showing that Montessori education fosters creativity. However, the cited studies do not appear to support this conclusion.

One of the studies (Dreyer & Rigler, 1969) measured creativity by Torrance's picture construction test and found that Montessori children had generally lower scores than their nursery school counterparts. The second study (Brophy & Choquette, 1973) tested 31 matched pairs of Montessori and traditional preschool children on a different measure of creativity: The Torrance Unusual Uses Test. Only one of the pairs showed a significant performance difference in favor of the Montessori child. The overwhelming majority of pairs showed no statistically significant difference. The third study that McGrath cites is that by Miller and Dyer (1975), which demonstrated that disadvantaged children who had received a preschool Montessori education were superior in divergent thinking to children who had received three different types of preschool education.

If divergent thinking is synonomous with creativity, then this last study could be interpreted as suggesting that Montessori education may develop creativity. Yet the other two studies seem to bear little evidence to support McGrath's conclusion that this is the case. At best, it may be possible to say that Montessori education does not inhibit creativity.

On social cognitive tasks and memory problems, Yussen, Mathews, and Knight (1980) found that the Montessori curriculum "exerts some influence on cognitive skills beyond the narrow bounds of the ones ostensibly taught in the classroom" (p. 136). However, the impact was not uniform or easily predictable.

Chattin-McNichols (1981), reviewing, among other research, a longitudinal study by Miller and Dyer (1975) noted that Montessori subjects had declined less in IQ scores than had the other three experimental groups and had the highest IQ scores at the end of the experiment. However, the mean IQ of the control group had increased, and results are therefore difficult to interpret.

In summary, these types of studies are relatively inconclusive in many cases, contradictory in others. For example, Sciarra and Dorsey, cited by McGrath (1980), showed cognitive gains in direct proportion to the number of years spent in a Montessori program, whereas White, Yussen, and Docherty (1976) found that children tested after 6 months of Montessori education tended to perform as well on certain cognitive tasks as children tested after 18 months. Other problems in research methodology are apparent. In a study by Reuter and Yunick (1973), a lower rate of adult-child interaction was reported for Montessori subjects; however, the child-adult ratio was 12:1 in Montessori schools as compared with 3.5:1 in comparison schools.

Few of the experimenters appear to have taken account of the amount of time spent by Montessori subjects on specific Montessori activities, and thus research has generally failed to examine the extent to which Montessori schools are an experimentally homogeneous group. It appears likely that there are great differences in the implementation of Montessori method within Montessori schools.

Miezitis (1971) has cited a study by Starr and Banta in which Montessori pupils were measured on the amount of time they were engaged in using didactic materials. A wide variation was observed. The researchers reported that individual children spent from 1% to 21% of the available school day with didactic materials (an average of 12%). Two classrooms were observed: a highly structured one, where 10% to 21% of the time was spent with didactic materials, and a relatively unstructured one, where 1% to 7% of the time was spent with didactic materials. In the structured class, 90% of the didactic activity was self-initiated by the pupil and unaided by the teacher, whereas in the unstructured class this was so for only 56% of the didactic activity time. Clearly, in studying the effect of the Montessori school on groups of children, it is necessary to measure the amount of time working with didactic materials as well as the amount of time engaged in practical life activities and in teacher-initiated and teacher-controlled group work. Starr and Banta's work does suggest that the Montessori method may be experienced more vividly by some children than by others. A wide amount of variation was also noted by the present authors when visiting Montessori schools.

Another unexamined variable is the training and experience of the teacher. This may be a most important variable since some teachers have taken only a few weeks of summer training followed by an internship. There appears to be little useful data on this matter. In a study by Caldwell et al. (1981), 17 Montessori teachers in Wisconsin were found to have a mean educational level of 5.1 years beyond high school, as compared with 4.8 years for "traditional" teachers. No information was provided as to the relevance of the education. In the Miller and Dyer (1975) longitudinal study, the Montessori teachers were apparently graduates straight from college. They had no teaching certification and received 8 weeks of Montessori training. Teachers in the non-Montessori comparison groups received 4 or 8 weeks of training in the method they were to teach, but apparently all had previous teaching experience.

Miller and Dyer's (1975) study of the effects of four preschool programs, including Montessori, is a model of good early intervention research, involving as it does random assignment of subjects to treatments, observation of the intervention process, simultaneous replication of treatments, longitudinal data, data on a variety of measures, and a control group. The general finding of this study was that preschool children in all treatments made early gains and that control children caught up by the end of second grade. Unfortunately, there were only two schools representing the Montessori method, as compared with four schools representing each of the other three methods. McGrath (1980), reviewing Miller and Dyer (1975), stated that, at the end of second grade, children who had had a Montessori preschool education were superior to the three other groups on certain measures. The present authors are not able to agree completely with McGrath's interpretation. What Miller and Dyer said is that Montessori males were the highest of all groups on five variables: IQ, curiosity, teachers' ratings of ambition, and both reading and mathematics achievement. However, they concluded that "the magnitude of these score differences would not justify an uncritical acceptance of Montessori [preschool education]" (p. 132).

Sheldon White, in a comment included in the Miller and Dyer (1975) study, concluded that, "there is no finding of lasting difference attributable to different kinds of [preschool] kindergarten programs — just possibly some interaction effects on the 'non-cognitive' measures that are complex, small in magnitude, and difficult to interpret" (p. 169). This was not to say that there were no lasting effects from the preschool education programs; White pointed out that the preschool child, in addition to developing cognitively, is also constructing his or her own theories about self and others, society, and politics. It remains to be seen whether we can or wish to attempt to measure the effects of preschool on these other aspects of the development of the young child.

Jones and Miller (1979) followed up Miller and Dyer's (1975) study when the original subjects were in the sixth and seventh grades. A total of 140 of the initial 200 subjects were located and tested for IQ and school achievement. There was a slight trend toward superior achievement performance by Montessori subjects; however, most of the differences were not statistically significant. In general, it would seem important to remember that home environment is an influential factor in a child's achievement. It has been observed that Montessori education suits the aspirations of many parents, particularly those concerned with academic achievement and self-discipline. Phillips (1980) has also noted that the popularity of Montessori schools has risen in conjunction with more authoritarian modes of parenting.

In response to the contradictions in the research evidence, Chattin-McNichols (1981) has concluded that

> it seems important to begin to assess the effectiveness of the Montessori system in terms of goals of Montessorians, rather than measures of general academic progress or cognitive development. Goals which would probably be accepted as important by most Montessorians include autonomy, each child's sense of success in academic areas, self-concept, an understanding of mathematical and geometric concepts, and the development of a world-wide perspective on cultural subjects such as history, geography, and social studies. The focus so far has been too limited to comparative studies; more and better research is needed to examine variability within Montessori schools (p. 65)

TEACHER EDUCATION

Rambusch (1978) has made a withering criticism of Montessori teacher education. It is, she says, "based on an act of the heart, conversion, rather than an act of the mind, persuasion" (p. 5). She claims that the training she received in 1954 has not changed today, and the present authors can verify this from visits to training institutions. Training consists of lectures on Montessori principles[4] and anecdotes from Montessori's life, the taking of dictation on the use of the Montessori materials, the manipulation of these materials in order to practice the sequence of presenting the materials to the child, observation in Montessori schools, and teaching practice in Montessori schools.

The heart of the matter is this: Montessori teachers are inadequately trained by today's standard of teacher education. To begin with, they are not necessarily educated beyond high school level, and they need not have a teaching credential from a state authority. In the United States, the Montes-

---

[4] Fleege (1977) provides a sample list of such Montessori principles.

sori teacher may enter training straight from high school, following work experience with young children, or following an associate's degree at a junior or community college. In fact, many Montessori trainees do hold a 4-year degree when they begin Montessori training, but it is important to realize that they need not.

There are two principal types of training for Montessori teachers in the United States, and these are related to the organization with which the training program is affiliated. Affiliates of the *Association Montessori Internationale* (AMI) are approved by AMI at its Amsterdam headquarters. There are 5 training sites in Europe (Italy, France, Germany, the United Kingdom, Ireland), 4 in Asia (India, Pakistan, Sri Lanka, Japan), 1 in Canada, 1 in Mexico, and 10 in the United States. Courses typically run from 9 to 11 months, of which 5 to 6 months are spent in coursework and 4 to 5 months in practicum.

The content of the coursework is based heavily on Montessori's own writing, especially *The Absorbent Mind* (1961), *The Discovery of the Child* (1958), and *The Secret of Childhood* (1959). These works, written between 1936 and 1949, embrace the essence of Montessori's ideals: a mixture of philosophical and psychological statement. In many respects, she was ahead of other psychological theorists of her time, but as Phillips (1977) has pointed out, she also lagged behind her contemporaries, particularly with respect to measurement and methodology. Phillips remarked that Montessori's scientific approach is openly intermingled with mysticism and sentimentalism. This leads to "generalizations based upon no empirical evidence whatsoever, and often flying in the face of it. There are also many metaphysical assumptions mixed with her scientific pedagogy" (p. 63).

It is now the case that modern psychology has furthered insights into cognitive development. By this process, some of Montessori's ideas have been refined and substantiated, while others are now disputed or considered irrelevant. Despite such advances, Montessori teachers in training are given little or no access to information about modern developmental psychology. The syllabus of the recently established Australian Montessori Association (*Association Montessori Internationale*) course, for example, does not refer to any psychologist other than Montessori. The impact of theorists such as Piaget and the wealth of empirical evidence that supports and/or challenges his theory is ignored. Courses usually studied in a regular teacher education program—such as child development, educational psychology, sociology, curriculum development, special education, and multicultural education—are not taken by Montessori trainees. A course of study reported by Orem (1972) at the Montessori Institute of Atlanta, Georgia, is said to include some child psychology and child development, but very few semester hours are involved. Of the Midwest Montessori Teacher Training Center, he says, "Stress is placed on imparting the rationale underlying Montessori insights, materials and practices" (p. 121). It is quite clear that Montessori child development predominates heavily over modern child development, indicating that little modern child development theory is examined by teacher trainees. There is plenty of exhortation to observe but little skill training in modern techniques of how to observe or in what to use the observations for (Orem, 1974, p. 214). This is not considered by the present authors to be an adequate basis for a teacher education program.

Teacher training establishments affiliated with the American Montessori Society (AMS) appear to be more varied in their programs. In a few cases, training programs are offered through community colleges. Students typically enter these colleges straight from high school or as reentry students. However, the majority of training sites are established in conjunction with Montessori schools. A typical school-based training program consists of a summer session of 4 weeks followed by a year-long internship in which the intern works as a teacher's aide and attends occasional weekend seminars. The present authors' general impression of Montessori teacher education is that it is largely an oral tradition, that methods have not changed over the past few decades, and that modern insights into child development are ignored.

Evans (1975) notes that "Montessori teachers and administrators seem more concerned with perfecting their pedagogical technique, than with supporting a continuous enquiry into the validity of the methodological procedures involved" (p. 279). In addition to programs affiliated with AMI and AMS, many schools train their own teachers. Very little has been written about Montessori teacher education. One source is Orem (1972, 1974), whose works represent nearly all that has been written on the subject. The summaries of training programs Orem presents are, by and large, lists of materials together with methods for introducing them. Theoretical bases for the presentation and manipulation of such materials are largely ignored.

THE PLACE OF THE MONTESSORI METHOD IN EARLY CHILDHOOD EDUCATION TODAY

In view of the limitations and inadequacies of the Montessori method of education and teacher education, what is to be made of the Montessori debate? The present authors conclude that Montessori education, as practiced today, is misguided in its attempt to keep alive a system of education that may have been effective and appropriate in the past, but which, being fossilized, is inappropriate for the children of today.

Both educators and parents should be suspicious of a system that: (a) ignores recent educational thinking, especially in regard to using a modern understanding of child development to inform educational practice; (b) trains its teachers in isolation from all other teachers; (c) accepts a low standard of teacher preparation (as measured by level of intake, length of training, rigor of training, credentials of the trainers, and acceptability of credential); (d) conceptualizes teacher education as an exercise in learning how to present the Montessori materials to children; (e) defines education narrowly, paying scant attention to gross motor development, social skills, language and literature, creativity, and the arts; (f) uses a harsh, outmoded system of discipline; and (g) limits parental involvement.

The Persistence of Montessori Schools

It might be fairly asked, in the face of all these problems and inadequacies, Why do Montessori schools persist? Several factors account for the continuation of Montessori education.

1.   Montessori education has strong overtones of a religion. The adherents of the Montessori method have an almost mystical belief in its efficacy and preach eloquently on its behalf. Neither adherents nor converts are involved in questioning the method's basic assumptions and beliefs. Since the teacher training programs referred to above largely omit the study of theories of early childhood education and development on a comparative basis, there is little impetus towards rational enquiry or empirical research within the Montessori movement itself.

2.   The parents who select a Montessori school for their child usually have no previous experience in selecting a school and no standards of comparison. Parents, who are generally invited to pay a 30-minute observation visit to a classroom before enrolling their child, tend to be impressed by the orderliness of the environment and the eloquence of the director. One of the present authors spoke to two prospective parents after one such observation visit. The husband, a psychiatrist, was impressed; the wife, a primary school teacher, was not.

3.   Some parents are eager to give their children a good start in life, via education, and see the work ethic of present-day Montessori schools as matching their beliefs in the value of hard work and strong discipline. A parent said to one of the present authors of her 3-year-old son, "Well, they've got to learn to work hard in this world, and I'm pleased to find a school where they're made to work."

4.   Some Montessori schools have kept their name but branched out from the narrow curriculum of the orthodox Montessori school. These schools offer sand and water play, gross motor activities, storytelling, parental involvement in the classroom, and games and activities purchased from sources other than the Montessori educational suppliers. A teacher in one such school said, "A morning in the sandbox can be [the children's] work." This is not a typical Montessori concept and raises the question of whether some parents are misled about what is unique to Montessori education. That

some schools continue to use the name "Montessori" may mean no more than that they continue to display Montessori materials alongside other educational materials. In this case, children are free to select or to ignore these materials and may use them no more than a tiny fraction of the time, as indicated in Starr and Banta's study (cited in Miezitis, 1971).

5. Academics who take an interest in Montessori education are usually not trained and experienced early childhood educators, and they approach Montessori education from a theoretical point of view and in ignorance of alternatives.

6. Present-day early childhood educators, by and large, have ignored Montessori education. When they have looked into it they have noted that: (a) Many of the practices that are claimed to give special distinction to Montessori schools are fully incorporated into regular preschool programs; (b) Montessori teachers are poorly prepared as teachers and have a limited understanding of child development; (c) the Montessori classroom environment is frequently impoverished, rigid, and rule-bound; (d) music, dance, drama, literature, and poetry are neglected; (e) the role of the teacher in fostering language development and stimulating children's interests is not encouraged; (f) dramatic play, considered a tool for learning, is discouraged; and (g) discipline may be harsh and unsympathetic. Such educators have failed to point out these problems, an understandable lapse since they believe that early childhood education has assimilated all that is best in the thinking of Montessori. However, they fail to inform the public of these facts. Conversely, some Montessori schools resemble regular preschools, having added to their curriculum a wide range of modern educational activities and subjects; these schools also fail to inform the public of this deviation from the original Montessori design.

A Proposal for Montessori Teacher Education

When one returns to the writings of Maria Montessori, one is struck afresh with her intelligence, vision, wisdom, insight, and modernity. She was without any doubt a person ahead of her time, a remarkable innovator. She demonstrated that young children could learn academic and social skills and that young disadvantaged children could do so equally as well as those more advantaged. Her system of education flourished during her lifetime, lapsed, and is now experiencing a mild revival. Phillips (1977, 1980) has charted the rise, fall, and rise again of the acceptability of Montessori's viewpoint to psychologists, philosophers, and parents. Miezitis (1971) and McGrath (1980) have summarized empirical studies searching for relationships between Montessori education in the early years and achievement reflected in such variables as cognitive ability, academic skills, and personal learning styles. Such few comparisons as do favor Montessori education do not constitute a compelling reason to favor Montessori education for all children.

The level at which a study of the Montessori approach might be useful is at the postgraduate level, for students who already have early childhood teaching qualifications and who, in addition, have had some experience in teaching young children. In this case, a study of the contribution of Maria Montessori and her followers, together with some practical experience in using Montessori materials with young children, would give experienced teachers the opportunity to judge for themselves the efficacy of the special Montessori apparatus and to evaluate the particular teaching approach that she advocated. Students would then, as classroom teachers, be in a position to use selectively the Montessori materials and the Montessori teaching style if they so desired. Thus, skillful and experienced teachers could expand their repertoire of teaching techniques, which they would employ according to their professonal judgment.

REFERENCES

Almy, M. (1975). *The early childhood educator at work*. New York: McGraw-Hill.

Berk, L. (1976). How well do classroom practices reflect teacher goals? *Young Children, 33*(1), 64–81.

Beyer, E. (1966). Let's look at Montessori. In *Montessori in perspective* (pp. 49–59). Washington, DC: National Association for the Education of Young Children.

Brophy, J.E., & Choquette, J. (1973, March). *Divergent production in Montessori Children*. Paper presented at the biennial meeting of the Society for Research and Child Development, Philadelphia. (ERIC Document Reproduction Service No. ED 080 212)

Caldwell, C.A., Yussen, S.R., & Peterson, P. (1981). Beliefs about teaching in Montessori and non-Montessori preschool teachers. *Journal of Teacher Education, 32*(2), 41–44.

Chattin-McNichols, J.P. (1981). The effects of Montessori school experience. *Young Children, 36*(5), 49–66.

Dreyer, A.S., & Rigler, D. (1969). Cognitive performance in Montessori and nursery school children. *Journal of Educational Research, 62*(9), 411–416.

Edmonson, B. (1966). Let's do more than look – let's research Montessori. In *Montessori in perspective* (pp. 66–77). Washington, DC: National Association for the Education of Young Children.

Evans, D.E. (1975). *Contemporary influences in early childhood education* (2nd ed.). New York: Holt, Rinehart & Winston.

Elkind, D. (1983). Montessori education: Abiding contributions and contemporary challenges. *Young Children, 38*(2), 3–10.

Farrow, E., & Hill, C. (1975). *Montessori on a limited budget*. New York: Valley Offset.

Faulman, J. (1980). Montessori and music in early childhood. *Music Educators Journal, 66*(9), 41–43.

Fleege, V.B. (1977). *Standard Montessori operating procedures* (7th ed.). Unpublished manuscript, University of California at Los Angeles.

Gitter, L. (1970). *The Montessori way*. Seattle: Special Child Publications.

Howells, S. (1977). Scuola Montessori: Rome. *Australian Journal of Early Childhood, 2*(1), 35–36.

Jones, B., & Miller, L.B. (1979). *Four preschool programs: Their lasting effects.* (ERIC Document Reproduction Service No. ED 171 415)

Koche, M.B. (1973). *The Montessori manual of cultural subjects: A guide for teachers.* Minneapolis, MN: Denison.

Kornegay, W. (1981). *The American Odyssey of Maria Montessori.* (ERIC Document Reproduction Service No. ED 205 272)

Krogh, S.L. (1982). Affective and social development: Some ideas from Montessori's prepared environment. *Topics in Early Childhood Special Education, 2*(1), 55–62.

McGrath, H. (1980). The Montessori method of education: An overview of research. *Australian Journal of Early Childhood, 5*(4), 20–24.

Miezitis, S. (1971). the Montessori method: Some recent research. *Interchange, 2*(2), 41–59.

Miller, L.B., & Dyer, J.L. (1975). *Four preschool programs: Their dimensions and effects.* Chicago: University of Chicago Press.

Montessori, M. (1912). The Montessori Method (A.E. George, Trans.). London: William Heinemann.

Montessori, M. (1914). *Dr. Montessori's own handbook.* New York: Stokes.

Montessori, M. (1959). *The secret of childhood* (B. Carter, Ed. & Trans.). Bombay: Orient Longmans.

Montessori, M. (1958). *The discovery of the child* (M.A. Johnstone, Trans.). Madras: Kalakshetra Publications.

Montessori, M. (1961). *The absorbent mind* (C. Claremont, Trans.). Madras: Theosophical Publishing House.

Montessori, M. (1964). *The Montessori method* (American ed.). Cambridge, MA: Bentley.

Montessori, Mario M., Jr. (1976). *Education for human development* (P.P. Lillard, Ed.). New York: Schocken.

Montessori Institute of Los Angeles, Inc. (n.d.). *The Montessori method.* Available from author, 2918 Santa Monica Blvd., Santa Monica, CA 90404.

Orem, R.C. (1972). *Montessori today.* New York: Capricorn.

Orem, R.C. (1974). *Montessori: Her method and the movement – what you need to know.* New York: Putnam.

Phillips, S. (1977). Maria Montessori and contemporary cognitive psychology. *British Journal of Teacher Education, 3*(1), 55–68.

Phillips, S. (1980). New fashions in child rearing and education. *New Horizons, 62.*

Pinho, C. (1967). The Montessori teacher and the Montessori method. In R.C. Orem (Ed.), *Montessori for the disadvantaged* (pp. 143–146). New York: Capricorn.

Pitcher, E.G. (1966). An evaluation of the Montessori method in schools for young children. *Childhood Education, 42,* 489–492.

Rambusch, N.M. (1962). *Learning how to learn: An American approach to Montessori.* Baltimore: Helicon.

Rambusch, N.M. (1978). Montessori teacher training: The calypso paradigm. *The Constructive Triangle, 5*(3), 5–29.

Reuter, J., & Yunick, G. (1973). Interaction in nursery schools. *Developmental Psychology, 9*(3), 319–325.

Schweinhart, L.J., & Weikart, D.P. (1980). *Young children grow up.* Ypsilanti, MI: High/Scope.

Simons, J. (1980). *Preschools and Montessori preschools: A comparison.* (ERIC Document Reproduction Service No. ED 202 573)

Simpson, M.M. (1912). *Report on the Montessori method.* Unpublished manuscript. Teachers' College, Blackfriars, Sydney, Australia.

Smilansky, S. (1968). *The effects of sociodramatic play on disadvantaged preschool children.* New York: Wiley.

Ward, F.E. (1913). *The Montessori method and the American school.* New York: Macmillan.

White, J.M., Yussen, S.R., & Docherty, E.M. (1976). Performance of Montessori and traditionally schooled nursery children on tasks of seriation, classification, and conservation. *Contemporary Educational Psychology, 1,* 356-368.

Wiley, K., & Langford, P.A. (1981). Comparison of Montessori with traditional preschool education in Melbourne. *Australian Journal of Early Childhood, 6*(1), 24-25.

Yussen, S.R., Mathews, S., & Knight, J.W. (1980). Performance of Montessori and traditionally schooled nursery children on social cognitive tasks and memory problems. *Contemporary Educational Psychology, 5,* 124-237.

9

The Academic and Social Consequences of Grade Retention: A Convergent Analysis

Diane L. Plummer   **Marilyn Hazzard Lineberger**

University of Georgia   *Emory University*

William G. Graziano

University of Georgia

INTRODUCTION

One of the most influential institutions for the development of children is the elementary school. This influence extends beyond intellectual development into the general realm of social development (see Centra & Potter, 1980; Gump, 1980; Hetherington & Parke, 1979). In the Caswell and Foshay text *Education in the Elementary School* (1957), George Strayer presents an idealized view of the school: "The good elementary school is one in which children learn the tool of inquiry, respect for differences and open-minded avoidance of prejudice, the difficult relationship between freedom and responsibility, and the art of cooperating" (p. 6). According to Metcalfe (1981) the school is second only to the home as an institution that determines the growing individual's self-concept and his or her attitudes of self-acceptance or self-rejection (see also Hetherington & Parke, 1979). It has been consistently observed that the type of school, school organization, and teacher-pupil relationships all influence children's self-concepts (Metcalfe, 1981).

The school understandably has a diverse impact on children. It is here that the child's abilities to succeed in life are often formed, shaped, and maintained. Recently, administrators have begun to focus on the "basics" of education; it is hoped that by teaching the basics (e.g., reading, writing, and mathematical skills), the child will acquire the abilities to succeed in his or her subsequent academic career. However, the "back-to-basics" movement has a hidden aspect that presents a serious problem to the schools. Throughout the United States, educators have increasingly advocated the use of "minimum competence" as a criterion for grade promotion. This practice has important implications for children. The primary question is, if minimum competencies in the basics are the criteria for academic success, what is to be done with the students who do not meet these standards? The traditional answer to this question is to retain children in grade until they have reached the appropriate mastery level. It seems that this solution is not uncommon; approximately 1 million American children are involved in this process annually (Jackson, 1975).

The subject of grade retention has generated substantial theoretical, empirical, and practical attention for almost a century. However, at present, there are few conclusive statements regarding this widespread practice, and mixed results continue to abound in the literature. The term "grade retention" itself tends to evoke numerous definitions and rationales. A retained child has been defined as "a child who is compelled to repeat an entire year in the same grade, giving the child an added chance for classroom success" (Kerzner, 1982). Grade retention has been used synonymously with terms such as repeating, flunking, and nonpromotion. The year of retention has also been referred to as "a year to grow." Rationales for grade retention usually include below average performance on certain standards of academic achievement and/or "social maturity" (Plummer & Graziano, 1982). According to Eshel and Klein (1981), two school criteria are usually employed in retention decisions: (a) teachers' ratings or marks; and (b) performance on objective achievement tests. There are, however, several other factors that influence the retention decision. These factors have included: (a) various demographic factors of the child (e.g., socioeconomic level [Safer, Heaton, & Allen, 1977]); (b) the teacher's educational philosophy (e.g., whether or not a teacher endorses the "back-to-basics" philosophy [Bossing & Brien, 1980]); (c) school policy (e.g., the adherence to automatic promotion policy [Reiter, 1973]); and (d) the child's classroom behavior (Caplan, 1973).

These extraneous factors have also been confounding factors in empirical research. There are numerous possible explanations for this situation — most particularly, the fact that there is little available evidence on the topic and that which is available is often inconclusive at best. Researchers generally focus on the academic progress made by students who have been retained, but grade retention can affect children in other areas as well. Most important is the fact that there is no consistent, generally accepted basis for nonpromotion. Children may be retained due to deficiencies in academic performance or to deficiencies in "social maturity." Further, there may be no consistent relationship between the achievement and ability of the student and his or her nonpromotion. Surveys of student progress reveal that children with low achievement have been promoted and children with higher achievement have been failed (Jackson, 1975). Earlier reports also revealed that schools with higher average achievement levels often fail a larger percentage of students than do schools with lower average achievement levels (Caswell & Foshay, 1957).

As alluded to earlier, reports on nonpromotion yield mixed results with respect to effects on the child. These reports have, on occasion, supported the policy of nonpromotion (Ames, 1981; Chase, 1968), whereas contrasting research has discussed the detrimental effects of nonpromotion (Abidin, Golladay, & Howerton, 1971; Dobbs & Neville, 1967). Supportive studies have noted academic, social, and personal improvements in retained children. These studies have posited improvements in achievement, peer relationships, and self-concept. Nonsupportive studies, which outnumber supportive studies, have discussed the negative impact of nonpromotion.

Even though the literature on the effects of grade retention yields mixed results, statistics indicate that the general trends are somewhat consistent. For instance, Ayers (1909) reported the first comprehensive analysis on the progress of children from grade to grade. He concluded that the rate of grade retention was significantly higher in the first grade than it was for other grades, and that the rate of grade retention was higher for boys than for girls. These results have been replicated (Abidin et al., 1971; Caswell & Foshay, 1957; Coffield, 1954; Jackson, 1975; Keyes, 1911; Sandin, 1944). The major difference noted in this research has been the rate of grade retention variance in different cities and states, the range being between 2% and 20%. According to Jackson (1975), there are marked differences for nonpromotion for minority and nonminority students (respectively, 0.7% and 0.4% in Minnesota, Oregon, and Utah; and in Louisiana, 7.9% and 3.6%).

Dillon (1975) states that dropout rates and excessive absenteeism attest to the fact that school is an obstacle rather than a help for a large number of children who seek entry into the mainstream of American life. This segment of children may experience a sense of failure and alienation because for them failure is built into the educational system. In these cases the children face failure (and possible retention), which may suppress their future abilities and competencies. They start to feel unsuccessful, impotent, and alienated because of failure feedback; this feedback can lead to the humiliation and alienation of children in their early years in school. The process can create a self-fulfilling prophecy and reduce aspirations for children and teachers. Thus, school systems can inadvertently train children to expect to fail and to eventually see themselves as failures (Dillon, 1975). Similarly, according to Sandin (1944), grade retention serves as an official reminder, an indication to the child that he or she has failed in some important aspect.

An empirical investigation (Sandin, 1944) was designed to assess the emotional and social adjustment of regularly promoted and nonpromoted children. Sandin obtained information from observations in the classrooms and student records showing that nonpromotion resulted in children being placed with classmates who were younger, smaller, and, in many cases, less mature. He concluded that a student who is retained because of academic deficiencies continues to grow physically as well as socially (that is, in terms of his or her social attitudes and aspirations). Hence, Sandin found that children who had been retained did not consider their younger, regularly promoted classmates appropriate companions.

The effects of grade retention continue to deserve close scrutiny. Current attention should logically pursue the academic and social consequences of nonpromotion. Reviews of the literature prompt many questions: (a) Does retaining children in grade subsequently increase their academic performance? (b) What are children's perceptions of their peers who are retained? (c) Do other children discriminate against children who are retained? (d) Do retained children have different expectations about their performance, school, and teachers than do their nonretained counterparts? and (e) Is children's self-esteem affected by grade retention?

A thorough examination of the relevant information is needed. The present discussion will attempt to synthesize the results of empirical research – in other words, to provide a convergent analysis of available information. Specifically, the first section will summarize available data to ascertain the effects of grade retention on children's academic performance. The second section will present information about the social behaviors of children who have been retained; available data include information on how the perceptions of others can influence children's school performance and their interactions with peers. The third section will summarize data regarding the effects of grade retention on the child's self-esteem. Finally, in the fourth section, some conclusive statements and proposed directions for future research on the effects of grade retention will be offered.

ACADEMIC CONSEQUENCES OF GRADE RETENTION

Academic achievement is generally measured as scholastic success shown by the Comprehensive Tests of Basic Skills (Kerzner, 1982). The tests employed in this battery are standardized; thus, normative data are based on large populations and can be assumed to have adequate reliability and validity. On some occasions, grades assigned by teachers are used to evaluate academic progress. If a student evidences subaverage performance on the basic skills test (which includes areas such as reading and mathematics) and/or displays general academic difficulties in course work (e.g., failing to complete homework assignments), he or she may be retained and viewed as an academic failure. In the early years of schooling, this feedback may be especially problematic to the young child who has had an abundance of successful experiences prior to school (Dillon, 1975). After the initial encounter of failure, however, these target children may be involved in a vicious cycle of failure. One experience of failure tends to make subsequent failure that much easier (Dillon, 1975). The aforementioned cycle entails a label of failure by teachers and peers as well as internalized feelings of failure. In general, this cycle involves the following steps: (a) The student may think that he or she is a total failure because of a single unsuccessful episode in the academic area; (b) this feeling may be intensified due to teacher and peer group perceptions of academic failure; and (c) the perceived feedback by these significant others may support the target child's perception of self as failure. Important questions at this point are, if this cycle exists, is it changed, either positively or negatively, by nonpromotion? and, Does nonpromotion produce positive effects on or improve future academic performance? These questions have been vigorously debated in the literature.

Historical Overview

As early as 1840, the problem of nonpromotion was evidenced when elementary education was divided into eight grade levels (Bossing & Brien, 1980). If a student mastered the appropriate content area of a given grade, then he or she was promoted to the next grade level. Early in the 20th century, however, the prospect of nonpromotion was entertained because of growing concern about the student who could not master academic material at the designated grade level. The retention year, theoretically, would provide a chance for the child to catch up academically by being exposed to materials more suited to his or her academic ability. Thus, the child would have additional time to learn required material (Bossing & Brien, 1980). From the early 1800s to the 1930s, it was a common educational practice to require students to remain in grades where academic mastery was a problem and thus to provide time for the additional work needed (Hess, Martin, Parker, & Beck, 1978).

Numerous studies have been conducted to test the effects of nonpromotion on academic achievement. As early as 1911, Keyes conducted a 4-year study including 5,000 pupils in an identified school district. The results of this study indicated that, of the large number of retainees, 20% did better academically, 39% showed no change, and 40% actually did worse.

Several other early investigations generally support the findings of Keyes. Buckingham (1926) found that a small percentage (approximately one-third) of several thousand children did better academic work after repeating a grade. McKinney (1928) evaluated repeaters above the first grade and found that 35% did better work the second time, 53% did not improve, and 12% did poorer work. Klene and Branson (1929) equated children on the bases of chronological age, mental age, and sex, and, in turn, identified potential repeaters. Their results indicated that, as measured by achievement scores, potential repeaters profited more from promotion than did repeaters from nonpromotion. A study by Arthur (1936) again supported this early research trend. This investigator compared the achievement of 60 first-grade repeaters with the achievement of nonrepeaters of the same mental age (as based on intelligence testing), indicating that the average repeater did not learn more in 2 years than the average nonrepeater learned in 1 year.

In 1933, Farley, Frey, and Garland studied children with low IQs who repeated several grades. These students were compared with children who had the same ability as measured by IQ but who had not been retained. It was found that retained children were not doing as well in their school work as children of the same ability who had not been exposed to nonpromotion. These findings indicated that retention, in this case, was more likely to be a deterrent than an impetus to acceptable academic achievement. In another comparison study, Coffield's (1954) results indicated the long-range consequences of achievement and nonpromotion. Failed and promoted pupils who evidenced comparable achievement levels at the time of failure showed no significant academic differences when the achievement of both was measured at a later date (specifically, when pupils were in the seventh grade).

These very early studies appear, then, to indicate that repeaters actually achieve no better the second time in the grade than they do the first time. In fact, many students seem to do poorer work the second time. Of course, this very early research cannot be generalized to current school systems. However, it appears that the early trends in nonpromotion research are fairly negative in that the results indicate no positive benefits of retention. Saunders (1941) reviewed the early research regarding elementary school retention and offered these summary statements:

> From the evidence cited, it may be concluded that nonpromotion of pupils in elementary schools in order to assure mastery of subject matter does not accomplish its objectives. Children do not appear to learn more by repeating a grade but experience less growth in subject matter achievement than they do when promoted. (p. 29)

Subsequent research has basically been supportive of this earlier notion that retention rarely produces positive changes in academic achievement. For example, Dobbs and Neville (1967) evaluated the effects of nonpromotion on the achievement of 15 once-retained first graders and compared them with 15 never-retained second graders. These identified groups were matched on sex, race, age, socioeconomic level, mental ability, reading achievement, and type of classroom assignment. The investigators concluded that nonpromotion was not an aid to achievement.

Abidin et al. (1971) concurred with the premise of Dobbs and Neville (1967) and other retention researchers. Abidin et al. offered support for the ongoing deterioration of both achievement and ability level as a function of nonpromotion. Investigating a group of 85 students who had been retained in the first and second grade, these researchers found that decreases in both achievement and ability continued for this group through the sixth grade. The study also indicated that several nonacademic variables significantly influence the retention decision during the first 2 years of school. An analysis of the demographic data indicated that the parents of prospective retainees are crucial in this process. Among the demographic factors measured in this study were race, sex, socioeconomic level of family, initial intelligence, and father absence. It was suggested that sex, race, and socioeconomic status are crucial determinants in retention decisions. In addition, black male students from low socioeconomic families in which the mother worked and the father was absent were found to be likely candidates for retention. It should be emphasized that retained children evidenced continuing academic deterioration after their initial encounter with the failure process. This process was discussed by Glasser (1969), who noted that "once the child receives the failure label and sees himself as a failure, he will rarely succeed in school."

Further documentation of this notion was offered by Godfrey (1971), who presented the results of a 1970 research project by the North Carolina Advancement School comparing students who had been retained with those who had not been retained. Approximately 1,200 sixth- and seventh-grade students from 14 representative schools served as the sample population. The results indicated that nonretainees were reading at a 6.8 grade level. The students who had repeated one grade, however, were reading at a 5.2 level, whereas students repeating two or more grades had dropped to a 4.5 grade level. Regarding mathematical achievement, it was found that nonretainees averaged in the 27th percentile. One-time repeaters averaged in the 10th percentile, and chronic repeaters (those who had repeated grades two or more times) were in the 5th percentile. In comparing nonretainees with those students once or twice retained, Godfrey found results indicating that years of retention can be an academic handicap to students in terms of decreasing their performance. This implies that subsequent failures could be a detriment to academic performance. The theoretical principle of retention allowing students to catch up is once again challenged.

Potential Benefits Versus Negative Effects

Before reaching final conclusions about the effect of grade retention, an examination of the contrasting literature is in order. In 1973, Reiter reviewed the literature on the policies of automatic promotion versus rigid retention for academically deficient pupils. These extreme positions did not offer a via-ble solution to pupils' problems. However, promotion appeared to have fewer disadvantages than retention. Generally, it was noted that repeaters evidence motivational problems in that they appear to be somewhat discouraged by their actual and perceived failure. In addition, when compared with nonrepeaters, the repeaters did not fare better at the end of their schooling.

One could therefore logically question whether retention, or the threat of retention, serves as a motivating force to facilitate academic performance. The motivational aspects of nonpromotion have been treated as a subcomponent of academic achievement. Several teachers believe that children are prompted to work by the threat of nonpromotion. In an effort to test this hypothesis, Otto and Melby (1935) evaluated the performance of second- and fifth-grade students who received different information about retention at the beginning of the school semester. These investigators found that telling children at the beginning of a semester that all of them would be passed to the following grade the next term did not change their behavior (i.e., this information did not make students less motivated to work or learn). More specifically, regarding criteria for change, these children did as well on a comprehensive achievement test as did children who throughout the semester were reminded of, or threatened with, the possibility of nonpromotion. Other research findings (Caswell, 1933; Farley et al., 1933) indicate that nonpromotion does not serve as a motivating factor; instead, nonpromotion may be more of a deterrent than an impetus to acceptable achievement levels. Furthermore, there is evidence to suggest that the threat of nonpromotion primarily motivates children to work if they are in no real danger of being retained (Kowitz & Armstrong, 1961).

Nonpromotion, however, has not consistently produced universally detrimental effects on children's achievement. As Saunders indicated in his 1941 review, following nonpromotion, the majority of children studied did not receive higher grades as judged by teachers or score higher on group achievement tests. Yet this evidence is not conclusive. Three studies reviewed by Saunders indicated that nearly one-third of the children displayed favorable academic gains during the retained year (Buckingham, 1926; Keyes, 1911; McKinney, 1928). Additionally, Lobdell (1954) stated that approximately 69% of retainees may be expected to evidence good or fair progress when and if careful selection criteria are employed. This notion has been supported by recent literature.

Since 1965, researchers in the retention area have postulated that maximal learning can occur in retainees if proper steps are taken. According to these reports, the crucial issue relates to how the individual student is treated in the school. The issue of treatment relates to the processes of promotion and retention alike (Reiter, 1973). For example, humanistic treatment of a pupil indicates that the student is valued and worthy of creative provision of appropriate learning tasks that will produce academic success. In this case, special reward systems could be implemented for the retainee who evidences academic progress. These rewards might include verbal reinforcement that would enhance the child's self-esteem.

In an extensive 2-year study, Sandoval and Hughes (1981) conducted a research project for two purposes: (a) to identify characteristics of children who profited from retention, and (b) to identify the factors in the retained group that facilitated success after failure. The subject sample in this study was 146 first graders who had been identified as potential repeaters. Of this number, 84 remained in the first grade and 62 were promoted. The researchers individually tested the children in an effort to assess academic achievement, perceptual-motor ability, interpersonal relationships, intelligence, and cognitive and physical development. In addition, parent and teacher interviews were conducted. The results of this extensive report indicated that the child's family background, early life experiences, physical size, and visual-motor development are, along with teacher philosophy, relatively unimportant determinants in whether or not the child evidences subsequent success from the repeated years. It appeared that the best predictors of successful retention outcomes are the child's initial status in three areas: academic skills, emotional development, and social skills. More specifically, when compared with less successsful retainees, successful retainees initially had the highest level of achievement (i.e., better academic skills), the highest self-concept (i.e., greater self-esteem), the best social skills (i.e., good interpersonal skills), and the most involved parents. Subsequent analysis indicated that, when comparing the successful retainees with a promoted group of children, the successful retained group was inferior to the promoted group only in mathematical achievement. In other measured areas, the successful retained group was equivalent to or, in the case of emotional adjustment, superior to the promoted group.

These results indicate that a successful nonpromotion may enhance the overall development of the child. However, Sandoval and Hughes (1981) warn readers to be cautious in accepting the results of their study concretely. Primary cautionary notes concern: (a) the data reduction procedures employed, which "simply selected variables with good psychometric properties and good correlations with other variables" (p. 150); and (b) the fact that this study evaluated retainees for only 1 year after nonpromotion.

Kerzner (1982) also investigated the educational merit of retaining low-achieving elementary school students in the same grade for a designated time period. The subjects in this study were 56 students who had progressed and completed one grade beyond the retained grade. The progress of this group was evaluated by their performance on the Comprehensive Tests of Basic Skills. Both preretention and postretention test scores were compared. The results revealed some positive aspects of retention. It was found that, overall, retention was academically beneficial to students in all grades observed; however, retained children in second or third grades appeared to have evidenced the greatest positive effects.

Other researchers also support the positive aspects of nonpromotion. Ames (1981) stated that retention is generally not accompanied by emotional or social difficulties. Even further, Ames suggests that retention tends to result in improved grades. Many teachers and parents thus support retention because they feel the positive aspects of the process outweight the negative.

Chase (1968) also indicated that 75% of 65 first-, second-, and third-grade children studied had no emotional upset after retention and that only 16% had temporary emotional upheaval. It should be noted that, in this study, most parents (approximately 95%) were supportive of the retention decision and stated that they observed positive changes in their children after they were retained.

Special programs for retained children have been shown to be effective. One such innovative program in Virginia, The Greensville Program, addressed the issue of nonpromotion and achievement. This program, implemented by Owens and Ranick (1977), set forth a strict ground rule: "No students would be promoted until they showed, on achievement tests, the mastery of the skills for their grades" (p. 531). This achievement-oriented program has produced respectable success rates—that is, the number of retainees is declining and achievement test scores are increasing. More specifically, this program, which began in 1973, showed that not only was the number of students retained in grade declining, but achievement tests scores had risen. Students previously scoring in the bottom 20 to 30% nationwide on achievement tests had risen to the top 50 to 60%. In addition, students displayed a more positive attitude about testing, their IQ scores increased, and the dropout rate declined. A similar guideline, one that does not suggest promoting students who are 1 year or more below grade level, has been incorporated in the New York City schools ("Must We Promote," 1974). These programs or guidelines support, in essence, the notion of retention as a motivating factor.

Qualifications on the Research

With the aforementioned in mind, one may wonder about the role of nonpromotion in academic achievement. Unfortunately, there are no straightforward answers to the questions raised. Research in this area supports both sides of the argument; some investigations support the retention policy, while the majority oppose it. Haddad (1979), for example, states that educational expenditures are poorly made when a student repeats a grade. Haddad further states that supporters of nonpromotion believe or assume that (a) academic factors determine success and failure, (b) achievement tests are reliable and valid, (c) some skills are best learned at designated grade levels, and (d) children who are placed at similar developmental levels are at an advantage emotionally. To compound an already complicated problem, as stated previously, nonacademic factors also play a crucial role in the retention decision. Classroom conduct (Caplan, 1973) as well as socioeconomic status (Safer et al., 1977) have been cited as two such factors.

It should be noted that, generally, studies that support grade retention have included qualifying remarks. These studies do not suggest that nonpromotion is good for all low-achieving students. Recent research has suggested an appropriate time for retention (very early in the student's academic career—e.g., first grade) (Kerzner, 1982) as well as an appropriate student for retention (those who have learned some academic material, particularly reading; good self-concepts; and adequate social skills) (Sandoval & Hughes, 1981). Even further, some researchers (Bocks, 1977; Bossing & Brien, 1980) suggest a more human approach to retention that seeks to accentuate the positive aspects of retention and the positive aspects of the student. Specifically, Bocks (1977) has suggested that teachers should individualize their academic programs. This process may aid teachers in preparing lessons for the children in their classes, and familiarity may also help teachers to determine the special needs of each student. Further suggestions have been made by Bossing and Brien (1980), who indicate that support from parents, teachers, and the principal is essential when making the decision to retain a child. Parents, for example, should be knowledgeable about the child's progress throughout the year. A possible retention decision should be discussed with the parents early in the academic year, perhaps at a mid-year conference. This process should make the parents more comfortable with the retention decision, and, in turn, the parents may facilitate adjustment for the child.

GRADE RETENTION AND CHILDREN'S SOCIAL DEVELOPMENT

In order to understand the potential effects of grade retention on children, it is necessary to consider the different areas of children's lives on which retention can have an impact. The young child is not an automated being in which the only expected impact of grade retention is on the intellect, but rather a growing social organism. As such, the influence of the school on intellectual and social development must be examined simultaneously.

As previously stated, Sandin (1944) designed a study in which he assessed the social and emotional adjustment of regularly promoted and nonpromoted students. The findings showed that children who had been retained did not consider their new, younger classmates appropriate companions. Sandin concluded that this difference, as well as others (e.g., differences in behavior, interests, and likes and dislikes) between the nonpromoted students and their new classmates creates a barrier to good social relations. In particular, Sandin stated that students who were retained isolated themselves from their younger counterparts. This type of social isolation was compounded further by the fact that retained students were not able to socialize during school hours with their preferred companions from the upper grades, who were more like them in many respects than were their academic peers. Hence, nonpromoted students are not placed in an optimum social environment. According to Sandin,

> The difference between these groups of students as to attitudes and feelings indicated that the general outlook of the slow-progress pupils (i.e., retained) toward the school environment was not as favorable or as indicative of a happy adjustment as that of their regularly-promoted classmates. Many of them, (i.e., those who were retained) wanted to quit school and were easily discouraged or considerably worried about their future school progress. (p. 135)

Similarly, Caswell and Foshay (1957) concluded that the nonpromoted will suffer from depression and discouragement. The personality of the child is affected, most often unfavorably, by nonpromotion (cf. Finlayson, 1975). The explanation of this phenomenon offered by Caswell and Foshay (1957) is that children cannot discover the relationships between their activities and outcomes and hence do not see a road to success. This ambiguity will inadvertently lead to distrust of social and/or academic abilities and very often to expectations of further failure.

The studies by Caswell and Foshay (1957) and Sandin (1944) are important because they suggest that peer reactions may have a strong influence on a child's adjustment to school. If retained children are rejected or are targets of discrimination in their new classes, then academic and familial problems associated with retention will be compounded, and self-evaluation may suffer further.

Johnson (1981) reported that children who have experienced chronic failure in school (i.e., failed at least 3 years) develop feelings of learned helplessness. On the other hand, some investigators have claimed that nonpromotion is not detrimental to the child (e.g., Chase, 1972; Saunders, 1941). These mixed results suggest the possibility of other mediating factors that could affect the relationship between grade retention and the social development of children.

Status Generalization

The notion that the child is affected by factors other than purely academic ones is further corroborated by research suggesting that peers play an important role in the socialization of children (Graziano & Shaffer, 1979; Gump, 1980; Hetherington & Parke, 1979). Peer influence, like school influence, extends beyond intellectual development into the general realm of social development (Centra & Potter, 1980). In other words, peers can serve as models for comparisons as well as reinforcers for behaviors defined as appropriate by the peer group. Accordingly, those youngsters who engage in behaviors valued by their peers are reinforced (i.e., rewarded) for doing so, while those youngsters who do not behave in this manner are generally not well-liked by their peers (Graziano & Shaffer, 1979).

The implications of such findings are that status differences evoke differential evaluations about individuals and provide a basis for inferring differences in other capacities or characteristics possesed by the individual. Assumptions made about a person on the basis of his or her status category seem to be of two kinds. *Specific* expectations are formed about capacities that are relevant to the interaction itself; *general* expectations (also referred to as *diffuse* expectations) are formed about capacities that may extend beyond the context of the interaction (Berger & Fisek, 1970). The process of status generalization could help in determining how relevant and/or irrelevant factors could operate to influence children's perceptions of their peers. Several investigations have observed that children have conceptions that appear to be stereotyped about appropriate occupations for males and females, and for peers younger and older than themselves (e.g., Feather, 1975; Graziano, Musser, Rosen, & Shaffer, 1982; Thelen & Kirkland, 1976). Furthermore, children assume different statuses and roles within the peer group. These group-defined attributes determine the relationship of each child to other members of the group (Graziano & Shaffer, 1979).

An illustration will clarify this point: In accordance with status generalization theory (Webster & Driskell, 1978), children could possibly perceive a child who has been retained as having lower status than their regularly promoted counterparts. These differential status evaluations would determine the relationship between retained and nonretained children (cf. Walster & Walster, 1975). For instance, it is possible that the grade-retained child who performed as well as the nonretained child on a school-related task would be evaluated less favorably by his or her peers.

An extensive investigation by Plummer and Graziano (1982) provides a test of the aforementioned implications. Plummer and Graziano predicted that: (a) children who are regularly promoted would be preferred for a school-related task such as helping work math problems (i.e., specific expectations); and (b) regularly promoted children would also be preferred for a school-irrelevant task such as playing in a playground (i.e., diffuse expectations). These hypotheses were tested using a sample of 219 children: 105 second graders (65 females and 40 males) and 114 fifth graders (53 females and 61 males). A total of 46% of the population had been retained in grades, while 54% had not been retained.

The data indicated that 75% of the sample chose the retained target child to help them with the academic task. Spontaneous comments the children made explained these unexpected results. The children stated that since the child had repeated a grade, he or she would have more experience and would be in a better position to help them than the nonretained child. However, post hoc tests showed significant differences between the nonretained fifth graders' responses and all other participants' responses. These results showed that the nonretained fifth graders preferred other nonretained children to help them with the academic task. Differential social cognitions are suggested by these results. The older children seem to focus on the implications of being retained, whereas the younger children seem to reason that being retained and older implies more experience, hence more helpfulness. Nonetheless, given that the majority of the children preferred the retained older target child to assist them, it was concluded that there was no support for the prediction as stated.

Support was revealed for the second prediction, however. The majority (55%) of the children in this study preferred to play with the nonretained younger target child rather than the retained older target child. Significant main effects for grade status and grade were revealed. The nonretained raters preferred the younger nonretained play partner more often than they preferred the retained partner; the retained raters preferred the retained partner more often than they preferred the nonretained partner. Furthermore, the younger children (second graders) preferred the retained older target child more often than did the older fifth graders. It appears that younger children would prefer to play with someone older, whereas older children would prefer a same-age playmate. Again, since the majority of the children had a significant preference for the nonretained play partner, it was concluded that there was support for the diffuse-expectation hypothesis.

These findings are noteworthy in that they suggest that age can influence peer evaluations. Specifically, whereas the older retained child may be evaluated more positively by younger children, he or she may not be rated as positively by same-age peers. Hence, grade retention could hinder the retained child's social relations with same-age peers.

Furthermore, the results of this investigation are particularly noteworthy for two other reasons. First, the participants were not told that the stimulus children had been retained in grades. This was done so that the stimulus children would not be labeled as retained and thus create a response bias in the sample population. Participants were shown two 13 × 9-cm Polaroid color snapshots and were asked, "Can you guess why these children are in the same grade and one is older than the other?" The responses to this question revealed significant main effects for grade status and grade. The nonretained participants reliably identified the retained stimulus children more often than did the retained participants. Similarly, fifth graders identified the retained stimulus children more often than did second graders. Duncan's multiple range test showed that these differences were significant at the .05 level. Overall, 56% of the sample guessed correctly, 23% missed, and 10% of the participants did not respond.

Second, the investigators designed a procedure to counterbalance the height and grade status of the stimulus children. The height of the stimulus children was manipulated independently of grade status since previous research has shown that height (size) can influence children's social judgments (e.g., Graziano, 1978; Graziano et al., 1982). Therefore, in one condition, the target children were labeled correctly. In other words, the taller child was labeled as older (9 and 12 years of age for second and fifth graders, respectively). In the other condition, the target children were labeled in the reverse order. In other words, the taller target child was labeled as younger (7 and 10 years of age for second and fifth graders, respectively), and the shorter target child was said to be older. A significant Condition × Gender disordinal interaction emerged, suggesting that male and female participants react differently to relative size. The female participants could identify the retained target child more often in the retained-shorter condition than in the retained-taller condition. However, this occurrence was reversed for males; they identified the retained target child less often in the retained-shorter condition than in the retained-taller condition.

As such, these data are significant because of the suggestion that children are aware of their retained peers and that differential perceptions are formed for retained and nonretained stimulus children even when height of the stimulus children is counterbalanced.

Equity Theory

If retained children are rejected or are targets of discrimination in their new classes, then academic and familial problems associated with retention will be compounded, and self-evaluation may suffer further. Although the precise mechanism responsible for such discrimination remains unclear, some clues may be found in the literature on equity theory. Equity theory states that judgments of deservingness are an integral part of resource exchanges that characterize social behavior. A social exchange is equitable when resources (outcomes) are dispensed in proportion to contributions or inputs (Walster, Berscheid, & Walster, 1973). Thus, a worker who does 20% of the work deserves 20% of the available resources.

From the perspective of equity theory, it could be argued that rejection and peer discrimination against the retained child may be seen as the deserved outcome for the input of poor school performance. By itself, this interpretation is too simplistic. The retained child may actually outperform his or her nonretained peers on at least some school-related tasks due to greater familiarity with some of the materials. If, however, the equity formulation is expanded to allow additional inputs beyond relative school performance, then the equity interpretation may be more plausible.

In naturally occurring circumstances, children are confronted with information about accomplishments within a context of other information that may be at least as salient as task performance (Graziano, 1978; Leventhal & Michaels, 1971; Thelen & Kirkland, 1976). It is these other salient, yet diffuse, items of information (e.g., size, race, grade status) that can function as inputs and hence mediators in children's perceptions of their peers (Graziano et al., 1982).

The results of these empirical equity studies suggest that task performance is not the only basis for children's judgments of deservingness (Leventhal & Michaels, 1971). Walster and Walster (1975) proposed that these contextual determinants (i.e., status attributes associated with the individual, such as physical strength, gender, and race) come to be seen as inputs. Thus, they are mediators in the distribution of resources.

Plummer and Graziano (1982) used an allocation task to assess the influence of children's grade status (i.e., retained or nonretained) in the distribution of resources. Students were shown color photographs of two unfamiliar children who were of the same race, sex, and grade as the participant. For second graders, one stimulus child (i.e., the child in the photograph) was taller and older than his or her counterpart. The student was told that the ages of the children in the photographs were 9 and 7 years, respectively. For fifth graders, the student was told that the stimulus children's ages were 12 and 10 years, respectively. Underneath each stimulus child's photograph was a printed portion of a story that the stimulus child allegedly had read. The students were asked to give each stimulus child as many prize chips as they thought he or she should have for reading the story. It was predicted that, given comparable task performance, the regularly promoted stimulus child would receive more rewards than would children who had been retained. Accordingly, the students observed the retained child when he or she had read more than, less than, and the same as his or her nonretained counterpart.

The data indicated that evidence of discrimination occurred in the reward-allocation task when the retained and nonretained child's performances were equal. Results suggest the subtle influences grade status could have on children's perceptions of their peers. Both second and fifth graders allocated fewer prize chips to the taller retained child than to his or her nonretained counterpart, even though their performance was equal (i.e., they had read the identical portion of the story). There was a notable exception to this occurrence, however. The nonretained second-grade raters allocated more prize chips to the taller retained child in the dyad. Intuitively, this can be understood: Size is a more salient (i.e., highly visible) cue to the younger raters and is thus more likely to influence their judgments than is task performance (Graziano et al., 1982). In contrast, older children (fifth graders) are more aware of "social cues," and from the aforementioned results, they appear to have lower expectations about the grade-retained child than about the non-retained child.

It was concluded that there was some support for the predictions that the retained child would be the recipient of discriminatory acts. The retained children received fewer rewards even when their performance was equal to that of the nonretained children; however, this effect appears to be moderated by the height of retained children. As noted earlier, this investigation also showed that retained children were not preferred for the school-irrelevant task, yet they were preferred for the school-relevant task. Noteworthy findings were that these effects can be enhanced or lessened by the height of the retained target child in comparison with that of the nonretained target child and by the grade status and grade of the raters.

When holding sex of first graders constant, Asbury (1975) found that underachievers (i.e., those whose performances are below their grade level) were selected less frequently by their peers than were other children and that these underachievers had a lower level of personality adjustment than did their counterparts. These results are consistent with the conclusions of Chase (1972). Chase proposed that a child who does not compete successfully in school could develop problems in living and in coping with his or her environment. This proposal is not inconsistent with Chase's (1972) additional conclusion that nonpromotion is not as detrimental as previously believed. Chase clarifies her position by stating that careful selection of the child who is retained and consistent monitoring of that child's progress is necessary to alleviate or decrease the possible negative effects of grade retention.

Peer Perceptions and Relationships

These studies and others outlined earlier suggest another way, in addition to equity theory and status generalization, to consider peer reactions to children who have been retained. It is conceivable that a grade-retained child is seen as somehow different by his or her nonretained peers. However, little information is available on the ways children interact with other children who are seen as being different from themselves (cf. Hartup, 1979; Lippitt, Polansky, & Rosen, 1952). For example, Lougee, Goldman, and Hartup (1977) note that most knowledge of peer relations is based on studies in which children are highly similar to each other in age, race, gender, socioeconomic status, mental and physical capabilities, etc. In particular, when grade-retained children interact with their new classmates, a special case of naturally occurring mixed-age interaction may be observed.

Established literature now demonstrates that children's interactions do differ in same-age and mixed-age contexts (Furman, Rahe, & Hartup, 1979;

Goldman, 1981; Graziano, French, Brownell, & Hartup, 1976; Shatz & Gelman, 1973). The bulk of this research has stressed the potential ameliorative and therapeutic effects of mixed-age interaction. For example, Furman et al. (1979) found that by pairing a socially withdrawn older child with a younger partner, the socially withdrawn older child becomes more socially interactive with agemates.

Ameliorative effects may indeed occur in dyadic interaction, but there is also the possibility that the larger social context can make mixed-age interactions detrimental to the individual older child. In the natural ecology of elementary schools, for example, mixed-age interaction occurs when children are retained in grade. Such grade retention may or may not ameliorate academic differences, but evidence suggests that unless explicit measures are developed and implemented, social development may be detrimentally affected. This information is further supported by research indicating that academic performance is highly related to social adjustment (e.g., Caswell & Foshay, 1957; Dillon, 1975; Entwisle and Hayduk, 1978; Plummer & Graziano, 1982; Sandin, 1944).

Plummer and Graziano (1982) predicted that children who were retained would have less favorable social cognitions and expectations about themselves and their school surroundings than would children who were regularly promoted. The results pertaining to this prediction indicated that retained and nonretained children did have different perceptions about their environment. However, the results of these measures are not conclusive. A total of 46% of the population did not give "codable" responses. Perhaps the students were not able to respond in such an abstract manner; support is suggested for this possibility in that more fifth graders (56%) than second graders (32%) responded. Nonetheless, interpretations of these results are difficult. Clearly, more research is needed in this area; such research would employ more concrete dimensions for the younger, less cognitively sophisticated student.

The possibility that grade retention does in fact influence children's perceptions about their peers has been substantiated. However, Plummer and Graziano (1982) also suggest that the grade status of the rater, the level of the rater's social cognition abilities (e.g., grade level), and the height of the retained child could mediate children's perceptions of their retained peers.

IMPACT OF GRADE RETENTION ON SELF-EVALUATION

In recent years, as part of the "back-to-basics" movement in education, questions have been raised about the socialization mission of the schools. Some writers have argued, for example, that schools should focus their attention on developing children's fundamental academic competencies rather than on developing "tangential" qualities like self-concept (see Lerner, 1981).

Nonetheless, there is evidence that qualities like self-concept are related to academic performance.

An Overview of Research

Wattenberg and Clifford (1964) successfully predicted reading achievement 2½ years beyond the time that measures of self-concept were procured from kindergarteners. Similarly, Lamy (1965) suggested that self-perceptions and IQ in kingergarten predicted reading achievement in first grade equally well. Brookover, Thomas, and Patterson (1974) also found that student self-conceptions of ability predicted school performance better than IQ. Entwisle and Hayduk (1978) provide data that further support the relationship between self-esteem and the school environment: Specifically, by the end of the third grade, even before the age competent reading and writing skills are acquired, children have developed fairly stable and complex self-images. How well children are doing academically at that age is a good long-term indicator of school performance. The implication of this finding is that school performance can be enhanced or weakened as a function of the student's self-esteem.

Unfortunately, most of these claims are difficult to evaluate since very few studies have systematically investigated the impact of grade retention on self-esteem. Finlayson (1975) assumed that the few studies done in this area were inadequate in the sense that they were retrospective and often "one-shot" assessments. According to Finlayson (1975), these types of investigations cannot answer the basic question—that is, Does school failure cause a poor self-evaluation, or does a poor self-evaluation cause school failure? The basic argument of the present analysis is that it is not beneficial to isolate these two factors. As stated previously, the literature suggests that academic performance is related to three factors: self-evaluation, self-expectations, and social adjustment. It is argued that whether or not a child is successful in school can be determined by the degree of consistency among these factors. For example, actual academic performance is said to influence children's self-evaluations and self-concept by gradually becoming a part of a reciprocal feedback system. That is, actual academic performance influences self-evaluation, which in turn influences subsequent academic performance.

At least two school-related factors may mediate the potential effects of grade retention on self-evaluations. The first of these is teachers' attitudes toward students and their performance (e.g., Adams, 1963; Barocas, 1974; Brophy & Good, 1970; Cooper, 1979; Lerner & Lerner, 1977; Rich, 1975; Rist, 1970; Seaver, 1975). Teacher expectations are considered a primary source of information about expected abilities that shape children's self-concepts—particularly the expectancies children hold about their capability for academic performance (Braun, 1976; Brophy & Good, 1974; Good, 1980; Weinstein, Marshall, Brattesani, & Sharp, 1980). Research indicates that achievement is affected in that the child internalizes information from the teacher-pupil interactions into self-expectations and transforms the expressions of those self-expectations into behavior and academic performance (e.g., Cooper, 1979; Weinstein et al., 1980).

A second school-related factor influencing children's self-evaluation is actual academic performance, which has been discussed earlier. Initially, it is argued, a child who fails academically suffers from a lowered self-evaluation (cf. Finlayson, 1975). If repeated failure occurs, the student subsequently may come to accept his or her substandard performances (see Johnson, 1981). As such, these students' self-evaluations may no longer become affected by grade retention, in the sense that being retained is consistent with their evaluations of themselves as poor academic performers.

A Study of Self-Concept

Support for this process is offered from the investigation by Plummer and Graziano (1982). As noted earlier, both retained and nonretained second and fifth graders' self-concepts were measured. It was proposed that the younger children (i.e., second graders) would have less experience in coping with grade retention and would not yet be cognitively sophisticated enough to handle the often subtle environmental implications of being retained in grade. Furthermore, it was proposed that any efforts to alleviate or decrease potential negative impacts of grade retention would be most effective at the earlier grade levels. In contrast, analysis of retained and nonretained children's self-evaluations in the fifth grade was assumed to provide a more concise assessment of the phenomenon. As well as having had more direct experience with both retained and nonretained peers than had the second graders, these older children had developed to the point of being able to process others' attitudes and expectancies about grade retention.

Following Katz and Zigler (1967), Plummer and Graziano (1982) employed a measure of difference between real self-concept (i.e., how children actually feel about themselves) and ideal self-concept (i.e., how children would like to be). This measure was labeled actual self-concept. A correlation matrix was constructed to determine the degree of relationship between each of the self-concept measures. As might be expected, the child's actual self-concept is highly correlated with the real self-concept measure ($r = .86$), and the actual self-concept is negatively related to the ideal self-concept measure ($r = -.24$).

Self-Concept Hypothesis

Actual self-concept. It was predicted that students who had been retained would have a lower actual self-concept than students who had not been retained. To test this hypothesis, the children's actual self-concept scores (i.e., discrepancy scores) were analyzed. Differences were found between the retained and nonretained participants; however, the differences were in the opposite direction of the prediction. Overall, retained participants' actual self-concepts were more positive than were those of the nonretained participants. There was also a significant grade status × grade interaction. Nonretained children, both second graders and fifth graders, had a lower actual self-concept than did retained second graders and fifth graders. In order to understand these results, it is necessary to review the components of the self-esteem measure separately. A discussion of these findings is presented below.

Real self-concept. This measure was used to index the children's perception of themselves (i.e., it is one component used to assess the children's actual self-concept). A grade status main effect indicated that participants who had been retained had a higher (more favorable) self-evaluation than did participants who had not been retained.

Ideal self-concept. This measure was used to assess how the children "would like to be" (i.e., their ideal self-images). The ideal self-concept component was also used to compute the children's actual self-concept. Therefore, theoretically, the closer children's real self-concept evaluation is to their ideal self-concept, the more likely it is that their actual self-concept will be more favorable than that of children who have a larger discrepancy between "how they are" (real self-concept) and "how they would like to be" (ideal self-concept).

The most pronounced effects were indicated by the univariate analysis of the children's ideal self-concept. Significant effects were revealed for gender and grade. Results indicated that the male participants had higher ideal standards than did the female participants. The fifth graders' ideal self-concept measure indicated that they had higher ideal standards than did the second graders.

Social concept. Part of the Katz and Zigler (1967) self-concept measure included a questionnaire for the assessment of children's opinion on how others saw them. This measure was utilized in the present study. The only significant effect revealed by the univariate analysis on the participant's social-concept measure was an experimenter's race × gender interaction. The results showed that black experimenters received responses that indicated a more favorable social concept from white male and black female participants than was obtained by the white experimenters. Subsequent analysis showed that white nonretained fifth-grade males had a social concept significantly lower than that of all other participants.

Based on previous research, Plummer and Graziano (1982) hypothesized that retained children would have a lower self-concept than would nonretained children. However, their data suggest that children who have been retained have an actual self-concept significantly higher than that for nonretained children.

There are two possible explanations for this finding. First, children who have been retained are placed in classrooms where the work could be repetitive. Hence, they could perform better in this situation than they did previously. Since they could also be doing comparatively better than their classmates, their self-esteem is higher. This possibility has received support by Strang, Smith, and Rogers (1978) in their investigation of the mainstreaming phenomenon. These investigators found that educationally gifted children, when placed in classrooms together, make comparisons with "similar others." Thus, their self-esteem is lower than when they are in a regular classroom, where their performance on academic tasks excels that of their classmates.

The fact that the results of Plummer and Graziano's (1982) study showed that both males and fifth graders had significantly higher ideal standards than did females and second graders, respectively, posed another interpretation. Males are typically expected to strive for perfection in all they do, whereas society expects complaisant females. It is also suggested that, as children get older, self-standards increase. Older children have learned to accept their faults and have had enough successful experiences to believe that their futures hold great promise. When the older children in this study were asked if they thought that they were smart, they would say no, but when asked if they would like to *be* smart, they would say yes. In contrast, the trend of the retained children's responses indicates marked consistency. When asked if they thought that they were smart, retained children would say no, and when asked if they would like to be smart, they would again say no. Since the actual self-concept is computed by the discrepancy scores between the real and ideal self-concept measures, the individual ideal standards of the children are important. It is possible that retained children have come to accept their below average performance in school (see Centra & Potter, 1980).

Plummer and Graziano (1982) contend that their data support the second explanation. Furthermore, in the particular school in which the investigation took place, retained children are not given "repetitive" work per se. Rather, they start the new year at the level they completed the previous year and work from there.

Taken together, these data suggest that the impact of grade retention is manifest in subtle ways. It is noteworthy that different effects of retention are obtained from younger and older children and are differentially elicited by different examiners. These data also suggest that the impact of mixed-age interaction is moderated by the larger social context in which the interaction occurs.

Considering the information outlined, it is not surprising to find that a child's success or failure in the school environment is not just a matter of a child's individual efforts or of effective or ineffective teaching, nor is it merely a matter of a favorable emotional climate at home. The child who does not compete successfully in school is likely to develop problems in living and in coping with his or her surroundings (Chase, 1972). Taken together, these studies suggest that intellectual and social development go hand-in-hand and that so-called tangential qualities like self-concept and self-evaluation may be very important for subsequent intellectual development.

CONCLUSIONS AND DIRECTIONS FOR FUTURE RESEARCH

Grade retention is a widespread policy in schools in the United States. The topic elicits diverse attitudes as well as diverse research findings. Investigations in this area of inquiry have focused on academic and social factors influenced by grade retention. Conclusive statements regarding these factors are difficult to make; evidence suggests that the impact of grade retention may be manifest in subtle but significant ways. Nonetheless, a convergent analysis allows for some important points to be made.

Academic Consequences

Children are usually retained in grade because they fall below certain standards of academic achievement or social maturity. The fact that an abundance of research indicates that retention does not necessarily lead to significant improvements in academic achievement makes it necessary for all those concerned to take a closer look at the policy of grade retention. Even further, it is important to note that grade retention may not guarantee that the student will reach minimum performance standards to advance to subsequent grades.

A subcomponent of academic achievement, threat of nonpromotion, does not appear to be a significant motivating factor for students. Additionally, many extraneous factors may influence the decision not to promote a child. The most notable of these factors have included socioeconomic status and classroom behavior. Furthermore, grade retention does not produce a homogeneous classroom for teachers. The results of these empirical investigations are therefore in direct contradiction to the reasons established for retaining a child. Research evidence has also revealed that there are no consistent, generally accepted criteria for the retention of a child in grade. One plausible explanation for the contradictory findings is that different schools in the same districts or in different cities or states use different retention guidelines. Given that these variations exist, an initial problem is to systematically reevaluate basic grade retention policies. Specific guidelines are needed that can be accepted by different schools in different regions.

Social Consequences

The second reason a child can be retained in grade is that of social immaturity. The fact that grade retention practices permit the child to be placed in classrooms with younger children suggests the possibility of creating a situation in which the child reaches a limited level of social maturity. For instance, a child who is retained in the second grade may eventually reach the maturity level of his or her nonretained second-grade counterparts; however, this same retained child is chronologically older and should have reached a higher level of development. So the question becomes, Where should such a child be placed in the subsequent school term? The answer to this question depends on four related factors: (a) the developmental level the child has reached during the retained year; (b) the developmental level in which his or her chronological agemates operate; (c) the availability of faculty or staff to assist the child in making social adjustments; and (d) the support available to the child outside of the school environment (i.e., from family, friends, or other organizations such as clubs and churches). In order to answer this question, a substantial amount of information must be obtained. Caution is warranted in that the decisions made could well have long-term effects on the child.

Research suggests that grade retention could possibly interrupt children's interactions with their peers. Although the mechanism responsible for these effects remains unclear, the literature on mixed-age interactions, equity theory, and status generalization provides some clues. Briefly, the literature on mixed-age groups suggests that children do react differently to children who are perceived as different from themselves. Equity theory provides information on how discriminatory or justifiable interactions may occur. For example, from this perspective, it could be argued that rejection and peer discrimination against the retained child may be seen as the deserved outcome for the input of poor school performance. Status generalization may then be the process that promotes understanding of how relevant and/or irrelevant factors might operate to influence peer interactions. It seems that status differences evoke differential evaluations about individuals and provide the basis for inferring differences in other (i.e., irrelevant) capacities or characteristics possessed by the individual.

These findings are further complicated by potential developmental trends affecting children's perceptions of retained and nonretained peers. It appears that younger children, due to their developmental level or their less sophisticated level of social cognition, are less discriminatory toward a retained child than are their older counterparts (e.g., they reward both retained and nonretained children equitably for their performances). Or it could be argued that size is a more valuable and salient factor to the younger child than to the older child (i.e., younger children hold the older and larger child in higher esteem than they do a same-size or younger child). If this difference between age groups is true, then it is possible that retaining a child in earlier grades could be less harmful to the child than retention at a later stage. These speculations warrant further research.

Self-Concept

Based on previous research, it can be assumed that retaining a child in grade could increase, decrease, or have no effect on his or her self-concept. However, current investigations suggest that these mixed results could be due to an intervening variable — namely, a child's self-expectations. The old adage, "You are what you think you are" can be applied here. It is proposed that the child who is not successful in school may come to doubt his or her abilities, and once these doubts are confirmed by retention in grade, further expectations of success are lowered. For instance, a child who does not expect to do well (i.e., has a low ideal self-concept) and who actually does not perform well (i.e., has a low real self-concept) will appear to have a high actual self-concept. Such a child's actual performance would be consistent with his or her low expectations. The individual ideal standards or self-expectations of children are important. In order for a child to excel, he or she must be motivated to do so and must believe that success is possible.

Implications for Educators

It is apparent that educators must rethink the policy of grade retention. In light of evidence against this policy, possible alternatives must be sought. Many alternatives have been proposed in the literature, yet well-meaning teachers continue to employ retention with the support of parents and school administrators. Perhaps teachers, parents, and school administrators are not convinced that there are problems related to nonpromotion. If this is the case, convincing evidence must be presented to them in formal (e.g., inservice training, parent conferences) and informal ways. It is further suggested that if retention is employed, rational decision making, parental attitudes, administrative and peer group attitudes, and the characteristics of the student and environment must be taken into account. There can be no simple solution to this complex problem.

Grade retention as a solution to the "minimal competencies" problem may itself pose further problems. The primary task for researchers is to isolate those factors that would minimize the potential negative effects of grade retention and maximize the benefits. For instance, so far it has been established that grade retention can be beneficial for the child if: (a) careful selections are made of children who will be retained; (b) retention is implemented when it will be most effective and least likely to have a negative impact on the child's social development; (c) systematic assessments are made of the child's academic and social progress; and (d) parents, teachers, and peers are supportive of the child (e.g., reward the child for academic progress and encourage cooperation and interactions with peers and involvement in extracurricular activities). These factors are important and must be considered if grade retention is to have a positive impact on the child's academic and social development.

REFERENCES

Abidin, R.R., Golladay, W.M., & Howerton, A.L. (1971). Elementary school retention: An unjustifiable, discriminatory and noxious educational policy. *Journal of School Psychology, 9,* 410–417.

Adams, S. (1963). Toward an understanding of inequity. *Journal of Abnormal and Social Psychology, 67,* 422–436.

Ames, L.B. (1981, March). Retention in grade can be a step forward. *Educational Digest,* pp. 36–37.

Arthur, G. (1936). A study of the achievement of sixty grade 1 repeaters as compared with that of non-repeaters of the same mental age. *The Journal of Experimental Education, 5,* 203–205.

Asbury, C. (1975). Maturity factors related to discrepant achievement of white and black first graders. *Journal of Negro Education, 44*(4), 493–501.

Ayers, L. (1909). *Laggards in our school.* New York: Sage Foundation.

Barocas, R. (1974). Referral rate and physical attractiveness in third grade children. *Perceptual and Motor Skills, 39,* 731–734.

Berger, J., & Fisek, M. (1970). Consistent and inconsistent status characteristics and the determination of power and prestige orders. *Sociometry, 33,* 287–304.

Bocks, W.M. (1977). Non-promotion: "A Year to Grow?" *Educational Leadership, 34*(5), 379–383.

Bossing, L., & Brien, P. (1980). *A review of the elementary school promotion/retention dilemma.* (ERIC Document Reproduction Service No. ED 212 362)

Braun, C. (1976). Teacher-expectation: Sociopsychological dynamics. *Review of Educational Research, 46,* 185–213.

Brookover, W., Thomas, S., & Patterson, A. (1974). Self concept of ability and school achievement. *Sociology of Education, 37,* 271–278.

Brophy, J., & Good, T. (1970). Teacher's communication of differential expectations for children's classroom performance: Some behavioral data. *Journal of Educational Psychology, 61,* 365–375.

Brophy, J., & Good, T. (1974). *Teacher-student relationships.* New York: Holt, Rinehart, & Winston.

Buckingham, B.R. (1926). *Research for Teachers.* New York: Silver Burdett.

Caplan, P.J. (1973). The role of classroom conduct in the promotion and retention of elementary school children. *The Journal of Experimental Education, 41*(3), 8–9.

Caswell, H.L. (1933). *Nonpromotion in elementary schools* (Field Studies, No. 4). Nashville, TN: Division of Surveys and Field Studies, George Peabody College for Teachers of Vanderbilt University.

Caswell, H., & Foshay, A. (1957). *Education in the elementary school.* New York: American Book Co.

Centra, J., & Potter, D. (1980). School and teacher effects: An interrelational model. *Review of Educational Research, 50,* 273–291.

Chase, J.A. (1968). A study of the impact of grade retention on primary school children. *Journal of Psychology, 70,* 169–177.

Chase, J. (1972). Differential behavior characteristics of nonpromoted children. *Genetic Psychological Monographs, 86,* 219–277.

Coffield, W.H. (1954). *A longitudinal study of the effects of nonpromotion on educational achievement in the elementary school.* Unpublished doctoral dissertation, Iowa State University, Ames.

Cooper, H. (1979). Pygmalion grown up: A model for teacher expectation communication and performance influence. *Review of Educational Research, 49,* 380–410.

Dillon, S.V. (1975). Schools with failure and alienation. *The Journal of School Health, 45*(6), 324–326.

Dobbs, V., & Neville, D. (1967). The effect of non-promotion on the achievement of groups matched from retained first graders and promoted second graders. *The Journal of Educational Research, 60*(10), 427–474.

Entwisle, D., & Hayduk, L. (1978). *Too great expectations.* Baltimore: The Johns Hopkins University Press.

Eshel, Y., & Klein, Z. (1981). Development of academic self-concept of lower-class and middle-class primary school children. *Journal of Educational Psychology, 73*(2), 287–293.

Farley, E., Frey, A., & Garland, G. (1933). Factors related to the grade progress of pupils. *Elementary School Journal, 24*(3), 186–193.

Feather, N. (1975). Positive and negative reactions to male and female success and failure in relation to the perceived status and sex-typed appropriateness of occupations. *Journal of Personality and Social Psychology, 31,* 536–548.

Finlayson, H. (1975). *The effect of nonpromotion upon the self-concept of pupils in primary grades.* (ERIC Document Reproduction Service No. ED 155 566)

Furman, W., Rahe, D., & Hartup, W. (1979). Rehabilitation of socially withdrawn preschool children through mixed-age and same-age socialization. *Child Development, 50,* 915–922.

Glasser, W. (1969). *Schools without failure.* New York: Harper and Row.

Godfrey, W. (1971, October). The tragedy of failure. *North Carolina Education,* pp. 10–11.

Goldman, J. (1981). Social participation of preschool children in same- versus mixed-age groups. *Child Development, 52,* 644–650.

Good, T. (1980). Classroom expectations: Teacher-pupil interactions. In J. McMillan (Ed.), *The social psychology of school learning* (pp. 79–122. New York: Academic Press.

Graziano, W. (1978). Standards of fair play in same-age and mixed-age triads in relation to chronological age and incentive condition. *Child Development, 47,* 707–714.

Graziano, W., French, D., Brownell, C., & Hartup, W. (1976). Peer interaction in same- and mixed-age triads in relation to chronological age and incentive condition. *Child Development, 47,* 707–714.

Graziano, W., Musser, L., Rosen, S., & Shaffer, D. (1982). Standards of deservingness in same-race and mixed-race situations. *Child Development, 53,* 938–947.

Graziano, W., & Shaffer, D. (1979). The role of peers in the socialization process: A theoretical overview. In D.R. Shaffer, *Social and personality development* (pp. 514–544). Monterey, CA: Brooks/Cole.

Gump, P. (1980). The school as a social institution. *Annual Review of Psychology, 31,* 553–582.

Haddad, W.D. (1979, March). *Educational and economic effects of promotion and repetition practices.* (ERIC Document Reproduction Service No. ED 195 003)

Hartup, W. (1979). Children and their friends. In H. McGruk (Ed.), *Child social development.* London: Methven.

Hess, F., Martin, W., Parker, D., & Beck, J. (1978). *Promotion versus non-promotion: A policy review.* (ERIC Document Reproduction Service No. ED 158 398)

Hetherington, E., & Parke, R. (1979). *Child psychology: A contemporary viewpoint.* New York: McGraw-Hill.

Jackson, G. (1975). The research evidence on the effects of grade retention. *Review of Educational Research, 45,* 613-635.

Johnson, D. (1981). Naturally acquired learned helplessness: The relationship of school failure to achievement behavior, attributions, and self-concept. *Journal of Educational Psychology, 73,* 174-180.

Katz, P., & Zigler, E. (1967). Self-image disparity: A developmental approach. *Journal of Personality and Social Psychology, 5,* 186-195.

Kerzner, R.L. (1982). *The effect of retention on achievement.* Unpublished master's thesis, Kean College of New Jersey. (ERIC Document Reproduction Service No. ED 216 309)

Keyes, C. (1911). *Progress through the grades of city schools.* New York: Bureau of Publications, Teachers College, Columbia University.

Klene, V., & Branson, E.P. (1929). Trial promotion versus failure. *Los Angeles Educational Review Bulletin, 7*(5), 6-11.

Kowitz, G.T., & Armstrong, C.M. (1961). The effect of promotion policy on academic achievement. *The Elementary School Journal, 61,* 435-443.

Lamy, M. (1965). Relation of self perceptions of early primary children to achievement in reading. In J.J. Gordon (Ed.), *Human development readings in research,* Chicago: Scott Foresman.

Lerner, B. (1981). The minimum competence testing movement: Social, scientific, and legal implications. *American Psychologist, 36,* 1057-1066.

Lerner, R., & Lerner, J. (1977). Effects of age, sex and physical attractiveness, academic performance, and elementary school adjustment. *Developmental Psychology, 13,* 585-590.

Leventhal, M., & Michaels, J. (1971). Locus of cause and equity motivation as determinants of reward allocation. *Journal of Personality and Social Psychology, 17,* 229-235.

Lippitt, R., Polansky, N., & Rosen, S. (1952). The dynamics of power. *Human Relations, 5,* 37-64.

Lobdell, L.O. (1954). Results of a nonpromotion policy in one school district. *Elementary School Journal, 54,* 333-337.

Lougee, M., Goldman, J., & Hartup, W. (1977, March). *Group compositions: Effects on the social behavior of children.* Paper presented at the biennial meeting of the Society for Research in Child Development, New Orleans, LA.

Metcalfe, B. (1981). Self-concept and attitude to school. *British Journal of Educational Psychology, 51,* 66-67.

McKinney, H. (1928). *Promotion of pupils, a problem in education administration.* Unpublished doctoral dissertation, University of Illinois, Urbana.

Must we promote children who can't read? (1974). *American School Board Journal, 161*(2), 21.

Otto, H.J., & Melby, E.O. (1935). An attempt to evaluate the threat of failure as a factor in achievement. *Elementary School Journal, 35,* 588-596.

Owens, S.A., & Ranick, D.L. (1977, March). The Greensville program: A commonsense approach to basics. *Phi Delta Kappan,* pp. 531-533.

Plummer, D., & Graziano, W.G. (1982). *The impact of grade retention on the social development of elementary school children.* Unpublished manuscript, Psychology Department, University of Georgia, Athens.

Reiter, R.G. (1973). The promotion/retention dilemma: What research tells us. *Philadelphia Office of Research and Evaluation, 7416,* 1-23.

Rich, J. (1975). Effects of children's physical attractiveness on teachers' evaluations. *Journal of Educational Psychology, 67,* 599–609.

Rist, R. (1970). Student social class and teacher expectations: The self-fulfilling prophecy in ghetto education. *Harvard Educational Review, 40,* 411–451.

Safer, D., Heaton, R., & Allen, R.P. (1977). Socioeconomic factors influencing the rate of nonpromotion in elementary schools. *Peabody Journal of Education, 54*(4), 275–281.

Sandin, A. (1944). Social and emotional adjustments of regularly promoted and nonpromoted pupils. New York: Teachers College, Columbia University.

Sandoval, J., & Hughes, G.P. (1981). *Success in nonpromoted first grade children. Final Report.* (ERIC Document Reproduction Service No. ED 212 371)

Saunders, C. (1941). *Promotion or failure for the elementary school pupil.* New York: Teachers College Press.

Seaver, W. (1975). Effects of naturally induced teacher expectancies. *Journal of Personality and Social Psychology, 28,* 332–342.

Shatz, M., & Gelman, R. (1973). The development of communication skills: Modification in the speech of young children as a function of the listener. *Monographs of the Society of Research in Child Development, 38* (5, Serial No. 152), 1–37.

Strang, L., Smith, M., & Rogers, C. (1978). Social comparison, multiple reference groups, and the self-concepts of academically handicapped children before and after mainstreaming. *Journal of Educational Psychology, 70,* 487–497.

Thelen, M., & Kirkland, K. (1976). On status and being imitated. *Journal of Personality and Social Psychology, 33,* 691–697.

Walster, E., Berscheid, E., & Walster, G. (1973). New directions in equity research. *Journal of Personality and Social Psychology, 25,* 151–176.

Walster, E., & Walster, G. (1975). Equity and social justice: An essay. *Journal of Social Issues, 31,* 21–43.

Wattenberg, W., & Clifford, C. (1964). Relation of self-concepts to beginning achievement in reading. *Child Development, 35,* 461–467.

Webster, M., & Driskell, J. (1978). Status generalization: A review and some new data. *American Sociological Review, 43,* 220–236.

Weinstein, R., Marshall, H., Brattesani, K., & Sharp, L. (1980, September). *Achieving in school: Children's views of causes and consequences: A preliminary report on methodology.* Paper presented at the annual meeting of the American Psychological Association, Montreal.

10

Preschool Social Education Curricula in West Germany: The Situation-oriented Approach

Frithjof M. Oertel

University of Hannover, West Germany

INTRODUCTION

Kindergarten work in West Germany (i.e., formal education for 3- to 6-year-old children) has changed dramatically during the past 10 to 15 years. These changes can best be seen in the development, implementation, and evaluation of curricula that have been widely accepted within the frame of kindergarten teaching. In fact, the whole reform movement can be described primarily as a shift from *function-oriented* approaches to *situation-oriented* approaches in both kindergarten and preschool work.[1] To introduce the following discussion of situation-oriented curricula, it is first helpful to draw a contrast between these two very different approaches.

A Function-oriented Classroom

Let us go back to the early 1970s. We are in a typical Protestant kindergarten classroom in Hannover, where a single teacher is working with a homogeneous group of 5- to 6-year-olds. Other teachers "play" with a group of much younger children and with another intermediate group. Between these groups contact is minimal. The older group of children is organized by the most able of teachers, whose aim is to give them serious preparation for schooling at all cost. The kindergarten has to work constantly to stem criticism that it is neg-

---

[1] The term "situation-oriented approach" is used in this discussion in two ways. It refers generally to all varieties of the approach, but — if so noted — it also indicates specifically the curriculum devised by Oertel and colleagues.

lecting the intellectual capacities of the children: The children must be readied for learning how to read, write, and count. This process includes training in different skills or functions: motor skills, cognitive skills, verbal skills, social skills, etc. The training follows operationalized objectives, is a step-by-step approach that involves all the children as a group, and proves learning success by testing. Those children who are deprived socially and intellectually are seen as being especially in need of basic knowledge and skills.

Today the kindergarten teacher is worried. Although everything has been done to promote psychomotor skills, some children are still retarded in their progress. They do not even know how to fold a sheet of paper diagonally. So the teacher prepares an exercise on how to fold a house out of paper, hoping that the children will not only obtain training in psychomotor skills, but also concentrate on one specific material. The sheets of paper are laid out, and the teacher demonstrates how to fold them. The children admire the results. Some are ready to learn how to fold a house. The teacher repeats the demonstration step by step. At the beginning, everybody is eager to follow, but soon some children become frustrated and begin talking to each other. Heinz seems to have no success at all. He destroys his product: "Rats!" he cries. Others are struggling, but Karin is moving right along: "I've got it!" she cries out. Karin receives most of the attention of the teacher and the group. "I'll take this home to show Mom," she says. And so the lesson goes on . . .

A Situation-oriented Classroom

Now let us go to the beginning of the 1980s. The picture in many kindergarten classrooms has changed. We are in a typical situation-oriented classroom in Garbsen, near Hannover, and the teacher is working with a heterogeneous group of 3- to 6-year-old children. Within the kindergarten are three heterogeneous subgroups of children, all with equal status. Every year, part of the group leaves to enter the first grade, and new children come to the group. There is contact among the groups, with interaction varying according to interests. Each group develops its own program according to the needs and the situations that occur. The kindergarten teacher thinks that enabling children to deal competently and autonomously within their life situations is the most important learning process in life and is therefore also the most effective preparation for school. The training of functions and skills is limited to the situations in which these skills are needed. Situations such as getting to know one another and one another's families, developing group life, exploring surroundings, dealing effectively with the time outside kindergarten, and solving problems in the neighborhood are considered of primary importance. Classroom work is a continuing process of social learning, and criticism that the kindergarten should incorporate more direct preparation for reading, writing, and counting is answered according to the situation-oriented, personality-centered approach: "Those are not the skills we are here to teach. Let the elementary school do its job, and we will do ours," the teacher would probably answer.

Today the kindergarten teacher observes a scene among the children. The youngsters are role-playing a situation between a security guard and children playing outside a house. "Quick, let's run away," some children cry out, looking around in fear. The child playing the part of the security guard comes nearer: "Damn it, children," he says, "get out of the way. This is not a playground." He shakes his fist in the air, threatening, "I'll tell your parents!" At first, the teacher is mildly amused, but as the children interact she becomes more seriously interested. She realizes that this is not only play; the children are acting out a real experience with a security guard who attacks them verbally whenever they ride their bicycles or roller skate near the house.

Some hours later the kindergarten teachers sit together as a team. They discuss a new theme—the situation "Playing in the Neighborhood." Lots of information is exchanged: how the parents deal with this situation, experiences of visits with children of the group in different families, the living conditions within the families, how parents deal with dangers on the street, etc. Different projects follow in the next weeks, including mutual visits in the families; special excursions to the neighborhood (to different houses, apartments, modern high-rise buildings, farms); playing kindergarten games at home (my fantasy playground or playhouse). Slowly, problems within this situation are dealt with, and the attitudes of children, parents, and teachers change. The neighborhood is influenced to more fully accept playing children; the situation "Playing in the Neighborhood" is, as these kindergarten teachers would call it, "democratized" (i.e., it gives way to the needs and interests of the children and their parents).

Obviously, these classrooms, described here very briefly (see Kolbe & Wurr, 1981, Chapters 2 and 3), are different. The next section deals specifically with the following questions: What are the major aspects of the reform movement? Which different phases can be described and analyzed? and, How can the present state of preschool education in West Germany best be understood? The third section in this discussion is an in-depth study of the situation-oriented approach—its general characteristics and its different schools—outlining criticisms from both within and outside the educational community. To answer these criticisms, arguments from basic research are addressed in a separate section. A concluding statement then refutes the essence of the criticisms, gives new perspectives, and stresses the relevance of the situation-oriented approach for kindergarten work not only in West Germany but also in similar industrialized countries in the east and west and especially in Third World countries, where the methodology of this approach for developing the early childhood curriculum has already met with some success.

INSTITUTIONALIZED PRESCHOOL EDUCATION IN WEST GERMANY: THE REFORM MOVEMENT

Overview

At the end of the 1960s and the beginning of the 1970s a euphoric discussion of reform was started in West Germany. The primary question addressed was, What constitutes the ideal preschool education? Educational politics had discovered preschool education. Several factors had come together: different interests and expectations, sociopolitical motifs, research findings, and economic considerations (see Hemmer & Obereisenbuchner, 1979, Chapter 1). It was felt that each child should have equal opportunity in education, all people's capacities should be discovered and developed to the highest possible level, and, perhaps most important, the educational level of our industrialized society should be uplifted in order to facilitate technological development in the future. Within this discussion, kindergarten teachers came under heavy attack. They were accused of neglecting the preschool child's cultural development and capacity to learn. Intellectually demanding programs were called for (see Lückert, 1974, pp. 189–273). Those parents who didn't accept the authoritarian practices of traditional pedagogy founded a counter-institution, the *Kinderladen*, which spread rapidly within the Federal Republic (Breiteneicher, 1971). The German Education Council, while accepting kindergarten as the beginning level of the educational system, considered it necessary to limit kindergarten education to 3- to 4-year-olds and to send 5-year-olds to elementary school (Deutscher Bildungsrat, Bildungskommission, 1970). Many institutions and political parties, as well as public opinion, supported this proposal. In fact, this proposal marked the beginning of an unprecedented reform movement within the history of early childhood education. The proposal did not limit itself to the development of preschool education as a specific academic field, but also included planning, implementing, and evaluating many model projects aimed at identifying optimal learning situations for 5-year-olds. In addition, this proposal fostered the development of curriculum materials, some of which are in use throughout Germany today. In all of these areas, the reform movement provided not only the impetus for change but also some specific proposals for that change.

The academic field.   Preschool education in the beginning of the 1970s was closely tied to elementary education. Facilitating later schoolwork and helping children get a good start in school were of primary concern, and this understanding was reflected in the model projects and the kinds of curriculum materials developed (Belser & Bauerjee-Schneider, 1972).

Toward the beginning of this 15-year reform, another interpretation of preschool education, as "institutionalized education before school" specifically for 3- to 6-year-olds, gained increasing recognition. The emphasis here was on social education and on the development of social skills. Because kindergarten education stopped imitating elementary education and began to find its own identity, preschool education during this period became increasingly synonymous with kindergarten education. This identity provided emphasis on the socialization process, a characteristic that clearly distinguishes kindergarten from elementary education (Küchenhoff & Oertel, 1976).

Preschool education today has an even larger meaning. It addresses the child's total learning experience from the beginning of life to the beginning of first grade. In addition, it includes the effects of various institutions on young children, interactions inside and outside the family, and other academic disciplines that have a bearing on preschool education, and it is distinct from elementary education as well as from the fields of social work and social education. Preschool education is a discipline in its own right, concentrating on what is good for children before school age. As such, it concerns all educational sciences and deals with the fundamental questions of how people learn and begin to develop their own identities (Kossolapow, 1977).

The model projects.   Although one of the original goals of the reform movement was to draw a new boundary between kindergarten and elementary school, the model projects produced results that led politicians from all sides to keep the division as it was. The first strike in this direction was the evaluation of 47 projects by a team of administrators and experts (Bund-Länder-Kommission für Bildungsplanung, 1976). These projects explored different settings: specific age groupings for 5-year-olds in kindergartens, preclasses that included classes of 5-year-olds in the elementary school (the equivalent of the American kindergarten), and special programs integrating 5- and 6-year-olds in the elementary school. The study avoided a clear decision against the original goal, indicating that all model projects have positive effects and that political authorities should therefore ensure participation of all children in preschool institutions. While such a result might have indicated that there was no need to change the boundary between kindergarten and elementary school, a strictly comparative study of preclasses for 5-year-olds at school and kindergartens with heterogeneous groupings, the results of which were published later, established the superiority of the kindergarten program over preclasses (Minister für Arbeit, Gesundheit und Soziales des Landes Nordrhein-Westfalen, 1977; Strätz & Schmidt, 1982). Reversing their earlier positions, the *Länder* (state) governments in West Germany (with the exception of the city-states) concurred in the late 1970s in the decision to keep 5-year-olds in the kindergartens, which would then be increasingly restructured in family groupings. The reasons for this altered decision were the long-term intellectual and general effects on children of kindergarten work and, more specifically, advantages of social learning exhibited by kindergarten children as compared with children in preclasses.

The curriculum materials. During the reform movement, the kindergarten evolved from an endangered species into a widely accepted institution for 3- to 6-year-olds. It legitimized itself as an institution clearly distinct from elementary school. These changes did not occur simply because of the great number of kindergartens established (today almost all children of this age group can attend a kindergarten). A wider understanding of the meaning of preschool education and the positive results of the model projects were also helpful in bringing about this new situation. In addition, the success of such programs was the result of fundamentally new insights into educational concepts. In fact, the newly developed materials and educational approaches — the shifting from function-oriented approaches to situation-oriented approaches and their consequences — were the primary reasons. In this respect, the reform can be subdivided into three phases.

Three Phases of Curriculum Work

Phase 1 — curriculum development: Prevalence of the function-oriented approach. During the first half of the 1970s, when sending 5-year-olds to school was being debated in the ways outlined above, initial programs in the different *Länder* concentrated on working conditions and curriculum reform in kindergartens (Arbeitsgruppe Vorschulerziehung, 1974). This was the period of developing new curricula. Building on current theories of preschool education, many function-oriented materials were developed (cf. Belser & Bauerjee-Schneider, 1972; Nitz, 1972). While other approaches were only in the making, function-oriented curricula dominate the scene not only within the model projects but outside as well. These function-oriented curricula were intended to teach the child systematically — i.e., by proceeding step-by-step in such fundamental areas as perception, language, and cognitive skills — in all areas where educational psychologists felt able to operationalize instruction. The materials were handed out in files. "Training in files" therefore became synonymous with whatever seemed to be important in preschool education.

Traditional kindergarten work also continued, but it was perceived as having no relevance. The real work was the daily period of training in files. During that period, every child in the so-called "preschool group" within the kindergarten or in any other preschool institution had to participate. Parents had to obtain information if their child was ill so that the child could do his or her training in files at home, and the training in files had to be repeated as many times as necessary. Great emphasis was placed on mastery of information and on measuring this mastery through testing. Preschool education was considered a necessary prerequisite for beginning reading, writing, and mathematics in the first grade. But, as can be seen from the following description, these curriculum materials also produced serious problems. Specifically, problems centered around five characteristics of the materials and their implementation:

1. Learning in its narrowest sense was required. Teachers, parents, and children had to assume duties and follow the standard program as they do at the elementary school level.
2. The learning materials were not easily adapted to playing, yet playing is the characteristic way in which children of preschool age learn.
3. Achievement was stressed, thus endangering the harmonious development of the child's whole personality.
4. The cognitive domain of the personality received absolute priority over the social-emotional and interactive domains, and this emphasis jeopardized the child's motivation.
5. There was virtually no transfer of functions, capabilities, and skills from the teaching situation to the real-life situations where they were needed (see Oertel, 1976).

Before this phase came to an end, and especially since many different school and kindergarten settings were included, difficulties with this approach were discussed at large. Even where highly structured lessons, homogeneous groupings, priority to the cognitive domain, and training and learning as a duty for the whole group were incorporated within an institution, it was not easy to use function-oriented materials. Teachers and administrators encountered many difficulties that could be solved only by using authority.

Phase 2—curriculum implementation: Prevalence of the situation-oriented approach.   In the second half of the 1970s, the results of work with models in the different *Länder* were exchanged and tested in a nationwide trial program (Bund-Länder-Kommission für Bildungsplanung und Forschungsföderung, 1982). This program, a unique experience in West German educational politics, included about 15,000 children and was charged with finding methods that could be widely used and transferred to everyday kindergarten work. The exclusive concentration of this program on kindergarten work, combined with a diminishing interest in sending 5-year-olds to school, made it apparent that the function-oriented materials widely included in the federal trial program had no chance within the enlarged kindergarten model group. Specifically, kindergarten teachers, for the sake of their children, refused to "function" (i.e., to follow prescriptions day after day, to imitate school settings, to separate children from each other, and to assign duties to children of this age). Although function-oriented instruction was found to enhance test results at the beginning of the child's school life, its effects proved not to last very long. In addition, the overall activities of kindergarten teachers with their children seemed to be of much more importance than the training in files. And finally, a new approach being widely discussed had brought out materials that strengthened social learning processes in the natural surroundings of the child.

In contrast to the large quantity of function-oriented materials developed previously, alternative project materials, although scarcely represented, won increasing acceptance. As has been briefly sketched in the introduction, these situation-oriented materials do not concentrate on teaching basic skills or functions. Instead, they draw on real-life situations and enrich children through multifaceted educational techniques (such as stories, pictures, role playing, games, and discussion). The teacher may choose whatever is appropriate to the group situation, the children's interests, his or her own educational skills, the financial means of the institution, and so forth. The educational proposals are regarded as enriching the child's life experiences (and probably those of the parents), as well as broadening the child's ability to manage real-life situations, chance to solve problems adequately, and inclination to interact socially. Real-life situations (for example, how to use the television, how to deal with quarreling among friends, or how to begin first grade) are an important part of this process. Social learning is central to such materials, and while the results of such learning cannot be measured easily, in the long run children profit personally in terms of their self-concept and social adjustment. Self-confidence, social competence, and mastery of facts are concurrently developed. Kindergarten work in heterogeneous groupings profit from this approach, and in fact more and more kindergartens in the federal trial program rediscovered the logic of a family-like grouping of children (Almstedt & Kammhöfer, 1980).

On the whole, then, the implementation phase inadvertantly promoted the situation-oriented approach and its materials all over the country. Articles in handbooks described the new kindergarten as a situation-oriented institution (Mörsberger, Moskal, & Pflug, 1978).

Phase 3 — curriculum evaluation: Acceptance of the situation-oriented approach. During the past few years, those materials that had been successfully tried out on a federal basis were revised and implemented nationally within the projects of the different *Länder*. Because only situation-oriented materials had won wide acceptance, only those materials were given a chance for revision. Three schools, or approaches, especially received general recognition; these schools have produced materials now ready for use throughout the 1980s. The first of these schools is the *situation approach,* characterized by 28 teaching units developed under the direction of Jürgen Zimmer (1973) by a working group in preschool education at the German

Youth Institute in Munich. The second school is the *situative approach,* described by Erna Moskal and her working group at the Ministry of Labor, Health, and Social Order in Dusseldorf in a set of guidelines for the planning process in kindergarten work (Minister für Arbeit, Gesundheit und Soziales des Landes Nordrhein-Westfalen, 1983). Finally, the *situation-oriented approach,* developed by the author and his colleagues at the University of Hannover (Oertel, 1982, 1983), provides eight teaching units. Although the materials produced by these groups vary, sometimes fundamentally, all three schools emphasize the child's social learning and make use of real-life situations in their curricula. Table 1 details the major works and goals of these three approaches; a subsequent section of this discussion will be devoted to an in-depth study of the materials presented by these schools.

How Things Stand Today

The end of the evaluation phase has brought the reform movement to an end. Apart from research work carried out on specific questions (for example, that concerning handicapped children or children of foreign workers), the research concentrated on curriculum work has stopped completely. While the new approach seems to be widely accepted, it is not firmly established. The present economic crisis makes it more difficult to realize the approach: Kindergarten personnel are reduced, more children are taken into groups, paid time for the planning of educational activities is limited, and virtually no funds are available for the necessary inservice training of kindergarten teachers. Higher professional standards for kindergarten teachers are seen as being controversial. And finally, as the crisis goes on, special interest groups are raising criticisms.

THE SITUATION-ORIENTED APPROACH

General Aspects of the Situation-oriented Approach

Although the situation-oriented approach includes different schools (whose specific characteristics, scientific backgrounds, implications for curriculum development, and kindergarten institutions are explained in Table 1 and will be dealt with at greater length shortly), these schools have certain common characteristics. Among these are the following assumptions:

1. Learning especially in early childhood, is a matter of experience (cf. the "learning by doing" approach of John Dewey). The kindergarten should therefore be seen and structured primarily as a field of experiences for building a way of life through projects, activities, field trips, etc.

Table 1 Schools of the Situation-oriented Approach

	Type of Approach		
	Situation Approach	Situative Approach	Situation-oriented Approach
1. Author and developmental group	Jürgen Zimmer and the Working Group in Preschool Education of the German Youth Institute at Munich, composed of about 30 experts in the field and kindergarten teachers and social educators of Hesse and Rhineland-Pfalz.	Erna Moskal, in connection with a mixed working group of the Ministry of Labor, Health, and Social Order at Dusseldorf in Nordrhein-Westfalia	Frithjof Oertel and his co-workers W. Dichans, S. Böse, R-Chr. Bracke, R. Bührlen-Enderle, M. Dedekind, H.L. Fichtner, A. Gerke, and W. Liekefett, in cooperation with kindergarten teachers and social educators of Lower Saxony – a project carried out at the University of Hannover.
2. Title of materials	*Curriculum Soziales Lernen: Didaktische Einheiten für den Kindergarten* [Social Learning Curriculum: Teaching Units for Early Childhood Education] (Arbeitsgruppe Vorschulerziehung, 1980).	*Arbeitshilfen zur Planung der Arbeit im Kindergarten* [Aids for the Planning of Kindergarten Work] (Minister für Arbeit, Gesundheit und Soziales des Landes Nordrhein-Westfalen, 1983).	*Elementare Sozialerziehung: Praxishilfen für den Kindergarten* [Elementary Social Education: Practical Aids for Kindergarten Work] (Oertel, 1982), *Konzept und Methoden elementarer Sozialerziehung: Materialien für die Aus- und Fortbildung der Erzieher* [Concept and Methods of Elementary Social Education: Materials for the Training of Kindergarten Teachers] (Oertel, 1983).
3. Main content	Twenty-eight units dealing with subjects such as television, handicapped children, children of foreign workers, and children in the hospital. Units are subdivided into in-	Eight chapters and three appendices. Chapters include "Kindergarten as an Institution in its Own Right," "Planning and Evaluation of Educational Work," "Methods and	Eight units, including "Entering Kindergarten," "We Get to Know Each Other," "The Kindergarten Group," "Everybody Has a Family," "Exploring Our Surroundings," "What

	troduction, materials to analyze the situation, educational proposals, cooperation of parents and other adults, and use of didactic materials.	Organizational Structures of Educational Work," "Tasks and Forms of Work with Parents," "Teamwork," "Materials for Kindergarten Work," "Children in Specific Situations," and "Cooperation with Primary School and Other Educational Institutions." Appendices include "Fundamental Perspectives in Education," "Prescriptions of the Law," and "Contributions of the Institute of Social Education."	We Do Outside of Kindergarten Time," "People Here and in Other Places," and "We'll Go to First Grade." Units include general aids for planning, proposals for practical work, and hints on other materials (picture books, stories, play materials, handbooks for kindergarten teachers, etc.).
4.	Important accompanying literature and other relevant materials	Seventeen situation films to accompany different teaching units. Also Zimmer (1973), Arbeitsgruppe Vorschulerziehung (1973–1976), and Colberg-Schrader and Krug (1977, 1980).	Merker, Rüsing, and Blanke (1980).	Film on conflict education at the preschool level (brochure, 2 × 2 slides, and cassette). Also Küchenhoff and Oertel (1976), Oertel (1978).
5.	Target group	Primarily kindergartens and training institutes.	Primarily all kindergartens and training institutes in Nordrhein-Westfalia.	Primarily the individual kindergarten teacher and social educators, personnel of training institutes, and preschool experts.
6.	Educational aims and overall goals for the child	Autonomy and competence (solidarity), capacity to manage life situations in social contexts.	Self-confidence, communication skills, discovery and understanding of one's surroundings, articulation and management of changing life situations.	Self-competence, social competence, and factual competence (a competence set); development of forms of social contact; resolution of conflicts; understanding of societal structures in everyday life; management of conflicts and life situations.

(Continued)

Table 1 (Continued)

		Type of Approach	
	Situation Approach	Situative Approach	Situation-oriented Approach
7. Methodological approach	"Projects" (field trips, activities, group reports, and documentaries) and "plays" (mostly role playing or simulation games) accompanied, prepared, or evaluated by discussion. Planning processes with children and parents, opening of kindergarten work to the community.	Development of play and "free activities," work in differing small groups, introduction of play and work materials, flexible use of time and space, mixture of direct and indirect methods.	Themes developed by playing, telling stories, showing pictures, preparing collages. From time to time, excursions and smaller activities. Treatment by discussion, repeated playing, and creative work; introduction of themes into periods of free play.
8. Process of planning	Choice and analysis of present and future real-life situations by researchers and others involved; continued analysis of situations, resulting in immediate changes. Linkage between social learning and technical skills within this process; cooperation among parents in defining goals, analyzing situations, and organizing the child's learning processes. Mutual learning of parents, teachers, and children for close contact between kindergarten and community.	Observation and its structuring, defining themes, developing themes according to learning fields.	Choice of situation among the teaching group (observation and collection of information), analysis of the situation (documentation and judgment), decisions about relevant aims, methodological orientation, and evaluation following implementation.

9.	Project history	1971–75: Development of materials in Hesse and Rhineland-Pfalz. 1976–78/79: Federal trial program, including the 9 participating *Länder.* Formation of special evaluation group for the program. 1979–80: Revision.	1974: Publication of materials. 1976–78/79: Federal trial program in 8 *Länder.* Specific evaluation of materials by an internal evaluation group. Revision for use in the 1980s.	1970–71: Prepatory stage. 1972–75: Development of materials in Lower Saxony. 1976–78/79: Federal trial program in 7 *Länder.* Specific evaluation in Lower Saxony. 1980–81: Revision.
10.	Scientific background	Robinsohn, Dewey, Illich, and Freire. Reaction against function- and "discipline-" oriented approaches and traditional kindergarten work.	Reaction against function-oriented approaches, subject orientation, content orientation, but also against too much action in the classroom.	Roth, Hentig, and the new social studies in the United States. Reaction against systematic learning in preschool education and traditional social education.

2. Growth can best be achieved through everyday life situations involving habits, conflicts in interactions, and fundamental childhood problems. Exercises isolated from real life are ineffectual.

3. Learning in real-life situations means including the whole personality of the child and holistic striving for self-confidence, social competence, and mastery of facts (Roth, 1971). The child has to learn to handle situations more and more independently.

4. Intense participatory observation of the everyday life of the child and his or her activities in the group is essential if the teacher wants to use the situation-oriented approach.

5. Situation-oriented work depends on constant communication within the teaching team. Innovative experiences depend on cooperation.

6. Everyday life in a kindergarten is not made up of a series of isolated activities. Instead, it is a total experience in which each activity is carefully planned to contribute to the overall goal of making the child able to act adequately in life situations. However, the situation-oriented approach requires flexibility on the part of the teacher to meet the needs and interests of the individual children involved.

7. Playing and learning can be regarded as intertwined rather than separate; the multifaceted situations of role playing and role interpreting stimulate identity formation in the child (Mead, 1968).

8. Free play and instruction are equally important opportunities for learning by experience. Experiences with themselves, other children, and adults, as well as with their natural and cultural surroundings, may help children learn to handle their own situations.

9. A flexible response to the specific needs and interests of children is necessarily included in educational planning. Individual participation is never mandatory.

10. Social education (about forms of social contact, conflicts in the group, and social structures, especially in the immediate environment) is central to the situation-oriented approach; all work can be integrated into this general field (Oertel, 1977a, 1977b).

11. Mixed-age groups in kindergarten facilitate social experiences. Children in heterogeneous groups can meet with friends at different stages of development; they can learn (and are stimulated to do so by the situation itself) how strongly people vary because the variety is greater; they can help and care for one another; and, finally, they can participate in the program as they feel comfortable. No child is forced to meet a standard set for his or her age group because standards, if they exist, are not made explicit.

12. A flexible arrangement of room structures and surroundings can enhance the opportunities of the children to provide their own experi-

ences. In principle, every field of children's activity can be represented within the classroom.

13. Equipment, toys, books, etc., should always be selected according to the general theme, perhaps in cooperation with parents and children. Such themes may be "The Group Life," "Exploring the Surroundings," "Children of Foreign Workers," "Children Come to School," and so forth.

14. Instead of a fixed schedule (weekly, monthly, or yearly), an open plan clearly oriented to the needs and interests of individual children is preferable.

15. Finally, the teacher is not the all-knowing expert but a partner of children and parents, ready to benefit from their knowledge, their ideas, and their abilities to open up opportunities for learning by experience and to ensure learning.

The situation-oriented approach cannot be planned only on a day-to-day basis. It is a continuing process that starts as an idea but slowly comes to include all facets of the learning process. Step by step, through action and reflection, the whole educational institution undergoes an innovative process. This process can be explained in greater detail according to the different schools of the approach.

Schools of the Situation-oriented Approach

The situation approach: Starting with the social sciences.   The situation approach (see Table 1, first column), initiated by Jürgen Zimmer, is an original curriculum development approach that, in comparison with the other two schools, puts the greatest emphasis on the social sciences. Consulting with kindergarten teachers, social science researchers have chosen and analyzed children's present- and future-life situations and have presented their analyses to teachers. The teachers have then continued the developmental process by transforming the analyses into teaching units, giving parents and children equal chance to contribute to the teaching/learning processes. In particular, parents and their children are encouraged to contribute to the choice of analyses and activities, to help make decisions about educational aims, and to assist in determining the concrete parts of the group work referring to life situations. Through these different projects, specific parts of the social reality (such as playgrounds, hospitals, and schools) are presumably influenced in order to meet children's needs and to facilitate their efforts to deal adequately with these situations. The underlying idea is to open the kindergarten to the community and to democratize the community through kindergarten initiatives. Teaching units may last several months; sometimes several units are dealt with at the same time.

In the beginning, the situation approach was directed primarily toward the content of the teaching process and the teaching/learning relationship per se. However, during the federal trial program, it became clear that the working conditions in the kindergarten strongly affected the implementation process. The model projects utilizing this approach had excellent working conditions (i.e., two adults in a group of children, time for educational planning, extra rooms to subdivide groups, educational equipment, etc.). Adherents of this approach therefore fight for better working conditions for all kindergartens, asserting that improved conditions will provide better chances to realize the curriculum. Thus, this approach can also be considered the most politicized of the three.

The situative approach: Starting with the socialization process. The situative approach (Table 1, second column), represented by Erna Moskal and her colleagues, started from very traditional kindergarten background and educational planning and has tried to inject innovation into them. According to this approach, the kindergarten teacher works within the everyday situations in the early childhood group (how the children play and what they talk about and look at) and tries to enlarge on these activities. A curriculum, if considered a book of preplanned activities, is not necessary. Every teacher has to find his or her own way.

Sometimes this approach is strikingly similar to traditional kindergarten work, but the fine examples presented in the literature (Merker, Rüsing, & Blanke, 1980) demonstrate that innovation is possible. These examples lean heavily on the play activities of the children. Situations from outside in the community seem to be integrated into play centering on stores, banks, families, teachers, materials, etc. Thus, the community can be considered to be represented; however, no special changes, either in the community or in the kindergarten's working conditions or type of educational planning, are expected.

The federal trial program has shown that kindergarten teachers really need a curriculum if they want to function effectively. Without special inservice training, guidelines are not enough. Although guidelines made it easy to get started in the process of implementing the situative approach, they were soon left behind in order to act and reflect on more demanding programs.

The situation-oriented approach: Integrating socialization, situation, and social sciences. The situation-oriented approach (Table 1, third column), developed by the author and his colleagues at the University of Hannover, started as a mutual exchange between some scientists and many kindergarten teachers. Originally, the teachers were unable to fulfill the demands of social and educational scientists and were dissatisfied with the scientists' work. Slowly, from visit to visit, from observation to observation, from one bit of unit to the next, a mutual understanding between teachers and scientists was developed. This understanding led to a curriculum out of which the scientists developed frames of reference (the understanding of social education, the theory/practice module for curriculum development, and the integration of curriculum work as a part of the overall kindergarten concept). The teaching units per se were the results of the teachers' exchange processes, action, and reflection. The curriculum was designed to give equal attention to the child, the theme (situation), and the discipline. Every effort was made to ascertain the proper balance.

The federal trial program demonstrated the usefulness of this integrative position. Materials could be revised to reflect a greater openness to the situation and flexibility for the learner. The curriculum, the development of which is considered only one part of the activity of the teacher, will not be undermined if other aspects of the kindergarten do not change. Although this approach begins with traditional work and with the everyday situations that can be observed in the group, innovation within the whole setting is the final goal. The community cannot be completely excluded from these changes.

Criticisms of the Situation-oriented Approach

Although widely used and accepted, situation-oriented approaches have encountered severe criticism from the very beginning, and the criticism has increased in the past few years. Some of this criticism has come from the researchers who introduced these approaches. Some of the questions raised by such researchers are enumerated below.

1. What is meant by the term "situation"?
2. Can the situation chosen be fundamentally — not only pragmatically — justified?
3. How far-reaching should the analysis of the situation be?
4. To what degree is it really possible to allow parents and children to participate in the process of analyzing situations and implementing situational learning?
5. Are all interpretations of situations (for example, "Playgrounds in the Neighborhood") acceptable? If not, how can the inappropriate ones be recognized?
6. After a careful analysis of the situation, what should be included in the teaching process?
7. Can education adequately answer to all the different levels of socialization that can be found in a group of children?

8. How can generally accepted overall goals be managed to keep the full support of the group?
9. To what extent can education really be combined with the play of children?
10. What are the measurable effects of the approach on children's development?

Although the questions have been formulated, research to date has discovered only some of the answers, and the funding of research in this field has come almost to an end.

Other fundamental criticism comes from outside the research community involved with the situation-oriented approach. These major points have been collected, reorganized, and annotated (Höltershinken, 1982). The criticisms are worthy of consideration and will be answered point by point.

Religious arguments. Fundamental criticisms come from religious educators (Kaufmann, 1974) who find the situation-oriented approach anthropologically unsound, especially when implemented according to the situation approach. These critics assert that the overall goals of autonomy and emancipation underlying the situation-oriented approach should be revised. Indeed, these goals are not giving sufficient notice to the goal of developing the social responsibility of every individual in a given society; and, in fact, a revision of the goals has been accomplished by the authors' addition of "solidarity" to the overall goals.

The basic human activity of managing one's situation, the argument goes, is overstressed to the exclusion of culture, tradition, history, and the value-bound behavior that is influenced by these factors (see Colberg-Schrader & Krug, 1980). In other words, the human being is not seen by these critics as being as "free" as the situation-oriented approach implies.

Regardless of their derivation, the overall goals of situation-oriented approaches and their emphasis on socialization can be justified when seen from a broader perspective. Learning is fundamentally social learning; it is a continuing dialogue and an interactive process. It makes sense, therefore, to start formal education with a strategy that first approaches the socializing process at home and tackles real-life situations — their analyses, enrichment, and changes. Descriptions of this process include labels like "autonomy," "self-, social, and factual competence," "self-reliance," and so on. It is the social dimension as a general learning field that is of concern. This definition of learning has nothing to do with actionism, social technology, lack of tradition and history, or avoidance of value questions. There may be dangers in these trends, but these reproaches stem from different interpretations of learning in general.

Arguments from social critics. Arguments come next from scientists who are very critical of our present society. They point out that the approach has not developed a theory of society. Asserting that real-life situations shouldn't be taken as final states that one can choose voluntarily in order to manage, these critics argue that real-life situations have to be changed through actions according to a developed concrete utopia. Changing one's individual life situation, step by step, doesn't satisfy these critics. They fear that these efforts will simply result in society's stagnating at its present level (Geulen, 1975).

If critics point to a lack of a utopian model of society implicit in the approach, they must remember that while they have a right to present their views, they must not force their own solutions on all people. Human beings should not be expected to accept only one perspective. The interpretation and definition of situations and their results require long-term discussion within every learning group. Otherwise, teachers, students, and parents would be subject to foreign will and would never become self-defining human beings. Defining processes cannot be predetermined for all times and environments; they must be experienced and developed cooperatively. The situation-oriented approach is a process approach emphasizing methodology and not content. It is, therefore, open to everyone's interpretation.

Criticisms based on developmental psychology. Other critics (Göckeler, 1981) stress a lack of orientation toward developmental psychology. They claim that the participation of 3- to 6-year-old children, along with their parents, in the analysis of situations is psychologically unsound, arguing that children cannot be equal to adults in analyzing situations. Children, these critics claim, have different views of reality; it is possible that they would define real-life situations in ways radically different from the interpretations of adults. However, in kindergarten programs utilizing the situation-oriented approach, the role of children involved in analyzing and developing the situation differs dramatically from the role of adults. In their own way, within their level of understanding, children *can* participate. Admittedly, it is difficult to make socialization processes and educational proposals compatible, as even the authors of these approaches agree, but it is worth the effort (see Zimmer, 1973, p. 43). Developmental theories and empirical data have also shown that, although psychologists have been minimally involved in creating the situation-oriented approach, this method does not demand achievement beyond the ability of the 3- to 6-year-old child. Certainly, participation requires interactive capacities leading to the phase of concrete operations. The development of materials for preschool learning tasks is central to this approach. However, a simple adherence to Piaget's approach is inadequate because egocentrism and social learning seem to be mutually exclusive at this age. The development of the learning processes of preschool children has to be fundamentally refined.

Arguments concerning Neo-Marxian influence. Finally, some critics actually fear a Neo-Marxian influence on kindergarten work resulting from the situation-oriented approach (Maier, 1980). This almost irrational criticism has to do with the orientation of the approach toward Piaget's findings that children develop their moral judgments in different stages. To these critics, this means a refusal of classical ethical thinking within the churches, especially within the Catholic church. Criticisms also concern the theory of Habermas, in which ethical positions cannot be simply stated by authority (religion, church, or party) but must be developed through human communication.

To refute these claims, it can be argued that the ethical norms of any religious denomination or social group are not lost when children are involved in the development of their own system of values. Condemning this as a Neo-Marxian approach is absurd. For the children's sake, the perspective of special interest groups must be rejected. Such views may be presented, but, because the structure of thinking, speaking, and acting is not merely an adapting process, they will not be accepted.

While space does not allow for a specific answer to all of the criticisms of the situation-oriented approach, it may be noted that they are to some extent self-contradictory. In addition, these arguments are bound to specific disciplines and interests, and in many cases ask too much of the theoretical background and practical realization of the approach. An educational approach can never solve all problems and be acceptable to all interest groups. However, these criticisms include the main points of the present discussion of preschool education in West Germany and point out some of the inherent dangers.

The next section will deal fundamentally with the scientific background that supports the situation-oriented approach. This background will make clear that the approach is essential for competence formation and identity development during the child's preschool years. Social learning is the fundamental agent of change in the child's early development. If this point can be illuminated, even the most profound skepticism about situation-oriented curricula should disappear.

ARGUMENTS FOR THE PRIORITY OF SOCIAL EDUCATION IN EARLY CHILDHOOD

First argument: *Changes in curriculum development and research (i.e., in applied research) are reactions to worldwide trends in basic research.* The shift toward situation-oriented curricula from function-oriented (also called "discipline-oriented") curricula has been described in didactic literature as a shift toward: (a) process versus product orientation; (b) interactionistic versus behavioristic learning; (c) teachers and learners being treated as subjects rather than objects; (d) curriculum development by teachers themselves rather than by experts; (e) decentralized versus centralized decision making; (f) context-bound curriculum as opposed to curriculum materials neutral to contexts; and (g) task orientation rather than knowledge orientation (Becker & Haller, 1974; Deutscher Bildungsrat, Bildungskommission, 1974; "Thema: Offene Curricula," 1973).

Those in West Germany and elsewhere who have chosen situation-oriented curricula (which has become more and more the majority position in Germany), have also chosen a change in the models of basic research. They have rejected positivistic or behavioristic positions in favor of relativistic, phenomenological positions: Humans cannot be seen as complex machines that can be conditioned under scientific control to the right behavior for the improvement of humankind. On the contrary, individuals must be seen as active beings defining themselves in a continuing interaction with their surroundings, through experiences that force them to organize, differentiate, and restructure perceptions again and again but bring them to no more than relative truth in the process (Breadmore, 1980). The situation-oriented approach has to be seen in the light of a tradition that stresses social learning, interaction, and communication as basic to learning processes.

Second argument: *Recent efforts to describe the development of the child tend to emphasize the mutual exchange of biological and societal factors in development, describing not only their existence but also their intertwined effects at every step of development as well* (Peukert, 1979). Whenever scientists in West Germany today try to describe the development of the child or even aspects of the child's behavior—for example, playing (Hebenstreit, 1979)—they draw from theories of different origins in order to avoid a one-sided picture. Mostly, elements of cognitivism (Piaget, Bruner) are combined with those of psychoanalysis (Freud, Erikson) and symbolic interactionism (Mead, Goffman, Krappmann). Parmentier (1979) shows us some biological tendencies in Freud and Piaget. He explains that two extreme positions of learning are no longer acceptable: learning as a process of actualizing a genetic potential (as in maturation theory) and learning as a result of influences from outside (as in behavioristic learning theory). To Parmentier, learning is a defining process based on symbolic interactionism:

Each definition of a situation which a human being makes is based on his desire to perceive the situation as it really is. But the reality of the situation is unknown. You can never grasp a situation in itself—except from its definition through the thinking and acting human being. Whether there are situations independent of "defining" processes of the human being can never be known by this human being. . . . Defining situations, therefore, can never be an act of reflection, like looking into a mirror. But at the same time it cannot be a simple projection either. In both cases the activity of the human being would be limited to the continual repetition of what already exists, be it within the subject or in the environment. Instead, I am considering the definition of a situation as an undertaking in which subjective and objective moments of reality are intertwined. The situation thus defined is the expression of reality reworked by the human being. (pp. 26–27)

Learning in itself is therefore an interactive process; in its fundamentals, it is situation-oriented social learning.

Third argument: *A critical analysis of theories and empirical data concerning the development of competence and identity formation in early childhood shows that the development of interactive competencies must have priority over cognitive and verbal competencies.* In order to clarify the process of identity formation in children, a brief description of development in the cognitive, language, and interactive domains follows. With respect to the cognitive domain, Piaget (1967), and Bruner (1970) describe the cognitive capacities in early childhood as preoperational and rigid with respect to context and situation. But the cognitive structure of young children can be changed, as has been demonstrated, especially by Russian psychologists (Galperin, 1969; Leontjew, 1973; Wygotski, 1974). Children can partially use abstract thinking, and special studies prove that egocentric speech has the sense of dialogue rather than monologue. Such speech can be seen functioning positively as cognitive self-direction in problematic situations:

This means that thinking and control behavior have to be considered with Wygotski as an internalization of language and of the control behavior of the language community of the child; egocentric speech is typical of the transitional stage from external speech to internal thought. (Peukert, 1979, p. 99)

Speech development accordingly precedes cognitive development.

As concerns the language domain, the acquisition of language cannot be explained acceptably as a simple conditioning process (cf. the disagreement between B.F. Skinner and Noam Chomsky at the end of the 1950s). Although the rate of biological or genetic determinants should not be discounted, language development is seen today as the learning of complex action sequences that increasingly find verbal expression. Language cannot be considered a system of symbols with which an objective reality can be copied; instead, it represents a "way of life," a "practice through use" (Wittgenstein, 1967). Consequently, verbal acts have to be seen as actions in situations having consequences. New research approaches demonstrating this understanding show that the child, from his or her earliest attempts at speaking, tries to structure interaction. For the child, every verbal act has meaning depending on cognitive knowledge. Through problems of interaction with responding persons, the child is forced to give up naive routines of interaction and to develop syntactical differentiation (Miller, 1976). In the child between the ages of 3 and 6, verbal behavior becomes more and more independent of its context, paralleling the development of the child's interactive capacities and his or her insight into different perspectives on situations.

In the interactive domain, research into the development of interactive competencies in early childhood clearly demonstrates that the hypothesis of egocentrism in early childhood must be revised. Role taking does not require concrete operational thinking. Although much empirical data indicates that the preschool child is unable to clearly distinguish between his or her own perspective and the perspectives of others, this result should be interpreted very carefully. A revised model of social competence, according to Flavell (1974), shows that elementary knowledge of different perspectives in visual and affective perception and experiencing exists at a very early age. An individual has to consider the perspective of others in order to fulfill personal intentions. However, role-taking abilities are used to different degrees according to the difficulty of a task (i.e., a person may have the competencies but may not necessarily use them). It is difficult for preschool children to anticipate and heed the emotions and perspectives of other children as clearly as they perceive their own. An adult can interpret a child's behavior adequately only by seeing the situation through the child's eyes. Children need to be taught to actualize and develop further their capabilities for changing their perspectives. Interactive experiences thus have an effect on both speech and thinking.

Fourth argument: *An analysis of basic research in early childhood demonstrates that social learning deserves peeminence in early childhood education (Peukert, 1979).* The fundamental areas in early childhood development, as defined in this literature, include: (a) shifting from egocentrism to sociocentrism; (b) ensuring one's role in appropriate age and sex groups; and (c) learning empathy (i.e., reflecting on one's own role in relation to others). These steps are all overall goals of social learning. The process of development from a preoperational to a concrete operational stage in thinking, speaking, and interacting "can be seen as a process in which interactive potentials lead to a differentiation of syntactical structure and a clearer verbal description of complex situations. In the cognitive domain this potential helps the transition to reversible operations (Piaget) . . . and to a continuing decentralization of perspectives of perception" (Peukert, 1979, p. 167). The situation-oriented approach can certainly aid in this process.

Fifth argument: *The structure of interactive processes in early childhood must be set up in accordance with the overall goals of social learning.* Such social learning must be seen as occurring within a situation-oriented context:

1. The development of the child must be seen as an interactive process in which the reactions of the child are affected by the actions he or she has

learned to expect from adults and in which the actions of adults are shaped by the reactions they expect from the child.

2. The whole personality of the child, in all its dimensions, must be included.
3. Different stages of development (for which the cognitive theory of Piaget, if modified, is still the best frame of reference) must be taken into account by the teacher.
4. Learning must be interpreted as a dialectical process that necessitates continual restructuring of the thinking process in the attempt to cope with problems. Educational processes and programs must be shaped in order to envision the child today in terms of his or her potential for the future.

CONCLUSION

Preschool education in West Germany can be seen in terms of several perspectives resulting from various aspects of the reform movement during the past 15 years. The present situation of the kindergarten, which serves 3- to 6-year-old children, can best be demonstrated in the development, implementation, and evaluation of its programs. Three stages of development have been described, and today's predominant situation-oriented approach has been characterized and illustrated through description of its different schools.

This approach and its instructional materials have legitimized preschool education as an academic field and given it an educational perspective in its own right. One hopes that this bodes well for preschool education in the 1980s. Criticism of the approach, mostly the result of the economic crisis and political conservatism, cannot stand up to research findings. The basic principles of the situation-oriented approach have been justified scientifically. After years of applied research — development, implementation, evaluation, and revision of educational concepts and materials — the approach is now ready for worldwide use. Its materials are appropriate for preschool institutions in any country with an industrialized society similar to West Germany's. In theory and practice, its methodology may be used for curriculum development throughout the world.

REFERENCES

Almstedt, L., & Kammhöfer, D. (1980). *Situationsorientiertes Arbeiten im Kindergarten: Bericht über ein Erprobungsprogramm* [Situation-oriented work in kindergarten: A report about a trial program]. Munich: Juventa Verlag.

Arbeitsgruppe Vorschulerziehung. (1973–1976). *Anregungen* [Stimulations] (Vols. 1–3). Munich: Juventa Verlag.

Arbeitsgruppe Vorschulerziehung. (1974). *Vorschulische Erziehung in der Bundesrepublik: Eine Bestandsaufnahme zur Curriculumentwicklung* [Preschool education in the Federal Republic of Germany: A stocktaking of curriculum development projects]. Munich: Juventa Verlag.

Arbeitsgruppe Vorschulerziehung. (1980). *Curriculum Soziales Lernen: Didaktische Einheiten für den Kindergarten* [Social learning curriculum: Teaching units for early childhood education]. Munich: Deutsches Jugendinstitut, Kösel Verlag.

Becker, H., & Haller, H.D. (1974). *Das Curriculum: Praxis, Wissenschaft und Politik* [The curriculum: Practice, theory, and political implications]. Munich: Juventa Verlag.

Belser, H., & Bauerjee-Schneider, K. (1972). *Curriculum — Materialien für die Vorschule* [Curriculum materials for the preschool]. Weinheim und Basel, West Germany: Beltz Verlag.

Breadmore, J. (1980, December). *Humanistic education: What it means.* Paper contributed to the World Council for Curriculum and Instruction World Conference on Education, Development Academy of the Philippines, Tagaytay City.

Breiteneicher, H.J. (1971). *Kinderläden: Revolution der Erziehung oder Erziehung zur Revolution* [Kinderladen. Revolution of education or education for the revolution]: Reinbek, West Germany: Rowohlt Verlag.

Bruner, J.S. (1970) *Der Prozeß der Erziehung* [The process of education]. Berlin and Düsseldorf: Berlin Verlag, Pädgogischer Verlag Schwann.

Bund-Länder-Kommission für Bildungsplanung. (1976). *Fünfjährige in Kindergärten, Vorklassen und Eingangsstufen: Bericht über eine Auswertung von Modellversuchen* [Five-year-olds in kindergartens, preschools, and introductory classes: An evaluative report about model projects]. Stuttgart: Ernst Klett Verlag.

Bund-Länder-Kommission für Bildungsplanung und Forschungsförderung. (1982). *Erprobungsprogramm in Elementarbereich: Bericht über eine Auswertung von Modellversuchen* [A trial program in early childhood education: An evaluative report about model projects]. Bühl, West Germany: Konkordia GmbH für Druck und Verlag.

Colberg-Schrader, H., & Krug, M. (1977). *Arbeitsfeld Kindergarten: Planung, Praxisgestaltung, Teamarbeit* [The kindergarten as a field of work: Planning, practice formation, teamwork]. Munich: Juventa Verlag.

Colberg-Schrader, H., & Krug, M. (1980). *Lebensnahes Lernen im Kindergarten: Zur Umsetzung des Curriculum Soziales Lernen* [Life-oriented learning in kindergartens: The practice of the social learning curriculum]. Munich: Kösel Verlag.

Deutscher Bildungsrat, Bildungskommission. (1970). *Strukturplan für das Bildungswesen* [A structural plan for the educational field]. Bonn: Bundesdruckerei.

Deutscher Bildungsrat, Bildungskommission. (1974). *Zur Förderung praxisnaher Curricullum-Entwicklung* [Fostering practice-oriented curriculum development]. Stuttgart: Ernst Klett Verlag.

Flavell, J.H. (1974). The development of inferences about others. In T. Mischel (Ed.), *Understanding other persons* (pp. 66–116). Oxford: Rowman & Littlefield.

Galperin, P.J. (1969). Die Entwicklung der Untersuchungen über die Bildung geistiger Operationen [The development of research about the forming of cognitive operations]. In H. Hiebsch (Ed.), *Ergebnisse der sowjetischen Psychologie* [Results of Russian psychology] (pp. 367–405). Stuttgart: Ernst Klett Verlag.

Geulen, D. (1975). Probleme vorschulischer Curriculumentwicklung für den Bereich der sozialen Handlungsfähigkeit [Problems of preschool curriculum development in the domain of capacities for social action]. In A. Baumgartner & D. Geulen (Eds.), *Vorschulische Erziehung* [Preschool education] (Vol. 2, pp. 13–73). Weinheim und Basel, West Germany: Beltz Verlag.

Göckeler, J. (1981). *Zur Integration der Entwicklungspsychologie Piagets in den Bezugsrahmen des situationsorientierten, vorschulischen Curriculumansatzes* [The integration of the developmental psychology of Piaget into the frame of reference of the situation-oriented approach to preschool curricula]. Unpublished manuscript, University of Dortmund, West Germany.

Hebenstreit, S. (1979). *Spieltheorie und Spielförderung im Kindergarten* [Play theory and the promotion of play in kindergartens]. Stuttgart: Ernst Klett Verlag.

Hemmer, K.P., & Obereisenbuchner, M. (1979). *Die Reform der vorschulischen Erziehung: Eine Zwischenbilanz* [The reform of preschool education: An intermediate evaluation]. Munich: Juventa Verlag.

Höltershinken, D. (1982). Grundsätzliche Fragen und Probleme situationsorientierter Kozepte und Materialien für die Arbeit in Kindergärten [Fundamental concepts and materials for early childhood education]. In *Pädagogische Konzeptionen und Materialien für die Arbeit in Kindergärten: Situationsorientierte Ansätze* [Educational concepts and materials for early childhood education: Situation-oriented approaches]. Freiburg: Zentralverband Katholischer Kindergärten und Kinderhorte Deutschlands e. V., Karlsstr. 40, 7800 Freiburg, West Germany.

Kaufmann, H.B. (1974). *Fragen zur Curriculumkonzeption der "Arbeitsgruppe Vorschulerziehung"—Bildungsplanung und Erziehungsauftrag im Elementarbereich: Der Beitrag der Evangelischen Kirche* [Questions concerning the curriculum approach of the working group for preschool education—Educational planning and the educational task in early childhood education: The contribution of the Protestant Church]. Munster: Comenius-Institute.

Kolbe, G., & Wurr, R. (1981). *Funktionsansatz und Situationsansatz in der Praxis des Kindergartens: Fallanalysen und pädagogische Perspektiven* [Function-oriented and situation-oriented approaches in the practice of early childhood education: Case studies and educational perspectives]. Stuttgart: Ernst Klett Verlag.

Kossolapow, L. Vorschulerziehung [Preschool education]. (1977). In H. Rombach (Ed.), *Wörterbuch der Pädagogik* [Dictionary of educational science] (Vol. 3). Freiburg: Herder Verlag.

Küchenhoff, W., & Oertel, F. (Eds.). (1976). *Der niedersächsische Modellversuch zur Sozialerziehung in Kindergärten: Ein Erfahrungsbericht* [The Lower Saxony model of social education in kindergartens: A report]. Hannover: Schroedel Verlag.

Leontjew, A.N. (1973). *Probleme der Entwicklung des Psychischen* [Problems of psychic development]. Frankfurt: Fischer Athenäum.

Lückert, H.R. (Ed.). (1974). *Begabungsforschung und Bildungsförderung im Vorschulalter* [Research on and promotion of talents in early childhood]. Darmstadt, West Germany: Wissenschaftliche Buchgesellschaft.

Maier, M.F. (1980). *Entwicklungslogik und Reziprozität kommunikativer Ethik: Eine inhaltsanalytische Untersuchung zum Einfluß kritischer Theorie (Habermas) auf die Gestaltung Curricula im Elementarbereich—unter besonderer Berücksichtigung des Begründungszusammenhangs Piaget—Habermas* [The logic of development and the reciprocity of communicative ethics: A content analysis on the inference of critical theory (Habermas) on the design of curricula in early childhood education with special reference to the frame of reference Piaget—Habermas]. Frankfurt: Haag und Herchen Verlag.

Mead, G.H. (1968). *Geist, Identität und Gesellschaft* [Mind, self, and society]. Frankfurt: Suhrkamp Verlag.

Merker, H., Rüsing, B., & Blanke, S. (1980). *Spielprozesse im Kindegarten* [Processes of playing in early childhood]. Munich: Kösel Verlag.

Miller, M. (1976). *Zur Logik der frühkindlichen Sprachentwicklung: Empirische Untersuchung und Theoriediskussion* [The logic of language development in early childhood: An empirical study and discussion of theory]. Stuttgart: Ernst Klett Verlag.

Minister für Arbeit, Gesundheit und Soziales des Landes Nordrhein-Westfalen. (1977) *Modellversuch 1970–2975: Abschlußbericht* [Model project 1970–1975: Final report]. Dusseldorf: Author.

Minister für Arbeit, Gesundheit und Soziales des Landes Nordrhein-Westfalen. (1983). *Arbeitshilfen zur Planung der Arbeit im Kindergarten* [Aids for the planning of kindergarten work] (rev. ed.). Dusseldorf: Author.

Mörsberger, H., Moskal, E., & Pflug, E. (Eds.). (1978). *Der Kindergarten: Handbuch für die Praxis in drei Bänden* [The kindergarten: Practical handbook in three volumes]. Freiburg: Herder Verlag.

Nitz, C. (1972). *Praxis der Vorschulerziehung* [Practice of preschool education] (Vols. 1–2). Wolfenbüttel, West Germany: Georg Kallmeyer Verlag.

Oertel, F. (1976). Bemerkingen zu einigen Ansätzen vorschulischer Curriculumentwicklung im Bereich Bewegungserziehung/Sport [Comments on some approaches to preschool curriculum development in the field of movement education/sports]. *Sportunterricht, 25,* 37–41.

Oertel, F. (1977a). Konflikt, Konflikterziehung [Conflict, conflict education]. In H. Rombach (Ed.), *Wörterbuch der Pädagogik* [Dictionary of educational science] (Vol. 2, pp. 280–183). Freiburg: Herder Verlag.

Oertel, F. (1977b). Sozialerziehung [Social education]. In H. Rombach (Ed.), *Wörterbuch der Pädagogik [Dictionary of educational science]* (Vol. 3, pp. 165–167). Freiburg: Herder Verlag.

Oertel, F. (1978). *Bericht über die landesspezifische Zwischenauswertung der Erprobung von "Elementare Sozialerziehung" (ES) im Jahre 1976* [Report about the Lower Saxonian trial program for elementary social education in 1976]. Available from Sonderdruck der Projektgruppe, Universität Hannover, Fb. Erziehungswissenschaften, Bismarckstraße 2, 3000 Hannover 1, West Germany.

Oertel, F. (Ed.). (1982). *Elementare Sozialerziehung: Praxishilfen für den Kindergarten* [Elementary social education: Practical aids for kindergarten work] (Vols. 1–2). Munich: Juventa Verlag.

Oertel, F. (1983). *Konzept und Methoden elementarer Sozialerziehung: Materialien für die Aus- und Fortbilung der Erzieher* [Concepts and methods of elementary social education: Materials for the training of kindergarten teachers]. Munich: Juventa Verlag.

Parmentier, M. (1979). *Frühe Bildungsprozesse: Zur Struktur der kindlichen Interaktion* [Early educational processes: The structure of interaction in early childhood]. Munich: Juventa Verlag.

Peukert, U. (1979). *Interaktive Kompetenz und Identität: Zum Vorrang sozialen Lernens im Vorschulter* [Interactive competence and identity: The priority of social learning in early childhood]. Dusseldorf: Patmos Verlag.

Piaget, J. (1967). *Psychologie der Intelligenz* [Psychology of intelligence]. Stuttgart: Rascher Verlag.

Roth, H. (1971). *Pädagogische Anthropologie* [Educational anthropology] (rev. ed., Vols. 1–2). Hannover: Schroedel Verlag.

Strätz, R., & Schmidt, E.A.F. (1982). *Die Wahrnehmung sozialer Beziehungen von Kindergartenkindern* [The perception of social contacts between children of kindergarten age]. Köln, West Germany: Verlag W. Kohlhammer.

Thema: Offene Curricula [Theme: Open curricula]. (1973). *Zeitschrift für Pädagogik, 19*(3).

Wittgenstein, L. (1967). *Philosophische Untersuchungen* [Philosophical studies]. Frankfurt: Suhrkamp Verlag.

Wygotski, L.S. (1974). *Denken und Sprechen* [Thinking and speaking]. Reutlingen, West Germany: S. Fischer Verlag.

Zimmer, J. (Ed.). (1973). *Curriculumtwicklung im Vorschulbereich* [Preschool curriculum development] (Vols. 1–2). Munich: R. Piper Verlag.

11

Characteristics of the Journal Literature in Early Childhood Education

Ann Lukasevich
Edward G. Summers

University of British Columbia, Canada

As the number of professionals working on behalf of the care, development, and education of young children increases, the published information related to early childhood education continues to expand. A literature is a body of thought expressed in published writings; a publication can be defined as anything in the form of text. Thus, the literature of early childhood education consists of journal articles, books of all types, dissertations, and a plethora of fugitive materials such as conference papers, research reports, curriculum guides, and the like. Although all types of literature in early childhood education are important sources of information, this discussion concentrates on the analysis of the journal literature because, since their inception in the 17th century, journals have been widely regarded as premier sources in carrying the new ideas and concepts in a field, and they reflect the major mechanism for transmitting and evaluating knowledge (Meadows, 1980).

An increasingly important collection of journal literature related to early childhood education has emerged, particularly within the past 10 years. This discussion addresses a number of issues related to journals as the primary conveyors of the information and state of the art in early childhood education. First, bibliometric techniques are applied to a collection of journal articles to identify the most important journals publishing information on early childhood education. Second, the journal article collection is examined to determine whether the production of information follows the same bibliometric regularity observed for the literature of other disciplines. Third, the time distribution of the published journal articles is analyzed to pinpoint quantitative trends in past publication and to predict possible future trends in the production of information. Finally, a general analysis is conducted, using descriptors employed by the Educational Resources Information Center

(ERIC) database, to ascertain topics that appear frequently in the early childhood education literature.

Specifically, the first three sections of the discussion describe the development of the collection of journal articles and the bibliometric analysis of the journals producing these articles. The fourth section analyzes thhe temporal distribution of the journal articles and offers some suggestions on past and future trends in publication. To determine current topics that appear frequently in the early childhood literature, the fifth section presents an exploratory analysis based on the descriptor postings from ERIC's computerized information database.

DEVELOPING THE COLLECTION OF JOURNAL ARTICLES

The use of published literature to indicate information activity in a discipline falls under the heading of bibliometric analysis (Narin, 1976). Such analysis has gained great popularity, particularly within the past two decades, as abstracting and indexing services have grown to handle the information explosion and as the contents of such indexes have been organized into computerized, machine-readable bibliographic databases. Potter (1981) states that bibliometrics is "the study and measurement of the publication patterns of all forms of written communication and their authors" (p. 5). Bibliometric methods have good validity because the data studied are an unobtrusive record that can be analyzed unrelated to subjective opinion and bias.

To develop the collection of early childhood education journal articles, ERIC's *Current Index to Journals in Education (CIJE)* computer tape database was searched through the services of the Educational Research Service and Computing Center of the Faculty of Education at the University of British Columbia. This search produced articles that had been assigned the term Early Childhood Education as a major descriptor. In the *Thesaurus of ERIC Descriptors* (Educational Resources Information Center, 1982), the term Early Childhood Education is defined as "activities and/or experiences that are intended to effect developmental changes in children, from birth through the primary units of elementary school (Grades K–3)" (p. 71). The descriptor first appeared in the ERIC *Thesaurus* in 1966. *CIJE* provides good overall coverage of the education-related literature and systematically monitors and announces the information published in approximately 800 journals. Computerized databases like *CIJE* are good sources for bibliometric studies because the articles included have been uniformly indexed according to agreed-upon lexicographical definitions and because the retrieved items conform directly to the formulated search question. Thus, content is systematically controlled in indexing and retrieval, and high relevance can be attained in searching. Depending on content, up to six major descriptors are assigned to each article. Searching under major descriptors, which index only the primary focus or subject of a document, ensures that only the most relevant documents related to the topic of the search are retrieved (Educational Resources Information Center, 1974).[1]

The computer search yielded 1,424 journal articles posted to the major descriptor Early Childhood Education in *CIJE* from 1969 through the first quarter of 1983.[2] The articles were hand-sorted by journal title and also were tabulated by their date of publication.

IDENTIFYING THE MOST IMPORTANT JOURNALS

If the journal literature on a topic for a particular time period is searched and the retrieved articles are tabulated, a pattern emerges in which the journals can be ranked by the volume of articles each produces. Looking more closely at the results of the computer search revealed that one journal contributed 170 articles and that 110 journals contributed only one article each. The distribution of articles over journal titles is presented in Table 1. Journals are ranked from those contributing the greatest number of articles to those contributing only one or two articles each.

The first column in Table 1 gives the rank of the journal, the second column indicates the cumulative percentage of journals, and the third column records the number of articles contributed by each journal. From the figures in the third column, it is apparent that the number of articles contributed by each successive journal decreases rather rapidly. The bottom-ranked 155 journals, producing one or two articles each, have been truncated to conserve space in the table. (The 45 journals ranked 89 through 132 contributed two articles each, and the 100 journals ranked 133 through 242 contributed one article each.)

The fourth column reports the running total for the articles retrieved. The first line of this column shows 170 articles contributed by the first-ranked

---

[1] The term Early Childhood Education is assigned by ERIC as a major descriptor when the subject of the document is that educational level (ie., the field of early childhood education). This term may also be assigned as a minor descriptor to other documents relating to children from birth to age 9 that do not discuss the field of early childhood education in general but that might, for example, concern research, curriculum materials, or teaching methods associated with this age group. For more complete information on searching the ERIC database, see the latest edition of the *Thesaurus of ERIC Descriptors* (Educational Resources Information Center, 1984).

[2] An additional 1,218 journal articles were indexed with the term Early Childhood Education as a minor descriptor but were not included in this study.

journal. The 308 articles indicated in the second line reflect the total number of articles contributed by the first- and second-ranked journals, and so on down the table. A total of 1,424 articles were contributed by the 242 individual journals.

To further clarify, a fifth column has been added to present the cumulative percentage of articles contributed by ranked journals. Figures in this column were created by dividing the number of articles in the fourth column by the total number of articles. As these figures indicate, the first three journals contributed approximately one-fourth of the articles on this topic produced by the 242 journals for the period 1969–82. In addition, these three journals represented a very small percentage of the total number of journals.

If important journals are defined as those that contribute the highest volume of articles for a given period of time, Table 1 suggests that the first 31 journals would be of major importance.[3] These 31 titles produced approximately two-thirds, or 954, of the articles published during this period. The titles and their publication counts are represented in Table 2. These journals represent a wide range of disciplines, cover many special interests, and vary markedly in terms of their research or practical content.

BRADFORDIAN CHARACTERISTICS OF THE JOURNAL LITERATURE

Bibliometric analyses of collections of journal literature in many disciplines have established the existence of certain patterns of regularity in the publication of information. This regularity is characterized by the concentration and dispersion of items of information over different sources—in this instance, the dispersion of the 1,424 articles across the 242 journals. On any given topic, a large number of relevant articles will be concentrated in a small number of journal titles. The balance of the articles will be dispersed over a large number of titles. The initial statement of this phenomenon was made by Bradford (1934, 1950), and Bradord's Law has been found to operate in collections of journal literature from many disciplines (Garfield, 1980). For example, Asai (1981) assessed the characteristics of 11 different bibliographic databases, including from 68 to 534 source journals, and found that the distribution of articles over sources closely approximated that predicted by Bradford's Law. Brookes (1977) suggests that this pattern operates for even small collections of journal titles. Summers (1983) recently reported Brad-

---

[3] It should be noted that article productivity is only one measure of the importance of a journal. Importance could also be measured by subjective opinion contributed by members in the discipline who use the journals and by citation counts (Smith, 1981), to name but two other methods reported in the literature.

Table 1 Distribution of Articles by Source Journals for the Early Childhood Education Journal Literature

Journal Rank	Journal Cumulative Percentage	Articles	Cumulative Articles	Article Cumulative Percentage
1	.004	170	170	.119
2	.008	138	308	.216
3	.012	57	365	.256
4	.016	48	413	.290
5	.020	42	455	.319
6	.024	39	494	.346
7	.028	32	526	.369
8	.033	31	557	.391
9	.037	25	582	.408
10	.041	24	606	.425
11	.045	24	630	.442
12	.049	23	653	.458
13	.053	22	675	.474
14	.057	21	696	.488
15	.061	20	716	.502
16	.066	19	735	.516
17	.070	18	753	.528
18	.074	18	771	.541
19	.078	18	789	.554
20	.082	18	807	.566
21	.086	16	823	.577
22	.090	16	839	.589
23	.095	15	854	.599
24	.099	15	869	.610
25	.103	14	883	.620
26	.107	14	897	.629
27	.111	13	910	.639
28	.115	13	923	.648
29	.119	12	935	.656
30	.123	10	945	.663
31	.128	9	954	.669
32	.132	9	963	.676
33	.136	9	972	.682
34	.140	8	980	.688
35	.144	8	988	.693
36	.148	8	996	.699
37	.152	7	1003	.704
38	.157	7	1010	.709
39	.161	7	1017	.714
40	.165	7	1024	.719
41	.169	6	1030	.723
42	.173	6	1036	.727
43	.177	6	1042	.731
44	.181	6	1048	.735

Table 1   (Continued)

Journal Rank	Journal Cumulative Percentage	Articles	Cumulative Articles	Article Cumulative Percentage
45	.185	6	1054	.740
46	.190	6	1060	.744
47	.194	6	1066	.748
48	.198	6	1072	.752
49	.202	5	1077	.759
50	.206	5	1082	.759
51	.210	5	1087	.763
52	.214	5	1092	.766
53	.219	5	1097	.770
54	.223	5	1102	.773
55	.227	5	1107	.777
56	.231	5	1112	.780
57	.235	4	1116	.783
58	.239	4	1120	.786
59	.243	4	1124	.789
60	.247	4	1128	.792
61	.252	4	1132	.794
62	.256	4	1136	.797
63	.260	4	1140	.800
64	.264	4	1144	.803
65	.268	4	1148	.806
66	.272	4	1152	.808
67	.276	4	1156	.811
68	.280	4	1160	.814
69	.285	4	1164	.817
70	.289	4	1168	.820
71	.293	4	1172	.823
72	.297	4	1176	.825
73	.301	3	1179	.827
74	.305	3	1182	.830
75	.309	3	1185	.832
76	.314	3	1188	.834
77	.318	3	1191	.836
78	.322	3	1194	.838
79	.326	3	1197	.840
80	.330	3	1200	.842
81	.334	3	1203	.844
82	.338	3	1206	.846
83	.342	3	1209	.849
84	.347	3	1212	.851
85	.351	3	1215	.853
86	.355	3	1218	.855
87	.359	3	1221	.857
88	.363	3	1224	.859
89–132	.549	2(45 × 2)	1314	.922
133–242	1.000	1(110 × 1)	1424	.999

Table 2   Important Core Publications for Early Childhood Education

Journal	Articles
Young Children	170
Childhood Education	138
Day Care and Early Education	57
International Journal of Early Childhood	48
Instructor	42
Journal of Experimental Child Psychology	39
Elementary School Journal	32
Developmental Psychology	31
Teacher	25
Child Development	24
Compact	24
Science and Children	23
Phi Delta Kappan	22
National Elementary Principal	21
Australian Journal of Early Childhood	20
Children Today	19
American Education	18
Journal of Genetic Psychology	18
Education	18
Perceptual and Motor Skills	18
Theory into Practice	16
Educational Leadership	16
Children	15
Exceptional Children	15
Child Care Quarterly	14
Merrill-Palmer Quarterly	14
Grade Teacher	13
Educational Horizons	13
Educational Product Report	12
School Science and Mathematics	10
Elementary English	9

fordian characteristics in the field of reading, as based on a collection of 865 articles from 204 journals appearing in an annual summary of research on reading for 1979.[4]

If, following Bradford's Law, one takes a collection of journal articles on a topic and ranks the journals in decreasing order of productivity, the journal titles can be divided into three zones such that each zone contributes about the same number of articles. For example, using a collection of 1,332 articles from 326 ranked journals in applied geophysics, Bradford (1950) found that the first 9 titles contributed 429 articles, the next 59 titles contributed 499 arti-

---

[4] A good description of both the theoretical and practical aspects of Bradford's Law can be found in Drott (1981).

cles, and the final 258 titles contributed 404 articles. The importance of this finding lies in the observed regularity. Specifically, a small core of highly productive journals produces one-third of the articles. To get the next third, one has to search five times as many titles, and to obtain the last third, one would have to search five times again as many titles. Thus, the relationship from zone to zone is geometric according to the following series (where 1 is the number of journals in the first zone and n is a proportional multiplier):

$$1 : n : n^2 \ldots n^{10}$$

Thus, journal literature collections demonstrated to be essentially Bradfordian in their distribution have a nucleus of high-producing journals, a second zone of relatively high-producing journals, and a long tail of journals producing a very small number of articles.

Bibliometric Regularity in Early Childhood Education Journals

The collection of early childhood education journal articles follows the bibliometric regularity of Bradford's Law, with Table 1 being divided into three approximately equal zones of 494, 460, and 470 articles. If Bradford's Law is operating as expected, the first zone should include 6 source journals, the second 24, and the third 96, using a proportional multiplier of 4 in the geometric progression. In reality, the number of source journals in the three zones is 6, 25, and 211. Thus, the results are close to those predicted for the first two zones and somewhat disproportional with respect to the third.[5] Results in this third zone are undoubtedly influenced by the high number of journals producing only one or two articles on the topic. It can be concluded that, at this stage in the development of early childhood education, the distribution of pertinent journal literature approximates the regularity of other areas, with considerable dispersion across the low-producing journals. These results are not surprising, but rather are typical of an emerging field such as early childhood education, in which a spurt of interest has come from many disciplines (behavioral psychology and cognitive development, to name but two). This distribution of literature also suggests the possibility that the field could, in the future, split into several strong subinterest areas, such as compensatory education, psychosocial development, and pedagogical practices.

---

[5] Drott (1981) presents several reasons why Bradford's Law is usually an approximation and seldom produces the exact predicted values. Several techniques have also been reported that can be used to statistically test the goodness of fit between the actual and predicted values. Among others, these include chi-square, several approaches based on regression analysis, and the Kolmogorov-Smirnov test. For our purposes, a general estimate of the goodness of fit is sufficient.

Implications for Retrieval

The results of this bibliometric analysis have important implications for retrieving information in early childhood education. Monitoring a small core of journals will allow one to keep abreast of much information, but a good deal of material will be scattered across a wide variety of low-producing journals. The low-producing journals also have a tendency to change considerably year by year. It is almost impossible for individuals, and even libraries, to maintain adequate collections to cope with this scatter of journal literature. Thus, there is a definite need for services like ERIC's *CIJE* to provide access to information. Computerized retrieval, based on coordinate indexing and Boolean logic, enhances the information dissemination capabilities of such indexes. Activities by ERIC Clearinghouses to generate state-of-the-art reviews and synthesis papers on important topics in early childhood education also provide a valuable service for the field in light of the diversity of the available information.

To illustrate the problem of bibliometric scatter in retrieving information, journal titles were collated from the 38 articles posted to the major descriptor Handicapped Children in the collection of 1,424 *CIJE* articles.[6] The 38 articles appeared in 22 separate journals; 7 articles appeared in 3 journals located in the first zone, 11 articles appeared in 3 journals located in the second zone, and 20 articles appeared in 16 journals located in the third zone. The scatter would have been even greater if the search had not used the major descriptor designation. With dispersion like this and without the aid of services like those provided by ERIC, it would be very difficult for an individual to retrieve a reasonably complete collection of journal articles about handicapped children and early childhood education. The range of journals producing information on this one topic is staggering, including research and nonresearch journals, journals located in several countries and reflecting a wide variety of disciplines, and journals representing many interests and professional groups.

TEMPORAL DISTRIBUTION OF THE JOURNAL LITERATURE

Figure 1 is based on the data arising from the tabulation of publication dates for the 1,424 articles cumulated across the time period from 1969 to 1982. There is a linear rise in articles published between 1969 and 1972, a sharp exponential increase to 1978 and a leveling off in publications from that point onward. The figure represents the logistic sigmoid S curve typical of litera-

---

[6] The term Handicapped Children become an invalid descriptor as of March 1980 but still may be used to search for ERIC postings entered prior to that date. The descriptor Disabilities or narrower terms should be used to retrieve documents entered in ERIC after March 1980.

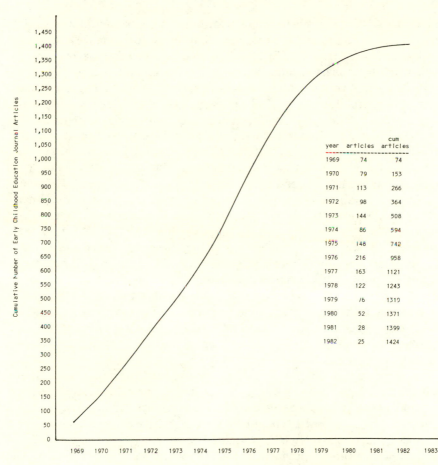

year	articles	cum articles
1969	74	74
1970	79	153
1971	113	266
1972	98	364
1973	144	508
1974	86	594
1975	148	742
1976	216	958
1977	163	1121
1978	122	1243
1979	76	1319
1980	52	1371
1981	28	1399
1982	25	1424

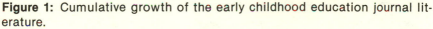

Figure 1: Cumulative growth of the early childhood education journal literature.

ture growth in developing specialties that encounter a sharp increase in interest. What is perhaps most notable about this figure is the dramatic doubling of literature production for the period 1974–78. The overall growth pattern approximates that outlined by Crane (1972), who suggests that a logistic pattern of growth in a discipline includes four dimensions; a slow beginning, exponential growth, linear growth, and continued slow irregular growth. A significant number of authors with interest in early childhood education entered the literature during the dramatic growth period of the middle and late 1970s.

It would be interesting to speculate as to the causes for the pattern of increase illustrated in Figure 1. Undoubtedly, broader interest in early childhood education — stimulated by societal concerns for children and sociological and political factors — has had its influence. The economics of recession and research and development funding patterns no doubt have played a role as well. It seems reasonable also to assume that the more recent leveling effect may be attributed to the same factors. It should be noted that the leveling effect may not be as sharp as indicated because some publications produced in the 1980s may not yet have entered the ERIC system through *CIJE* at the time this search was made (in early 1983). However, even allowing for this possibility, there is a definite leveling off in production of articles after 1978.

It is interesting to speculate whether the growth curve for the future will follow this same logistic pattern. If literature production is maintained at the asymptotic values, it perhaps would indicate that the field of early childhood education has reached a mature stage where the level of interested individuals remains fairly stable and the related production of literature is somewhat constant. One could also predict a decline in the literature. However, a decline would be unlikely since it would suggest either that the problems in the field have been solved or that interest in solving these problems has declined. Most likely, this leveling effect is temporary, and increases in literature production will occur. Although the volume of such increases perhaps will never equal that of the 1970s' "golden age" of funding and activities, irregular linear increases, rather than exponential increases, will be typical. Exponential growth cannot be maintained indefinitely and, as the pace of innovation in an area of interest slackens, it can be observed that concomitant declines in literature production occur.

The question also arises as to whether or not the information growth in early childhood education literature is, in reality, a growth in knowledge per se. Undoubtedly, the knowledge base has also increased as information has expanded. Investigators have pointed out that, with an exponential increase in article production, there is a substantial probability that knowledge has also increased, although this increase is undoubtedly linear rather than exponential (Tague, Beheshti, & Rees-Potter, 1981). It has been suggested that in a body of literature the number of really significant papers produced is roughly the square root of the total number of papers (Tague et al., 1981, pp. 126-127). Further investigation of this assertion would make interesting research, and a number of suggestions could be drawn from research in information science and the sociology of knowledge in developing a scale for rating the "significance" of a work.

CURRENT TOPICS IN THE JOURNAL LITERATURE

The bibliometric discussion to this point has been largely statistical in nature. However, an important question arises as to the substantive content of the indexed articles and the general topics appearing in the recent early childhood education literature. An in-depth content analysis of the articles is outside the scope of this discussion. Nonetheless, an indication of general trends can be obtained by analyzing the ERIC descriptors used in indexing. The descriptors provide a framework for "sorting" the information contained in the ERIC materials. The framework is flexible because the documents can be assigned more than one descriptor, depending on their content. In ERIC, an average of nine descriptors are assigned to each item indexed.

For this analysis, descriptor counts for the early childhood education articles indexed in *CIJE* were combined with those assigned to documents indexed in ERIC's other abstract publication, *Resources in Education (RIE)*. Obviously, it would not be productive to analyze all the descriptors used. It seemed reasonable to include for analysis only those descriptors that had been used 30 times or more across the time period 1969–82. A total of 216 descriptors appeared 30 times or more and accounted for approximately two-thirds of all the postings made to the materials in the two ERIC indexes. The 216 descriptors were first empirically sorted and organized into clusters of reasonably related concepts. Then, 10 broad categories were created to provide a general heading for the sets of descriptors. With this method, the major categories were essentially defined by the literature itself.

Table 3 presents the 10 categories with the appropriate descriptors ranked by the number of times they were posted in indexing the *CIJE* articles and *RIE* documents. The separate descriptors can be thought of as representing various subcategories within the broader categories. The classification appears reasonably valid and provides a useful framework that captures the general thrust and dimensions of the early childhood education journal and report literature. Heavy emphasis has been given to discussions of developmental characteristics, program development, and special needs of children. Also, the considerable volume of articles containing information on teaching and learning, measurement and evaluation, teachers, and parental concerns should be noted. A relatively small number of articles were assigned descriptors in the research category.[7]

An interesting analysis could be made of individual descriptors or groups of descriptors to determine the ebb and flow of interest in various topics across the 1969–82 time period. To accomplish this, the number of documents indexed to each descriptor would be broken down by date of publication to show how publications were distributed across the topics and time frame. A table would then be created to give predicted publication distributions in which predictors were based on knowledge of the subtotals for the topics and years. The equation used in this case would be the familiar formula used to calculate the contingency tables in the Chi-square statistical

---

[7] After the introduction of a new publication type coding system in September 1974 for *RIE* and in August 1979 for *CIJE*, the ERIC single-word descriptor Research became invalid for use except on documents that discussed research itself as a topic.

Table 3   Early Childhood Education Categories and Descriptor Usage

Age/Grade Level

Preschool Children	338	Elementary School Students	78
*Preschool Programs	268	*Primary Grades	69
Preschool Education	262	Primary Education	66
Kindergarten	207	Nursery Schools	62
Elementary Education	142	Children	60
Kindergarten Children	107	Grade 1	52
Infants	111	**Preschool Learning	41
Preschool Curriculum	94	*Infancy	40
Early Experience	80		

Publication Types

Instructional Materials	178	Guidelines	65
Literature Reviews	94	Teaching Guides	52
Curriculum Guides	86	Resource Materials	50
Annotated Bibliographies	83	Conference Reports	40
Bibliographies	80	*Resource Guides	32

Research

Research	121	Research Projects	54
Educational Research	110	Research Needs	41
Longitudinal Studies	74	Data Collection	32
Research Methodology	66	Behavioral Science Research	31
Tables (Data)	61		

Developmental Characteristics

Child Development	422	Motor Development	66
Cognitive Development	353	Sex Differences	64
Language Development	227	Cognitive Processes	62
Social Development	159	Childhood Needs	54
Self Concept	131	Perceptual Development	50
Play	112	Sex Role	49
Emotional Development	85	Values	43
Nutrition	79	Physical Development	41
Age Differences	75	Interpersonal Competence	37
Intellectual Development	73	Psychomotor Skills	36
Concept Formation	72	Developmental Stages	34
Skill Development	68	Developmental Psychology	31

Programs

Program Evaluation	403	Health Services	59
Program Descriptions	343	*Program Planning	58
*Day Care Services	209	Government Role	55
*Day Care Programs	164	Federal Legislation	52
Program Development	132	State Programs	48
Federal Programs	126	Financial Support	47
**Child Care	123	Child Welfare	45
Program Effectiveness	104	Delivery Systems	42

Table 3   (Continued)

Programs

*Compensatory Education Programs	95	Program Administration	40
**Educational Programs	95	Experimental Programs	40
*Child Care Centers	91	Policy Formation	39
Home Visits	78	Educational Legislation	39
Demonstration Programs	77	Cost Effectiveness	33
Home Programs	73	Educational Finance	33
Family Day Care	67	Needs Assessment	32
		Program Design	30

Special Needs

Disadvantaged Youth	229	Cross Cultural Studies	38
**Handicapped Children	172	Socioeconomic Influences	38
**Exceptional Child Education	137	Disabilities	36
Foreign Countries	127	Educationally Disadvantaged	35
Bilingual Education	78	English (Second Language)	35
Compensatory Education	60	Cultural Differences	34
Special Education	52	*Exceptional Children	33
Low Income Groups	49	*Mentally Handicapped	33
Exceptional Child Research	48	Minority Groups	32
Learning Disabilities	44	American Indians	30
Mexican Americans	40		

Measurement/Evaluation

Comparative Analysis	104	Observation	46
Evaluation Methods	97	Screening Tests	42
Questionnaires	61	Classification	40
**Measurement Instruments	59	Achievement Tests	37
Classroom Observation Techniques	56	Testing	33
Evaluation	52	Surveys	32
Evaluation Criteria	48	Measurement Techniques	32
Interaction Process Analysis	48	Educational Assessment	31
Student Evaluation	46	Formative Evaluation	30

Learning and Instruction

Intervention	242	Reading Instruction	44
Learning Activities	192	Communication Skills	43
Educational Objectives	197	Learning Theories	42
Teaching Methods	177	Thought Processes	42
Models	139	Learning Readiness	41
Curriculum Development	127	Language Arts	40
Academic Achievement	125	Educational Television	38
*Teaching Techniques	116	Problem Solving	37
Educational Philosophy	89	*Regular Class Placement	37
Classroom Environment	87	Perceptual Motor Learning	37
Learning Processes	84	Curriculum Design	36
Environmental Influences	82	Memory	36

(Continued)

Table 3   (Continued)

Learning and Instruction

Educational Theories	80	Educational Diagnosis	36
Behavior Change	73	Learning Experiences	35
Reading Readiness	70	Beginning Reading	35
Individualized Instruction	62	Identification	34
Educational Policy	61	Standards	34
Behavioral Objectives	59	Basic Skills	34
Curriculum	59	Reinforcement	33
Objectives	58	Concept Teaching	33
Open Education	57	Art Education	33
Educational Innovation	53	*Performance Based Education	33
Educational Needs	53	Diagnostic Teaching	33
Educational Environment	52	Mathematics Education	32
Educational Change	51	Sex Stereotypes	32
Motivation	50	Peer Relationship	31
Science Education	48	Educational History	31
Learning	46	Individual Differences	31
Toys	45	Educational Development	30

Teachers

Teacher Education	229	Teacher Attitudes	69
Teacher Role	161	Teacher Behavior	50
Student Teacher	101	Teacher Education Curriculum	50
Relationship		Paraprofessional School	50
Preschool Teachers	79	Personnel	
*Child Care Workers	77	Teacher Aides	43
Inservice Teacher Education	76	Staff Role	39
*Performance Based Teacher	75	*Staff Improvement	35
Education		Certification	33

Parents

Parent Participation	342	Parent Teacher Cooperation	61
Parent Education	213	Community Involvement	56
Parent Child Relationship	151	Family Environment	53
Parent Role	115	Mothers	51
Parent School Relationship	87	Parents	41
Parent Attitudes	79	Family Influence	31
Child Rearing	64		

Note. For current information on ERIC descriptor use, see the *Thesaurus of ERIC Descriptors* (10th ed.) (Educational Resources Information Center, 1984).

*These descriptors were downgraded by the ERIC *Thesaurus* to "use" references in 1980 (with the exception of Exceptional Children and Regular Class Placement, which were downgraded in 1978).

**These invalid (or "dead") descriptors are no longer used in indexing but may be used to search for database entries prior to September 1980.

test. In order to measure the degree to which the observed values deviated from the predicted values, standardized Z scores would be calculated. The greater the absolute value of Z, the greater the difference between the actual frequency of the topic and the predicted frequency. Such an analysis would allow a determination of changes in the pattern of topics appearing over time and would permit an estimation of which apparent changes in interest were due to chance factors and which were, in reality, true changes. Publication pattern anomalies would also be dramatically highlighted.

SUMMARY AND CONCLUSION

This discussion has examined characteristics of the journal literature in early childhood education indexed with the term Early Childhood Education as a major descriptor in ERIC's *CIJE* publication for the period 1969–82. A body of 242 journals publishing articles on early childhood education was identified, and core and peripheral journals were defined according to their frequency of article publication. The Bradfordian regularity of the distribution of articles across journals was demonstrated, and related implications for effective retrieval of information were discussed. In addition, analysis of the temporal distribution of article publication revealed the approximate pattern of linear and exponential growth in article production that took place across the time period. Possible future trends in publication of information were discussed, and an empirical analysis of the ERIC descriptors used in indexing was conducted to highlight the various topics and issues consistently appearing in the recently published journal and report literature in early childhood education. Finally, some suggestions were made to guide further research to determine the statistical significance of the publication patterns observed in the analysis of ERIC index terms.

The results of the analysis have indicated the general characteristics of the journal literature and have illustrated the significant increase in interest in and publication of information that took place in the 1970s. No doubt the quantity, diversity, and complexity of the literature published on this topic will continue to increase as society pursues issues and opportunities and selects priorities in advocating improved education for young children in the 1980s. The published literature provides both the information base and the forum for pursuing future significant issues in early childhood education. It is hoped that the ideas explored in this paper will aid professionals in their understanding and use of the wealth of journal literature available to the field.

REFERENCES

Asai, I. (1981). A general form of Bradford's distribution: The graph oriented approach. *Journal of the American Society for Information Science, 32,* 113–119.

Bradford, S.C. (1934). Sources of information on specific subjects. *Engineering, 137,* 85–86.

Bradford, S.C. (1950). *Documentation.* Washington, DC: Public Affairs Press.

Brookes, B.C. (1977). Theory of the Bradford Law. *Journal of Documentation, 33,* 180–209.

Crane, D. (1972). *Invisible colleges.* Chicago: University of Chicago Press.

Drott, M.C. (1981). Bradford's Law: Theory, empiricism and the gaps between. *Library Trends, 30,* 41–52.

Educational Resources Information Center. (1974). *ERIC processing manual.* Washington, DC: National Institute of Education. (ERIC Document Reproduction Service No. ED 092 164)

Educational Resources Information Center. (1982). *Thesaurus of ERIC descriptors* (9th ed.). Phoenix, AZ: Oryx Press.

Educational Resources Information Center. (1984). *Thesaurus of ERIC descriptors* (10th ed.). Phoenix, AZ: Oryx Press.

Garfield, E. (1980). Bradford's Law and related statistical patterns. In E. Garfield, *Essays of an information scientist* (pp. 476–483). Philadelphia: Institute for Scientific Information.

Meadows, A.J. (Ed.). (1980). *The scientific journal.* London: Aslib Publications.

Narin, F. (1976). *Evaluation bibliometrics: The use of publications and citation analysis in the evaluation of scientific activity.* Cherry Hill, NJ: Computer Horizons.

Potter, W.G. (Ed.). (1981). Bibliometrics. *Library Trends, 30,* 3–172.

Smith, L.C. (1981). Citation analysis. *Library Trends, 30,* 83–106.

Summers, E.G. (1983). Bradford's Law and the retrieval of reading research journal literature. *Reading Research Quarterly, 19,* 102–109.

Tague, J., Beheshti, J., & Rees-Potter, L. (1981). The law of exponential growth: Evidence, implications and forecasts. *Library Trends, 30,* 125–145.

How to Obtain ERIC Documents

Within the chapters of this volume, citations that are assigned ED numbers are indexed and abstracted in ERIC's *Resources in Education (RIE)*. Complete copies of most ERIC documents cited here are available in ERIC microfiche collections at approximately 700 libraries in the United States and other countries. For a list of ERIC collections near you, write ERIC/EECE, College of Education, University of Illinois, 805 W. Pennsylvania Ave., Urbana, IL 61801.

ERIC Documents may be ordered in either paper copy (PC), a photocopy of the original, or microfiche (MF), a transparent film card containing up to 98 pages of text. Please include ED number and specify PC or MF. Document prices given in *Resources in Education (RIE)* are subject to change. The current price schedule is provided below.

Paper copy (per ED number): 1–25 pp., $1.80; 26–50 pp., $3.60; 51–75 pp., $5.40; 76–100 pp., $7.20. Add $1.80 for every additional 25 pp. or fraction thereof.

Microfiche (per ED number): 1–480 pp., $.75.

Prices shown do not include mailing, which must be added to all orders. First class postage (for all MF orders up to 32 MF): $.22 for 1–3 MF: $.39 for 4–8 MF; $.56 for 9–14 MF; $.73 for 15–18 MF; $.90 for 19–21 MF; $1.07 for 22–27 MF; $1.24 for 28–32 MF. UPS charges (for 33 or more MF and all PC orders): $1.74 for 1 lb; $2.16 for 2 lbs; $2.57 for 3 lbs; $2.99 for 4 lbs. (Each pound equals 75 PC pages or 75 MF.)

Send order and check to ERIC Document Reproduction Service, 3900 Wheeler Avenue, Alexandria, VA 22304-5110.

The ERIC System and ERIC /EECE

The Educational Resources Information Center/Elementary and Early Childhood Education Clearinghouse (ERIC/EECE) is part of a system of 16 clearinghouses sponsored by the National Institute of Education to provide information about current research and developments in the field of education. The clearinghouses, each focusing on a specific area of education (such as junior colleges, teacher education, languages and linguistics), are located at universities and other institutions throughout the United States.

Each clearinghouse staff searches systematically to acquire current, significant documents relevant to education. These research studies, conference proceedings, curriculum guides, program descriptions and evaluations, and other publications are abstracted and indexed in *Resources in Education (RIE)*, a monthly journal. *RIE* is available at libraries, or it may be ordered from the Superintendent of Documents, United States Government Printing Office, Washington, DC 20402. The documents themselves are reproduced on microfiche by the ERIC Document Reproduction Service for distribution to libraries and individuals.

Another ERIC publication is *Current Index to Journals in Education (CIJE)*, a monthly guide to periodical literature that cites articles in more than 800 journals and magazines in the field of education. Most citations include annotations. Articles are indexed in *CIJE* by subject, author, and journal contents. *CIJE* is available at libraries or by subscription from Oryx Press, 2214 North Central at Encanto, Phoenix, AZ 85004.

The Clearinghouse on Elementary and Early Childhood Education (ERIC/EECE) publishes topical papers, bibliographies, resource lists, and bulletins for persons interested in child development, child care, and childhood education (for children from birth to age 12). The clearinghouse staff also answers individual information requests. For more information, write ERIC/EECE, College of Education, University of Illinois, 805 W. Pennsylvania Ave., Urbana, IL 61801.

The ERIC Clearinghouses

ADULT, CAREER, AND
  VOCATIONAL EDUCATION
Ohio State University
1960 Kenny Road
Columbus, OH 43210
  (614) 486-3655

COUNSELING AND PERSONNEL
  SERVICES
University of Michigan
School of Education, Room 2108
Ann Arbor, MI 48109
  (313) 764-9492

EDUCATIONAL MANAGEMENT
University of Oregon
1787 Agate Street
Eugene, OR 97403
  (503) 686-5043

*ELEMENTARY AND EARLY
  CHILDHOOD EDUCATION
College of Education
University of Education
805 W. Pennsylvania Avenue
Urbana, IL 61801
  (217) 333-1386

HANDICAPPED AND GIFTED
  CHILDREN
Council for Exceptional
  Children
1920 Association Drive
Reston, VA 22091
  (703) 620-3660

HIGHER EDUCATION
George Washington University
1 Dupont Circle N.W., Suite 630
Washington, DC 20036
  (202) 296-2597

INFORMATION RESOURCES
Syracuse University
School of Education
Huntington Hall, Room 030
Syracuse, NY 13210
  (315) 423-3640

JUNIOR COLLEGES
University of California
  at Los Angeles
Mathematical Sciences Building,
  Room 8118
405 Hilgard Avenue
Los Angeles, CA 90024
  (213) 825-3931

LANGUAGES AND LINGUISTICS
Center for Applied Linguistics
1118 22nd Street, N.W.
Washington, DC 20037
  (202) 429-9292

READING AND
  COMMUNICATION SKILLS
National Council of Teachers
  of English
1111 Kenyon Road
Urbana, IL 61801
  (217) 328-3870

RURAL EDUCATION AND
  SMALL SCHOOLS
New Mexico State University
Box 3AP
Las Cruces, NM 88003
    (505) 646-2623

SCIENCE, MATHEMATICS,
  AND ENVIRONMENTAL
  EDUCATION
Ohio State University
1200 Chambers Road, Room 310
Columbus, OH 43212
    (614) 422-6717

SOCIAL STUDIES/SOCIAL
  SCIENCE EDUCATION
Social Science Education
  Consortium, Inc.
855 Broadway
Boulder, CO 80302
    (303) 492-8434

TEACHER EDUCATION
American Association of Colleges
  for Teacher Education
One Dupont Circle, N.W., Suite 610
Washington, DC 20036
    (202) 293-2450

TESTS, MEASUREMENT, AND
  EVALUATION
Educational Testing Service
Rosedale Road
Princeton, NJ 08541
    (609) 734-5176

URBAN EDUCATION
Teachers College, Columbia University
Institute for Urban and
  Minority Education
Box 40
525 W. 120th Street
New York, NY 10027
    (212) 678-3433

---

*ERIC/EECE is responsible for acquiring research documents on the social, psychological, physical, educational, and cultural development of children from the prenatal period through pre-adolescence (age 12). Theoretical and practical issues related to staff development, administration, curriculum, and parent/community factors affecting programs for children of this age group are also within the cope of the clearinghouse.